Why Do You Need This New Edition?

If you're wondering why you should buy this new edition of *Writing with Confidence: Writing Effective Sentences and Paragraphs*, here are 10 good reasons!

❶ *Writing with Confidence* is now part of the new **VangoBooks** program! Clean, simple, smart, and efficient, VangoBooks represent a very different type of textbook—one that you will actually want to read. VangoBooks will not bog you down with information; they will not weigh down your backpack, and at about half the cost of a traditional textbook, they will not break your budget.

❷ A **new chapter on exemplification** teaches students how to support and illustrate their claims.

❸ Newly added **"Templates,"** interactive writing guides, help students make claims, support them with examples and explanations, and effect transitions.

❹ **"Revision Guidelines"** and interactive **"Revision Checklists"** assist students in responding specifically to their work and the work of their classmates as they move from the early to the final drafts of their writing.

❺ **Five new high-interest readings** that offer rhetorical models and topics for analysis, discussion, and writing.

❻ **New suggestions for writing** follow each reading selection.

❼ A **new appendix on using portfolios** enables students to easily and efficiently reflect on and revise their work.

❽ **Expanded treatment of pronouns** is incorporated in Chapter 8, along with a new appendix section listing types of pronouns with examples of each.

❾ **New exercises with fresh thematic content** are added and/or replace less popular exercises.

❿ Did we mention the price? It will not break your budget and is worth every penny.

PEARSON
Longman

Writing with Confidence

Writing Effective Sentences and Paragraphs

Ninth Edition

Alan Meyers

Harry S Truman College

New York   San Francisco   Boston
London   Toronto   Sydney   Tokyo   Singapore   Madrid
Mexico City   Munich   Paris   Cape Town   Hong Kong   Montreal

To Brad, Sarah, and baby Dylan

Acquisitions Editor: Matthew Wright
Development Editor: Ann Hofstra Grogg
Marketing Manager: Thomas DeMarco
Senior Supplements Editor: Donna Campion
Senior Media Producer: Stefanie Liebman
Production Manager: Eric Jorgensen
Project Coordination, Text Design, and Electronic Page Makeup: Elm Street
    Publishing Services
Cover Design Manager: Nancy Danahy
Cover Designer: Nancy Sacks
Cover Image: Max Alexander © Dorling Kindersley
Photo Researcher: Rona Tuccillo
Senior Manufacturing Buyer: Alfred C. Dorsey
Printer and Binder: RR Donnelley & Sons Company—Owensville
Cover Printer: Phoenix Color Corporation

For permission to use copyrighted material, grateful acknowledgment is made to the copyright holders on p. 465, which are hereby made part of this copyright page.

Library of Congress Cataloging-in-Publication Data
Meyers, Alan, 1945–
    Writing with confidence: writing effective sentences and paragraphs/alan meyers.—
9th ed.
        p. cm.
    Includes index.
    ISBN-13: 978-0-205-61780-7
    ISBN-10: 0-205-61780-8
    1. English language—Rhetoric. 2. English language—Sentences. 3. English language—
    Paragraphs. 4. English language—Grammar. 5. Report writing. I. Title.

PE1408.M52 2009
808′.042-dc22

                                                                                2008006185

Please visit us at www.pearsonhighered.com

ISBN-13: 978-0-205-61780-7
ISBN-10: 0-205-61780-8

1 2 3 4 5 6 7 8 9 10—DOM—11 10 09 08

Brief Contents

Detailed Contents

Rhetorical Contents

The following list classifies the reading selections and student essays according to the rhetorical modes they employ or include. Many of the additional readings are mixed modes.

The Writing Process

Hints and Help for Writers

TIPS AND SHORTCUTS

IF YOUR FIRST LANGUAGE IS NOT ENGLISH

COMBINING AND REFINING SENTENCES

WORKING WITH VERBS

TEMPLATES

Preface

In recent years, practices in English composition instruction have changed significantly. Terminology has changed, reading and writing have become more integrated, portfolio assessment is increasingly commonplace, and, thanks to the pioneering work of Gerald Graff and Cathy Birkenstein, templates are becoming an important pedagogical aid. This ninth edition of *Writing with Confidence* reflects this evolution—and more. Specifically, each rhetorical mode chapter includes the following:

1. **New terms**—*claims*, *support*, and *explanation*—that bolster students' understanding of the topic sentence and thesis statement, as well as the unity, coherence, and development of the paragraph and essay.
2. **Templates** that guide students in making claims, support them with examples and explanations, and effect transitions. Students fill in their own content within the template and modify the template for use in their paragraphs and essays.
3. **Interactive revision checklists** that assist students in responding specifically to their work and the work of their classmates as they move from the early to the final drafts of their writing.

The ninth edition also features these changes:

4. A new **chapter on exemplification** that instructs students on how to support and illustrate their claims.
5. **Five new high-interest readings** that offer rhetorical models and topics for analysis, discussion, and writing.
6. **New suggestions for writing** based on each reading selection.
7. An **appendix on using portfolios** that enables students to reflect on and revise their work.
8. **Expanded treatment of pronouns** incorporated in Chapter 8 and in a new appendix section listing types of pronouns, with examples of each.
9. **New exercises** with fresh thematic content.

Along with these additions and changes, the new edition retains its most popular and effective features: its student-centered and often humorous style; the straightforward instruction in the writing process; the thorough coverage of each rhetorical mode for both paragraphs and essays (including professional and student models); the architectural theme and "blueprints for success"; the extensive treatment of grammar and mechanics within the editing process, concluding with two parallel "Editing for Mastery" passages; the continuous discourse exercise content focused on unusual and unique people, events, and natural phenomena; the attention to the needs of students whose first language is not English; and the handy "Tips" boxes interspersed throughout the text.

CONTENT OVERVIEW

- **Unit I: Building Your Writing Skills.** These four chapters provide lively, straightforward instruction in the writing process for both paragraphs and essays. Separate chapters address the reasons for writing; a six-step writing process that begins with discovery and ends with proofreading; the shape and form of the paragraph; and the connection between paragraph and essay.

- **Unit II: Building and Repairing Sentences.** This five-chapter unit addresses essential skills in revising for clarity and correctness. The unit begins with identifying and eliminating fragments, continues with ways to join sentences correctly, and ends with identifying and correcting comma splices and run-ons. More than a fix-it kit, however, the unit offers a variety of ways to join clauses and phrases through coordination and subordination.

- **Unit III: Revising with Care: Building on the Framework.** Chapters in this unit cover the most important grammatical and mechanical issues to consider in the editing stages of the writing process: subject-verb agreement, past-tense and past-participle verb forms, pronoun forms, use of modifiers, adjective and adverb forms, consistency, concrete language, concise language, and ways to write concretely and concisely.

- **Unit IV: Writing Types of Paragraphs: Shaping the Structure.** The ten chapters in this unit address the rhetorical modes—now including exemplification—as well as report, summary, and response writing. Each chapter includes a professional or student model followed by discussion questions; an explanation of paragraph order; a visual "blueprint" of that order; a sequential guide through a single writing assignment; a revision checklist that promotes collaborative revision; a student model; and additional writing assignments.

- **Unit V: Editing for Grammar and Mechanics: Finishing the Job.** This section includes five chapters of additional help with punctuation, spelling, sound-alike and look-alike words, and issues aimed primarily at non-English dominant, or ESL, writers: articles, prepositions, verb constructions, and phrasal verbs.

- **Reading Selections.** These sixteen high-interest essays, five of which are new, provide models of the rhetorical modes, practice in close reading, questions for analysis, and prompts for additional writing, including writing in response to the readings.

- **Appendixes.** These include the aforementioned portfolio instruction; definitions of pronouns, with examples; a list of common irregular verbs; commonly misspelled verbs; and common expressions using prepositions. In addition, at the back of the book are answers to chapter exercises (odd-numbered items only) and a glossary.

CONTINUING FEATURES

The following features make *Writing with Confidence* a valuable and flexible tool for both instructor and student.

- **Clear and Simple Explanations.** Discussions of the writing process, grammar, and mechanics offer practical instruction in drafting and revising paragraphs, essays, and sentences, while increasing facility with language and eliminating errors. The text highlights and explains key terms and lists them again in a glossary at the back of the book. The extensive grammatical instruction minimizes terminology, telling students only what they need to know to revise their work.

- **Guidance Throughout the Writing Process.** Chapter 2 introduces the "Six Steps to Successful Writing and Revising," Chapter 3 applies that process to the paragraph, and Chapter 4 extends it to the essay. Each of the ten chapters on types of paragraphs and essays then guides students through the drafting and revision of their work.

- **Integrated Approach to the Rhetorical Modes.** Instead of viewing the rhetorical modes as ends in themselves, this book strengthens the field's increasing recognition of modes that are often mixed and combined in essays and even paragraphs. While the text continues to focus on paragraphs, students are urged to see paragraphs of description, narration, comparison–contrast, and others as one means by which they can achieve a larger purpose in writing. Questions for analysis and writing assignments also encourage students to regard the modes within the context of purpose and audience.

- **Chapter on Summary and Response.** Students in composition and many other classes are often asked to write a summary and response to a reading, and this chapter shows them how. They learn the important skills of summarizing objectively without plagiarizing and then stating and developing a response. This chapter illustrates and provides instruction in both skills, separately and in combination. As with each writing chapter in the book, it takes the student through a series of steps in planning, drafting, revising, and editing—all with an eye toward practical application.

- **High-Interest Exercises and Models.** Engaging with materials in connected discourse, students gain competence in composing, revising, and editing sentences within a meaningful context. This entertaining subject matter serves a more serious purpose as well: demonstrating that people write to communicate ideas, and if ideas are worth saying, they are worth saying well. Selections include biographies of Diamond Jim Brady, Alexandra David-Neel, Sequoyah, Jesse Owens, Dian Fossey, and Abraham Lincoln as well as accounts of the origins of the wedding cake, the teddy bear, and the "Happy Birthday" song.

- **Chapter Goals.** These chapter openers address student aims instead of merely foreshadowing chapter heads.

- **Multifaceted Presentation of Each Paragraph Mode.** Professional and student models exemplify the organization of paragraphs (and essays). The first model in each chapter is followed by discussion questions and then a step-by-step guide through a single, well-developed piece of writing.

- **Prompts for Writing Assignments—and Assignments Based on Readings.** Visual prompts inspire student writing, as do suggestions for writing that follow each of the readings—both within chapters and in the Reading Selections at the end of the book. In every case, at least one of these prompts requires a written response to the reading.

- **Chapter-Ending Summary Boxes.** These highlighted summaries help students identify and review the important points to practice, and serve as additional reference aids in revising and editing.

- **Tips Boxes.** Interspersed throughout the chapters are helpful tips on practical matters and strategies for remembering key points.

- **ESL Boxes and Chapters for ESL Students.** Special tips boxes address key issues for students whose first language is not English, and chapters on word order and articles and prepositions provide comprehensive additional instruction.

- **"Blueprints" for the Structure of the Paragraph, Essay, and Each Rhetorical Mode.** These in-chapter summaries, based on the architectural theme of the book, provide graphical representations of typical structures of writing.

- **"Blueprints for Success."** These end-of-unit graphs and charts provide clear and useful summaries of the major concepts, strategies, and practices in each unit.

- **Flexible Approaches to Instruction and Learning.** The Additional Writing Assignments and Final Writing Assignments in each chapter on the rhetorical modes provide options for essay assignments. And answer keys for odd-numbered items in each exercise and for the first "Editing for Mastery Exercise" provide options for independent, self-paced study.

- **Collaborative Activities.** These suggestions for group or paired work expand learning opportunities. Each paragraph writing assignment includes Revision Guidelines that encourage peer response and editing. Predicting activities throughout the text provide additional opportunities for collaboration while stressing the interrelationship between writer and reader.

- **Mastery Learning Capabilities.** Using a Mastery Learning approach, students complete a section on grammar and mechanics, evaluate their understanding and application of the concepts, restudy parts of the section if necessary, and then engage in further evaluation. The two Editing for Mastery exercises in each of these chapters and the parallel test forms in the ancillary testing package can serve as useful tools in this approach.

- **Attention to Matters of Style.** Chapter 16 explores ways to make writing more lively, vivid, and direct. It offers practice in writing strong verbs, adjectives, and expressions; eliminating unnecessary repetition of words and ideas; and avoiding clichés.

- **Comprehensive Treatment of Verbs.** Focusing on one of the most troublesome hurdles for novice writers in their first or second language—verbs—the book devotes four chapters to verb tenses, verb forms, verb phrases, and phrasal verbs.

- **Attention to the Special Needs of Students.** Unit V is a handbook-like section on punctuation, consistency, verb formation and use, quoting, spelling, apostrophe use, double negative correction, hyphenation, capitalization, articles, and prepositions.

- **Glossary.** Key terms are highlighted in the text and defined in the glossary at the back of the book.

- **Full Test Bank.** The ancillary materials include two parallel forms of multiple-choice quizzes, two parallel forms of sentence writing quizzes, and two parallel forms of paragraph editing tests. Additionally, the *Test Bank* includes both a midterm and a final examination.

THE TEACHING AND LEARNING PACKAGE
FOR *WRITING WITH CONFIDENCE*

A combined Instructor's Manual/Test Bank package is offered to adopters of this edition. These components have been crafted to ensure that the course is a rewarding experience for both instructors and students. The **Instructor's Manual** contains teaching tips, overhead transparency masters, additional exercises and tests, and answers to all in-text questions. The **Test Bank** contains a wealth of additional quizzes, tests, and exercises—keyed to each chapter in the student text. The Instructor's Manual and Test Bank is printed on $8\frac{1}{2} \times 11$ paper, perforated for easy removal and copying. ISBN 0-205-61784-0

THE PEARSON DEVELOPMENTAL
WRITING ANCILLARY PACKAGE

In addition to the book-specific supplements discussed above, Pearson offers a wealth of instructor and student ancillaries to complement *Writing with Confidence*. Please visit our online catalog at www.pearsonhighered.com/devenglish or consult your Pearson Arts & Sciences Representative for options that best suit your interests.

Multimedia Offerings

Q: Do your students have trouble transferring skill and drill lessons into their own writing or seeing errors in others' writing? • Would you like constant awareness of your students' progress and work in an easy-to-use tracking system? • Would a mastery results reporter help you to plan your lectures according to your class' weaknesses? • Do you want to save time by having work automatically graded and feedback supplied?

My WritingLab (**www.mywritinglab.com**)   MyWritingLab is a complete on-line learning system with *better* practice exercises to make students better writers. The exercises in MyWritingLab are progressive, which means within each skill module students move from literal comprehension to critical application to demonstrating their skills in their own writing. The 9,000-plus exercises in the system do rehearse grammar, but they also extend into the writing process, paragraph development, essay development, and research. A thorough diagnostic test outlines where students have not yet mastered the skill, and an easy-to-use tracking systems enables students and instructors to monitor all work in MyWritingLab.

Penguin Discount Novel Program

In cooperation with Penguin Putnam, Inc., Pearson is proud to offer a variety of Penguin paperbacks at a significant discount when packaged with any Pearson title. Excellent additions to any English course, Penguin titles give students the opportunity to explore contemporary and classical fiction and drama. The available titles include works by authors as diverse as Toni Morrison, Julia Alvarez, Mary Shelley, and Shakespeare. To review the complete list of titles available, visit the Pearson-Penguin-Putnam Web site: http://www.pearsonhighered.com/penguin.

ACKNOWLEDGMENTS

As always, I am grateful for the support of my colleagues at Truman College and the City Colleges of Chicago. I am especially grateful to my students, who continually teach me how the writing process works and should be addressed. I especially thank the students who have contributed paragraphs and essays to the text: Linder Anim, Bozena Budżyńska, Victor Ciurte, Mirham Mahmutagic, Veronica Fleeton, Ehsan Ghoreishi, Iman Rooker, Mark Schlitt, Sara Sebring, Jane Smith, Amra Skocic, Erica Teal, and Tuyet-Ahn Van. Again, Professor Patricia W. Kato of Chattanooga State Community College, Chattanooga, Tennessee, deserves my special thanks for providing several of the reading selections and student paragraphs for the book. And so does Professor Sherry F. Gott of Danville Community College, Danville, Virginia, who provided Jane Smith's student essay.

Again, I want to acknowledge Gerald Graff and Cathy Birkenstein's contribution to the profession through their groundbreaking work with templates, which I have adapted for my purposes in this edition.

And, of course, I thank the reviewers of the manuscript for their insights, suggestions, and even enthusiasm, which have helped guide this revision: Joan Cashion, Marymount College; Deborah Fontaine, Okaloosa-Walton College; Dr. Beatrice Mendez Newman, The University of Texas-Pan American; Julia Nichols, Okaloosa-Walton College; and Kari Sayers, Marymount College, Palos Verdes.

I also thank all those who have worked so diligently in the copyediting and production of the text. I thank my acquisitions editor, Matt Wright, for laying the foundation for this edition. I thank the production team: Martha Beyerlein and the staff at Elm Street Publishing Services and Longman Production Manager Eric Jorgensen. But most importantly, I express my deepest indebtedness to my development editor, Ann Hofstra Grogg, whose analytical mind, keen eye for detail, and passionate commitment to excellence have guided me through many editions of this text.

Finally, I thank my family: my wife and best friend, Ann, who has been my loving and supportive companion for more than four decades; and my children, Sarah and Bradley, whose accomplishments both professionally and personally give me so much pride.

ALAN MEYERS

Building Your Writing Skills

The word *writing* comes from a verb. That means it's an activity—a process.

Therefore, you shouldn't think of writing as merely a "paper," an "assignment," a "story"—some *thing* that magically emerges from the hands of a genius. Yes, some people have a natural gift for writing. But it was Thomas Alva Edison (an elementary-school dropout) who said, "Genius is 1 percent inspiration and 99 percent perspiration." All of us can write, provided we're willing to engage in the process.

Writing is a way to produce language, which you do naturally when you speak. You say something, think of more to say, perhaps correct something you've said, and then move on to the next statement. Writing isn't much different, except that you take more time to think about your subject, the person or people you'll be discussing it with, and the goal you hope to achieve in that discussion. You also take more time to form your words and then change them until they clearly express your thoughts.

The four chapters in this unit will show you how to engage in the writing process. They'll discuss why you write (and there are plenty of good reasons), how to discover and organize your thoughts, how to capture them on the page, and how to revise and rewrite them so they achieve your goals. These chapters suggest ways to make your writing interesting, direct, and clear.

Don't worry if you're new to, or unsure about, the writing process. The lessons in this unit will take you through it step by step. Follow those steps and you can indeed write well—and with confidence. ■

Why Write?

Let's start with a basic point: writing is speaking to others on paper—or on a computer screen. If you can speak, you can write. Yes, writing is partly a talent, but it's mostly a *skill,* and like any skill, it improves with practice. Writing is also an *action*—a process of discovering and assembling your ideas, putting them on paper, and reshaping and revising them. We'll examine the writing process in Chapter 2, but here we'll look briefly at

- the relationship between speaking and writing
- the ways you can build confidence in your writing
- the ways you choose to write
- the ways you can use writing

SPEAKING AND WRITING

When you speak, you don't just make sounds. You say *words* that *mean* something. You speak because you want to share an idea, give information, express a greeting, state an opinion, or even send a warning. That is, you speak because you have

1. something to say: *a subject*
2. a reason for saying it: *a purpose*
3. someone to say it to: *an audience*

When you speak, you can see and hear your listeners. They respond to you, and you respond to them. You answer their questions, restate ideas, and even change the subject if it bores them. You use your voice and body to emphasize and clarify your ideas. You raise or lower your voice, talk quickly or slowly, and pause for effect. You point with your hands, shrug your shoulders, wink your eye, grin, or frown. And when you speak, you also find your thoughts coming into focus. You correct yourself, restate your ideas, illustrate your opinions, or even change your mind. In short, you're both stating and examining your ideas as you say them aloud.

Writing is much like speaking—a way to discover and communicate your ideas. Unlike speaking, however, it doesn't happen all at once. You cannot see and hear your readers, so you must predict their reactions. You must think about a subject that will interest them and try to present it in an interesting way. You must consider if an idea won't be clear to your readers and then try to make it clear. You must anticipate their questions and then try to answer them. Because you cannot emphasize your ideas through your body and speaking voice, you must pay more attention to your word choice. You must present your ideas in a logical order. You must read what you write and then rewrite it until you express your meaning strongly and clearly. In short, you must choose your language carefully, arrange it carefully, and punctuate it carefully.

You cannot do all of these things at once. Any good paragraph or essay goes through many stages before it's finished. First, you may simply explore ideas as you put them into words, lists, or charts. Afterward, you write a first draft and let it sit for a while. Then you can question and challenge it, and probably rewrite it. Perhaps you'll revise and polish your ideas and language in several drafts until you're confident that your audience will understand and care about what you have to say. You must fine-tune your message *before* you send it out.

That's what this book will help you do.

WRITING WITH CONFIDENCE

Now in its ninth edition and in print since 1979, *Writing with Confidence* has helped hundreds of thousands of people build and improve their writing skills. In fact, many of the model paragraphs and themes you'll see in the following chapters were written by students who used this book. They learned to write with confidence, and you can, too.

Perhaps you've had problems with writing in the past—getting started, organizing your thoughts, finding the right words, or mastering the rules of grammar and punctuation. Perhaps you even struggle with writing in English if it's your second (or third, or fourth) language. This book is designed to give you the best chance to improve. It divides the writing process into a series of small steps that you can master:

- ways to begin thinking about writing
- ways to explore and expand your ideas freely
- ways to shape those ideas into a plan
- ways to compose a first draft
- ways to review and revise the draft
- the way to produce final copy

Later sections of the book will give you additional help:

- suggestions for fixing problem sentences and combining sentences for variety
- strategies for organizing paragraphs and essays
- readings to serve as models of strong writing and as prompts for your own essays
- advice on mastering additional grammatical and mechanical matters

As you follow the program in *Writing with Confidence*, you should discover that, although writing is rarely easy, it need not be painful and can even be fun. Flip through the pages of this book and you'll discover that many of the exercises discuss unusual people, places, animals, and events. When you revise the sentences in these exercises, you'll see how your improvements make subjects become clearer and more alive. In short, you'll learn how ideas worth reading about can get even better.

Remember that writing is a process. Remember, too, that writing is a skill that, like all skills, improves with practice. This book is filled with exercises that give you that practice. Doing them will build your confidence in your writing.

FINDING THE RIGHT WAY TO WRITE

Writing is a personal process, and no two people approach it in exactly the same way. So you should determine what works for you. Do you write best in the morning or at night? Do you write by hand or on a computer, or a combination of both? But there's one thing that you should never do: sit down to write a paper the night before it's due. You *cannot* do your best under those circumstances. Because writing is a process, you must give yourself time to work through the process.

Some writers are great planners. They see where they're going and get there with only small changes in their plans. Other writers are discoverers. They need to reach their destination by writing and then rewriting many times. But every writing task is different. Therefore, you might be a great planner in one situation, a great discoverer in another. In general, though, you should begin with a plan and then discover ideas along the way. You don't have to solve every problem before you begin. In fact, people who try that often experience *writer's block.*

The first step in planning is to prepare a schedule. Allow yourself time to list some topics, mull them over, and then choose one. Let ideas occur to you in the shower or on the way to class, and jot them down whenever you can. (You'll see specific ways to do this in Chapter 2.) Give yourself time to write a first draft, put it aside, and return to it a day or two later. You may spend three hours on an assignment, but they could be spread out in half-hour segments over five days. If you do your work in small steps, you'll accomplish something in every session. That will help you build your confidence.

WRITING FOR EVERY REASON

Now that we've looked briefly at the writing process, let's go back and answer the question in the title of this chapter: why write?

Writing to Work

We live in a technological world, where many jobs have been sent abroad to less-developed countries and mega-malls have replaced the corner mom-and-pop stores. Today's economy requires that you write more than ever before. And with computers now a part of almost every job, word processing and e-mailing are essential skills.

Getting and keeping a job these days usually involves good writing skills. You'll get a job partly by writing a strong letter of application and résumé. You'll keep a job by writing clear memos and reports. If you're an office worker, you'll write memos and letters. If you're a health-care professional, you'll write clear records, memos, and orders. If you're a lawyer, you'll write legal briefs and documents.

Writing to Learn

Right now, of course, you're a college student, and your main job (or one of your main jobs) is to succeed in school. To do that, you need to take notes and write clear essays, reports, and answers to examination questions—and even an occasional letter or e-mail home.

For success in college, you should make note taking a habit. The physical act of writing will help you learn. Begin by taking notes on your readings; mark up your texts with questions, reactions, and reminders. If you have questions, write them down and bring them to class to get answers. And, of course, take good notes on your class lectures. Take notes on your assignments, too, so you know what's expected of you and when it's expected. These practices will help not only your writing but also your success as a student.

Keeping a writing log or subject journal can give your learning a big boost. You can record your progress in learning, jot down questions to ask your instructors, and explore your thoughts about new concepts and materials. Some students use a double-entry journal in which they summarize reading or lecture notes on the left-hand column or page and explore their reactions and questions to this material on the facing right-hand column or page.

Writing to Communicate

With so many computers connected to the Internet these days, people are e-mailing coworkers, friends, and relatives regularly. Why make a long-distance telephone call (and connect to an answering machine) when you can send a quick computer message or get in a chat room to exchange messages? Students are e-mailing their professors to find out about classroom assignments—and to submit them. They're e-mailing classmates to discuss and work together on homework. They're also sharing text messages about soccer practices and clubs, gossip, and philosophies of life. People are applying for jobs, conducting business, staying in touch, and even falling in love—all by writing!

In spite of computers, there will always be a place and need for the personal letter. A handwritten note from a friend, cousin, child, or parent is, and will continue to be, the best way to communicate important thoughts at important times. No matter what the content, the real message is, "I care about you and want to keep in touch." These writing practices pay off in ways that can't be measured in dollars or grades, only in the success of human relationships.

Writing for Yourself

There is another reason to write—for yourself—and this reason will last a lifetime. In this sense, all of us are writers. We write to explore our ideas, plans, sorrows, and dreams. We write to record what we've learned and done, or need to learn or do. We write to communicate with friends and relatives. We write to record family histories so our children and grandchildren can know and appreciate their heritage. We write for our own growth and pleasure. If you haven't ever written for pleasure, you may discover that, as your writing voice gains power and strength, writing can indeed be a joy.

Many writers like to keep a personal journal. It might be just a diary in which you summarize your daily activities ("Studied math for two hours, took a break to talk to Ron, and then started work on the biology project due Friday"). But the best journals serve as places to record your concerns and interests, to keep tabs on your questions and plans, to capture what surprises or puzzles you, to blow off steam, and to work through a problem and find a solution.

Take just ten minutes a day. Describe funny, dramatic, or troubling events, or examine interesting places or people. Even if you never do anything more with your journal, it will give you personal satisfaction and continual practice with writing. Often, however, college students find that their journals do become starting points for essays. They're resources for ideas that constitute the first step in the writing process. With a number of ideas already on paper, you won't have to take time searching for new material.

No matter what reason you choose to write, remember this: Good writers follow one universal practice—they write a lot.

GETTING A HEAD START

Begin the writing process now. List some topics for later writings. What has made you think, made you dream, made you mad? Jot down a few ideas. Then consider (but don't worry if you cannot yet answer) these questions on each topic: Why do I want to capture those ideas and express them? To whom do I want to tell them?

_____

_____

_____

_____

_____

_____

_____

_____

The Writing Process
Laying the Foundation

Writing with confidence comes from engaging in a *process* of writing. The page you're reading right now is the finished product of many hours of composing and revising. You don't see the papers that went into the wastebasket along the way: the notes, the false starts, the early drafts, and the later ones. You don't see the changes made in response to student reactions, the advice from professors who use this book in their classes, and the comments of editors. But the process does work, and it will work for you, too. In this chapter, you'll examine the steps in that process. They'll cover

- ways to gather and shape ideas
- ways to get your first draft on paper or in the computer
- ways to revise and edit your work

WRITING WITH CONFIDENCE IN SIX STEPS

No two writers approach writing in exactly the same way. But they do tend to follow a series of actions that look something like this:

1. Exploring ideas
   a. Considering subject
   b. Considering purpose
   c. Considering audience
2. Prewriting—using one or more of these methods
   a. Brainstorming
   b. Clustering
   c. Freewriting
3. Organizing
   a. Selecting
   b. Outlining
4. Writing a first draft
   a. Writing quickly to capture ideas
   b. Inserting notes and new ideas in the margins

5. Revising the draft
   a. Reviewing
   b. Reading aloud
   c. Predicting
6. Producing the final copy
   a. Editing
   b. Copying over
   c. Proofreading and copying over again

STEP 1: EXPLORING IDEAS

Remember that writing is like speech, and speaking includes discovering ideas as you say them. So before you sit down to write, let your mind speak freely. Thoughts will occur to you at odd times and in odd places—while walking the dog, traveling to work, stretching out on the couch. When inspiration happens, capture it by writing on whatever you can—napkins, scraps of paper, or even the back of your hand.

Eventually, though, you should focus your exploration more systematically. As in speaking, you must have something to say, a reason for saying it, and someone to say it to. Ask yourself three questions:

- What is my subject?
- What is my purpose?
- Who is my audience?

Take notes on your answers.

Your Subject

Ask yourself, *what is my **subject**, and what do I know about it?* The most interesting subjects to your audience are those that you also find most interesting. Choose a subject that you care about and know about (or can find out about). Then you'll have something interesting to say, and you'll say it more clearly and confidently.

College assignments sometimes give you freedom to choose your subject. Often, though, you must select and then narrow your subject from an assigned general topic. For example, suppose you're asked to describe a job you know well. Ask yourself:

- What jobs have I done or do now?
- What do I know about these jobs?
- Which jobs (or parts of one job) do I feel strongly about? What do I love or hate? What parts make me angry or happy?

E X E R C I S E I   Exploring a Subject

Start thinking about a job as the potential subject of a paragraph. If you've never had a job, choose a "job" you've been responsible for at home. Explore your ideas. Jot notes in the margin or on a separate sheet of paper. Answer the questions above, and then answer the following:

- What jobs have I done or do now?

- What do I know about these jobs?

- Which jobs (or parts of one job) do I feel strongly about? What do I love or hate? What parts make me angry or happy?

- What tools or materials do I use in my job?

- How do I perform each task?

- Which tasks are most interesting or boring?

- What examples or little stories best illustrate these points?

Your Purpose

Now ask yourself, *what is my purpose?* Communicating always has a purpose: to inform, to persuade, or to entertain—or maybe to do all three. You could, for example, *inform* your classmates about some procedures at your job. You could also *persuade* your classmates that they should find (or avoid) a job like yours. Or you could simply *entertain* your classmates with examples of odd incidents you've experienced at your job.

E X E R C I S E   2   Defining Purpose

Each of the following sentences could begin a paragraph. Read the sentence and then predict the purpose of the paragraph. Will it probably inform, entertain, or persuade? There may be more than one possibility. Be prepared to explain your answers.

1. Before November 18, 1883, when the railroads instituted Standard Time and time zones, the time of day varied from city to city and town to town. *to inform*

2. There must be better ways to resolve differences than going to war.
   _____

3. More Americans, from both the North and the South, died during the Civil War (620,000) than in all of our nation's other wars combined, from the Revolution to the present. _____

4. The history behind the naming of the months of the calendar is fascinating.
   _____

5. The Roman Emperors Julius and Augustus Caesar each added a month to the year, and named them, of course, after themselves. _____

6. Beginning with California in 1994, many states have now banned smoking in all workplaces and restaurants, but it's high time for all the other states to do the same.

_____

EXERCISE 3   Exploring Purpose

COLLABORATIVE ACTIVITY I

Comparing Revisions
Discuss the sentences you wrote in Exercise 3. Does each accomplish its purpose? If not, how could it be revised?

Revise one of the sentences from Exercise 2 so that it begins three different paragraphs: one that informs, one that entertains, and one that persuades. For example:

> a. (to inform) Before November 18, 1883, when the railroads instituted Standard Time and time zones, the time of day varied from city to city and town to town.
>
> b. (to entertain) Before the railroads instituted Standard Time and time zones in 1883, nobody knew when trains would arrive, and the results were chaotic.
>
> c. (to persuade) Although it may seem trivial, the switch to Standard Time and time zones on November 18, 1883, revolutionized life in this country and throughout the world.

Your Audience

Ask yourself, *who is my **audience?*** The answer will help you determine the content and purpose of your writing. For example, you might need to explain a great deal to a reader who's unfamiliar with your subject, but a lot less to a reader who knows your subject well. Or you might need to provide a lot of evidence to persuade a reader who doesn't agree with your ideas or point of view, but provide far less for someone who tends to agree with you.

EXERCISE 4   Adjusting for Audience

For each of the following topics, list two or three points you would include if you were writing to the different audiences specified.

1. Topic: the benefits of controlled diets

a. Audience: overweight adults

   better health, better appearance, feeling of well-being

b. Audience: athletes

   _____

2. Topic: the role of personal Web sites on the Internet like MySpace

a. Audience: people between the ages of 12 and 30

   _____

b. Audience: people between the ages of 40 and 70

   _____

3. Topic: the reasons for requiring helmets for motorcycle riders

   a. Audience: riders of motorcycles

   _____

   b. Audience: motorcycle manufacturers

   _____

EXERCISE 5   Recognizing Purpose and Audience

Read this passage and then answer the questions that follow. Record your answers below or in your journal. Your instructor may also ask you to discuss them with classmates.

No Problem, But It Needs a Solution
Bill Cosby
* * * *

When your fifteen-year-old son does speak, he often says one of two things: either "Okay," which, as we know, means "I haven't killed anyone," or "No problem."

"No problem" has been my son's philosophy of life. Two years ago, he was one of the top ten underachievers in our state and whenever you asked him how he was doing in school, he always said, with simple eloquence, "No problem." And, of course, his answer made sense: there *was* no problem, no confusion about how he was doing. He had failed everything; and what he hadn't failed, he hadn't taken yet. (Undoubtedly, F's had even been penciled in for next year.) He had even failed *English.*

His failing his native tongue piqued my curiosity, so I said, "How can you fail English?"

"Yeah," he replied.

Hoping to get an answer that had something to do with the question, I said again, "Please tell me: how can you fail English?"

"I don't know," he said.

"Son, you didn't really fail *English,* did you? You failed handing in the reports on time, right? Because you can understand people who speak English, can't you? And when you talk, *they* can understand *you,* can't they? So the teacher *understood* what you had written but just didn't care for the way you put it, right? You just failed *organization,* right? I mean, the teacher who failed you in English said, 'He can do the work,' right? It's just that you don't *want* to do it yet. And all it'll take is maybe leaving you out in the wilderness with no food or money in the middle of winter. . . . [until] you're ready to study."

"No problem," he said.

1. What's the writer's main purpose: to inform, persuade, or entertain? Or is it some combination of these purposes? _____

2. Who's the audience for this little article? Would you expect to find it in a college textbook, a newspaper, or in a popular magazine? What reasons can you give for your answers? _____

3. What point (or points) is the writer making? _____

4. What's the writer's attitude toward his son? Does he have more than one attitude? How do you know? _____

STEP 2: PREWRITING

The second step of the writing process involves capturing your thoughts on paper or on the computer screen. Jot down whatever comes to mind. Don't worry about spelling or punctuation or exact meanings, because you will probably change your mind and your phrasing later anyway. This step is called **prewriting.** It's a time to relax, to let the words flow, to see your ideas take shape. The process can even be fun!

Brainstorming

One way to capture your thoughts is by **brainstorming**, or listing thoughts as they come to you. Here's an example from a student who has been asked to describe a job:

> Deliver pizza for Guido's Glorious Pizzas
> Pay: minimum wage plus tips
> work nites, 6 to 10
> boss is impatient
> must use cell phone
> hate some customers
> fraternity guys who always are partying, forget to tip
> fussy lady who makes me take back cold pizza
> drunk guy who answers bell after six rings

You might also brainstorm a second (or even a third) time to generate more ideas.

Clustering

In **clustering,** you put your topic in a circle in the middle of the page and then add related ideas as they occur to you. These related ideas are also called *branches*.

my job
delivering pizza

You can then add more branches as more ideas occur to you. A completed diagram might look like this:

Freewriting

Another way to get started is through **freewriting.** You simply write about the subject without worrying about sentence structure, spelling, logic, and grammar. Write it as you would speak it. Use abbreviations and shortcuts so you can get your ideas down fast. Here's an example:

> Work part time delivering pizza for Guido's Glorious Pizzas. Nites 6 to 10 three days during week and on Saturday eve. Drive an old beater held together with duct tape and chewing gum. Have to have a cell phone because new orders come in all night, I need directions, and some customers won't open the door unless I call. Customers are a pain. One woman, I'll call her Fussy Ms. Fritzy, is very impressed with herself. Every time I deliver a pizza, she gives me a hard time. It's cold, it's not what she ordered, it smells funny. (Of course, she keeps on ordering.) All her gold bracelets and fancy hairdos. Once she looked in the box and told

> me she wanted triple extra cheeze, not double. And told me to give her a discount or take it back. What could I do? Either give the discount or eat the pizza myself. Another customer, Wobbly Wally, takes 4 mins to anser the door-after I ring the bell six times. Beer can in his hand and breathe to kill any infectious disease. I think I could give him cheese on cardboard and he wouldn't know the diffrence. Fumbles to find money, gives me a $20 bill and doesn't count the change. The fab fraternity four are another pleasure. Their always partying. The music is so loud my teeth rattle when one of them opens the door. They wear T-shirts with cutoff sleeves and bellys hanging out over their pants. They grab the pizza, pay me, and give me a thank you but never a tip. I guess it's not a bad job, it beats digging ditches.

Don't think of your freewriting as disorganized. It's just a way to get your creative juices flowing and put ideas into words that you can look at, expand on, change, or omit.

EXERCISE 6   Prewriting a Paragraph

Return to the job you chose to explore as a subject in Exercise 1, or choose another job, hobby, or skill you know well. Consider how the topic might interest your classmates. Consider your purpose: will you inform, persuade, or entertain? Then do a brainstorming list, a clustering diagram, and a freewriting page so that you can sample each of these techniques. See which ones you find most useful.

STEP 3: ORGANIZING

With your ideas roughly captured in words, you can select from and organize them.

- Underline or highlight the most promising ideas in your brainstorming list. Then rewrite the list, putting related ideas together. Add to the list as more ideas occur to you.
- Choose the part of the clustering diagram that seems most promising. Do a second clustering diagram that explores those ideas in greater detail.
- Circle or highlight the most promising parts of your freewriting. Base a second or even a third freewriting on them. Focus more narrowly on your subject and add more details.

Selecting

Once you've narrowed your focus and generated more ideas, you can choose the ones that fit your purpose and audience. For example, the pizza delivery writer might decide that his purpose is to entertain classmates who also have part-time jobs—and to make the point that his job really isn't so bad. So he'd select only the most humorous information. That's the customers he typically serves: Fussy Ms. Fritzy, Wobbly Wally, and the fraternity boys. He'd then omit unimportant details or ones that drift off his point—perhaps the ones about his cell phone and maybe even his working hours. And he would generate more details to develop the humor.

Outlining

After deciding to focus on customers, the pizza delivery writer can make a rough outline. It might include about three examples and details in categories according to customer. The outline would look something like this:

Fussy Ms. Fritzy

  Answers door with gold bracelets dangling from her arm and $90 perm

  Complains about the pizza

    One time: too cold

    Another time: it smells funny

    Another time: wants a discount

Wobbly Wally

  Have to ring door bell six times

  Arrives after 4 minutes

  Always has beer can in hand

  Breath that could kill

  Almost unconscious

  Fumbles to find money, gives me $20 and doesn't count the change

The Fab Fraternity Four

  Always partying

  Loud music

  T-shirts with cutoff sleeves and bellies hanging out over their pants

  Never tip me

Of course, he could arrange the details in other ways: in a time sequence, perhaps with each stop on a typical delivery night, or as a comparison of the best and worst customers. There are many ways to organize paragraphs, as later chapters in this book will explain.

EXERCISE 7   Selecting and Outlining

Return to the materials you generated in Exercise 6, and consider your purpose and audience. What point do you want to make, and to whom? Select your ideas by underlining, circling, or highlighting them. Arrange the ideas in an informal outline. If you discover that some parts of the outline are thin, generate some additional details for those parts.

STEP 4: WRITING A FIRST DRAFT

You've done some prewriting, selected your best ideas, and arranged them in some reasonable order. Now you can confidently begin the first draft. Don't worry about writing something "perfect." No one gets it right on the first try. Remember that writing is a process of self-discovery. New ideas will come to you, and you may discover a different and better arrangement of ideas. So write fast, as if you were speaking your words aloud. Circle words or sentences that you want to revise later. If a new idea occurs to you that belongs earlier in the draft, make a note about it in the margin, write it on a second sheet of paper, or mouse click to the spot you want to insert it. Here's an example of a first draft:

I have a part-time job delivering pizzas for Guido's Glorious Pizzas three nights a week and on Saturday nights. I can put up with driving an old beater held together with duct tape and chewing gum, but the customers can be a pain. One woman, I'll call her Fussy Ms. Fritzy, answers the door with dozens of gold bracelets hanging from her wrist and a puffed up $90 hairdo that must be left over from the 1950's. Every time I deliver a pizza, she gives me a hard time. She says it's to cold, or it's not what she ordered, or she claimed it smells funny. Once she opened the box and told me she wanted triple extra cheeze, not double. She even demanded a discount. I had to give her the discount or eat the pizza myself. Another customer, Wobbly Wally, takes 4 minutes to anser the door after I ring the bell six times. He always has a beer can in his hand and sort of sways back and forth as if he s on a ship in a storm. When he talks, his breath kills. I think I could give him cheese on cardboard and he wouldn't know the diffrence. He fumbles in the pockets of his torn pants to find money, gives me a $20 bill and doesn't count the change. The fab fraternity four are another pleasure. When I arrive with the pizza, their always partying. Every time they open the door, the music from the apartment is so loud my teeth rattle. They're a lovely bunch in their T-shirts with cutoff sleeves and bellies hanging out over their pants. One of them grabs the pizza, pays me, and thank me but never gives me a tip. I hate some of the customers, the job isn't too bad. It pays well enough, and it beats digging ditches.

EXERCISE 8   Drafting a Paragraph

Write a first draft based on the selecting and outlining you did in Exercise 7. If you compose by hand, write on one side of the page only, leave wide margins, and skip every other line so that you have room for additional changes. If you compose by computer, double- or triple-space and leave wide margins as well.

STEP 5: REVISING THE DRAFT

After completing your first draft, set it aside. Give yourself a chance to see it with fresh eyes later. It's hard to think about changing and correcting your work immediately after you finish a draft. You tend to read what you *think* you said, not what's actually on the page. If you've composed it on the computer, print out a hard copy to work on later.

Reviewing

When you go back to your writing, read it carefully. Study its organization, word choice, and details. You'll probably find some things to cut, as well as some things to add. Rearrange sections, rephrase sentences, and improve your word choice. Look at the words you circled earlier and correct the spelling of the words you keep. Make notes in the margins and above the lines. Write new sections and draw arrows to where they will go—or compose them on the computer. If necessary, make a clean copy before going any further. Here's a bit of the first draft on delivering pizza after the writer reviewed it:

COLLABORATIVE ACTIVITY 2

Predicting

Take turns reading your drafts aloud, following the procedures for predicting. Take notes on what others suggest or what you discover so that you can revise your draft fully.

> One woman, I'll call her ~~Fussy~~ Ms. Fritzy, answers the door with dozens of gold bracelets hanging from her wrist and a puffed up $90 hairdo ~~that must be left over~~ from the 1950's. Every time I deliver a pizza, ^complains that
> she ^~~gives me a hard time. She says~~ it's ^too ~~to~~ cold, or it's not what she ordered, or ~~she claimed~~ it smells funny.

Reading Aloud

Now read your work aloud. Listen hard. You'll probably hear mistakes to correct and discover improvements to make. Then read your work again—perhaps to another person—and repeat the process until you're satisfied that your writing is interesting and clear. Don't ask yourself and others, "Can this be understood?" but instead, "Can this be *mis*understood?"

Predicting

Remember, readers don't merely receive information; they actively attempt to find meaning for themselves. They *predict* what will follow from your opening sentences and then perhaps adjust their predictions as they read on. Your writing can benefit from predicting, too. Here's how to do it:

- Read the first sentence or two.
- Stop and think about (or hear) what your readers would expect to follow.
- Decide if the rest of the paragraph satisfies those predictions.
- Make notes on what to add, remove, or shift to satisfy those expectations.

Predicting is a valuable tool and should become a regular part of your revision practices.

Making a Clean Copy

You've reviewed, read aloud, and made predictions about your first draft. So you've probably come a long way toward doing a second draft. Now write it. You'll probably find more improvements to make as you write. Keep revising and copying over until you're satisfied with (or even proud of) what you've produced.

EXERCISE 9 Revising Your Paragraph

Now review the draft you composed in Exercise 8 one or more times. Make changes on the original version. Read your paper aloud so you can hear the words and rhythms of the sentences. Read the paper to someone else, too, and let the person make predictions and comments. Complete your revision by producing a clean copy incorporating all the changes and improvements you've made.

STEP 6: PRODUCING THE FINAL COPY

Once you're reasonably satisfied with your writing, you can begin the final copy. Prepare it according to guidelines your instructor gives you, or following the guidelines on pages 7 and 8. Before you're finished, however, pay attention to details you've ignored up until now.

Editing

You want people to judge your ideas, not your mistakes. So edit your work carefully. **Editing** requires that you carefully examine and look for errors in what you've written. This kind of attention during early stages of the writing process could freeze your creativity. In the heat of writing and revising, you probably don't want to stop and analyze sentence structure. But now in the final stages of the writing process, you can examine your work coldly and make changes. Check your work for misspelled words and words left out or repeated. Look for grammatical errors, missing word endings, incomplete sentences, and incorrect punctuation. Read the paper more than once. Copy it over or print it out again, including all your changes. This draft should be neat and legible—and represent your best effort.

Proofreading

This is the step in the writing process that students (and even some professional writers) may overlook or not treat seriously. **Proofreading** means carefully examining the last copy again, perhaps comparing it to the previous one. Did you include all your editing changes? Did you make any typographical errors? Read through the paper slowly. Place a ruler under each line to focus your eyes. Read the paper aloud. And then reread it. If necessary, make a new and completely clean copy—and then proofread that copy.

Here's the final draft of the paper on delivering pizza:

> I work part-time three weeknights and on Saturday night delivering for Guido's Glorious Pizzas. I can put up with driving an old beater held together with duct tape and chewing gum, but the customers give me worse indigestion than the pepperoni. One regular customer, Fussy Ms. Fritzy, answers the door with dozens of gold bracelets hanging from her wrist and a puffed up $90 hairdo from the 1950s. She always throws a tantrum. She complains the pizza is too cold, or it's not what she ordered, or it smells funny. Once she looked in the box and screamed that she wanted triple extra cheese, not double. She even demanded a discount. I cut the price by $2 rather than lose the sale and eat the pizza myself. Another customer, Wobbly Wally, takes four minutes to answer the door after I ring the bell six times. He arrives with a beer can in his hand and sways back and forth like a man on a ship in a storm. When he talks, his breath would kill just about any infectious disease. He's so delirious, I think I could give him cheese on cardboard and he wouldn't know the difference. He fumbles in the pockets of his torn pants to find money, gives me a $20 bill, and doesn't count the change. Finally, the Fab Fraternity Four are another of my least favorite regulars. They're always partying when I arrive with the pizza. Every time one of them opens the door, the loud music from the apartment makes my teeth rattle. He grabs the pizza, pays me, and gives me a thank you but never a tip. In spite of the customers, the job isn't too bad. It pays for my school tuition and books—and it beats digging ditches.

Notice that this final draft is livelier than the original. It sticks to the point. Its sentences are clear. Its examples are developed with interesting details.

You can get similar results by working your way through the steps in the writing process described in this chapter, which forms the core of the book. Return to this chapter every time you write, until the process becomes a habit— even an instinct. You, too, can write with confidence.

EXERCISE 10   Editing and Proofreading Your Work

Look over your revised paragraph from Exercise 9 carefully. Correct mistakes in spelling, grammar, and punctuation. Copy over the paper and proofread it more than once. Keep looking for errors. Make a final clean copy and proofread it, too.

IN SUMMARY   The Writing Process

1. Consider your subject, your purpose, and your audience.
2. Explore your ideas by putting them into words through brainstorming, clustering, or freewriting.
3. Decide what to include in your writing and how to organize those details.
4. Compose a first draft (and don't worry about making it perfect).
5. Take a break and then revise the first draft several times, perhaps after getting the reactions of other people.
6. Produce a clean copy when you are reasonably satisfied with your work.
7. Edit this copy and make another if you find errors. Check your corrections and proofread the copy again until your final copy is ready for your instructor.

CHAPTER 3

Writing a Powerful Paragraph

Building the Foundation

Now that you've seen how the writing process works, try applying it. This chapter shows you how to write a powerful paragraph. The process will also work for essays, but let's start with paragraphs—the building blocks of essays. In this chapter you'll practice

- choosing the topic
- drafting the topic sentence
- planning and writing the paragraph
- revising and strengthening the paragraph

WHAT IS A PARAGRAPH?

Throughout your college and working career, you'll sometimes need to write single paragraphs—for homework assignments, short essay answers, simple memos, and reports on various subjects. However, learning to write effective paragraphs is also an important first step in learning to write an effective essay. Paragraphs break down the main idea of the essay into smaller, easily understood parts. The first part relates logically to the second part, the second part relates to the third part, and so on. Without these smaller divisions, readers would have a hard time understanding all these ideas, and writers would have an even harder time expressing them.

In fact, you might think of a single paragraph as an essay in miniature. Just as an essay is a group of paragraphs that discuss one large idea, a **paragraph** is a group of sentences that discuss a smaller idea. And, like an essay, the paragraph generally contains an introduction, a body, and a conclusion.

1. The **introduction** catches your reader's interest, and it states the main point, or **claim,** in a **topic sentence.**
2. The **body** supports the main point or claim with explanations, specific details, or examples in three, four, ten, or even more sentences.
3. The **conclusion** often summarizes or ties together the ideas of the paragraph while bringing it to a graceful end.

All paragraphs share several other traits.

1. A paragraph *looks like a unit.* It begins with the first line indented (usually about a half-inch or about five spaces on a word processor). And each new sentence follows the preceding one *on the same line,* not on a new line.

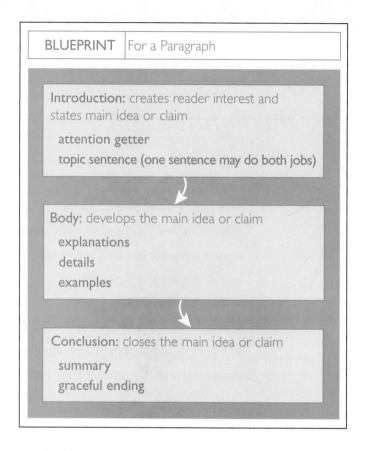

2. A paragraph *is a unit.* That means each sentence is related to and supports the claim or main idea of the topic sentence.

3. A paragraph *holds together.* That means each idea leads clearly and logically into the next.

In short, the structure of the paragraph presents its ideas in a form that's easy for readers to follow. We'll have much more to say about these traits later in this chapter.

EXPLORING AND PLANNING

Remember that the first step in writing is to explore ideas and choose a topic. And that topic has to be limited—or you'll have too much to say and too short a space to say it in.

For example, suppose you chose (or were given) the topic "the influence of television" for a one-paragraph essay. This subject can fill a long book. You could discuss television quiz shows, talk shows, cop shows, cartoon shows, comedies, documentaries, miniseries, movies, soap operas, news broadcasts, sports events, or commercials. And you could discuss the influence of any one of these on preschoolers, older children, teenagers, adults, or the elderly.

You therefore need to narrow the topic. Make a list of smaller topics, like this:

soap operas
Saturday morning cartoons

> the instant replay in sports
> beer commercials
> documentaries
> coverage of the Olympics

Notice that these narrowed topics are also more detailed and specific.

Then *select one topic*—perhaps "soap operas." Consider your attitude toward this topic—and write it as a question to answer in your paragraph:

> Are soap operas good or bad?

You might narrow the topic further by writing more questions:

> Is the way soap operas portray sexual relationships good or bad?
> Is the way soap operas portray sexual relationships good or bad for young people?

Your attitude will help you determine *your purpose* (probably to persuade) and *your audience* (probably people who are somewhat familiar with soaps). Now you can construct a full topic idea (you don't have to write it as a full sentence):

> how soap operas glamorize casual sex instead of lasting relationships

Notice the key terms in the topic idea: *soap operas, sex, relationships.* They're the ones to explore in the next step—prewriting—through brainstorming, clustering, or freewriting. If your ideas about the topic aren't entirely clear at this point, don't worry. They'll become clearer as you work, and you can change them later as you revise.

EXERCISE 1   Narrowing a Topic

Narrow each of the following broad topics to one that can be developed in a single paragraph.

1. A problem in the schools how poor attendance in the primary grades stops children from learning

2. Living in the city or the suburbs _____

_____

3. A popular trend today _____

_____

Examining Your Topic
Choose a topic you would
most like to write about
from Exercise 1. Discuss
your focus, purpose, and
intended audience. Also
discuss how to limit the
topic so that you can
develop it fully in a single
paragraph.

4. Women's roles and men's roles_____

_____

5. A favorite activity_____

_____

6. A family custom (or a custom from your native country)_____

_____

WRITING THE TOPIC SENTENCE

You don't merely absorb ideas from a page as you read. Instead, you work at understanding the writer's ideas. You *predict* what will come based on what you've already seen. For example, suppose you see this sentence at the beginning of a paragraph:

> Slavery was not the only cause of the Civil War in 1861.

What else would you expect to find in the rest of the paragraph?_____

_____

You'd probably expect an explanation of the other causes of the Civil War.

Each paragraph often contains one key sentence—usually, but not always, at or near the beginning of the paragraph—that makes a claim about a main point and suggests how the rest of the paragraph will support that claim or point. This is called the **topic sentence.**

General and Specific Statements

The topic sentence is usually the most general statement in the paragraph, and the rest of the sentences support it with more specific information. For example, which of these two sentences is probably the topic sentence?

> 1. Stan Harris, the drummer in the rock group *The Moving Violations*, is incredibly talented.
> 2. He plays the cymbals well.

You probably chose the first, more general one. It leads logically into explanations and examples of the drummer's talents. The second sentence—a more specific statement—isn't a good topic sentence because it's too difficult to develop. What could you say after "He plays the cymbals well"? Perhaps "He hits them with his drumsticks." That's not exactly a brilliant observation!

Here's a full paragraph based on the topic sentence:

> Stan Harris, the drummer in the rock group *The Moving Violations*, is incredibly talented. He plays the snare drums, the cymbals, the kettledrums, the bongos, the congas, and the xylophone—all in different rhythms and styles. He can set a strong tempo on the snares for hard rock, rumble on the kettledrums for big-band sounds, do fancy riffs on the cymbals, and

switch over to the bongos or congas for the Latin tunes. The great sound of his xylophone blends perfectly with the sounds of the lead and bass guitars. Audiences love his solos on any instrument, and his driving rhythms keep people on the dance floor. It is no wonder that *The Moving Violations* are the most popular band on campus. Catch them when you can.

EXERCISE 2   Identifying Topic Sentences

Underline the topic sentences in the following paragraphs. Be careful: not every topic sentence comes at the beginning.

What's the Name of That Street?

Paragraph A (1) <u>*Sesame Street*, the most popular kids' show in television history, was the bright idea of one person.</u> (2) In 1966, Joan Ganz Cooney worked for a television station in New Jersey. (3) One evening, she and a psychologist friend were sitting around in her apartment after dinner, discussing TV. (4) They had just read a report that very young children watched an average of twenty-seven hours of television a week. (5) Cooney and her friend agreed that if toddlers were going to spend so much time in front of the tube, it made sense to teach them something while they were there. (6) But how could she do it?

Paragraph B (1) Shortly afterward, Cooney thought she had found the answer. (2) She left her job and started the Children's Television Workshop. (3) Her plan was to create an entertaining and fast-moving educational show for preschoolers. (4) Actually, she based her ideas for the show on beer commercials and the hit show *Laugh-In*. (5) Cooney remembers, "Back then, kids were singing beer commercials. (6) We decided to use the idea of commercials to teach."

Paragraph C (1) A show that introduces preschool children to numbers and the letters of the alphabet might not seem like such a big deal today, but back then hardly anyone believed it would work. (2) Carroll Spinney, who plays Big Bird on the show, says that teachers "assumed preschoolers weren't ready to read. (3) So we seemed crazy, proposing to sell kids the ABCs, like other shows hustled sugarcoated breakfast cereals."

Paragraph D (1) NBC, CBS, and ABC thought the idea was too risky—especially when Cooney told them it would cost $8 million a year. (2) So Cooney looked for another way to pay for it. (3) She was in luck. (4) The federal government thought that the show would fit right in with its Headstart program and chipped in $4 million. (5) Cooney raised the rest from the public and from private foundations. (6) She needed every cent. (7) *Sesame Street* would be the most expensive program on television.

Paragraph E (1) Cooney and the show's producer, Jon Stone, wanted to create a setting that very young children from the inner city would recognize. (2) The producers didn't want the action to take place in a tree house. (3) That was because, as Stone says, "Kids learn best in a setting similar to their daily lives." (4) However, no one could think of a good set to build for the show. (5) Then one day Stone saw a commercial asking college students to be tutors in the inner city. (6) The brick and stone buildings in the commercial gave her the idea for the setting of *Sesame Street.*

Paragraph F (1) Choosing a name for the show was a much more difficult job. (2) The writers suggested *104th Street, Columbus Avenue,* and several other names, including *Sesame Street.* (3) Stone hated them all—especially *Sesame Street,* which reminded him of the corny expression used by magicians: "Open sesame!" (4) "Besides," he argued at one meeting, "*Sesame Street* will be too hard for little kids to pronounce." (5) As the time arrived to publicize the show, Cooney asked the writers what name they had come up with. (6) They hadn't thought of one. (7) "I guess we'll have to go with *Sesame Street,*" Stone sighed.

Paragraph G (1) Perhaps Cooney's most important decision was hiring Jim Henson. (2) He was a brilliant young man whose "Muppets" (part *marionette,* part *puppet*) starred in a Washington, D.C., TV show called *Sam and Friends.* (3) They had also been in commercials and had appeared on television elsewhere. (4) His first (and most famous) Muppet was Kermit the Frog. (5) When Henson was a college freshman, he made the green creature by cutting up his mother's old green coat, sewing it into a puppet, and adding the halves of a table tennis ball for eyes.

Paragraph H (1) *Sesame Street* first appeared on November 9, 1969. (2) The program received mixed reviews from the media. (3) Some critics liked it. (4) Many critics said that its fast pace would make kids restless and give them short attention spans. (5) But studies showed that preschool kids who watched *Sesame Street* were better prepared to enter school than kids who didn't. (6) Within a year, *Sesame Street* had more than 7 million regular viewers. (7) It has continued to be the most popular children's show in history, not only in the United States but throughout much of the world.

Making a Claim

The topic of a paragraph is different from its topic sentence. The topic is what the paragraph is "about." But the topic sentence makes a **claim** about the topic. That is, it makes a point that can be debated, that someone else could disagree with. The job of the body of the paragraph is to support or prove the claim. Together, the topic sentence and the supporting sentences answer the question, "So what?" Compare these sentences:

No claim:	Mr. Williams teaches chemistry. (So what? Who can argue with that?)
Claim:	Mr. Williams is an excellent chemistry teacher. (Well, you might think so, but I'm not sure. Tell me why.)

The body of the paragraph will explain why Mr. Williams is excellent.

TIPS

For Testing Topic Sentences

Test your topic sentence by disagreeing with it. If you cannot easily disagree with the topic, revise the sentence to express an attitude.

Weak: There are two movie theaters near campus. (Who can disagree with that?)

Strong: There are not enough movie theaters near campus. (Hmm. There are enough for most people.)

Expressing an Attitude or Opinion

Think of the claim in a topic sentence as expressing an attitude or opinion. For the example you've just seen, *excellent* expresses the writer's attitude or opinion. Compare these sentences:

No attitude:	Most high school graduates go on to college.
Attitude:	A person without a college degree today is at a disadvantage.
No attitude:	I've had a cat for several years.
Attitude:	My cat outsmarts me all the time.

Many topic sentences follow this pattern: *subject + stated or implied attitude or opinion.* Here are examples:

Subject	Attitude or opinion
Our quarterback has some	*unusual* abilities.
I	*enjoy* fishing in the Halifax River.
Mathematics courses	*challenge* me.

Attitude or opinion	Subject
It's *dangerous*	*not to wear seat belts.*

A strong topic sentence usually helps you write a strong body of the paragraph. But don't expect to get it perfect on the first try. You'll probably revise the topic sentence several times. The point of the paragraph may become clear to you only in the late stages of the writing process. You can compose the final version of the topic sentence then.

EXERCISE 3   Revising Topic Sentences

COLLABORATIVE ACTIVITY 2

Discussing Topic Sentences

Compare your revisions of the topic sentences in Exercise 3. List the most interesting revisions and report your findings to the class.

Each of these topic sentences fails to express an attitude or opinion. Rewrite each one so that its attitude or opinion is clear.

1. This paragraph will compare living on campus with going to a commuter college.
Living on campus offers students advantages that going to a commuter college cannot.

2. The topic that I want to discuss is popular music.

3. California has a lot of pet cemeteries.

4. An issue in the modern world is the spread of AIDS.

5. There are many different kinds of sports in the United States.

6. The subject of my paragraph is drugs.

E X E R C I S E   4   Writing Topic Sentences

Assume you'd written the following paragraphs but hadn't yet decided on their topic sentences. Read each paragraph and write its opening topic sentence.

Paragraph A. *The dog has had a long and important relationship with human beings.*

_____

The dog became the first trained animal and the only creature willing to live alongside human beings. Stone Age cave paintings in Spain show that cave dwellers hunted together with trained dogs as early as 10,000 B.C. Many thousands of years before then, however, dogs were working partners with men and women in Europe. The creatures prowled around campfires, ate garbage, and guarded their human "pack."

Paragraph B. _____

_____

The ancient Egyptians used their big dogs to hunt antelope. Some Egyptian kings and wealthy people kept dogs as pets. These pets were the first nonworking animals. In fact, one Egyptian ruler made 2,000 slaves take care of his sacred dogs. Later, the early Greeks used powerful dogs to track lions in Africa. Then, with the development of agriculture, dogs were taught to guard and herd livestock.

Paragraph C. _____

_____

Oddly enough, both dogs and cats came from the same ancestor, which lived 60 million years ago. There is plenty of evidence of the early taming of dogs. Strangely, however, there are no cave paintings or rock carvings of domestic cats. Cats did not appear in written and historical records until 2,000 B.C.

Paragraph D. _____

_____

The Egyptians were the first to tame the African wild cat. They closely associated this animal with their cat-headed goddess, Bast. The cat was a working deity, however. It had to earn its keep by protecting food from rodents. In fact, the cat prevented famine and disease so well that the punishment for killing a feline—even by accident—was death.

Paragraph E. _____

_____

Although Egyptians would not allow anyone to take cats from the country, felines had been smuggled out to all parts of Europe by 900 B.C. There they mated with local wild cats to produce two other breeds. People treasured these animals in the fourteenth century because the felines killed rats that spread the bubonic plague. Unfortunately, later, during the Middle Ages, when the cats were associated with witchcraft and other evils, people tortured and murdered the creatures.

EXERCISE 5   Writing Your Own Topic Sentences

Return to the topic you chose in Exercise 1 (and perhaps discussed in Collaborative Activity 1). Or, if you don't like that topic now, list five or more lessons you have learned or been taught outside school. You don't need to be a Great Philosopher. Instead, think about some small truths about childhood or parenthood, sportsmanship, working, dating, studying, being disciplined, succeeding or failing, saving or spending money. Look over your list and choose the topic you want to explore.

Then narrow its focus and write a preliminary topic sentence. Be sure that your sentence is general (not too specific) and that it makes a claim that expresses an attitude or opinion. Then brainstorm, cluster, or freewrite three to five details and examples that support your claim.

WRITING THE BODY AND CONCLUSION

You've selected a topic and narrowed it. You've examined your attitude toward it so that you can make a claim. You've drafted a topic sentence that opens the way for you to support your ideas. Now begin to develop them.

Generating Ideas

One way to support your topic sentence is to back it up with details. Explore your ideas through brainstorming, clustering, or freewriting. Here, for example, is a brainstorming list to support the topic sentence, "Soap operas set a terrible example for children."

> Too much sex, especially between unmarried people
> Too quickly into sexual relationships—boy meets girl, boy and girl take off clothes, boy and girl hop into bed
> Too many quick break-ups in relationships
>   Example: Tom and Terri on "General Anesthetic"
> Too many bad people tricking good people
>   Example: Wicked Wanda and Sucker Sam on "The Young and the Brainless"
> Too much emphasis on beauty-blonde hair, flat bellies, and Barbie Doll figures
>   Examples: every actress wakes up with perfect hair and fresh lipstick, bikinis are standard dress (when people wear clothes), and the men look like Greek sculptures
> How will children be misled by these shows?

Selecting and Organizing Ideas

After finishing your brainstorming list, clustering diagram, or freewriting page, choose the details that support your topic sentence. Arrange them in an informal outline, as Chapter 2 illustrated. Choose only the details that relate to your purpose. Don't use those that don't fit.

Look for ways to group the details:

- Does your topic sentence mention *reasons, ways, methods,* or some similar labeling word? If so, be sure you supply three or four reasons, ways, or methods.
- Could you make any ideas clearer or more interesting through examples? Provide those examples.
- Do you need to explain any ideas? Explain them.

Then organize your material in some appropriate way.

Developing Ideas

Developing ideas involves explaining, specifying, or illustrating—or some of each.

Explanations. Because the topic sentence of a paragraph usually expresses an attitude or opinion, you might need to explain the reasoning behind your opinion. Why do you think that way? What leads to that conclusion? You might also need to explain unfamiliar ideas to readers. Suppose, for instance, that you claim soap operas set a terrible example for children. You could explain that soaps appear in the late morning and early afternoon, when preschool children watch them with their caregivers. You could also argue that young people aren't emotionally prepared for the kissing and bed-hopping they see on the soaps. (Don't kids say "yuk" when that mushy stuff happens?) In fact, you could argue that these children will be influenced to become involved in sexual relationships long before they can handle them.

Specific Details. Specific information makes general ideas easier to understand and discuss. When, for example, you claim that soap operas are unrealistic, you can support that claim by describing the typical plot of *Most of My Children.* Infants are switched in the hospital at birth, brothers are presumed dead but then reappear, men learn that their sisters are actually their mothers, and every handsome married lawyer romances his beautiful young assistant.

Examples. Examples clarify and illustrate your general statements. For instance, to support your claims about casual sex on the soap operas, you might describe a scene on *One Life to Louse Up* where Trashy Trudy wears a slinky dress while she seduces Frisky Fred over a dozen oysters, a bottle of wine, and a set of silk sheets. You might discuss the episode on *Another Whirl* when Bruno the Body Builder comes home from the health club one afternoon to find his wife, Silvia, massaging the muscles of his best friend, Felix.

Looking at Paragraph Development

Let's look at a paragraph that is weak in development:

> Probably one of the biggest and most expensive meals of all time took place in 1905, when "Diamond Jim" Brady gave a party. Brady spent a lot of money to feed his guests, but, as usual, he ate the largest meal himself. His guests drank a lot of expensive champagne, and everyone agreed that it was a very nice party.

We don't learn very much about the party, and we don't care very much about it, either. The paragraph leaves many questions unanswered, too many claims unsupported, too many ideas unexplained or not illustrated. Just how big and how expensive was this meal the topic sentence discusses? Who was "Diamond Jim" Brady, and why did he give the party? Where was it? How many people attended, and how much did the party cost? What did Brady himself eat? How much did

Brady weigh? How much, how expensive, and what type of champagne did the guests drink? And why did everyone agree that the party was "very nice"?

Here's a revision of the paragraph, this time developed through explanations, specific details, and examples:

> Probably one of the biggest and most expensive meals of all time took place at a hotel in New York City in 1905, when the famous millionaire and the world's greatest eater, "Diamond Jim" Brady, gave a party in honor of his racehorse, Gold Heels. Brady invited only fifty guests, but the food bill came to $40,000. (That is $800 per person!) Since nobody could ever eat more than the 250-pound Brady himself, Diamond Jim's own meal probably came to several thousand dollars' worth. Here, for example, is what he ate—which, for him, was a typical meal. He started with three dozen oysters, followed by a half dozen crabs, two bowls of soup, seven lobsters, two ducks, two huge portions of turtle, a sirloin steak, and large helpings of assorted vegetables. For dessert, he consumed a platter of cakes, pies, cookies, and tarts, and topped it all off with a two-pound box of chocolates. Of course, all that food made him thirsty, so he guzzled a gallon or two of orange juice. Although Brady didn't drink any alcohol (he never did), he served his guests five hundred bottles of very expensive Mumm's champagne. When the meal was over, his guests said that they couldn't recall a nicer party given for a horse.

The second version of the paragraph is much longer than the first. But don't jump to the conclusion that the *quantity* of words provides the power of a paragraph. The *quality* of the information generates that power. A strong paragraph supports its central point through clear, persuasive, and lively explanations, details, and examples.

The amount of specific development to include depends on your answers to three questions:

1. How complicated is the topic idea? The more complicated it is, the more you must explain and illustrate the idea.
2. How much do your readers know about the topic? The less they know, the more information you must supply.
3. How interesting or entertaining should the paragraph be? Examples often enliven the paragraph.

Notice that the three questions relate to the three questions you should ask yourself at the very beginning of the writing process:

- What is my subject?
- What is my purpose?
- Who is my audience?

The answers will shape your writing from start to finish.

Writing a First Draft

Plunge in. There's no way to begin writing other than to write. Following your topic sentence, write one sentence, then another. Develop the topic idea with the explanations, specific details, and examples you gathered and organized. The paragraph should have seven to ten sentences, but don't pad it. And if you think of other information or better ways to present explanations, specific details, and examples, then change your plans.

Don't try to write a perfect first draft. You'll revise your draft later.

Writing a Conclusion

A paragraph's closing sentence often summarizes your claim and supporting information. Sometimes that means returning to the idea of the topic sentence, but don't just repeat the same words. Change the language to make the ending graceful.

Not every conclusion has to summarize, however. You might try ending your paragraph with a bang—with a quotation, a joke, a powerful example, a surprise. And, as with the first draft, expect to revise later.

E X E R C I S E   6   Planning Your Paragraph

Make an informal outline of the paragraph you planned in Exercise 5. The blueprint of the outline should look like this:

- *a preliminary topic sentence that makes your claim*
- *explanations that clarify or details that expand on the claim*
- *one or more examples of the claim and a discussion of each example*
- *a conclusion*

Fill in the blueprint below, or, if you need more room, make your own on a separate sheet of paper.

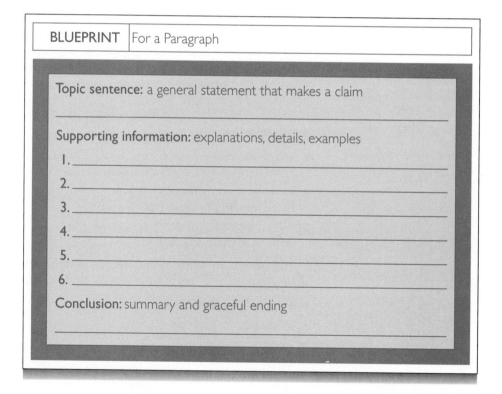

BLUEPRINT | For a Paragraph

Topic sentence: a general statement that makes a claim

_____

Supporting information: explanations, details, examples

1. _____
2. _____
3. _____
4. _____
5. _____
6. _____

Conclusion: summary and graceful ending

_____

E X E R C I S E   7   Drafting Your Paragraph

Now write the first draft. Select the strongest and most relevant details and examples you've numbered. You won't use all of them. Assume that your audience will be your classmates. Your purpose, however, will depend on the subject matter, which could be informative, entertaining (that is, amusing, shocking, or even frightening), or persuasive. The first draft should be about one handwritten page or half a computer-generated, double-spaced page.

REVISING THE PARAGRAPH

You want your readers to understand, appreciate, or be convinced by your message. So make it thorough and clear and help it move logically and smoothly from one idea to the next.

As you revise your paragraph, pay attention to **unity** and **coherence.** Adjust your topic sentence and your conclusion until every part of the paragraph—the introduction, the body, and the conclusion—fits together tightly.

Unity

A good paragraph has **unity.** That means that each sentence in the body supports the topic sentence. As you revise your paragraph, examine your first draft with an eye toward dropping details that don't belong. Almost every first draft contains some information that strays off the point.

For example, the claim of the paragraph "about" Diamond Jim Brady was that *his party was huge and expensive.* It doesn't mention Brady's collection of diamonds (it was large), his love affair with the actress Lillian Russell (she was large, too), or his success as a businessperson (yes, it was also large). These details may be interesting, but they don't belong in the paragraph. If the writer included them in early plans or drafts, they would have to be dropped later.

Key words in the topic sentence might help you test the unity in the body of the paragraph. Here, for example, is a short outline of a paragraph based on a topic sentence presented earlier in the chapter. Notice how the underlined words in the topic sentence provide a guide to the specific explanations, details, and examples that follow:

I enjoy the <u>peace</u> and <u>relaxation</u> of fishing in the Halifax River for <u>four reasons.</u>

First, it gives me a chance to get away from the pressure of my job.

    I work at a bank where I constantly . . .

    I become accustomed to a much more relaxing pace on the river . . .

    There's no clock to worry about . . .

Second, I can spend time with a friend, just talking and . . .

    We often discuss . . . while we . . .

Third, when a fish does bite, I can focus my attention only on . . .

    For example, last year, a twenty-pound bass . . .

Finally, I can go back to my tent, cook the fresh fish over a campfire, and spend a restful evening . . .

EXERCISE 8   Unifying a Paragraph

One sentence in each group strays off the point of its topic sentence. Underline the words in the topic sentence that suggest the type of support you'd expect to follow. Then draw a line through the sentence that doesn't belong.

1. *Topic sentence:* Before the fork was widely used in seventeenth-century Italy, people picked at their food in <u>a variety of ways</u>.

   a. They speared it with an eating knife.

   b. They scooped up their food in a spoon and lifted it to their mouths.

   c. ~~They ridiculed men who used forks as fussy and unmanly.~~

   d. They held food with three fingers because five was considered impolite.

2. *Topic sentence:* Around the time of Jesus, religious law listed a great many crimes that could be punished by stoning.

   a. A woman accused of adultery could be stoned.

   b. A man could be stoned for stealing.

   c. Anyone could be stoned for heresy—that is, disobeying religious laws or practices.

   d. The condemned person's accuser would step forward to "cast the first stone."

3. *Topic sentence:* The origins of nursery rhymes explain why some lyrics might not be suitable for young children.

   a. For centuries, the rhymes were known only as "songs" or "ditties" and were intended mainly for adults.

   b. Some rhymes were taken from crude folk ballads.

   c. In the 1820s, the lyrics of the rhymes were cleaned up because morals had changed.

   d. Many nursery rhymes started as drinking songs, jokes about religious practices, social satires, and the lyrics of romantic songs.

4. *Topic sentence:* Tecumseh (1768–1813) had all the qualities of a true leader of the Native American tribes.

   a. In the War of 1812, he was killed by a bullet through the heart from a member of the United States Cavalry.

   b. In battle, Tecumseh was fierce and fearless.

   c. In conversation, he was sophisticated and refined.

   d. In dress, he refused to wear the clothing of the whites, preferring simple buckskin with a tomahawk and a silver-handled hunting knife shoved under the belt.

5. *Topic sentence:* The superstition about bad luck on Friday the thirteenth came about for a number of reasons.

   a. Adam and Eve were supposedly expelled from the Garden of Eden on a Friday.

   b. Noah's great flood started on a Friday.

   c. Jesus was crucified on Friday.

   d. Twelve witches and the Devil—totaling thirteen—are necessary for a satanic meeting.

   e. But not all combinations of thirteen are deadly—a baker's dozen is thirteen, for example.

Coherence

An effective paragraph must also have **coherence.** The ideas in the paragraph must cohere, which literally means "stick together." So you must make the logical relationships between ideas clear.

You can strengthen coherence in a number of ways.

Logical Arrangement. Arrange your ideas in the most logical order. For example, the paragraph on fishing in the Halifax River describes the four reasons the experience is enjoyable. The paragraph also explains each reason before going on to the next; the explanation doesn't jump back and forth between ideas.

In revising, look carefully at your organization. Have you grouped together similar ideas? Should one idea come before another or follow it? What should you say first—or last?

Pronouns. Use pronouns to link ideas. **Pronouns** replace nouns and refer back to them. *It, this,* and *that* refer to a singular subject; *they, them, these,* or *those* refer to a plural subject. These references tie ideas together and help sentences mesh. But if a pronoun (*he,* for example) can refer to more than one idea in a sentence ("my *brother* borrowed the car from my *father*"), you'll need to repeat the noun to avoid confusion (*my father* or *my brother,* whichever one you mean).

Reinforcement. Repeat key words or ideas in different ways as you move from sentence to sentence. For instance, in the Halifax River paragraph, the phrase *just talking* appears in one sentence, and *we often discuss* appears in the next. Readers can see that the second sentence develops the idea of the first.

Transitions. Use transitional words and phrases to explain relationships. A **transitional word** or **phrase** shows the logical relationship between one idea and another. For example, in the Halifax River paragraph, the words *first, second, third,* and *finally* label the reasons so that readers can easily identify them. The expression *for example* in one sentence clearly introduces an illustration.

Here's a list of other transitions. Consult it often as you write and revise:

> ### TIPS
>
> **For Achieving Coherence with Transitions**
>
> Try this test as you write. After each general statement in your paragraph, say "in other words," "for example," "to be specific," or some other transitional expression. You might not need the transition, but see if it increases the flow between ideas.

TRANSITIONS

For Counting: first, second, third, next, then, after that, finally

For Space Relationships: above, around, behind, below, beneath, beyond, close by, farther away, inside, outside, next to, over, under, underneath

For Time Relationships: after, afterward, after that, before, then, and then, finally, later (on), next, soon, as soon as, the next day, tomorrow, yesterday, a year ago, as, during, immediately, meanwhile, when, while, last night, in March, in 2004, on July 8

For Addition: additionally, also, and, furthermore, in addition, moreover, too

For Comparison: in the same way (manner), likewise, similarly

For Contrast: although, but, even though, however, nevertheless, on the other hand, yet, despite, still

For Emphasis: above all, especially, in fact, most important

For Illustrations: for example, for instance, in particular, such as

For Reasons: because, because of, due to, for, since

For Summary: and so, in other words, in short, in summary, to sum up, to summarize

E X E R C I S E 9   Looking for Coherence

Read the following paragraph, and answer the questions about it.

A Dark, Sweet History

(1) Although history does not prove where the chocolate chip cookie began, it evolved through a very long process. (2) At first, chocolate existed only as a liquid or a powder, not as a solid. (3) The long road to the chocolate chip cookie orginated in Mexico around 1000 B.C. when the Aztecs made a ceremonial drink, *xocoatl,* meaning "bitter water," from crushed cocoa beans. (4) Xocoatl later became *chocolatl* in other Mexican dialects. (5) After the Spanish had conquered Mexico about 2,600 years later, they introduced this drink to Europe, where the recipe remained unchanged until 1828. (6) That year, a candy maker in Holland tried to make a finer chocolate powder but instead created a creamy butter. (7) This discovery led to the world's first solid chocolate, produced by a British company in 1847. (8) Hard chocolate therefore became a reality, and the chocolate chip cookie a possibility. (9) From that point on, the origin of the cookie is less certain. (10) According to legend, the first chocolate chip cookie was baked around 1930 at the Toll House Inn, near Whitman, Massachusetts. (11) Ruth Wakefield, the inn's owner, was also its cook and baker. (12) One day, she added chocolate pieces to her butter cookies, creating the Toll House Inn cookie, which she sold nationally. (13) For chocolate bits, Mrs. Wakefield cut up the Nestle Company's large Semi-Sweet Chocolate Bar. (14) Nestle was impressed with her recipe and asked permission to print it on the wrapper of the bar. (15) Her reward would be a lifetime supply of free chocolate. (16) The cookie was so popular that in 1939 the company finally introduced Morsels, the packaged chocolate chips. (17) From a bitter drink of the Aztec Indians to the household delight of today, chocolate has come a long way.

COLLABORATIVE ACTIVITY 3

Discussing Coherence
Review your answers to Exercise 9. Discuss the way the paragraph achieves unity and coherence.

1. Where is the topic sentence? Underline it.

2. What expressions mark the passage of time? What other transitional expressions give coherence to the passage? Underline them.

3. What key words or ideas are repeated to provide coherence? Circle them.

4. What pronouns establish coherence? Put them in brackets. Look at the adjectives *this* and *that* before nouns. How do these expressions add coherence to the paragraph? _____

_____

5. How many groups or individuals were involved in the process of discovering, transmitting, manufacturing, and producing the ingredients of chocolate chip cookies? _____ What words or phrases identify the groups?

_____

_____

6. Which incident does the paragraph develop most specifically?_____

_____ Why? _____

_____

_____

Refining the Topic Sentence and Conclusion

A good topic sentence not only makes a claim, but also provides a brief "road map" for readers as they journey through the information supporting the claim. For example, suppose in collecting and examining information to support the topic sentence about Mr. Williams ("Mr. Williams is an excellent chemistry teacher") the writer settled on three reasons. The topic sentence can include that information:

> There are *three important reasons* why Mr. Williams is an excellent chemistry teacher.

Here are other topic sentences you saw earlier, now revised with roadmapping language that helps readers predict what will follow:

> Our quarterback has some unusual abilities *as a runner, a passer, a kicker, and even a receiver.*

> Mathematics courses challenge me *to study, analyze, and apply what I've learned.*

You don't have to draw the road maps as you write the topic sentence. Your route may become clear to you only in the later stages of writing. The map isn't always necessary, but it does help readers predict and therefore understand a long, complex paragraph. If you can see the road you're on only after you've traveled it, go back and refine your topic sentence. Your reader will never know you circled back from the end to the beginning.

Keep adjusting your topic sentence and its supporting details until they're perfectly in sync. Then take a look at the conclusion. Can you make it summarize better or end with a stronger punch? Can you shorten the conclusion if it drags on past the logical ending point?

Using Peer Review

Your peers—your own classmates—can be a useful resource as you revise a paper. They can make suggestions and ask you questions about things you hadn't considered.

Your instructor may ask that you form groups of three or four members to review each other's work, or you and some friends may decide to form one of your own. Always begin the peer review session by stating what you like in a paper.

COLLABORATIVE ACTIVITY 4

Responding in Peer Groups
Here's a way for peer groups of three or four members to work productively. Make enough photocopies of your writing for each member. The other group members will do the same. Then read each other's writing during class—or, if possible, ahead of time. Use the Revision Guidelines on page 38 to help you structure your comments. During discussion, take notes. These will help you improve your revision.

Then focus on what could be strengthened or improved. As a writer, you don't have to agree with the group's suggestions, but do consider them. If you find yourself saying, "What I meant to say was . . . ," then stop and write it down. What you meant to say is exactly what you should say.

The Revision Guidelines that follow and appear throughout the book for specific types of writing can structure the comments you make on another writer's papers. They can also help you structure your own revisions as you work alone.

REVISION GUIDELINES   Writing a Powerful Paragraph

1. What is best about the paragraph? What are its strengths?

2. Locate the topic sentence. Does it clearly make a claim that expresses a main point or opinion? What words express that point or opinion?

3. Should any sentences or parts of sentences be restated or reworded? How could they be revised?

4. Can any general ideas be explained more? How? Would examples help? Which examples?

5. Do any statements need examples to clarify their meaning? Are there places where examples might make the paragraph livelier?

6. Look at the end of each sentence and the beginning of the next. Is there a natural flow between sentences? If not, what transitional words or phrases could be added—*therefore, however, because, when, despite, later,* and so on? Should something be deleted or shifted to another location in the paragraph?

7. Look at the beginning and ending sentences of the paragraph. Is the relationship between them clear and logical, or does the paragraph stray off the point? If so, how could the problem be corrected?

8. What would readers *do* with the information in the paragraph? That is, how does the paragraph answer the "So what?" question? Should the paragraph be rearranged or changed to answer that question better?

9. Is the conclusion effective? Does it summarize? Does it end powerfully? How could it be revised if it drags on or strays off the point?

E X E R C I S E   1 0   Arranging a Paragraph

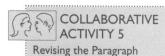

COLLABORATIVE ACTIVITY 5

Revising the Paragraph
Compare the paragraphs you wrote in Exercise 10. Have one person as "secretary" compose a paragraph that incorporates the best ideas of everyone. Submit this revised copy to your instructor.

The following information is totally disorganized. It has no unity or coherence. Number the information in the most logical order. Then compose a paragraph based on the information. Begin with the most likely topic sentence (you can revise it later). Rewrite the other sentences as necessary to create unity and coherence. Add transitions and repeat key terms as necessary. Finally, create a topic sentence and a conclusion.

Most humans are right-handed.

The practice dates back to the fifteenth century.

By studying portraits and drawings of buttoned garments, historians have traced the

reasons why men's clothes button from right to left while women's button from left

to right.

Most men found it easier to have clothes that buttoned from right to left.

Men generally dressed themselves at home, on trips, and on the battlefield.

Buttons were very expensive at the time.

Wealthy women had female servants who dressed them.

Most maids were right-handed.

It was easier to fasten their mistresses' garments if the buttons and buttonholes were reversed.

Maids faced the buttons head on.

The practice has never been changed.

EXERCISE 11   Revising Your Own Paragraph

Check for the unity and coherence in the paragraph you composed in Exercise 7. Look at the topic sentence: Is its point clear? Underline the words that make the claim. Add roadmapping language to the topic sentence if it's needed. (You might need to revise the topic sentence to account for all the information in the paragraph.) Examine the supporting information. Cross out any ideas that stray off topic, and make notes in the margins about where to add sentences or phrases that develop or clarify the point.

Then examine the paragraph for coherence. Should you insert transitional words in any places? Should you repeat any key terms? Have you used pronouns effectively? Are the pronoun references clear? Record your notes above the lines and in the margins. Then rewrite the paragraph.

EXERCISE 12   Editing and Proofreading Your Paragraph

Return to the paragraph that you revised in Exercise 11. Look it over carefully. Can any wording be strengthened? Are the grammar, spelling, and punctuation correct? Make final changes and corrections before writing a clean copy or printing a new computer copy. Then proofread. Submit the final copy to your instructor.

IN SUMMARY   A Paragraph

1. Is focused on a topic that can be developed fully in a short space;
2. Begins with an introduction that attracts the readers' interest;
3. Includes a topic sentence that is the most general statement in the paragraph, makes a claim, and expresses an attitude or opinion;
4. May include a "roadmap";
5. Develops the main point or supports the claim in the body with supporting explanations, details, and examples;
6. Arranges the supporting information in some logical way; and
7. Concludes with a summary or a graceful ending.

Writing an Effective Essay
Building a Larger Structure

Although you often need to write single paragraphs for school or work assignments, you'll write essays far more often. This chapter will teach you to write an essay confidently and efficiently by showing you how to

- plan and organize the essay
- compose and revise the essay

WHAT IS AN ESSAY?

After working with paragraphs, you can turn your attention to the **essay**—an organized discussion of a subject in a series of paragraphs. A single **paragraph** and the essay actually share many traits. The paragraph explores a limited topic, which it introduces in a topic sentence and then supports through explanations, specific details, and examples. The claim of the topic sentence unifies and shapes the content of the paragraph. The **essay** explores a much broader topic, which it introduces through the central claim in a **thesis statement** and then explains and illustrates in separate paragraphs. In other words, the thesis statement unifies and shapes the content of the entire essay.

An essay is not simply a longer version of a paragraph. The content of the essay is more complex and needs much more development. However, the essay is structurally similar to a single paragraph, for it contains three parts:

- The **introduction**—that is, the first paragraph of the essay—attracts the reader's interest, makes the central claim for the essay in a thesis statement, and often previews what follows.
- The **body**—usually at least three paragraphs but often more—develops or supports the thesis statement by breaking it down into smaller ideas or points, each of which is stated and supported in separate paragraphs. Therefore, in a well-organized essay, each body paragraph:
  1. introduces an idea through a topic sentence that develops the thesis statement
  2. develops the idea in the body sentences
  3. and then concludes with a transition to the next paragraph
- The **conclusion**—the last paragraph of the essay—ties all the ideas together and gracefully ends the paper.

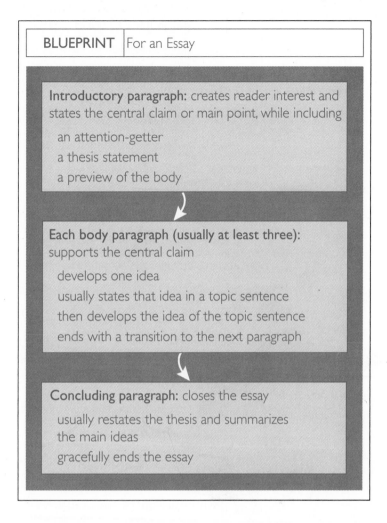

BLUEPRINT | For an Essay

Introductory paragraph: creates reader interest and states the central claim or main point, while including

an attention-getter
a thesis statement
a preview of the body

Each body paragraph (usually at least three): supports the central claim

develops one idea
usually states that idea in a topic sentence
then develops the idea of the topic sentence
ends with a transition to the next paragraph

Concluding paragraph: closes the essay

usually restates the thesis and summarizes the main ideas
gracefully ends the essay

E X E R C I S E I   Analyzing an Essay

Here's a final draft of an essay written by Linder Amin, a student from Ghana, who attended Truman College in Chicago while Michael Jordan was leading the Chicago Bulls basketball team to six National Basketball Association championships. Jordan played from 1984 to 2003, with two one-year retirements (the first to play professional baseball) and is generally regarded as the greatest basketball player of all time. Read the essay and then answer the questions that follow.

Michael Jordan, Superstar
Linder Anim

* * * *

(1) Michael Jordan has played for the Chicago Bulls for years, and everyone cheers for him. Fans have filled the seats at the United Center ever since he led the team to six NBA championships, and many millions have watched each of his games on TV. However, it is no wonder that he has attracted such admiration and fame. [**Thesis statement**] *Jordan possesses all the features of an athletic superstar: extraordinary attractiveness, incredible physical talent, and exemplary character.*

(2) [**Topic sentence**] *First of all, Jordan is a fine physical specimen of a man.* He is not only handsome, but he has a magnificent body on his 6½-foot frame. He always shaves his hair, which seems to symbolize his commitment to the game. With his broad shoulders and rippling muscles, he looks strong and formidable in his number 23 jersey.

(3) [**Topic sentence**] *Second, he is a talented athlete who has developed a game of speed, agility, and intelligence.* He quickly dodges the opposing team's defense and makes spectacular shots, sometimes as he falls away from the basket, other times when he drives toward it. As a result, he always scores a lot of points, which makes him the top scorer on the Bulls and also the rest of the NBA. The amazing part of it all is his "Air Jordan" moves, which rely on agility and leaping ability. He jumps up in the air and can stay there for a long time before coming down. He is also smart, and as the team captain he tries to keep his teammates as disciplined as he is on the court. Without Michael Jordan, the Chicago Bulls would not be where they are today.

(4) [**Topic sentence**] *Finally, Jordan is not only a great athlete, but also a gentleman on and off the basketball court.* As the team captain, he shows cool and controlled leadership and gentility. He never fights, and if any one of his teammates does fight, he immediately calms that person down. After each game, he always puts on a beautiful suit and his earring and politely answers questions from the press. He also donates money to charity for a variety of good causes. Jordan sponsors community services, too, such as basketball camps for kids.

(5) [**Conclusion**] Michael Jordan is a one-of-a-kind superstar. That is why people look up to him.

---

1. How many points does the thesis statement in the first paragraph introduce? _____ What is the function of the opening sentences of the paragraph that lead up to the thesis statement? _____

   _____

2. How are the topic sentences in the body paragraphs related to the thesis statement?

   _____

   Which words or phrases in these paragraphs are transitional? Circle them.

3. Identify the supporting details in the body paragraphs. How many details does each paragraph contain? **Paragraph 2** _____ **Paragraph 3** _____ **Paragraph 4** _____

4. The concluding paragraph consists of only two sentences. Why? _____

   _____

Reread the essay on Michael Jordan and pay special attention to its structure. The framing materials—the thesis statement, topic sentences, and conclusion—shape the whole essay. In fact, if you combined all these framing elements and removed the remaining material, you'd be left with a coherent paragraph:

> Michael Jordan possesses all the features of an athletic superstar: extraordinary attractiveness, incredible physical talent, and exemplary character. First of all, Jordan is a fine physical specimen of a man. Second, he is a talented athlete who has developed a game of speed, agility, and intelligence. Finally, Jordan is not only a great athlete, but also a gentleman on and off the basketball court. Michael Jordan is a one-of-a-kind superstar. That is why people look up to him.

Is this paragraph effective? Only as a summary. You can't develop its ideas very well in so short a space. A large topic such as Michael Jordan's abilities requires a multi-paragraph essay to explain and illustrate its ideas. At the same time, you usually can't expand a strong single paragraph into an essay.

Linder's essay is also graceful in style. Notice how she varies the word choice of her topic sentences instead of simply repeating the language of the thesis statement. Compare these versions:

> Thesis: Jordan possesses all the features of an athletic superstar: extraordinary attractiveness, incredible physical talent, and exemplary character.

Mechanical topic sentence	Graceful topic sentence
(1) First, Jordan is very attractive.	First of all, Jordan is a fine physical specimen of a man.
(2) Second, he has incredible physical talent.	Second, he is a talented athlete who has developed a game of speed, agility, and intelligence.
(3) Third, Jordan also has an exemplary character.	Finally, Jordan is not only a great athlete, but also a gentleman on and off the basketball court.

Linder's essay evolved through hard work in planning, writing, revising, responding to suggestions, and editing. You can do the same.

COMPOSING AN ESSAY

The process of writing an essay basically involves the same six steps you've followed for writing a paragraph:

1. **Exploring** your ideas (subject, purpose, and audience)
2. **Prewriting** to discover ideas and narrow the topic
3. **Organizing** and writing a preliminary thesis statement and topic sentences
4. **Composing** a first draft
5. **Revising** the draft
6. **Producing the final copy** through editing and proofreading

Getting Started

Let's take a look at how Linder composed her essay. She first generated and organized her ideas, probably by brainstorming, clustering, and/or freewriting. Then she outlined her ideas, including a preliminary thesis statement, preliminary topic sentences, and possible supporting details. Here's an outline. Notice that the thesis statement and topic sentences differ slightly from the ones in the essay.

Paragraph 1 thesis: Jordan has all the qualities of a superstar.

Paragraph 2 topic sentence: Jordan is a fine physical specimen.
Details: muscular, 6'6" tall, shaved head, handsome

Paragraph 3 topic sentence: He is a talented athlete who is quick and smart.
Details: quick, great jumper with "Air Jordan" moves, best scorer, cool headed

Paragraph 3 topic sentence: Jordan is also a gentleman on and off the basketball court.
Details: leader on court, never fights, dresses in suit, polite to press, supports charities and community groups

Concluding paragraph: Michael Jordan is one of a kind, and everyone looks up to him.

Developing the Thesis Statement

As you've seen in Linder's essay, the thesis statement is much like the topic sentence of a paragraph, which was discussed and illustrated fully in Chapter 3. Like the topic sentence, the thesis statement should

- be general enough to cover everything in the essay
- make a central claim that expresses an attitude or opinion

The thesis statement also sometimes includes an overview, or preview, of the body paragraphs that will follow. You can attach that preview onto the thesis statement through linking words such as *because, since,* or *by,* or with a colon [:]. Or you can write an entirely separate sentence.

Linder's essay on Michael Jordan evolved in this way. Linder began by quickly jotting down an opinion in a preliminary thesis statement:

> Michael Jordan has all the qualities of a superstar.

She later expanded the thesis by adding the preview:

> Michael Jordan possesses all the qualities of an athletic superstar: extraordinary attractiveness, incredible physical talent, and exemplary character.

When should you write your preview? That depends on when you see the shape of the whole essay most clearly. It may be in the planning stages. It may be in the revision stages. But don't worry if your first thesis statement isn't perfect. You can revise it many times, and at various points in the writing process.

EXERCISE 2   Considering Organization and Development

Examine each of the following thesis statements and predict the main supporting ideas you'd expect to find in the full essay—and the order in which they might be introduced.

1. The federal government of the United States is divided into three main branches— the legislative, executive, and judicial—each branch intended to provide "checks and balances" against the other branches.

    Paragraph 1 *A description of the role of the legislative branch and how it provides checks and balances against the remaining two branches.*

    Paragraph 2 _____

    _____

    Paragraph 3 _____

    _____

2. Few islands are as beautiful as Maui, Hawaii, with its powdery sand beaches, two majestic mountains, and its winding roads along the ocean on both the eastern and western sides of the island.

    Paragraph 1 _____

    _____

    Paragraph 2 _____

    _____

    Paragraph 3 _____

    _____

    Paragraph 4 _____

    _____

3. The personal computer, the Internet, and the cellular telephone have transformed the way we get our news, communicate, and view or listen to entertainment.

    Paragraph 1 _____

    _____

    Paragraph 2 _____

    _____

    Paragraph 3 _____

    _____

    Paragraph 4 _____

    _____

EXERCISE 3   Revising and Supporting Thesis Statements

Each of the following thesis statements fails to state a claim that could be developed in a logically organized and unified essay. Revise the thesis statement, underlining the key words of the point. If possible, include a preview of the supporting ideas in the body paragraphs.

1. Our college offers an introductory computer course. *Revision:* Our college's introductory computer course offers valuable instruction in basic word processing, database management, and Web searching.

2. I want to be a nurse. *Revision:* _____

   _____

3. I had a pet dog (or cat) for ten years. *Revision:* _____

   _____

4. I want to discuss reality shows on television. *Revision:* _____

   _____

EXERCISE 4   Generating Ideas for Your Essay

Begin work on an essay on why you admire a particular person: a public figure, a relative, a friend, a teacher, or anyone who's had a positive impact on your life or the lives of others. Compose a preliminary thesis statement—just something to get you focused. Then do some brainstorming, clustering, and/or freewriting to discover and produce ideas that develop the thesis. Remember: you're writing an essay, which is much longer and more complex than a paragraph, so generate as many ideas as you can—perhaps two pages' worth.

EXERCISE 5   Selecting Details and Outlining

✓ TIPS

For Writing a First Draft

1. Write fast and circle any parts that you want to revise later.
2. Don't worry about the exact language of the opening paragraph. You'll revise it later—after you've written the body.
3. The same advice applies to the conclusion!
4. If you get stuck for ideas in one paragraph, just make a brainstorming list. Then move on to the next paragraph.
5. Make notes in the margins about things to add or revise later.

Now organize your ideas. Can you select three or four main reasons why you admire the person? Can you find any details that explain or illustrate those reasons? Discard information that doesn't fit. If you don't find enough information that fits, do more brainstorming, clustering, or freewriting. Then write a rough outline of your essay, including an attention-getting opening, a thesis statement (which may have changed from your original version), topic sentences for each body paragraph, supporting details for the topic sentences (which you can merely list), and a concluding statement. Fill in the blueprint below, or, if you need more room, make your own blueprint on a separate sheet of paper.

BLUEPRINT	For an Essay

Introduction

   attention getter: _____

   _____

   thesis statement: _____

   _____

Body

1. Topic sentence: _____

_____

_____

Supporting details: _____

_____

_____

2. Topic sentence: _____

_____

_____

Supporting details: _____

_____

_____

3. Topic sentence: _____

_____

_____

Supporting details: _____

_____

_____

Conclusion: _____

_____

_____

Writing the First Draft

Now write your first draft. Include an introductory paragraph, at least three body paragraphs, and a concluding paragraph. If any body paragraphs contain only a few sentences, plan on revising them later—perhaps after you've gotten more ideas through brainstorming, clustering, or freewriting.

In your first paragraph, include an opening remark that will interest your readers, and a thesis sentence. In your concluding paragraph, return to the thesis statement of the opening paragraph—but don't just restate it. Vary the wording. And try to end with a punch: something upbeat or clever. Don't fret about writing either a perfect introduction or conclusion at this point, however. You will be revising the draft.

EXERCISE 6   Composing a First Draft

Write a first draft of your essay based on details you selected and outlined in Exercise 5. Your draft should be at least five paragraphs long, with an introduction, a body, and a conclusion.

Revising

Take a break. Then return to your essay with clear eyes and mind. Read it critically. What ideas are unclear or poorly worded? Which need more details or explanations? Do the paragraphs have unity and coherence? Does each paragraph lead smoothly to the next, or do some paragraphs seem isolated—like separate essays rather than parts of a whole? Revise the essay one or more times.

EXERCISE 7   Revising Your First Draft

Now revise the draft, according to the following Guidelines.

REVISION GUIDELINES   Writing an Effective Essay

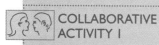 **COLLABORATIVE ACTIVITY I**

Peer Review
Read your essay aloud to others or photocopy it for others to read silently. Then listen to or read their responses. Use the Revision Guidelines as you critique each essay.

1. Does the first paragraph include an effective attention-getting introduction? If not, how should the opening be revised?
2. Does the first paragraph include a clear thesis statement that introduces the essay's central claim or main ideas? If the thesis isn't focused or is incomplete, how should it be revised?
3. Is the point of each body paragraph stated in a topic sentence? Is each topic sentence clear? If not, how should these paragraphs be revised?
4. Do all the details in each body paragraph support its topic sentence? Are there enough details? Are they arranged logically? It not, what should be eliminated, added, moved, or rewritten?
5. Are the transitions between paragraphs clear? Are the transitions within each paragraph clear? If not, what should be added or revised?
6. Does the final paragraph summarize the main ideas and end gracefully? If not, how should it be revised?

Editing and Proofreading

Edit the essay to correct errors in spelling, grammar, and punctuation—and to make any final adjustments in wording. Prepare a clean copy of the work according to the format your instructor specifies. Then proofread the essay more than once—and make a final copy, which you should proofread again.

EXERCISE 8   Editing and Proofreading

After revising your essay, edit it for correct spelling and punctuation, complete sentences, and clarity of ideas. Then make a clean copy and proofread it carefully for errors. Submit it to your instructor.

IN SUMMARY   An Essay

1. Begins with an introductory paragraph that attracts the readers' attention and states the central claim or main point in a thesis statement, often including a preview of the supporting ideas that will follow;

2. Continues with body paragraphs that discuss the supporting ideas, each stated in a topic sentence, followed by its support; and

3. Concludes with a restatement of the thesis and a graceful ending.

Write, Write, Write!

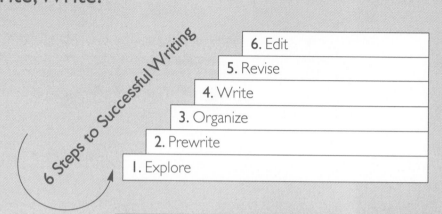

6 Steps to Successful Writing

6. Edit
5. Revise
4. Write
3. Organize
2. Prewrite
1. Explore

?

Three questions to ask when you begin

1. What is my SUBJECT?
2. What is my PURPOSE?
3. Who is my AUDIENCE?

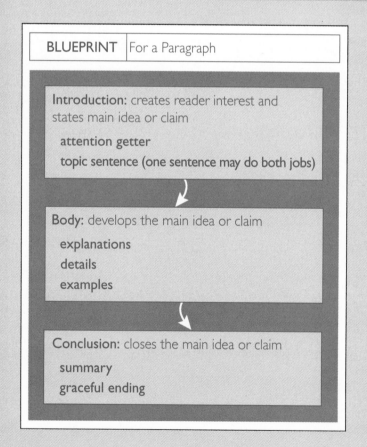

BLUEPRINT	For a Paragraph

Introduction: creates reader interest and states main idea or claim

- attention getter
- topic sentence (one sentence may do both jobs)

Body: develops the main idea or claim

- explanations
- details
- examples

Conclusion: closes the main idea or claim

- summary
- graceful ending

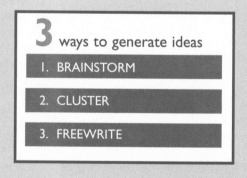

3 ways to generate ideas

1. BRAINSTORM
2. CLUSTER
3. FREEWRITE

The more you do it, the better you get!

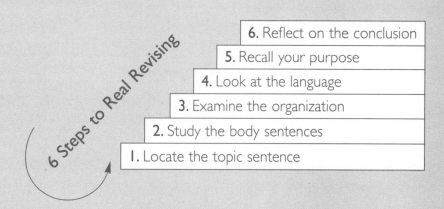

6 Steps to Real Revising

6. Reflect on the conclusion
5. Recall your purpose
4. Look at the language
3. Examine the organization
2. Study the body sentences
1. Locate the topic sentence

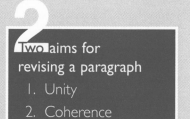

2 Two aims for revising a paragraph
1. Unity
2. Coherence

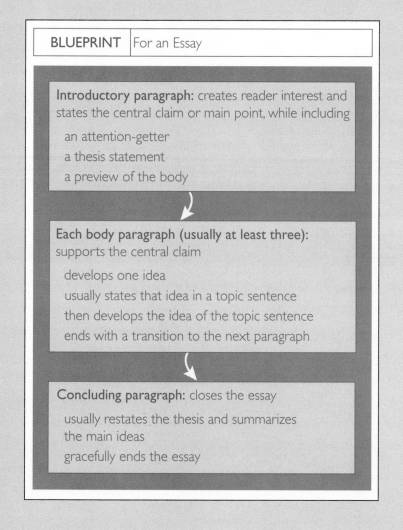

BLUEPRINT	For an Essay

Introductory paragraph: creates reader interest and states the central claim or main point, while including

an attention-getter
a thesis statement
a preview of the body

Each body paragraph (usually at least three): supports the central claim

develops one idea
usually states that idea in a topic sentence
then develops the idea of the topic sentence
ends with a transition to the next paragraph

Concluding paragraph: closes the essay

usually restates the thesis and summarizes the main ideas
gracefully ends the essay

THREE ways to develop the body of a paragraph

1. Explanations
2. Specific details
3. Examples

THREE traits of a topic sentence—or thesis statement

1. Makes a claim
2. Expresses an attitude
3. May include a "road map"

Building and Repairing Sentences

The chapters in Unit I have taken you through the writing process.

You've worked on writing and revising your ideas in the structure of paragraphs, and perhaps you've tried an essay. Now you can turn more of your attention to sentences. Developing confidence in your ability to notice and correct errors in sentence structure is important. You want readers to focus on the content of your ideas—not how you express (or fail to express) them. Eliminate the errors as you edit so that you can be judged on what you have to say, not on what the errors might say about you.

Unit II looks at ways to correct errors with incomplete sentences or improperly joined sentences, as well as a variety of ways to join them clearly, powerfully, and—above all—confidently. ■

CHAPTER 5

Recognizing Sentences and Fixing Fragments

Sentences are the basic units of expression. But if something is missing in the sentence—if it's only a fragment of a sentence—its idea will be confusing or even impossible to understand. This chapter will show you how to write complete sentences. It explains

■ the essentials of a sentence: a subject and a verb

■ ways to identify and fix sentence fragments

WHAT IS A SENTENCE?

Every **sentence** makes a complete statement. That means it must contain a **subject**—*who* or *what* the statement is about. And it must contain a **verb**—which begins the statement about what the subject *does* or *is*. The subject and verb usually go together at the beginning of a group of words called a **clause.** Most often, the subject comes first, and the verb follows the subject. Here are some examples:

Subject	Verb
President Abraham Lincoln	loved
He	saved
The turkey	was

As you can see, though, the subject and verb of a sentence don't complete the statement. That usually requires additional words that follow the verb:

Subject	Verb	Remainder of Clause
President Abraham Lincoln	loved	animals.
He	saved	a turkey's life.
The turkey	was	a gift for Christmas dinner.

This combination of *subject + verb + completion of the statement* is called an **independent clause.** It creates a full sentence. You can also combine two or more clauses in the same sentence, as you'll see in this unit. But right now, we'll concentrate on identifying the main elements of a single clause: the subject and the verb.

Identifying Subjects

The easiest way to identify the subject and verb is to look for both at the same time. Let's begin, however, with the **subject.**

The subject

- tells *who* or *what* the clause makes a statement about
- usually (but not always) appears at or near the beginning of the statement—before the verb, which tells what the subject *does* or *is*
- can be a **noun**—a person, place, idea, or thing
- can be a **subject pronoun**—a word used in place of a noun

Subject (*who* or *what*) + verb (*does* or *is*) = sentence

The following sentence, for example, makes a statement about the subject, *Tad Lincoln.* Notice that the verb *adored* follows the subject.

Tad Lincoln adored the turkey.

EXERCISE I   Identifying Subjects

*Underline the subjects **at the beginning** of each of these sentences. Ask yourself: Who or what does this sentence make a statement about?*

1. Tad Lincoln was only ten years old in 1863.

2. He adored the turkey and named it Jack.

3. The bird soon followed young Tad around the White House grounds.

4. Tad and his father agreed not to kill the animal.

5. Pardoning the White House turkey has since become an annual tradition for presidents.

Are these the words you underlined? Each one demonstrates an important trait of the subjects:

1. *Tad Lincoln* A subject can be a **proper noun**—a name that is capitalized.
2. *He* A subject can be a **subject pronoun.** The complete list of subject pronouns includes *I, we, you, he, she, it,* and *they.*
3. *bird* A subject can be a **common noun**—a noun that is not a name and so is not capitalized unless it begins the sentence.
4. *Tad and his father* A subject can be two or more nouns (or subject pronouns) joined by *and.*
5. *Pardoning the White House turkey* A subject can occasionally begin with an **-ing word** (a verb turned into a noun).

EXERCISE 2   Identifying Subjects

Try again. Underline the subject of each sentence. You'll find at least one example of the kinds of subjects explained in Exercise 1.

1. <u>Abraham Lincoln</u> faced attacks from all sides.

2. Southerners and Democrats hated him.

Abraham Lincoln

3. The Republican Party was divided over him in the election of 1864.

4. Some Republicans refused to support him.

5. Two of his generals ran against him.

6. Nevertheless, this tall, homely fellow from Illinois achieved greatness.

7. He was indeed a self-made man.

8. Studying law on his own, becoming a lawyer, and serving in the Illinois legislature led to his election to the United States House of Representatives in 1846.

9. The future president could also tell a good story around the general store—a great asset in campaigning for office.

Identifying Verbs

Now you can turn your attention to the **verbs** in clauses.
The verb

- says what the subject *does* or *is*
- usually has a **tense,** indicating if the verb discusses the past, present, or future
- usually follows the subject and begins a statement about the subject
- may contain more than one word

Subject	Verb	Remainder of Clause
Tom	*needs*	a new hairpiece or a large, floppy hat.
Albert	*has eaten*	the whole cake and part of the plate.

EXERCISE 3   Identifying Verbs

Circle the verbs in the following sentences. Ask yourself: What word or words begin a statement of what the subject does or is?

1. Lincoln was controversial throughout his presidency.

2. By today's standards, people might even consider Lincoln a racist.

3. Lincoln didn't free the slaves at the beginning of the Civil War for a simple reason.

4. He wanted to bring the South back into the Union quickly.

5. However, like other great presidents, he grew in office and took courageous positions.

6. In the fall of 1862, he drafted the Emancipation Proclamation, freeing the slaves in the areas still in rebellion as of January 1, 1863.

Are these the words you circled? Each one demonstrates an important trait of verbs:

1. *was* A verb usually has a tense. (*Was* is the past tense of *is*.)
2. *might* (even) *consider* The parts of a two-word verb may be separated by an **adverb** such as *even*.
3. *did*(n't) *free* A two-word verb often contains a negative such as *not* or *never*.
4. *wanted* This word expresses the tense of the action. Did you circle *to bring*? See below.
5. *grew* and *took* The subject performs *two actions* in *two verbs*, which are usually joined by *and*. (Indeed, a subject can perform two, three, or even more actions.)
6. *issued* This is another past-tense verb. Did you circle *freeing*? See below.

Sentence 4: *to bring,* an action word preceded by *to,* is an **infinitive.** It's formed from a verb but doesn't function as a verb. It never has a tense because something that's infinite cannot be limited to the past, present, or future.

Sentence 6: *freeing,* an *-ing* word, which is also formed from a verb. It usually doesn't function as a verb.

Infinitives and *-ing* words, although formed from verbs, normally function as other parts of speech. (Remember "Pardoning the White House turkey" in Sentence 5 of Exercise 1? *Pardoning* serves as a noun in that sentence.) Don't confuse infinitives and *-ing* words with verbs.

Helping Verbs. Verbs can include two, three, or even four words. In the examples that follow, *use* is the main verb, and the words before it are **helping verbs,** which help express the complete tense or content of the verb:

Main Verb	Main Verb with Helping Verbs		
use	am using	will be using	might have been using
uses	is using	would have used	should have been using
used	has used	might be using	could have been used
	did(n't) use	must be using	must have been used
	may use	may be using	
	will use	could be using	
	had used	will have used	
	can use	should be using	
	does use	must have used	

Note the one exception to the rule about –*ing* words. They're verbs when they follow the helping verb *to be:*

is going, am going, are going, was going, were going, will be going, etc.

Linking Verbs. Most verbs express action (*works, needed, has eaten*). However, a few verbs—called **linking verbs**—simply say that the subject *is* or *was* something. In other words, they give information about the subject. Here are examples:

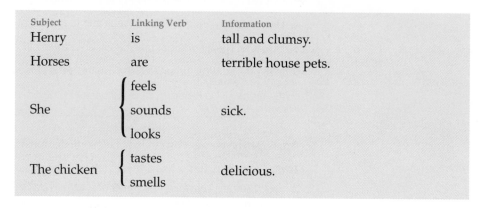

Subject	Linking Verb	Information
Henry	is	tall and clumsy.
Horses	are	terrible house pets.
She	feels / sounds / looks	sick.
The chicken	tastes / smells	delicious.

The most common linking verb is *to be.* The other common linking verbs represent the five senses—*look, sound, feel, smell,* and *taste*—and the verbs *become* and *appears.*

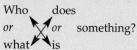

TIPS

For Identifying Subjects and Verbs

Every clause says that someone or something *does* or *is.* Therefore, one simple question should help you locate the subject and verb of each clause: *Who* or *what does* or *is? Who* or *what,* of course, will identify the subject of the clause. *Does* or *is* will identify the verb.

Subject Verb

Who   does

or   *or* something?

what   is

EXERCISE 4   Identifying More Verbs

Once more, circle the verbs in the following sentences. Also, put a box around any infinitives and any –ing words that don't function as verbs.

1. Lincoln (won) the election in 1860, (becoming) the sixteenth president of the United States.

2. He was also the first president to die from an assassin's bullet.

3. He would be the second president to die as a result of the zero curse.

4. From 1840 to 1960, any president winning an election in a year ending in zero did not leave the presidency alive.

5. William Henry Harrison (election of 1840) would die in April 1841 after being in office for only thirty days.

6. President James A. Garfield (election of 1880) was shot and killed by an assassin in 1881.

7. President William McKinley (election of 1900) held office for less than a year before dying at the hands of an assassin in 1901.

8. Warren G. Harding (election of 1920) and Franklin D. Roosevelt (1940) both would not live to the end of their terms.

9. And of course, John F. Kennedy (election of 1960) would have been the first to outlive the curse, except for a gunshot coming from the sixth floor of a building in Dallas, Texas, according to the Warren Commission Report.

EXERCISE 5   Writing Verbs

Complete the following passage with the past tense of one of the verbs in the box. You won't use all the verbs, and you may use one twice.

ask	be	call	do
face	free	have	hope
know	make	put	win

Lincoln (1) ___*faced*___ more serious problems than any other president. Therefore,

he (2) _____ some very serious and difficult decisions. While the members of

Congress were not meeting, he formed an army and (3) _____ thousands of people

in jail although he didn't charge them with crimes. Lincoln (4) _____ that this step

(5) _____ a violation of the United States Constitution, but it (6) _____ neces-

sary "in cases of rebellion or invasion."

At the beginning of the Civil War, many people in his political party

(7) _____ him to end slavery. In 1863, Lincoln (8) _____ the slaves. Still,

many people (9) _____ to stop the war by any means. They (10) _____

Lincoln a dictator. After four long years, the North finally (11) _____ the war.

EXERCISE 6   Identifying Subjects and Verbs

Here's a chance to apply all you've learned about recognizing subjects and verbs. In each of the following sentences, underline the subject(s) and circle the verb(s). Be certain you know why each sentence is complete.

1. Lincoln hoped to end the Civil War quickly, wanting to avoid needless bloodshed.
2. He asked one of his best military leaders, Robert E. Lee, to command the Union Army.
3. Instead, Lee resigned from the U.S. Army and accepted a commission in the Confederate Army.
4. This decision was not easy for Lee.
5. He had graduated from West Point and sworn allegiance to the United States.
6. He also hated slavery and had freed his own slaves.
7. Nor did he believe that states had the right to leave the Union.
8. But Lee was a native of Virginia.
9. "I have been unable to make up my mind to raise my hand against my native state, my relatives, my children and my home," he wrote.
10. Loyalty and duty called him to serve the Confederacy.

EXERCISE 7   Identifying Subjects and Verbs and Incomplete Sentences

Try it one more time. In each group of words below, underline the subject(s) and circle the verb(s). If any group is missing a subject or a verb, write "incomplete" in front of the number.

1. After her husband's assassination, <u>Mary Todd Lincoln</u> (invited) several spiritualists to the White House.

2. They comforted the grieving widow.

3. Years later in Chicago, Mary going to séances under an assumed name.

4. She would test the skills of the spiritualists.

5. Once, on a trip to Boston, attended a séance.

6. Used the name "Mrs. Tundall" to avoid recognition.

7. Her dead husband appeared before her during the séance.

8. She then visited the studio of William Mumler, a "spirit photographer."

9. Mumler produced a photograph of Mary with Abraham.

10. The president in the background with his hands on Mary's shoulders.

WHAT IS A FRAGMENT?

In Exercise 7, each item you found that's missing a subject or verb is a **fragment:** an incomplete statement that's written as if it were a sentence. Many times, it lacks a subject, a verb, or both.

Fragments occur for many reasons. Here are a few:

* You might be struggling to express an idea and therefore are not paying attention to the boundaries between sentences.
* You might be punctuating by ear, without understanding how punctuation works.
* You might be omitting subjects or writing only partial verbs.
* You might be unclear about the uses of joining words such as *although* and *because*.

No matter why a fragment occurs, however, you must be able to identify and eliminate it. And that's what we'll be doing in the rest of this chapter.

FIXING SIMPLE FRAGMENTS

✓**TIPS**

For Identifying and Fixing Fragments

If you suspect that something is a fragment, try changing it to a question. You can't change a fragment into a question.

Complete sentence: The election was close.
Question: Was the election close?

Fragment: A close election. *Question:* ????

A simple fragment is an incomplete clause. Let's take a look at several types:

* fragments missing a subject
* fragments missing a verb or part of a verb
* fragments beginning with infinitives or *-ing* words
* fragments that add details or examples

Missing Subjects

Suppose you write a statement in which the subject performs *two actions* expressed in two separate verbs. If you end the statement after the first verb, the second verb will be left hanging, without a subject, in a fragment. Here's an example:

Sentence   Fragment
In the 1850s, many people went to séances. And supposedly communicated with their dead relatives.

The fragment contains a verb, *communicated,* but doesn't have a subject. You could fix the fragment in at least two ways:

> **Combining:**   In the 1850s, many people went to séances and supposedly communicated with their dead relatives.
>
> **Adding a subject to the fragment:**   In the 1850s, many people went to séances. *These people* supposedly communicated with their dead relatives.

Missing or Incomplete Verbs

Some simple fragments result from writing incomplete verbs. Notice the missing helping verb in the following examples:

Incomplete verbs	Complete verbs
Spiritual mediums *putting* people in touch with the dead.	Spiritual mediums *were putting* people in touch with the dead.
Abraham Lincoln's wife Mary often *gone* to séances.	Abraham Lincoln's wife Mary *had* often *gone* to séances.

The most frequently omitted helping verbs are *to be (is, am, are, was, were)* and *to have (has, have, had).*

Infinitives and –*ing* Words

Infinitives and –*ing* words are formed from verbs and therefore seem to express action. However, they usually don't function as verbs but only introduce or continue a sentence. If they aren't attached to that sentence, they hang loose as fragments. Look at these examples:

> Sentence   –*ing* word fragment
> Mary Lincoln's young sons Willie and Eddie had died. *Sending her into deep despair.*
>
> –*ing* word fragment   Sentence
> *Refusing to accept her children's death.* Mary told her sister that they visited her each night.
>
> Infinitive fragment   Sentence
> *To console Mary after President Lincoln's death.* Several spiritualists visited her at the White House.

You can fix the fragments by attaching them to the complete sentences:

> Mary Lincoln's young sons Willie and Eddie had died, sending her into deep despair.
>
> Refusing to accept her children's death, Mary told her sister that they visited her each night.
>
> To console Mary after President Lincoln's death, several spiritualists visited her at the White House.

Hanging Details or Examples

Some fragments are simply details that continue the idea of the previous sentence. For instance, the detail fragment that follows this sentence does not contain a verb:

Sentence	Detail fragment
At a séance, people would sit in a dark parlor.	*With their hands on the table.*

You can fix the fragment by adding it to the sentence:

At a séance, people would sit in a dark parlor with their hands on the table.

EXERCISE 8 Fixing Simple Fragments

Find the fragments in this exercise. Then fix each one by supplying the missing subjects, verbs, or partial verbs, or by attaching the fragment to a complete sentence. Be careful: some sentences are complete.

1. Lincoln ^was^ shot at Ford's Theatre in Washington, D.C., on April 14, 1865.

2. Charles Leale the first doctor to reach the president's box.

3. Lifted Mary's head off the president's chest.

4. Mary now in a state of near collapse. Sat on a couch near her chair.

5. Leale asked a few soldiers to place the president on the floor.

6. Other doctors arrived in the president's box and were able to revive him. Using artificial respiration and some brandy and water.

7. Leale then said, "His wound is mortal. It is impossible for him to recover."

8. From the couch, Mary quietly moaned, "His dream was prophetic." (For more about Lincoln's dream, see Exercises 9 and 10.)

COLLABORATIVE ACTIVITY I

Writing and Correcting Fragments

Write five fragments of your own and exchange your work with a classmate who has also written five fragments. Correct each other's work and then discuss your results.

FIXING COMPLEX FRAGMENTS

You've looked at simple sentences that contain a single independent clause. Now you'll look at **complex sentences** that contain two clauses: one that depends on the other to make the meaning complete. If the two clauses are not joined together properly, one clause may be a fragment. There are two main types of these fragments:

- those beginning with words like *although* or *because*
- those beginning with words like *who, which,* or *that*

Although and *Because* Types

Find the subjects and verbs of the following clauses:

Because the doctors were trying to save the president
Although Mary Todd Lincoln could not help her husband

Each clause contains a subject and a verb, but the clauses don't make complete statements. They're **dependent clauses**—and sentence fragments—which depend on another clause to make a full sentence. After you read them, you want to ask, "What happened?" The words *because* and *although* at the beginning of a clause make that clause incomplete. These incomplete clauses must be attached to **independent clauses** and then could stand alone as a sentence.

✓ **TIPS**

For Identifying and Fixing Fragments

As you know, writing imitates speech. In writing, the punctuation represents pauses that occur with the rise and fall of our voices. The pitch of our voices *drops* at the end of a sentence, and that's where a period belongs:

This is a complete sentence. ↓

Notice how the pitch lowers at its end. ↓

When a sentence continues, the pitch of our voices *rises* at the comma.

Because this sentence is incomplete, ↑ . . .

If we want to make it complete, ↑, . . .

Read your sentences aloud as you edit your papers. If you hear your voice rise at the end of a sentence, look closely at that sentence. It could be a fragment (unless it is a question, which also ends with your voice rising).

> *Because* the doctors were trying to save the president, *they took him to the nearest house.*
>
> *Although* Mary Todd Lincoln could not help her husband, *she kissed him and begged him to speak.*

Although and *because* are only the most common words that introduce dependent clauses. There are many others:

after	if
although	once
as	since
as if	unless
as soon as	until
because	when
before	whether
even though	while

You can correct these dependent clause fragments in two ways.

1. Join the dependent clause to the sentence that precedes or follows it. This is usually the most common and best solution.

> *Fragments*
>
> A. *When President Lincoln finally passed away.* Mrs. Lincoln was waiting in the front room of the house.
> B. Nearly two hours passed. *Before she was in any condition to be taken back to the White House.*
>
> *Joined*
>
> C. *When President Lincoln finally passed away,* Mrs. Lincoln was waiting in the front room of the house.
> D. Nearly two hours passed *before she was in any condition to be taken back to the White House.*

Punctuation is very important. A comma follows a dependent clause that begins a sentence, but there's no comma before a dependent clause that ends a sentence.

2. Remove the joining word before the dependent clause and write the clause as a separate sentence. However, this solution often creates choppy sentences—and sometimes it simply doesn't work. Let's return to examples C and D above. Example C could be written as two sentences by removing *when*. But notice what happens to example D if *before* is removed to create two sentences. The original meaning of the statement changes and may not even make sense.

> C. (*with* when *removed*) President Lincoln finally passed away. Mrs. Lincoln waited in the front room of the house. (*Meaning unchanged*)
> D. (*with* before *removed*) Nearly two hours passed. She was in any condition to be taken back to the White House. (*Meaning changed*)

EXERCISE 9   Fixing Complex Fragments

Find the sentence fragments in this exercise. Fix each one either by joining it to the clause that completes its meaning or by rewriting it as a complete sentence. Place commas where they're needed. Be careful: one of the items does not contain a sentence fragment.

Lincoln's Terrible Dream

1. On the evening of April 11, 1865, President Lincoln and Mrs. Lincoln were talking with several friends. When Lincoln suddenly began to discuss his dreams. _On the evening of April 11, 1865, President Lincoln and Mrs. Lincoln were talking with several friends when Lincoln suddenly began to discuss his dreams._

2. He said that he had been unable to sleep well. Because he had had a terrible dream ten days earlier. _____

_____

3. Since he had been waiting for important messages from the battlefront. He went to sleep very late. _____

_____

4. In his dream, he heard soft sobs. As if a number of people were weeping. _____

_____

5. He left his bed and wandered downstairs. When the sobbing grew louder. Although the mourners were invisible. _____

_____

6. He kept going from room to room. Then he arrived at the East Room. _____

_____

(For more about this dream, see Exercise 10.)

Who, That, and Which Types

A second kind of complex fragment includes the words *who, that,* and *which.* Look at these examples:

> . . . *who* was a famous actor at the time.
> "Voices" *that* Mary Lincoln began to hear ten years later . . .
> . . . *which* was a place for the mentally ill.

These are also dependent clauses, so they're incomplete statements. You can complete their meaning in two ways:

1. Attach them to the words that make the statement complete, which usually immediately precede or follow them.

> *President Lincoln was assassinated by John Wilkes Booth,* who was a famous actor at that time.
>
> "Voices" that Mary Lincoln began to hear years later *were cited as evidence of her insanity.*
>
> *In 1875, she spent four months in a private hospital called Bellevue,* which was a place for the mentally ill.

2. Rewrite the clauses without *who, which,* or *that* and make them complete sentences. Again, this might not be the best solution if it creates short, choppy sentences.

> President Lincoln was assassinated by John Wilkes Booth. He was a famous actor at that time.
>
> In 1875, she spent four months in a private hospital called Bellevue. It was a place for the mentally ill.

Since the handling of *who, which,* and *that* in clauses is rather complicated, we'll return to it again in Chapter 8.

EXERCISE 10   Fixing More Complex Fragments

Find the sentence fragments in this exercise. Fix each one by joining it to the clause that completes its meaning. Be careful: one of the items does not contain a sentence fragment.

The End of Lincoln's Dream

1. In the East Room, Lincoln saw a platform. That held a corpse wrapped in funeral clothing. *In the East Room, Lincoln saw a platform that held a corpse wrapped in funeral clothing.*

2. All around the platform were many people. Who were crying. _____

3. One of the soldiers. Who were acting as guards. Told him that it was the president. Who had been killed by an assassin. _____

4. The crowd cried loudly with grief. That noise awoke Lincoln from his dream.

COLLABORATIVE ACTIVITY 2

Comparing Your Solutions
Share and compare the ways in which you've fixed the fragments in Exercises 9 and 10. If you have different solutions, list them, and then share your lists with the entire class.

5. Mrs. Lincoln was horrified by her husband's story. Which, the president reminded
   her, was only a dream. _____

   _____

   _____

E X E R C I S E   I I   Fixing Fragments

*Read the Tips box on page 63. Then read each of the following groups of words aloud.
Listen for the rise or fall of your voice. Label each item either S (for sentence) or F (for
fragment). Then punctuate it correctly—adding a period or a comma—and add the
words to make each fragment complete.*

____S____ 1. If you think the first part of the sentence is complete, you aren't noticing

  the rise in pitch at the comma.

_____ 2. When there's a rise in the pitch of your voice. _____

_____ 3. The result should be that you can tell when a sentence is complete.

  _____

_____ 4. Your ear is a pretty good judge of these matters. _____

_____ 5. With enough practice and repetition. _____

_____ 6. This exercise should give you a better idea about how sentences sound.

  _____

IN SUMMARY   ## To Recognize Complete Sentences

1. Identify the *subject* (*who* or *what* the sentence makes a statement about),
   usually found at the beginning of the clause.
2. Identify the *verb* (begins the statement of what the subject *does* or *is*),
   which usually follows the subject and has a tense—for example, past,
   present, or future.
3. Look for *helping verbs* to make sure the verb is complete.
4. See if the subject and verb fit logically together.
5. See if the words following the verb complete the statement.

To Fix Fragments

1. Make sure that each statement contains at least one subject and a
   complete verb.
2. Make sure that you don't mistake an *–ing* word or an infinitive for a verb.
3. Make sure that there are no hanging details or examples written as complete statements.
4. Make sure that a clause beginning with words such as *although* or *because*
   is attached to a clause that completes its idea.
5. Make sure that a clause beginning with words such as *who, that,* or *which* is
   attached to the words that complete its idea.

EDITING FOR MASTERY

Mastery Exercise 1

Eliminating Fragments

The following passage contains twelve fragments, excluding the example (which has been corrected for you). Find and fix them by following this procedure:

1. *Identify the subject(s) and the verb(s) in every clause.*
2. *Make any changes necessary in sentences that are incomplete. These changes can include*

   a. *supplying a missing subject or a missing (or incomplete) verb*
   b. *joining an incomplete sentence to another sentence (usually by removing a period between the two sentences and sometimes by changing the period to a comma)*
   c. *rewriting the fragment*

You don't have to rewrite the passage. Make all your changes above the lines.

The Death of Abraham Lincoln

(1) On Friday, April 14, 1865—Good Friday—Lincoln met with his cabinet (2) ^to ~~To~~ discuss lifting the blockade of the South. (3) Now that the war was over. (4) His mood was happy, and he telling everyone around him to look for a way to make the peace last. (5) By preparing a plan that would bring the Southern states back into the Union with very little punishment.

(6) That evening he and his wife went to see a play at Ford's Theatre in downtown Washington. (7) The Washington policeman guarding the president left his post. (8) Either to get a drink or a better view of the play. (9) When a pistol shot rang out. (10) Lincoln fell forward in his chair. (11) A man jumped from the president's box to the stage. (12) In the process breaking his leg. (13) He waved his gun and shouted something. (14) Then he escaped through a back exit and mounted a horse. (15) Which was waiting outside.

(16) Lincoln was taken to a house across the street from the theater. (17) Where he died the next morning. (18) Throwing the shocked nation into grief. (19) Although he was hated and opposed throughout the war years by many groups who criticized him for one reason or another. (20) Abraham Lincoln had finally become a hero of the entire nation.

(21) The assassin was soon discovered. (22) John Wilkes Booth, who was an actor. (23) After a huge manhunt, Booth was trapped in a barn on April 26, and shot and killed. (24) A military court sentenced four other captured conspirators to be hanged. (25) Including Mary Surratt, who was the owner of a boardinghouse.

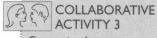

COLLABORATIVE ACTIVITY 3

Comparing Answers
Compare your changes and report them to the class.

Scorecard: Number of fragments found and corrected: _____

Mastery Exercise 2

Eliminating Fragments

The passage below contains twelve fragments (excluding the example, which has been corrected for you). Find and eliminate them by following this procedure:

1. *Identify the subject(s) and the verb(s) in every clause.*
2. *Make any changes necessary in sentences that are incomplete. These changes can include*

   a. *supplying a missing subject or a missing (or incomplete) verb*
   b. *joining an incomplete sentence to another sentence (usually by removing a period between the two sentences and sometimes by changing the period to a comma)*
   c. *rewriting the fragment*

You don't have to rewrite the passage. Make all your changes above the line.

So What If His Name Was Mudd?

(1) Dr. Samuel A. Mudd set the broken leg of a mysterious visitor in 1865 and wound up in prison with a life sentence~~.~~(2) ^*for*^ ~~For~~ assisting in the escape of President Abraham Lincoln's assassin. (3) Although four years later the White House pardoned Mudd. (4) In 1992, several of his descendants still trying to clear his name.

(5) The man who found his way to Mudd's country house on the morning of April 15, 1865. (6) He was actor John Wilkes Booth, who was wearing a false beard. (7) Booth had shot Lincoln and broken his leg when he jumped from the president's box. (8) In 1992, the Army Board of Correction of Military Records stirred up new interest in the good doctor. (9) By considering the Mudd family's appeal to remove his conviction from the books.

(10) The government's original case against Mudd has always been weak. (11) The military council had appeared to rig the trial. (12) The use of false and suspicious testimony, and the prosecution's refusal to admit evidence that was favorable to Mudd. (13) According to the evidence, Mudd was only a casual acquaintance of Booth's. (14) After the assassination when Booth looked for treatment at Mudd's house. (15) The doctor was unaware that Lincoln had been shot.

(16) The biggest supporter of Mudd's innocence was Louise Mudd Arehart, who was the youngest of Mudd's ten surviving grandchildren. (17) Arehart relied heavily on her grandmother's story of what happened. (18) When Booth came to the Mudd's house. (19) The grandmother became suspicious of Booth, who called himself Tyler. (20) When his false whiskers fell off as he left the house. (21) Mudd, who had been out, returned home. (22) He had learned of Lincoln's murder. (23) And the search for the assassin. (24) When soldiers arrived the following week, Mudd told them everything he knew and produced the boot he had cut from the stranger's injured leg. (25) On the boot was the name "J. Wilkes."

(26) Arehart and many other of Mudd's descendants appealed Dr. Mudd's case in 1992. (27) However, William D. Clark, who was the Assistant Secretary of the Army. (28) Refused to hear their appeal. (29) Announcing that the Board had no right to "settle historical disputes." (30) The fight to clear Mudd's name still continues.

Scorecard: Number of fragments found and corrected _____

CHAPTER 6

Joining Sentences Through Coordination

If you want to keep your readers interested—and sane—you need to create some variety in your sentences. If you don't, here's what happens:

> My sentences are short. They are simple. Each contains only one idea. They are too simple. They are choppy. They can't express complex thoughts. Short sentences get boring. They are all alike. They make me sound like a first-grader. I had better stop now. You will be glad to stop reading, too.

Sentence variety comes largely from joining sentences—clearly, logically, and correctly. This chapter will examine one way to join sentences called **coordination.** You'll learn how to

- join sentences by adding words
- join sentences by using punctuation
- use words and punctuation correctly

CONNECTING WORDS

One way to connect sentences is to add words that join them. A joining word is called a **conjunction** (like a junction that joins two roads). Notice how conjunctions connect each of the following pairs of words:

> John *and* I (two people, or subjects)
> tripped *or* fell (two actions, or past-tense verbs)
> a fat *yet* athletic man (two describing words, or adjectives)
> moved quickly *but* carefully (two words describing actions, or adverbs)

The Coordinating Conjunctions

In these examples, each pair of words is grammatically equal, or *coordinate* (co = equal, *ordinate* = level). The joining words are therefore called **coordinating conjunctions** because they join grammatically equal structures. There are only seven coordinating conjunctions in English, which you can memorize by remembering the words *fan boys:*

✓ **TIPS**
For Using Conjunctions
1. Beware of *then* and *also.* They might look like coordinating conjunctions, but they're not.
2. Don't join sentences with *plus.* It's a great term for mathematics, but it's not a conjunction.

For	But
And	Or
Nor	Yet
	So

JOINING SENTENCES WITH CONJUNCTIONS

Coordinating conjunctions can also join *two sentences* that are also grammatically equal structures. Remember that every sentence must have at least one independent clause—a subject and verb combination that can stand alone. Therefore, when you join two sentences with a coordinating conjunction, you create a single sentence with two independent clauses. That single sentence is called a **compound sentence.**

EXERCISE 1   Identifying Conjunctions

Find and underline the coordinating conjunctions in the sentences. Look carefully. One item does not contain a coordinating conjunction, so the two clauses are not correctly joined. Circle the word that incorrectly joins the two clauses.

COLLABORATIVE ACTIVITY 1

Analyzing Combined Sentences

Discuss the effect of each coordinating conjunction you've identified in Exercise 1. Which ones suggest an addition, an alternative, a change or qualification, or a negative? What other meanings do these conjunctions communicate as they join clauses? Which sentence with two independent clauses is incorrectly joined by a word that is not a coordinating conjunction?

1. Male babies often wear blue, and female babies wear pink.

2. Years ago, people wanted to protect their infant boys from evil spirits, so they dressed the boys in blue.

3. People associated blue with good spirits, for those spirits lived in the blue sky.

4. Of course, people cared about their female children, yet people did not care enough to dress them in blue.

5. Many years later, people still dressed the males in blue, but they chose pink for the females.

6. The superstition about evil spirits had disappeared, or people might have dressed their girls in blue also.

7. Very few parents today know the reasons behind these traditional colors, nor do parents care.

8. Some parents choose yellow, then color doesn't make any difference.

9. The color doesn't make any difference to the baby, and even the parents know that.

Using conjunctions correctly is important. They not only join two clauses, but they also *explain the logical relationship between the two clauses:*

Conjunction	Purpose
for	shows a reason (The second clause gives a reason for the first.)
and	shows addition

nor	shows a negative alternative (It is the negative form of *or*, and it must follow a clause containing a negative word such as *not*.)
but	shows contrast
or	shows an alternative or choice
yet	shows an unexpected contrast (It is similar in meaning to *although*.)
so	shows a result (The first clause results in the second.)

PUNCTUATING COMPOUND SENTENCES

Not every coordinating conjunction requires a comma. Here are the rules:

▶ **Place a comma before the coordinating conjunction** *that joins independent clauses.*

independent clause	coordinating conjunction	independent clause
Tom likes ice cream,	*but*	he likes pizza better.

▶ *Don't use the comma* **before coordinating conjunctions that merely join two words.**

word	coordinating conjunction	word
Tom likes ice cream	*and*	pizza.

EXERCISE 2   Combining Sentences

Join each of the following pairs of sentences with one of the seven coordinating conjunctions, preceded by a comma. Use each conjunction at least once.

Black Bart: Stagecoach Robber and Poet

1. It was August 3, ^ <ins>1877, and a</ins> <del>1877. A</del> stagecoach was traveling across California.

2. A man with a flour sack over his head stopped the coach. He pointed a rifle at the drivers.

3. The man told them to throw down their cash box. He did not harm anyone.

4. Later, someone found the box. That person was surprised.

5. The box contained an angry poem signed by "Black Bart." It also contained a note of apology saying, "Driver, give my respects to your friend, the other driver."

6. Black Bart continued robbing. He continued to leave humorous verses.

7. The stagecoach company was not amused. It offered a reward of $800 for his capture.

8. On Bart's last holdup, someone shot and wounded him. He tried to stop the bleeding with a handkerchief that he left behind.

9. Detectives learned Black Bart's real name by tracing the laundry mark on the handkerchief. The robber might have gone free.

10. He was Charles E. Bolton, an elderly gentleman with a white mustache, gold-headed cane, and fine clothes. He finally confessed to his crimes.

11. He also said, "I never robbed a passenger. I never treated a human being badly." (Use *nor,* and change the wording of the second clause.)

12. He was supposed to serve a long term in prison. His behavior was so gentlemanly that he was released four years later.

EXERCISE 3   Completing Sentences

Write a second independent clause that logically follows each coordinating conjunction.

1. The Internet has become very important today, and <u>many people now rely on it for</u> <u>e-mail and information.</u>

2. Nowadays, people are spoiled by the speed and convenience of e-mail, so

   _____

3. Many people also shop on the Internet, for it _____

   _____

 COLLABORATIVE ACTIVITY 2

Comparing Sentences
Discuss and compare your answers to Exercise 3. Did everyone write full and complete clauses? Do the clauses logically carry out the meaning of the coordinating conjunctions? List the best clauses, and then report your results to the class.

4. Companies without computer technology must change, or_____

   _____

5. Prices of computers continue to drop, yet_____

   _____

6. Ten years ago, hardly anyone used the Internet, but_____

   _____

7. Many people don't realize that their cars contain hundreds of computer chips, nor

   _____

EXERCISE 4   Writing Combined Sentences

Write seven combined sentences of your own, using a different coordinating conjunction— for, and, nor, but, or, yet, *and* so*—in each sentence. Use your own paper.*

JOINING SENTENCES WITH SEMICOLONS

There is only one punctuation mark that can join two sentences into one. This is the **semicolon (;).** Take a good look at the semicolon; notice that it's a combination of a period and a comma. Like a period, it signals the end of a complete statement. Like a comma, it signals that the sentence continues. But unlike a period or a comma, it joins two clauses into one sentence.

Use a semicolon when the logical connection between the two clauses is obvious and needs no explanation. Here are some examples:

> California is the most populous state in the United States; one out of every nine people lives there.
> Alaska has very long and cold winters; not many people want to live there.

Follow these rules to use semicolons properly and gracefully in your writing:

Never use a coordinating conjunction with a semicolon.
Don't capitalize the first word after the semicolon.
Don't overuse semicolons; your writing will sound too choppy.

EXERCISE 5   Writing Clauses After Semicolons

Complete each of the following sentences with a second independent clause that relates logically to the first. It may be an example, or it can present a contrast.

1. There is very little difference between "men's work" and "women's work" these days; *both sexes do a variety of jobs in all sorts of professions.*

2. Many doctors and lawyers are women;_____

_____

3. Most married women are no longer simply "housewives";_____

_____

COLLABORATIVE ACTIVITY 3

Discussing Your Combined Sentences

Compare your answers to Exercises 4 and 5. Then share your results with the class.

4. It's not unusual to see women in hard hats at construction sites;_____

_____

5. Many men work in what used to be "female" professions;_____

_____

6. Most women and men are probably happy about the changes in our society;_____

_____

Transitional Words After the Semicolon

Sometimes the logical connection between the two clauses joined by a semicolon needs a boost. Consider this example:

> Juan said he was so full that he could burst; he ate a second piece of cake. [Huh?]

That boost can come from adding a word directly after the semicolon to make the relationship clear.

> Juan said he was so full that he could burst; *however,* he ate a second piece of cake.

This additional word is called a **conjunctive adverb** because it's partly a conjunction and partly an adverb. That is, like a conjunction, it shows a link between two ideas. And, like an adverb, it explains *how* or *in what way* the ideas are related.

It's also called a **transitional word** because it establishes the transition (or movement) from one idea to another. Here's a list of common conjunctive adverbs.

Transitional word (conjunctive adverb)	Acts like this joining word (conjunction)	But in this way (adverb)
furthermore, moreover, also	and	in addition
however	but	in contrast
nevertheless	yet	in contrast
therefore, consequently	so	as a result
otherwise, instead	or	as an alternative
meanwhile, then, later, afterward	(none)	shows time relationships

Remember: the conjunctive adverb doesn't join two clauses; *the semicolon joins them.* As with the coordinating conjunctions, punctuation is important.

1. The semicolon comes first.
2. The conjunctive adverb comes next.
3. The comma comes last.

independent clause	transitional word	independent clause
Mario enjoyed quiet;	*nevertheless,*	he worked at the bowling alley.
Claudia studies during the week;	*however,*	she likes to go out on the weekends.

EXERCISE 6   Substituting Transitional Words

Rewrite each of the following combined sentences. Change the coordinating conjunction to a semicolon followed by a conjunctive adverb and a comma.

The Voyage of the Kon-Tiki

1. Thor Heyerdahl was born and raised in Norway, but he is most famous for his travel to Polynesia in the South Pacific. *Thor Heyerdahl was born and raised in Norway; however, he is most famous for his travel to Polynesia in the South Pacific.*

2. On an island in Polynesia in 1936, he learned the legend of a pale-skinned god Tiki who brought the ancestors of the natives from the West across the sea, so he logically concluded that they came from Peru in South America. _____
   _____
   _____
   _____

3. He wanted to prove that such a voyage was possible, so in 1947 he built a raft like the kind he thought the early natives used. _____

_____

_____

4. He made a forty-five-foot-long raft, which he called *Kon-Tiki*, out of nine huge balsa logs and bamboo, and he used only rope to hold the logs together. _____

_____

_____

5. Heyerdahl and a crew of six had to be incredibly skilled and brave, or they would never have made it on their 4,300-mile voyage across the open sea. _____

_____

_____

6. After 101 days, the raft reached the reefs off a Polynesian island, but the strong waves there smashed the cabin and broke the mast like a matchstick. _____

_____

_____

7. The boat was destroyed and the crew thrown into the water, yet they were able to wade their way to the palm-covered island. _____

_____

_____

8. People said that a flimsy balsa-wood raft couldn't possibly cross the Pacific Ocean, yet Heyerdahl proved them wrong. _____

_____

_____

EXERCISE 7   Writing Combined Sentences

Complete the following sentences after the semicolon by adding a transitional word, a comma, and a second independent clause. Use a different transitional word each time.

1. Last summer was the hottest in many years; *therefore, I spent most weekends at the beach.*

2. The legal drinking age in most states is twenty-one; _____

_____

3. The health-care industry offers many opportunities for employment; _____

_____

4. I have developed a real talent for flipping hamburgers at my job; _____

_____

5. Mr. Gottbucks owns a seventeen-room house in Florida; _____

_____

6. I can't persuade my cat, Tubby, to go on a diet; _____

_____

EXERCISE 8   Combining More Sentences

Combine each of the following groups of sentences, creating at least two independent clauses and omitting repeated words. Use both coordinating conjunctions and semicolons (and transitional words if necessary).

Harriet Tubman (1820–1913): Liberator of Slaves

1. Harriet Tubman was not even five feet tall. She was black. _Harriet Tubman was_ _not even five feet tall, and she was black._

2. She had been enslaved in Maryland. She became free in 1849 by escaping to

Philadelphia, Pennsylvania, where slavery was illegal. _____

_____

3. She was determined to help slaves gain freedom. She returned to the South.

_____

_____

4. She was the woman the slaves called "Moses." She led the slaves to the free states

in the North. _____

_____

5. No one knew how it happened. The slaves mysteriously disappeared and followed

her on secret trails. _____

_____

6. Tubman wasn't satisfied that only she was free. She had to help her family, her

friends, and finally strangers get away, too. _____

_____

7. She knew that she could be captured and made a slave in the South. She returned to

the South as many as nineteen times to free her people. _____

_____

8. She was a tender woman. She comforted the men and women who followed her on the long, painful journey by foot. _____

_____

9. She knew that runaway slaves who returned to their masters would endanger the others. Whenever they tried to turn back, she commanded them to continue on or die. _____

_____

IN SUMMARY   To Join Sentences with Coordination

- Use one of the coordinating conjunctions (*for, and, nor, but, or, yet, so*), preceded by a comma.
- Use a semicolon (;) when the logical connection between two clauses is obvious.
- Add transitional words such as *however, therefore*, and *nevertheless* after the semicolon if necessary.

EDITING FOR MASTERY

Mastery Exercise 1

Combining Sentences

Eleven of the following items contain two independent clauses that are not joined in any way. Join the clauses using either a coordinating conjunction or a conjunctive adverb, if necessary. Use correct punctuation. Be careful: Three of the items shouldn't be changed. (The first item has been done for you.)

Harriet Tubman and the Underground Railroad

1. Harriet Tubman was an expert on the routes to the North ^, for ^she knew every farmhouse and cottage along the way where the escaping slaves could get food and fresh clothing.

2. A farmer asked who was knocking on his door, Tubman would reply that it was a "friend with friends."

3. Her answer was a secret message it was her "ticket" on the Underground Railroad.

4. These messages and her courage led more than 300 slaves to freedom.

5. The railroad had no tracks or trains it took its passengers where they wanted to go.

6. Many people knew the term *Underground Railroad* by the 1830s it actually resembled a real railroad.

7. The "conductors" on the railroad freed the slaves from captivity they guided them at various points on their journey.

COLLABORATIVE
ACTIVITY 4
Comparing Answers
Compare your changes and
report them to the class.

8. There were "stations," where sympathetic men and women gave runaways food and fresh clothing.

9. The railroad's journeys even had timetables they showed when slaves would arrive or depart from a particular station.

10. Tubman usually made her trips during the long winter nights the slaves followed her along back roads and through the woods.

11. During the day, she hid them in barns, holes in the ground, swamps, and people's homes.

12. Tubman was a brilliant planner she carried fake passes to fool patrolmen who were looking for runaways, and she paid local blacks to take down the posters identifying the runaways.

13. Once, she had to travel through a town where one of her former masters lived she dressed as an old woman and walked slowly down the street carrying several live chickens tied with a string.

14. She turned a corner and saw her old master walking toward her she quickly released the string, ran after the chickens, and escaped.

Scorecard: Number of errors found and corrected _____

Mastery Exercise 2

Combining Sentences

Eleven of the following items contain two independent clauses that are not joined in any way. Join the clauses using either a coordinating conjunction or a conjunctive adverb, if necessary. Use correct punctuation. Be careful: Three of the items shouldn't be changed. (The first item has been done for you.)

The Workings of the Underground Railroad

1. No one knows where the term *Underground Railroad* came from ^; however ^it might have begun with an event in 1831.

2. That year in Kentucky, the owner of a runaway slave named Tice Davids chased after him Davids jumped into the Ohio River and swam across.

3. The master got into a small boat and followed the slave then he could not find Davids on the shore.

4. Nobody in the nearby town had seen or heard of the slave the master told friends that Davids must have gone off on an "underground railroad."

5. The Underground Railroad was very well planned in some places, in other areas, runaway slaves had to take care of themselves or rely on fellow blacks for aid.

6. For runaway slaves and a person who helped them, every step was dangerous.

7. Harriet Tubman usually led her runaways on Saturday night so that she could be two days ahead of her pursuers, who wouldn't find out about the escape until Monday.

8. Most runaways did not have guides like Tubman they traveled to the North by following the North Star.

9. On cloudy nights, the runaways couldn't see the stars they felt the trunks of trees for the moss that grew on the northern sides.

10. The hardest part of the journey for the slaves was through the South they had almost nobody to help them or hide them.

11. As the fugitives moved north, they might contact a representative of the Underground Railroad he would give them the name of a conductor to help them.

12. At each station, the fugitives would be hidden, given food and supplies, and then sent to the next station.

13. Fugitives reached a new station then they signaled to its conductor by knocking on a window or saying code words.

14. The Underground Railroad was an enormous success it helped as many as 60,000 slaves escape to the North or Canada.

Scorecard: Number of errors found and corrected _____

CHAPTER 7

Joining Sentences Through Subordination

As you saw in Chapter 6 on coordination, joining sentences helps you express logical relationships and achieve sentence variety. However, coordination alone cannot accomplish both these goals. For example, read the following paragraph, which relies heavily on the coordinating conjunctions *and, but,* and *so:*

> The 1912 Olympic Games were held in Stockholm, Sweden, *and* there was controversy during the pentathlon. This event involves five different skills, *and* one of them requires shooting a gun at a target. The American was competing for a gold medal, *and* he fired his gun, *but* the judges said that his bullet had completely missed the target. He didn't agree, *and* he claimed that his bullet had gone straight through a hole in the center, *and* the hole had been made by an earlier contestant. The judges did not accept his argument, *so* he lost. The contestant was an army lieutenant, *and* his name was George S. Patton.

Here's a clearer, more entertaining, and more graceful version:

> At the 1912 Olympic Games, in Stockholm, Sweden, a controversy occurred during the pentathlon. Among the five different skills in this event, one requires shooting a gun at a target. After an American competing for a gold medal fired his gun, the judges said that his bullet had completely missed the target. He didn't agree, claiming that his bullet had gone straight through a hole in the center made by an earlier contestant. The judges did not accept his argument, so he lost. The contestant was an army lieutenant named George S. Patton.

WHAT IS SUBORDINATION?

Coordination joins equals, but not all ideas are equal. In the following sentence, for example, is the first idea as important as the second?

> I came home from work, and I found an eight-foot cobra snake in my living room.

If you answered yes, perhaps you live in a rather strange neighborhood! These ideas shouldn't be joined by *and.* They need to be joined in a way that expresses their inequality. Here are two possibilities:

> *When I came home from work,* I found an eight-foot cobra snake in my living room.
>
> *After coming home from work,* I found an eight-foot cobra snake in my living room.

Now the less important idea is *subordinate* (*sub* = lower, *ordinate* = level) to the more important one. This chapter explains, in detail, how you can combine sentences with **subordination.**

SUBORDINATING WITH CLAUSES

One type of subordination creates a **dependent clause**—which, as its name suggests, depends on an independent clause to complete its meaning. The dependent clause contains the less important idea. The independent clause contains the more important idea.

Like an **adverb,** the dependent clause often tells when, why, or where the idea in the independent clause takes place. So these dependent clauses begin with words like *when, because,* and *where.* Read the following two sentences, for example:

> Albert sits down for dinner. He can eat seven pizzas.

You could join them by subordinating the less important idea, introducing it with *when:*

> *When* Albert sits down for dinner, he can eat seven pizzas.

Now the first clause merely says when the second, and more important, action occurred. And this first clause can no longer make a complete statement:

> *When* Albert sits down for dinner, . . . (what happens?)

The joining word *when* subordinates the clause it introduces. We therefore call it a **subordinating conjunction.**

Combine the following two sentences with the subordinating conjunction *because:*

Albert had some serious indigestion.

He ate seven pizzas with sausage and anchovies.

_____

_____

And combine these two sentences with the subordinating conjunction *where:*

There is food.

You will find Albert.

_____

TIPS
For Detecting Fragments
Clauses beginning with *because* and *where* will be fragments unless they're attached to independent clauses that tell the main action.

(What happened?) . . . *because* he ate seven pizzas with sausage and anchovies.

Where there is food, . . . (what will happen?)

Are these the sentences you wrote?

> Albert had some serious indigestion *because* he ate seven pizzas with sausage and anchovies.
>
> *Where* there is food, you will find Albert.

Joining clauses with *when, why,* and *where* not only gives you more ways to express logical relationships. It also helps you create sentence variety.

EXERCISE 1   Identifying Subordination

Each sentence in this exercise contains a dependent clause and an independent clause. Label them DC and IC. Then find and underline the subordinating conjunction that begins that dependent clause.

Jesse Owens

✓

TIPS

For Using *Although*

Although is a conjunction; it joins clauses:

   Although the class was very difficult, I really learned a lot.

But *however* is a transitional word that doesn't join anything (notice where the semicolon and comma go):

   The class was very difficult; *however,* I really learned a lot.

The Triumph of Jesse Owens

1. In 1936, <u>when</u> the Olympic Games began in Nazi Germany, Adolf Hitler wanted them to prove his theories of Aryan (white) superiority.

2. However, after a twenty-two-year-old African-American named James Cleveland ("Jesse") Owens had competed in the track-and-field events, the young man personally ripped those theories to pieces.

3. At the beginning of the track-and-field events, Owens felt tense because a German had won a gold medal the day before and received Hitler's enthusiastic congratulations.

4. But later the same day, when one of the African-American athletes won a gold medal, Hitler did not shake his hand but hurried out of the stadium.

5. Although Hitler claimed he left to escape a light drizzle, the meaning of the German dictator's action was obvious.

6. If Hitler felt bad about a black man winning a medal, Jesse Owens would soon make him feel much worse.

7. When the track-and-field events were over, Jesse Owens had won four gold medals, breaking or equaling *nine* Olympic records.

Common Subordinating Conjunctions

The last exercise introduced you to many of the subordinating conjunctions. Here's a more complete list, divided into categories:

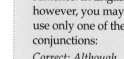

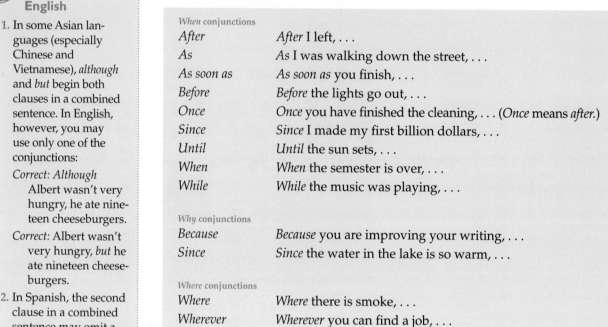

When conjunctions	
After	*After* I left, . . .
As	*As* I was walking down the street, . . .
As soon as	*As soon as* you finish, . . .
Before	*Before* the lights go out, . . .
Once	*Once* you have finished the cleaning, . . . (*Once* means *after*.)
Since	*Since* I made my first billion dollars, . . .
Until	*Until* the sun sets, . . .
When	*When* the semester is over, . . .
While	*While* the music was playing, . . .

Why conjunctions	
Because	*Because* you are improving your writing, . . .
Since	*Since* the water in the lake is so warm, . . .

Where conjunctions	
Where	*Where* there is smoke, . . .
Wherever	*Wherever* you can find a job, . . .

Other subordinating conjunctions set up a contrast or condition:

Contrasting conjunctions	
Although	*Although* you look honest, . . .
Even though	*Even though* the test was difficult, . . .
Whereas	*Whereas* many people thought the world was flat, . . .

Conditional conjunctions	
If	*If* I have the opportunity, . . .
Unless	*Unless* he stops playing that music so loudly, . . .

If Your First Language Is Not English

1. In some Asian languages (especially Chinese and Vietnamese), *although* and *but* begin both clauses in a combined sentence. In English, however, you may use only one of the conjunctions:

   Correct: Although Albert wasn't very hungry, he ate nineteen cheeseburgers.

   Correct: Albert wasn't very hungry, *but* he ate nineteen cheeseburgers.

2. In Spanish, the second clause in a combined sentence may omit a subject pronoun because it's part of the verb (for example, *tengo* means "I have"). In English, however, the second clause must include a stated subject:

   Correct: Albert didn't eat the last hamburger because *he* didn't want to be impolite.

Punctuating Dependent Clauses

Here are the rules for using commas with adverb dependent clauses:

▶ **Place a comma after a dependent clause** *at the beginning of a sentence.*

subordinating conjunction	dependent clause,	independent clause

When the alarm clock rings in the morning, I put the pillow over my head.

▶ **Do not use a comma before a dependent clause at the end of a sentence (but you may use a comma before a long clause beginning with the words *unless*, *although*, or *since*).**

> independent clause   *subordinating* conjunction   dependent clause
> I put the pillow over my head *when* the alarm clock rings in the morning.
> but
> I always get to work on time, *although* my hair may not be combed or my shirt buttoned.

EXERCISE 2   Joining and Punctuating Sentences

Read each pair of sentences. Then join them with a subordinating conjunction that best expresses the logical relationship between the sentences. The conjunction can come before either the first or the second sentence. Place a comma where it is needed.

COLLABORATIVE ACTIVITY 1

Comparing Combined Sentences
Compare your answers to Exercise 2. Did everyone use the same subordinating conjunctions? Did you agree on the placement of commas? Report your results to the class.

Jesse Owens's Most Remarkable Day

1. No one was surprised at Jesse Owens's success in the 1936 Olympics. ^ ~~He~~ *because he* had done something even more remarkable a year earlier.

2. He competed in the Big Ten Championship on May 25, 1935. He had the greatest day in the history of modern track competition.

3. He didn't think he would even be able to participate. He had strained his back a few weeks earlier.

4. He could not even jog at the warm-up before the meet. He decided to compete in the 100-yard dash.

5. He got off to a perfect start. He finished the dash in 9.4 seconds, matching the world record.

6. His coach advised Owens to take only a single long jump. He leapt almost 27 feet and beat the world record by nearly a half-foot.

7. Owens won the 200-yard dash in 20.3 seconds. He set another world record.

8. Owens finished the 220-yard low hurdles in 22.6 seconds. He broke an 11-year-old world record.

9. Owens completed four events in forty-five minutes. He set three world records and tied another.

COLLABORATIVE ACTIVITY 2

Writing Combined Sentences
Write two dependent clauses. Then, in your group, combine all of the clauses into a single list. Work by yourself for a few minutes to add independent clauses and create complete sentences. Now compare and discuss your results. Share three or four with the class.

EXERCISE 3   Writing Sentences with Dependent Clauses

Each of these sentences is incomplete, so complete the sentences. Be sure that your idea contains both a subject and a verb. Add a comma wherever it is needed.

1. When you are in the neighborhood, *please come to my place and visit me.*

2. I can give you a place to stay if _____

3. Since California has many earthquakes _____

4. _____ after an earthquake happens.

5. _____ although everyone knows about the danger.

6. People live in California because _____

SUBORDINATING WITH PHRASES

You can also subordinate an idea by making it a **phrase**—a group of words that don't include a complete subject and verb. (See Chapter 13 for a discussion of modifying phrases.) Here's an example of a *when* clause changed into a phrase:

> *dependent clause*
> *After the Native American Jim Thorpe* became the most famous athlete in track
>
> *independent clause*
> and field, *he competed* in the 1912 Olympic Games in Stockholm, Sweden.
>
> *phrase*   *independent clause*
> *After becoming the most famous athlete* in track and field, *the Native American Jim Thorpe competed* in the 1912 Olympic Games in Stockholm, Sweden.

Notice three things:

- The phrase begins with *after*.
- The verb *became* converts to an *–ing* word: *becoming*.
- The subject of the adverb clause, *Jim Thorpe,* moves to the independent clause.

Change the dependent clause to a phrase in this sentence:

While Thorpe won all five events in the pentathlon, he also won all ten events in the decathlon.

_____

_____

Is this what you wrote?

> While winning all five events in the pentathlon, Thorpe also won all ten events in the decathlon.

You can't convert every dependent clause into a phrase—just those that begin with the conjunctions *after, while, when, since, before,* and *although.* Here are a few more examples:

> *After*
> *While* ⎱ *triumphing in the Olympics,* Thorpe became a national hero.
> *When*   ⎰
> *Since*
>
> *Before entering the Olympics,* Thorpe was relatively unknown.
> *Although coming from a poor background,* Thorpe would achieve national fame.

✓ **TIPS**

For Detecting Fragments

Notice that the dependent clauses beginning with *because* and *where* can no longer make complete statements:

(What happened?) . . . *because* he ate seven pizzas with sausage and anchovies.

Where there is food, . . . (what will happen?)

In fact, some phrases can drop the conjunction and begin with an *–ing* word:

> *Entering the Olympics,* Thorpe was relatively unknown.

 Like a dependent clause beginning a sentence, a phrase that begins a sentence requires a comma.

EXERCISE 4   Revising Sentences

Each of the following sentences contains a dependent clause and an independent clause. Rewrite each sentence, changing the dependent clause into a phrase.

Jim Thorpe at a goal-kicking exhibition

Jim Thorpe (1887–1953): A World-Class Athlete

1. When people think about the origins of great athletes, people would never expect James Francis Thorpe to have become one of the best in history. *When thinking about the origins of great athletes, people would never expect James Francis Thorpe to have become one of the best in history.*

2. Before Jim Thorpe came to the Carlisle Indian School in Pennsylvania, he lived in Oklahoma Territory as a member of the Sac and Fox Tribe._____

_____

_____

3. Although Thorpe planned to become a tailor at Carlisle, he attracted national
    attention as a track-and-field athlete._____

    _____

    _____

4. In 1912, Thorpe won six of seven events while he was leading the tiny Carlisle team
    to an overwhelming victory over the much larger team from Lafayette._____

    _____

    _____

5. While he continued to compete in track and field, he became an all-American runner,
    place kicker, and defensive player in football._____

    _____

    _____

6. After he enjoyed such success in football, he went on to play major league baseball.

    _____

    _____

EXERCISE 5   Combining Sentences

Combine each of the following pairs of sentences using when, while, although, after, *or* before *plus an –ing word.*

1. Jim Thorpe breezed through the five events in the pentathlon in the Olympics. He
    won the decathlon so easily that it shocked the world. *After breezing through*
    the five events in the pentathlon in the Olympics, Jim Thorpe won the decathlon
    so easily that it shocked the world.

2. Thorpe received a bronze bust of himself from King Gustov of Sweden, who called
    him the greatest athlete in the world. Thorpe said only, "Thanks, King."_____

    _____

    _____

COLLABORATIVE ACTIVITY 3

Comparing Combined Sentences
Compare your answers to Exercise 5. Did you combine sentences in more than one way?
    Now combine the sentences using semicolons and coordinating conjunctions. See how many ways you can devise for joining the clauses. Report your results to the class.

3. The world learned that Thorpe's Olympic medals had been taken away from him. The
    world was astonished._____

    _____

    _____

4. In 1913, the Amateur Athletic Union (AAU) took back Thorpe's Olympic medals. It
    claimed he had played baseball for money in 1909 and 1910._____

    _____

    _____

5. Thorpe played for only a few dollars. He was technically a professional who should not have competed in the "amateur" Olympic Games. _____

_____

_____

6. The AAU refused to change its ruling. It finally awarded Thorpe his medals—in 1973, sixty years later, and twenty years after he had died. _____

_____

_____

IN SUMMARY   To Join Sentences with Subordination

1. Use a subordinating conjunction such as *if, when, although,* or *because* to relate a less important idea to a more important one.
2. Make the less important idea into a phrase beginning either with a word such as *when, while,* or *after* or with an *–ing* word.

EDITING FOR MASTERY

Mastery Exercise 1

Eliminating Sentence-Joining Errors

The following passage contains ten errors related to joining sentences (excluding the first error, which has been corrected as an example). Some sentences are actually fragments. Some sentences contain incorrect punctuation or are missing commas. Find and fix the errors by making any necessary changes above the line.

Jesse Owens Defeats Hitler

(1) Because Adolf Hitler wanted to turn the 1936 Olympics into a gigantic show of Nazis superiority. (2) ~~A~~ *,the* German dictator built a huge Olympic complex, including a 100,000-seat stadium just outside the city of Berlin. (3) Hitler was thrilled when in the opening parade, the Austrians gave him the Nazi salute. (4) The Bulgarians drew loud cheers. (5) When they marched like Nazi storm troopers. (6) But the German crowd jeered the Americans; because they didn't salute or dip their flag to Hitler.

(7) Hitler's joy disappeared on the second day of the track-and-field events when the American Jesse Owens broke into the lead in the 100-meter run. (8) Although his fellow African-American teammate Ralph Metcalfe challenged him strongly, but no one caught Owens as he won the gold medal.

(9) The following morning as the qualifying trials were held for the broad jump. (10) Owens fouled on his first and second attempts. (11) He had only one chance left, and he was obviously tired. (12) Because he had just run the heats of the 200-meter dash.

COLLABORATIVE ACTIVITY 4

Comparing Corrections
Appoint someone to read this passage aloud so you can hear where errors occur. Then make corrections, discuss them, and report them to the class.

(13) When Owens felt a hand on his shoulder. (14) He turned around to face Luz Long, a tall, blue-eyed German broad jumper. (15) Long suggested that Owens begin his jump a few inches before the starting board. (16) The grateful Owens did so and qualified with almost a foot to spare.

(17) Later that afternoon, Owens set an Olympic record on his second jump. (18) Although, Luz Long tied it on his next-to-last try. (19) Owens, however, was just warming up and lengthened the Olympic record on his fifth and sixth attempts. (20) After landing on his final jump. (21) Owens was congratulated by Long.

(22) While collecting four gold medals in all. (23) Owens didn't receive a single word of praise from Adolf Hitler. (24) Indeed, Owens and his nine African-American teammates outscored every other national team and won thirteen medals, eight of them gold. (25) Their triumph was enough to make Hitler's theory about the purity of white blood run thin.

Scorecard: Number of errors found and corrected _____

Mastery Exercise 2

Eliminating Sentence-Joining Errors

The following passage contains ten errors related to joining sentences (excluding the first error, which has been corrected as an example). Some sentences are actually fragments. Some sentences contain incorrect punctuation or are missing commas. Correct each error by making any necessary changes above the line. You may need to read the entire paragraph before you decide where to make corrections.

Mildred "Babe" Didrikson Zaharias: The Greatest Woman Athlete

(1) Although women weren't expected to perform as well as ^men. (2) Mildred "Babe" Didrikson Zaharias could outthrow, outrun, and outhit just about anyone of any sex.

"Babe" Didrikson in the javelin event, Xth Olympics, 1932

(3) While standing at home plate; she could throw a baseball and hit the left-field wall on one bounce. (4) She was incredibly skilled in tennis, bowling, and basketball. (5) She won more than fifty major golf tournaments, including three women's national opens. (6) "Babe" Didrikson Zaharias was also one of the best track-and-field performers of all time. (7) Because she was so talented in so many ways. (8) This native of Beaumont, Texas, was named the greatest woman athlete of the first half of the twentieth century.

(9) Babe Zaharias attracted national attention in 1930 in Dallas, as she won both the baseball throw and the javelin. (10) Although she finished second in the long jump, but her jump was good enough to top a world record. (11) In 1931, she continued her record-breaking performances in New Jersey; where she threw a baseball 296 feet and won both the 80-meter hurdles and the long jump.

(12) These performances turned out to be just a warm-up for the 1932 Olympics in Los Angeles. (13) Zaharias threw the javelin more than 143 feet for a new Olympic and world record. (14) She ran the 80-meter hurdles in less than 12 seconds while setting another Olympic and world record. (15) Although her high jump was good enough to break another world record. (16) She was disqualified for "diving" over the bar and finished in second place.

(17) After dominating women's track-and-field for a decade. (18) She became a world-champion golfer. (19) This led to one of the greatest comebacks in sports history. (20) Even though Zaharias had a cancer operation in 1953. (21) She won the women's national open in 1954. (22) In fact, she triumphed in every contest. (23) Until she finally lost her battle with cancer and died in 1956.

Scorecard: Number of errors found and corrected _____

CHAPTER 8

Joining Sentences with Pronouns

The previous two chapters showed you a number of ways to combine sentences in a confident, mature style. This chapter will introduce you to additional ways of joining sentences, with **pronouns**—words that replace nouns.

We'll be looking at how to

■ join sentences with pronouns that make one clause dependent on another

■ join sentences by making one clause function as a noun

■ join sentences by making a clause into a phrase

RELATIVE CLAUSES

TIPS

For Using Relative Pronouns

Beware of *in which.* Some writers love the expression *in which* because they think it sounds elegant. But the result often makes no sense.

Unclear: The topic *in which* we discussed today was capital punishment.

Clear: The topic *that* we discussed today was capital punishment.

Use *in which* only when *in* fits logically within the sentence:

Uncombined sentences: I want to discuss a subject. I am interested *in it.*

Combined sentences: I want to discuss a subject in which I am interested. (*In it* becomes *in which.*)

The following two sentences are short and choppy, almost sounding like the writing of a child:

I talked to a counselor. She was very helpful.

These sentences are begging to be combined—in this case by replacing *she* with a different kind of pronoun, *who:*

I talked to a counselor *who* was very helpful.

We call *who* a **relative pronoun** because it *relates* the information *was very helpful* to a noun, *counselor.*

Here are two more short, choppy sentences:

Our car needs to be replaced. It is ten years old.

Join them by replacing the pronoun *it* with another relative pronoun, *which:*

Our car, *which is ten years old*, needs to be replaced.

Now join the following two sentences by changing *they* to *that.*

I bought three chairs. *They* look beautiful in my living room.
Combined _____

Is this what you wrote?

> I bought three chairs *that* look beautiful in my living room.

Clauses beginning with the relative pronouns *who, which,* or *that* are therefore called **relative clauses.** They are **dependent clauses** because they cannot stand alone as sentences. And they function like **adjectives** because they describe nouns or pronouns.

- *Who* describes people (and sometimes animals).
- *Which* describes things.
- *That* describes either people or things.

Placement of Relative Clauses

A relative clause most often directly follows the noun or pronoun it describes. Otherwise, the sentence may not be clear:

> *Poor:*   Bill bought a car for his daughter *that cost a fortune.* (What cost a fortune—the daughter or the car?)
>
> *Better:*   Bill bought his daughter a car *that cost a fortune.*

E X E R C I S E   1   Combining Sentences

Combine each of the following sentences by adding the relative pronouns who, which, *or* that *above the lines to turn one sentence into a relative clause.*

The Origins of April Fool's Day

1. Throughout France in the early sixteenth century, New Year's Day was celebrated on March 25. It began the spring season. _Throughout France in the early sixteenth century, New Year's Day was celebrated on March 25, which began the spring season._

2. People would celebrate for a week by exchanging gifts at parties and dinners. These ended on April 1. _____

3. However, in 1564, King Charles IX moved the date of New Year's Day back to January 1. It was the beginning of the new (and more accurate) Gregorian calendar. _____

4. Nevertheless, for many of the French, gift-giving and parties continued to occur on April 1. They resisted the change. _____

5. Some people made fun of these conservatives by sending foolish gifts and invitations to parties. The parties didn't exist. _____

_____

6. After the French became comfortable with January 1 as the beginning of the year, they continued to play jokes on April 1. It became a tradition. _____

_____

7. Two hundred years later, the English adopted the custom. It then went on to reach the American colonies. _____

_____

Commas with Relative Clauses

The way you punctuate relative clauses can determine the meaning of a sentence. Here's why.

Restrictive Clauses. Read the following sentence:

> You can't start a car *that has a dead battery.*

If you remove the relative clause beginning with *that*, what's left?

> You can't start a car . . .

The meaning is no longer the same. The original sentence with the relative clause *restricts* the meaning of the car to the one with a dead battery—and not any other car. Therefore, we call it a **restrictive relative clause.** The pronoun *that* always begins a restrictive relative clause.

Remember that commas *separate* ideas—but the information in restrictive relative clauses is essential to meaning, so it must not be separated from the words it relates to.

▶ **Don't put commas around a restrictive relative clause.**

Nonrestrictive Clauses. Many relative clauses are not essential to meaning. Remove the relative clause from the following sentence, and see if the remaining idea is unclear.

> My new car, *which I bought in October,* started every day in the coldest weather.
> My new car . . . started every day in the coldest weather.

In this case, the basic meaning of the sentence doesn't change. The relative clause "which I bought in October" just adds a bit of extra information—the kind of information you might include in parentheses. Because that information doesn't restrict meaning in a particular way, we call the clause a **nonrestrictive relative clause.**

▶ **Put commas around a nonrestrictive relative clause, in the same place as parentheses would go:**

> My new car, *which I bought in October*, started every day in the coldest weather.
> My new car *(which I bought in October)* started every day in the coldest weather.

The pronouns *who* or *which* often begin a nonrestrictive relative clause. Enclose these clauses in commas. But *which* or *who* can begin restrictive relative clauses, too. So test the meaning of the clauses by temporarily removing them from the sentence. If the meaning is still clear, then use commas around the relative clause. For more practice with punctuating relative clauses, see Chapter 27.

EXERCISE 2   Punctuating Relative Clauses

Underline the relative clauses in the following sentences and then place commas around the relative clauses that need them.

The Blessing After the Sneeze

1. "God bless you" is an expression <u>that people everywhere say after someone sneezes.</u>

2. The practice of blessing someone which began in Greece in the fourth century B.C. can be traced to the philosophers Aristotle and Hippocrates.

3. They observed many people who seemed to sneeze just before dying from illness.

4. Therefore, to save sneezing people from dying, they recommended blessings that included "Long may you live!" and "May you enjoy good health!"

5. The Romans who had basically similar ideas continued the practice of the Greeks.

6. However, "God bless you" which is a Christian expression began for a different reason.

7. During the sixth century, there was a terrible plague that killed many people in Italy, so the Pope asked people to pray for the sick.

8. Therefore when people with the illness sneezed, their friends and relatives replaced "May you enjoy good health" with a stronger prayer which was "God bless you."

 COLLABORATIVE ACTIVITY I

Comparing Combined Sentences

Compare your answers to Exercises 1 and 2. In Exercise 1, did you all combine the sentences in the same way? In Exercise 2, did you agree on the placement of commas? Report your results to the class.

Relative Pronouns as Subjects

The relative pronouns *who*, *which*, and *that*, can serve as subjects of their clauses:

> Dr. Dunn is the professor *who* teaches modern languages.
> Our car, *which is ten years old*, needs to be replaced.
> You have to take a course *that* fulfills the natural science requirement.

As subjects, these pronouns begin the relative clause and are followed by the verb.

> Subject word order: Relative pronoun + verb

EXERCISE 3   Completing Sentences with Relative Clauses

Complete each of the following sentences. Some are missing only verbs; some are missing subjects and verbs. Insert commas where necessary.

TIPS

For Using Relative Pronouns

Beware of fragments. A relative clause doesn't make a complete statement.

Fragment: The cat that sleeps on top of the television set . . . (*does* or *is* what?)

Fragment: The instructor who gives killer assignments . . . (*does* or *is* what?)

Fragment: The watch, which Tonya gave me for graduation, . . . (*does* or *is* what?)

When you write a *who, which,* or *that* clause, be sure it's attached to an independent clause.

1. The accomplishment that I most want to achieve in the next few years *is to finish my college education and get a good job.* _____

2. People who don't eat meat _____ _____

3. In July the temperature in Arizona which often reaches more than 110 degrees _____ _____ _____

4. _____ which many students major in _____ _____

5. The older chairs and desks that are falling apart _____ _____

6. _____ who live in New York _____ _____

Relative Pronouns as Objects

Here are three more examples of sentences that could be combined with relative pronouns:

> Please give this form to the man. You will see *him* at the front desk.
> You must fill out several forms. You can get *them* from the receptionist.
> This is a form. You need to write your name and address on *it*.

The pronouns *him, them,* and *it* in the second sentences are objects, so the relative pronouns that replace them must also be objects. In this case, the relative pronouns have three forms:

- *Whom* relates to people.
- *That* relates to people, things, or ideas.
- *Which* relates to things or idea, and is used most often when it follows a preposition.

>   O   S   V
> Please give this form to the man *whom* you see at the front desk.
>   O   S   V
> You must fill out several forms *that* you can get from the receptionist.
>   O   S   V
> This is the form *on which* you need to write your name and address.

Since the object, represented by the relative pronoun, has now shifted to the beginning of the clause, you have to be careful not to repeat the object a second time:

> Please give this form to the man *whom* you see [him] at the front desk.
> You must fill out several forms *that* you can get [them] from the receptionist.
> This is the form *on which* you need to write your name and address [on it].

In fact, you can omit the object pronoun in many sentences, except when it follows a preposition.

> Please give this form to the man (whom) *you see at the front desk.*
> You must fill out several forms (that) *you can get from the receptionist.*
> BUT
> This is the form *on which* you need to write your name and address.

E X E R C I S E   4   Combining Sentences with Object Pronouns

In each pair of sentences below, the second sentence contains an object pronoun. Combine each pair, making the second sentence a relative clause while omitting the object pronoun (and the relative pronoun if the combined sentence is clear without it).

The Origins of Thanksgiving Day

1. Most people in the United States know the story of Thanksgiving. They celebrate it on the fourth Thursday of November. *Most people in the United States know the story of Thanksgiving, which they celebrate on the fourth Thursday of November.*

2. A ship called the *Mayflower* left Holland in 1620, carrying 102 people. People called them Pilgrims. _____

   _____

3. On December 11, 1620, after four months at sea, it landed at a place. We now call it Plymouth, Massachusetts. _____

   _____

4. By the next fall, forty-six Pilgrims were dead from disease. Hundreds of local Indians had died from it as well._____

   _____

5. The survivors, however, were thankful because food was abundant. They had harvested it. _____

   _____

6. The Pilgrims celebrated for three days with local Indians. The Indians had befriended them. _____

   _____

Relative Clauses with *Whose*

Here are two more sets of sentences that could be combined:

> On Thanksgiving Day, we recall the people. Their ship arrived on the shores of North America on December 11, 1620.
> That ship carried 102 passengers. It name was the *Mayflower*.

Their and *its* in the second sentences above show possession. Therefore, they must be replaced by the possessive form *whose*, which refers to either people or things:

> On Thanksgiving Day, we recall the people *whose ship* arrived on the shores of North America on December 11, 1620. That ship, *whoes name* was the *Mayflower*, carried 102 passengers.

EXERCISE 5   Combining Sentences with *Whose*

Combine each of the following sentences, making the second one into a relative clause beginning with whose.

1. You're the man. Your car is parked on my lawn. *You're the man whose car is parked on my lawn.*

2. Those are the chairs. Their legs are broken. _____

3. Pardon me, but are you the student? Your books are lost. _____

4. You must be the person. Your daughter just started school. _____

5. Relative clauses will be confusing. Their meaning is unclear. _____

6. I bought a used car. Its tires need to be replaced. _____

NOUN CLAUSES

Here are two short, choppy sentences begging to be combined. Do so by using one of these pronouns: *who, which, that,* or *what.*

> I know something. You said it.
> *Combined* _____

Is this what you wrote?

> I know *what* you said.

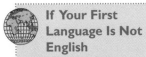

If Your First Language Is Not English

In English, the object pronoun always comes *after* the verb as in this example:

I heard *some news.* I *was* very excited about *it.*

But if you combine these two sentences, the relative pronoun replaces the object *it.* Be careful to remove *it* from the combined sentence:

       object

I heard some news *that* I *was* very excited

     second object

about i̶t̶.

Speakers of Eastern European languages, especially Russian, often confuse *what* with *that.*

Incorrect: I see the chair *what* I want.

Correct: I see the chair *that* I want.

Notice that "what you said" replaces "something"—the *object* of the verb "know." An object is a noun—or, in this case, a pronoun. So we call a clause beginning with *what* a **noun clause.**

A noun clause can also be the subject of a sentence. Compare these examples:

Sentence with a noun subject	Sentence with a noun clause
His behavior *annoyed me.*	*What he did* annoyed me.

Other joining words can begin noun clauses:

He told me $\begin{cases} where \\ how \\ that \\ when \\ why \end{cases}$ I should go.

He asked me $\begin{cases} if \\ whether \end{cases}$ he should go.

E X E R C I S E   6   Writing Noun Clauses

Complete each of the following sentences.

1. We know what *you want.* _____

2. I told you that _____

3. Do you have what _____

4. My friend asked me if _____

5. What doesn't make any sense _____

6. What will make Maria sad _____

E X E R C I S E   7   Combining Sentences

Combine each of the following groups of sentences into one sentence, using appropriate methods of both coordination and subordination.

The Origins of New Year's Day

1. Our word *holiday* comes from a word. It means "holy day." All celebrations used to be religious. *Our word holiday comes from a word that means "holy day," for*

    all celebrations used to be religious.

2. New Year's Day is the oldest "holy day." It began a long time ago. The calendar didn't exist. _____

_____

3. The first New Year's festival began in the city of Babylon. It was the capital of ancient Babylonia. Babylonia is now part of Iraq. _____

_____

4. Late in March, Babylonians had a huge festival. They wanted to celebrate the new year at a particular time. It was the beginning of spring. _____

_____

5. The Babylonians also performed a play. It was to honor the goddess of fertility. They had an enormous parade. It included music, dancing, and performers. The performers wore costumes. _____

_____

6. The idea behind the holiday began to change with the Romans. They created a calendar. It celebrated the new year on March 25. _____

_____

7. Roman rulers and government officials changed the months and years. They made the months and years longer. They wanted to lengthen time. The time was when their terms of office lasted. _____

_____

8. Members of the Roman Senate met in 153 B.C. They knew something. They had to set the date of the new year on January 1. _____

_____

9. Roman emperors continued to change the calendar. They changed it for the next century. In 46 B.C., Julius Caesar adjusted the calendar. The year now dragged on for 445 days. _____

_____

10. The Catholic Church disapproved of any "pagan" (non-Christian) festivals. These celebrated the planting of seeds. The Church eliminated the new year holiday.

_____

_____

COLLABORATIVE ACTIVITY 2

Comparing Combined Sentences
Compare your answers to Exercise 7. How many different but correct ways to combine these sentences did your group come up with? Report your results to the class.

11. The holiday came back during the Middle Ages. The British celebrated it on March 25. The French celebrated it on Easter Sunday. The Italians celebrated it on Christmas day. _____

_____

12. These differences continued until about 400 years ago. The date of January 1 was finally agreed on. _____

_____

_____

PHRASES

How would you combine the following sentences?

> The eight-foot-tall man must be a basketball player. He is wearing Nikes and a jersey.
> The Rolls Royce is my second car. It is parked in the alley.

One possibility is to combine them with *who* or *that* clauses:

> The eight-foot-tall man *who is wearing Nikes and a jersey* must be a basketball player.
> The Rolls Royce *that is parked in the alley* is my second car.

But the combined sentences would be just as clear (and shorter) if you eliminated *who* or *that* and the verbs that follow them:

> The eight-foot-tall man *wearing Nikes and a jersey* must be a basketball player.
> The Rolls Royce *parked in the alley* is my second car.

These shorter versions of combined sentences now contain **phrases**—groups of two or more words—instead of clauses.

Try combining these sentences without using *who, that,* or *which:*

> Many high school students have read *Great Expectations.* It is a novel written by Charles Dickens.
> The book was made into a movie. The movie was made in 1998.
>
> 1. _____
> 2. _____

Is this what you wrote?

> Many high school students have read *Great Expectations,* a novel written by Charles Dickens.
> The book was made into a movie in 1998.

These combined sentences contain four types of phrases—all of which describe or rename nouns:

- phrases beginning with an *–ing* word (*wearing* Nikes and a jersey)
- phrases beginning with a *noun (a novel)*—technically called an **appositive,** which adds identifying information to the noun that precedes it
- phrases beginning with a *past participle* (*written* by Charles Dickens)
- phrases beginning with a **preposition** (*in* 1998).

Consider these choices when you combine sentences.

EXERCISE 8   Combining Sentences

Combine each of the pairs of sentences using the methods described in this chapter.

A Sticky Solution

1. The idea for Velcro began in 1941. It started with an unlucky accident that happened to the wife of Swiss manufacturer George de Mistral. _The idea for Velcro began in 1941 with an unlucky accident that happened to the wife of Swiss manufacturer George de Mistral._

2. The zipper on her dress jammed and would not unjam. They were at a formal affair.

3. A few months later, de Mistral thought of a better way to fasten fabrics. He was on a hunting trip with his dog.

4. The dog's ear became covered with burrs. They came from brushing against some weeds.

5. De Mistral noticed tiny hooks on their ends. He was examining the burrs under a microscope.

6. Sixteen years later, this principle led to the manufacture of Velcro. It was little burrlike hooks on fabric. (*Hint:* Place the second idea after *principle* and use commas.)

IN SUMMARY   To Join Sentences Using Pronouns or Phrases

1. Use the relative pronouns *who, whom,* or *that* in a relative clause describing a person. *Whom* can function only as an object pronoun and often can be omitted from the sentence.
2. Use the relative pronouns *which* and *that* in a relative clause describing a thing or idea.
3. Put commas around a nonrestrictive relative clause.
4. Use *whose* as a possessive word before a noun in sentences such as "I found a book *whose cover* is torn."
5. Use *what* or *that* to create a clause that functions as a noun.
6. Whenever possible, change relative clauses into phrases.

EDITING FOR MASTERY

Mastery Exercise 1

Eliminating Sentence-Joining Errors

The following passage contains ten errors related to joining sentences (excluding the first error, which has been corrected as an example): incorrectly used relative pronouns, sentence fragments, incorrectly punctuated relative clauses, and incorrectly used noun clauses. Find and fix them. Correct each error by making any necessary changes above the line.

The First Thanksgiving: 1621

(1) The Pilgrims ^who ~~Which~~ settled in Plymouth in 1620 had suffered through a difficult first year, when more than half of them had died. (2) But after the harvest the following fall, there were many things what they were thankful for. (3) They had plenty of food and they were alive, mostly because of the help of one person: an English-speaking Pawtuxet Indian named Squanto, whom would stay to help them until his death two years later.

(4) As a boy, Squanto had been captured by explorers to America. (5) Who sold him into slavery in Spain. (6) He escaped to England, spent several years working for a wealthy merchant, and returned to his native Indian village just six months before the Pilgrims landed. (7) During the first year what the Pilgrims were in Plymouth, he had helped them build houses and grow crops of corn and barley. (8) In the fall of 1621, the Pilgrims elected a new governor, who's name was William Bradford. (9) He declared a day of thanksgiving in their small town. (10) Which had seven private homes and four public buildings.

(11) According to Governor Bradford's own *History of Plymouth Plantation,* the celebration lasted three days. (12) The day before it began, he sent "four men fowling," and they returned with "a great store of wild turkeys." (13) However, the "turkeys" in which they found may not have been actual turkeys. (14) Although wild turkeys did live in the forests, "turkey" in those days meant any form of bird, who included ducks and geese.

(15) The Pilgrims invited the chief of the Wampanoag tribe, Massasoit, and ninety of his braves. (16) The four Pilgrim women and two teenage girls whom the previous winter had not killed prepared the feast—for ninety-one Indians and fifty-six settlers.

Scorecard: Number of errors found and corrected _____

COLLABORATIVE ACTIVITY 3

Comparing Corrections
Appoint someone to read the passage aloud so you can hear where errors occur. Make corrections, discuss them, and report them to the class.

Mastery Exercise 2

Eliminating Sentence-Joining Errors

The following passage contains ten errors related to joining sentences (excluding the first error, which has been corrected as an example): incorrectly used relative pronouns, sentence fragments, incorrectly punctuated relative clauses, and incorrectly used noun clauses. Correct each error by making any necessary changes above the line. You may need to read an entire paragraph before you decide where to make corrections.

The Birth of the National Holiday

(1) October 1777 was the first time ^that ~~What~~ all the thirteen colonies joined in a common thanksgiving holiday. (2) Which celebrated an important victory over the British during the Revolutionary War. (3) However, the colonies celebrated this holiday only once.

(4) In 1789, that was the year of his inauguration the first president, George Washington, proclaimed Thanksgiving as a national holiday, but the thirteen states didn't accept the proclamation. (5) For one thing, many Americans, felt, that the hardships of a few early settlers weren't important enough to commemorate. (6) Certainly the new nation had bigger events what deserved a celebration. (7) In fact, Thomas Jefferson, which became president in 1801, actually condemned a national recognition of Thanksgiving.

(8) The creation of the day that we now celebrate nationwide it was mostly because of the work of a magazine editor who's name was Sarah Joseph Hale. (9) Mrs. Hale, whom edited the *Boston Ladies' Magazine* in 1827, wrote that the country should observe a Thanksgiving holiday. (10) When *Ladies' Magazine* merged with *Godey's lady's Book,* Mrs. Hale became the editor of the most popular woman's magazine in the country, with 150,000 readers. (11) She continued to write strong editorials in favor of a Thanksgiving celebration.

(12) Additionally, for almost forty years, she wrote hundreds of letters to governors, ministers, newspaper editors, and each president. (13) She always made the same request. (14) Which was that the last Thursday in November should be a time to "offer to God our tribute of joy and gratitude for the blessings of the year."

(15) Finally, national events turned Mrs. Hale's request into a reality.

(16) By 1863, the Civil War had divided the nation in two. (17) Mrs. Hale's final editorial appeared in September of that year, right after the Battle of Gettysburg. (18) Although the Northern states had won the battle, many soldiers on both sides had lost their lives. (19) This persuaded President Abraham Lincoln to issue a proclamation on October 3, 1863, in which set aside the last Thursday in November as a national Thanksgiving Day.

Scorecard: Number of errors found and corrected _____

Repairing Run-ons and Correcting Comma Splices

Good writing depends on strong sentences—sentences that are clear, concise, interesting, and easy to read. To write strong sentences, you need to be aware of all the options open to you for combining them. You need to recognize and avoid combinations that don't work, too.

This chapter will show you how to correct two common errors in sentence-joining:

■ clauses joined by nothing at all

■ clauses joined by nothing but a comma

RUN-ON SENTENCES

What joins the two independent clauses in each of the following sentences?

> My friend John is a bit weird he wears six rings in his nose.
> We saw an early movie then we had a pizza later at Guido's.

Nothing joins them. The first clause simply runs on into the second. These are **run-on sentences**—two independent clauses with nothing linking them together—a very confusing and serious error.

You can repair run-ons in a number of ways. In some cases, you need only insert a conjunction or semicolon. In other cases, you need to rewrite the sentence a bit:

1. Add a coordinating conjunction (see Chapter 6):

> My friend John is a bit weird, *for (so)* he wears six rings in his nose.

2. Add a semicolon (see Chapter 6):

> My friend John is a bit weird; he wears six rings in his nose.

3. Add a semicolon and a transitional word (see Chapter 6):

> We saw an early movie; *afterward,* we had a pizza at Guido's Glorious Pizza.

4. Rewrite the sentence to eliminate a clause:

> My *weird* friend John wears six rings in his nose.

5. Rewrite the sentence and add a relative pronoun to create a dependent clause (see Chapter 8):

> My friend John, *who* wears six rings in his nose, is a bit weird.

6. Add a subordinating conjunction to create an adverb dependent clause (see Chapter 7):

> *After* we saw an early movie, we had a pizza at Guido's Glorious Pizza.

7. Rewrite the clauses as separate sentences:

> We saw an early movie. Then we had a pizza at Guido's Glorious Pizza.

If you find a run-on sentence as you edit your work, experiment with different corrections until you find one that best expresses your meaning.

EXERCISE 1   Revising Run-on Sentences

Rewrite each run-on sentence in this exercise to eliminate the error. Use a variety of solutions: coordinating conjunctions, subordinating conjunctions, semicolons and transitional words, relative pronouns, or complete revisions of the sentences.

Canine Convict Number C2559

1. Pep was a male Labrador retriever he belonged to neighbors of the governor of Pike County, Pennsylvania. *Pep, who was a male Labrador retriever, belonged to neighbors of the governor of Pike County, Pennsylvania.*

2. Pep was a friendly dog ~~,~~ *but* he went wild and killed the governor's cat one hot summer day. _____

3. The governor was furious ~~,~~ *therefore* he put Pep on trial and sentenced the dog to life imprisonment. _____

4. The poor beast went to the penitentiary in Philadelphia *;* the warden gave him an ID number like the rest of the cons. _____

5. The story has a happy ending *,* Pep's fellow inmates loved him *,* and he could switch cellmates at will. _____

COLLABORATIVE ACTIVITY I

Comparing Combined Sentences

Compare your answers to Exercise 1. Make a list of the different solutions for each item. Report your results to the class.

6. Pep spent six pleasant years in prison (forty-two dog years) then he died of old age.

_____

_____

_____

COMMA-SPLICED SENTENCES

TIPS

For Avoiding Run-ons and Comma-spliced Sentences

Watch out for *then* and *also*. They often show up, trying their hardest to be conjunctions. But they can't be used to join sentences.

Incorrect: I took a quick shower, then I headed off to class.

Correct: I took a quick shower, *and then* I headed off to class

Incorrect: I have a quiz on Thursday, also I have to finish my math assignment.

Correct: I have a quiz on Thursday, and I have to finish my math assignment.

What joins the two independent clauses in these sentences?

> Albert wasn't satisfied with just three pizzas, he ate seven.
> Albert eats six meals a day, however, he never gains any weight.

Commas don't join the clauses—because commas *separate* ideas. And *however* can't join clauses—because *however* is a *transitional* word. So nothing joins the clauses. They're **comma-spliced sentences**—two independent clauses with a comma between them but no joining word.

Just as you shouldn't splice together electrical wires with masking tape, you shouldn't splice together sentences with commas. The electrical wires should be joined securely in a *junction* box; the sentences should be joined securely with a *conjunction*.

Comma-spliced sentences occur far more frequently than run-ons. That's because writers hear a pause between ideas and mark it with a comma instead of a period. Like run-on sentences, though, comma-spliced sentences often confuse and annoy readers. Repair these damaged sentences in the same way you repair run-ons:

1. Insert conjunctions.
2. Insert semicolons (with transitional words if necessary).
3. Insert relative pronouns to create relative dependent clauses.
4. Rewrite the sentences.

(For additional practice with punctuating sentences, see Chapter 27.)

EXERCISE 2   Revising Comma-Spliced Sentences

Label each item here with CS (for comma splice) or OK (because it is correct as is). Then repair each comma-spliced sentence, using a variety of solutions.

The Loyal Dog

 COLLABORATIVE ACTIVITY 2

Comparing Combined Sentences

Compare your answers to Exercise 2. For the items that are OK, explain what makes these sentences complete and correct. Report your results to the class.

_____ **1.** Eisaburo Ueno was a college professor at Tokyo University, he had a dog named Hachi. _Eisaburo Ueno, a college professor at Tokyo University, had a dog named Hachi._

_____ **2.** Every morning he went to a railroad station near his home his dog always accompanied him. _____

_____

CS __ 3. Every evening he returned on a train, Hachi was always there to greet him.

_____

_____

_____

cs __ 4. One day in 1925 Professor Ueno had a heart attack at school, then he died.

_____

_____

Cs __ 5. Hachi lived for ten more years, he went to the train station every evening and patiently waited for his master. _____

_____

_____

_____

OK __ 6. When the professor didn't arrive, the dog sadly went back to Ueno's family.

_____

_____

_____

as __ 7. Hachi always met the evening trains, he became a familiar sight to Japanese travelers. _____

_____

_____

_____

CS __ 8. Finally, Hachi died at Shibuya station, he was still hopeful that the professor was on the next train. _____

_____

_____

_____

CS __ 9. Today a statue of Hachi sits outside of Shibuya station where people put wreaths around the statue's neck and leave small gifts. _____

_____

_____

_____

_____**10.** In 1987, Japanese filmmakers made a movie about Hachi, the dog

that has become a national symbol of loyalty and devotion. _____

_____

_____

E X E R C I S E   3   Eliminating Sentence-Combining Errors

Each of the following items contains one or more run-ons or comma splices. Correct the errors above the lines. You don't have to rewrite the sentences.

The Death of Dian Fossey: The Lonely Woman of the Forest

1. It was a quiet morning at Karisoke Research Station in Rwanda, ^*but* noises suddenly broke the silence.

2. A group of men stormed into the cabin of Wayne McGuire, he was an American graduate student, they woke him up.

3. They kept on repeating in Swahili that Dian was dead, it was a language he did not know well, he finally understood them.

4. He found Dian Fossey's body lying next to the bed in her cabin, her face had been slashed from forehead to mouth.

5. It was four days later, the fifty-four-year-old woman was buried in the station's animal cemetery, in a spot next to the graves of some mountain gorillas that she loved so dearly.

6. Dian Fossey had spent her life studying the mountain gorillas, also she had saved them from extinction.

7. McGuire was accused of the crime and fled the country, however, there were other, more obvious suspects.

8. Fossey had made friends with the mountain gorillas, at the same time she had made enemies in Rwanda.

IN SUMMARY   To Repair Run-ons and Comma Splices

1. Add a coordinating conjunction (*and, but, or, for, so, nor, yet*).
2. Add a semicolon and, if necessary, a transitional word (*however, therefore, nevertheless*, and so forth), followed by a comma.
3. Use a subordinating conjunction (*because, when, if, although*, etc.) to create an adverb dependent clause.
4. Use a relative pronoun (*who, which, that*) to create a relative dependent clause.
5. Make one clause a phrase.
6. Rewrite the sentence.
7. Write the two clauses as two separate sentences.

EDITING FOR MASTERY

Mastery Exercise 1   *Eliminating Sentence-Combining Errors*

The following passage contains ten run-on or comma-spliced sentences (excluding the example, which has been corrected for you). Find and fix the errors.

Dian Fossey's Crusade to Save the Gorillas

(1) Dian Fossey's closest friends praised her as a warmhearted, completely dedicated woman.; ^ in fact, they called her "Queen of the Apes." (2) She worked most of her life to save the East African mountain gorillas, consequently, they are a less endangered species. (3) Today there are 650 mountain gorillas alive in the world, there were only 250 in the mid-1970s.

(4) Although people used to think that gorillas were all like King Kong, Dian Fossey's research changed that idea. (5) She began by watching these gentle giants from a safe distance, later on she moved among them. (6) She imitated their grunting sounds and body language, also she nibbled on the wild celery they loved and scratched them.

(7) Fossey's desire to live among the gorillas was understandable, she had been a lonely child who loved animals. (8) However, she couldn't have any pets except a goldfish when it died, she cried for a week.

(9) She saw gorillas on her first trip to East Africa in 1963, she described them as "big and imposing but not monstrous at all." (10) She left Africa, then she returned four years later and established the Karisoke Research Station in Rwanda.

Dian Fossey (photo by Peter G. Veit for the National Geographic Society)

COLLABORATIVE ACTIVITY 3

Comparing Corrections
Appoint someone to read the passage aloud so you can hear where errors occur. Make your corrections, discuss them, and report them to the class.

(11) Fossey loved the gorillas but constantly chased after poachers, they were killing the animals. (12) When she caught the poachers, she took away their weapons and even whipped them. (13) She also fought the Rwandan authorities, who wanted to make the gorilla's home into a tourist attraction. (14) Fossey said that the gorillas were not zoo attractions, she threatened to shoot any tourist approaching her station. (15) She made many enemies among the Rwandans, and her murder has never been solved.

Scorecard: Number of errors found and corrected _____

Mastery Exercise 2

Eliminating Sentence-Combining Errors

The following passage contains ten run-on or comma-spliced sentences (excluding the example, which has been corrected for you). Correct each error above the lines.

The Talking Gorilla

(1) For centuries, people have dreamed of communicating with animals, ^*and* the most likely candidates for communication have always been apes. (2) Not surprisingly, the first animal to fulfill that dream was a female gorilla named Koko, she was born at the San Francisco Zoo on July 4, 1971. (3) In 1972, a psychology student named Francine Patterson began the gorilla's incredible education. (4) Patterson taught Koko American Sign Language, the friendly 290-pound beast quickly became a good student.

(5) Patterson and her assistants started by teaching Koko the signs for food, drink, and other things. (6) Eventually Koko was able to use language more creatively. (7) For instance, she was taught that *dirty* referred to her bowel movements, soon she used it to describe people and events as well. (8) She later chose her own meaning for certain signs, for example, *good* meant "yes" and *lip* meant "woman." (9) She learned to make jokes, also she was interviewed on television—and even on the Internet.

(10) Koko has been studying for more than twenty years, she has learned about 900 different signs. (11) Researchers wanted to see if she could pass on her language skills to another ape, therefore they began looking for a mate for her in 1983. (12) Koko didn't find a mate until 1994. (13) Then she met Ndume, he was from a Chicago zoo, and they were immediately attracted to each other.

(14) There are critics of Patterson's experiments with Koko, they complain that the gorilla has never learned grammar or how to ask a question. (15) However, there is no doubt that Koko and other gorillas can answer questions, usually with one-word signs. (16) The human dream of communicating with animals started long ago, it has come true with a friendly ape named Koko.

Scorecard: Number of errors found and corrected _____

Essentials of a sentence = an independent clause
subject + verb + completion of statement

A sentence fragment is

(NO SUBJECT) + VERB

SUBJECT + (NO VERB)

SUBJECT + INCOMPLETE VERB

SUBJECT + VERB (NO COMPLETION OF STATEMENT)

4 ways to fix a fragment

Add a missing subject.

Add a missing verb.

Complete an incomplete verb.

Complete the statement following the verb.

A run-on sentence is

FIRST SENTENCE SECOND SENTENCE (nothing joins them)

A comma-spliced sentence is

FIRST SENTENCE , SECOND SENTENCE (a comma incorrectly joins them)

8 ways to repair run-ons and comma splices (correctly joining two sentences into one)

- FIRST SENTENCE , **coordinating conjunction** (*and/but* etc.) SECOND SENTENCE.

- FIRST SENTENCE ; SECOND SENTENCE.

- FIRST SENTENCE ; **conjunctive adverb** (*however/therefore* etc.), SECOND SENTENCE.

- **Subordinating conjunction** (*when/although* etc.) FIRST SENTENCE now a dependent clause , SECOND SENTENCE.

- FIRST SENTENCE **subordinating conjunction** (*when/although* etc.) SECOND SENTENCE now a dependent clause.

- FIRST SENTENCE , (*when/although* etc.) SECOND SENTENCE now a dependent clause.

- FIRST SENTENCE , **relative pronoun** (*who/which/that/whom/whose*) + verb (or subject + verb) from SECOND SENTENCE.

- FIRST SENTENCE . SECOND SENTENCE.

Joining sentences: one question to ask

Are the statements equal or unequal?
- Equal ⟶ join by coordination
- Unequal ⟶ join by subordination

Four ways to join sentences by subordination

FIRST SENTENCE , subordinating conjunction (*when/although* etc.) SECOND SENTENCE now a dependent clause.

Subordinating conjunction (*when/although* etc.) FIRST SENTENCE now a dependent clause, SECOND SENTENCE.

FIRST SENTENCE + phrase (formerly SECOND SENTENCE)

Phrase (formerly FIRST SENTENCE) , SECOND SENTENCE.

Three ways to join sentences by coordination (making both sentences into one)

FIRST SENTENCE , coordinating conjunction (*and/but* etc.) SECOND SENTENCE

FIRST SENTENCE ; SECOND SENTENCE

FIRST SENTENCE ; conjunctive adverb (*however/therefore* etc.), SECOND SENTENCE

To make a subject + verb into a phrase, make the verb incomplete by adding *–ing*.

Comma Do's

1. before a coordinating conjunction that joins two sentences
2. after a dependent clause beginning a joined sentence
3. around a nonrestrictive clause

Comma Don'ts

1. on either side of a conjunctive adverb
2. between two independent clauses

Semicolon Do's

1. between two closely related joined sentences
2. before a conjunctive adverb after the semicolon in joined sentences

COORDINATING CONJUNCTIONS

For	But
And	Or
	Yet
Nor	So

SUBORDINATING CONJUNCTIONS

although	after
if	before
because	while
when	(for more, see p. 84)

CONJUNCTIVE ADVERBS

furthermore	nevertheless
moreover	therefore
	otherwise
also	meanwhile
however	(for more, see p. 75)

Revising with Care: Building on the Framework

The previous unit focused on sentences—ways to ensure they're complete, correctly joined, and joined in ways that create variety and interest as you edit your writing. This unit looks more deeply into the parts of the sentence: the words and phrases that make sentences work—and work for *you.* It begins by showing you how to identify the elements of the sentence as you revise and edit: the subject, the verb, and the completion of the statement that follows the verb.

It then shows you how to identify and correct errors in the forms of verbs, nouns, pronouns, adjectives, and adverbs. It shows you how to place words so sentences are clear and correct. It shows you how to maintain consistency in verb tense and word order. It also shows you how to select strong verbs and adjectives while eliminating unnecessary words. In short, it shows you how to master the small matters that make a big difference in the way readers respond to your message. ■

Making Subjects and Verbs Agree

Readers should pay attention to your ideas, not to unexpected and confusing word forms. But readers can be confused if the subjects and verbs of sentences don't fit together. With a singular subject, you need a singular verb; with a plural subject, you need a plural verb. This agreement between subjects and verbs is sometimes difficult because English has some unusual word forms and tricky situations. This chapter will show you how to overcome the difficulties as you edit. You'll learn

■ how to make subjects and verbs work together

■ how to recognize exceptions that can trip you up

WHAT IS SUBJECT-VERB AGREEMENT?

As you know, subjects can be nouns or pronouns. They can be **singular:** representing one person, place, or thing. Or they can be **plural:** representing more than one. In other words, nouns and pronouns have **number.** Likewise, the verbs that work with subjects can have singular or plural forms. A singular subject goes with a singular verb, and a plural subject with a plural verb. That's **subject-verb agreement,** and without it, some sentences can sound pretty odd.

Look, for example, at the following two sentences written in the **present tense,** which discusses habitual actions or states, or actions that are happening now:

> I *are* reading a fascinating book.
> He *am* a charming man.

They sound unnatural and unclear because the verbs don't match the subjects. This is what you'd expect to see:

> I *am* reading a fascinating book.
> He *is* a charming man.

Here's one more sentence:

> One of the kittens *are* awake.

How many kittens are awake? The sentence may be confusing because the verb *are* agrees with the wrong word, *kittens*—not with the actual subject, *one*. The correct subject-verb agreement clears up the confusion:

> One of the kittens *is* awake.

Subject-verb agreement occurs only in tenses that deal with the present, and with just one verb in the past tense, which we'll discuss in Chapter 11. Right now, we'll focus on the present-tense agreement.

SUBJECTS

TIPS

For Determining Verb Agreement with Nouns: The Rule of One –s

Plural verbs never end in –s, but most plural nouns do. So, if the noun subject ends in –s, the verb usually does not. If the verb ends in –s, the noun subject usually does not.

Singular: noun (no –s) + verb with –s

The *student studies* in the library.

Plural: noun with –s + verb (no –s)

The *students study* in the library.

In English sentences, the subject generally comes before the verb, and the form that the verb takes depends on its subject. So we'll begin by looking at the singular and plural forms of the most common kind of subject: nouns. You'll need to be able to recognize them to check subject-verb agreement.

Nouns as Subjects (and Objects)

A *singular* noun, which usually doesn't end in –s, takes a verb that ends in –s:

> A *jaguar is* the fastest animal on earth.
> A *professional baseball player owns* several jaguars—the driving kind.

A *plural* noun, which normally ends in –s, takes a verb without an –s ending:

> *Jaguars are* members of the cat family.
> Many professional *athletes make* millions of dollars.

The –s ending for plural nouns—whether they're subjects or objects—is important, for it tells readers that you mean more than one. And the –s ending on present-tense verbs is important, for it reminds readers that your subject is singular.

EXERCISE I   Choosing Correct Noun Forms

Some of the nouns throughout the following sentences should be plural. Change them by adding –s or –es endings. (One sentence contains no errors.)

Facts About Zebras

1. It's not unusual to see 1,000 zebra^s together at one time.

2. They're very social animal.

3. They generally live in short grassy area or open fields.

4. A family group consists of one male (called a stallion), several female (called mares), and many infant.

5. The female are not equal; the dominant mare leads the pack and the other follow behind her in single file.

6. And the family stays together, even when they join large herds.

7. Although lion and hyenas prey on zebra, these striped horses are extremely brave.

8. The male often form a semicircle to protect their families.

9. The lions will sometimes come out second best, because zebras can deliver powerful kick.

EXERCISE 2   Choosing Correct Verb Forms

Decide whether the subject of the sentence is singular or plural. Then write the appropriate present-tense form of the verb supplied in parentheses.

Facts About Leopards

1. Leopards normally (hunt) _____*hunts*_____ at dusk and throughout the night.

2. These beautiful cats often (stay) ____*stays*____ hidden during the day or (lie) _____*lies*_____ in high branches of trees.

3. A male leopard normally (live) _____*lives*_____ alone, and (join) _____*joins*_____ a female only for mating.

4. Their spotted bodies (make) ____*make*____ wonderful camouflage, so the big cats attack their prey by surprise.

5. A single bite from a leopard usually (kill) _____ the prey.

6. Then the leopard (take) _____ it up in a tree and has a leisurely meal.

Irregular Plurals

English is a very old language in which grammar was originally much more complicated. Singular nouns used to form their plurals in a number of ways. The regular practice of simply adding –s to the ends of nouns is actually a fairly recent change. But a few nouns stubbornly hold onto their ancient plural forms, without –s endings, so they are **irregular.** Here are some examples:

Singular	Plural
child	children
man	men
mouse	mice
foot	feet

Some words, taken from other languages, retain the plural forms of those languages:

phenomenon	phenomena
crisis	crises
medium	media

Some other nouns have identical singular and plural forms, such as these:

sheep	fish	deer

Still other nouns have only plural forms:

clothes	scissors	pants	shorts

Finally, a few nouns are singular even though they end in *–s:*

mathematics	physics (and all other nouns ending in *–ics*)	news

EXERCISE 3   Making Irregular Nouns Plural

Change the following singular nouns to plurals. Use a dictionary if you're uncertain.

1. woman _____

2. goose _____

3. louse _____

4. datum _____

5. tooth _____

6. person _____

Pronouns as Subjects

A **pronoun** takes the place of a noun. Like a noun, it can be singular or plural and can serve as the subject of a verb:

	Singular + verb		Plural + verb	
First person	I	run	we	run
Second person	you	run	you	run
Third person	he	*runs*	they	run
	she	*runs*		
	it	*runs*		

Notice that only the *third-person singular* subject pronouns (*he, she,* and *it*) require a verb ending in *–s:*

he ⎫	
she ⎬ works, eats, itches, yawns, wiggles, giggles
it ⎭	

EXERCISE 4   Writing Verbs with Pronoun Subjects

Look at the pronoun subject of each sentence. Then write the present-tense form of the verb in parentheses that agrees with the subject.

1. We (deserve) ___*deserve*___ an award for talking to crazy Eddie.

2. She (wear) _____ the most attractive orange and red polka dot shoes.

3. They (own) _____ a lovely house in the suburbs of Antarctica.

4. He (scratch) _____ his ear with his salad fork.

5. It often (rain) _____ through my roof in the spring.

6. You (know) _____ how to charm people.

7. I always (write) _____ elegant and beautiful sentences in these exercises.

Subjects Joined by *and*

Any combination of nouns and pronouns joined by *and* also makes a plural subject, which is called a **compound subject**. Note the following examples:

Subject	Verb without –s
a candle and a prayer	
Juan and I	*go, make, seem*
ice cream, cake, candy, and Alka Seltzer	

A compound subject, like a plural noun or pronoun, requires a plural verb.

Only the word *and* joins two subjects. *Or, nor,* and prepositions such as *with* or *in* do not make a compound subject:

> The little old lady with seven dogs *is* a grandmother. (Only the woman is a grandmother—not the seven dogs.)
> One in a million people *is talented* enough to play professional basketball. (Only one is talented enough—not a million.)
> A roll of thunder or a flash of lightning *is* not a sure sign of rain. (*Or* signals a choice between the two subjects; it doesn't join them. The sentence means "a roll of thunder *is* not" or "a flash of lightning *is* not"—and the verb agrees with the second and last choice.)

Compare these three sentences:

> *Maria,* along with her friend, *works* part time on weekends. (Only Maria is the subject of this sentence.)
> *Maria and her friend work* part time on weekends. (*And* joins the two subjects of this sentence.)
> Neither Maria nor her friend *works* full time on weekends. (*Nor* signals a negative choice, and the verb agrees with the second and last choice.)

TIPS

For Keeping Contractions Straight

You need to examine *to be* verbs carefully as you edit, for you can make two common errors when writing their contractions:

1. You might leave off the –'s, the –'m, or the –'re. Change "*He* a good man" to "*He's* a good man."

2. You might confuse the contractions with sound-alike or look-alike words: *we're* with *were, you're* with *your, it's* with *its,* and *they're* with *their* or *there.*

TIPS

For Remembering Compound Subjects: The Rule of *And*

When two subjects are joined by *and*, the verb needs to be plural.

Subject *and* subject = verb without –s

EXERCISE 5 Writing Verbs After Compound Subjects

Decide whether the subject of the sentence is singular or plural. Then write the appropriate present-tense form of the verb supplied in parentheses.

1. The gold pen and the silver bullet (belong) *belong* _____ to me.

2. That purple jacket and yellow tie (go) _____ *go* _____ together beautifully.

3. Five scoops of ice cream with only two bananas, nuts, and syrup (make)

_____*makes*_____ a wonderful low-fat treat.

4. After sixty-two years of marriage, Mr. and Mrs. Wilson (look) _____*look*_____ at

each other with great affection—although they can't see too well.

5. The money in the safe, under the mattress, and on top of the refrigerator (seem)

_____*seem*_____ to be mine.

6. The use of compound subjects (become) _____*becomes*_____ quite easy to

master with a little practice.

SPECIAL PRESENT-TENSE VERBS

The verbs *to be, to do,* and *to have* deserve special attention because they occur so often and take unusual forms. You need to know those forms well.

To Be

To be (is, am, are) is the most common verb in the English language. It always precedes –*ing* words in verb phrases:

> I *am looking* for an honest man.
> Arnie *is looking* for a quick buck.

And it often serves as a linking verb:

> The photographs *are* beautiful.
> I *am* beautiful in all of them.

Here are the present-tense forms of *to be* and their **contractions** (that is, their shortened forms with apostrophes replacing omitted letters):

Subject	Verb	Contractions	Negative contractions
I	*am*	*I'm*	
he, she, it (or singular noun)	*is*	*he's, she's, it's*	*isn't*
we, you, they (or plural noun)	*are*	*we're, you're, they're*	*aren't*

COLLABORATIVE ACTIVITY I

Checking Agreement
Write five sentences with blanks for verbs. Make the subjects as varied as you can. Exchange papers and fill in the blanks with appropriate present-tense verb forms. Discuss your answers.

EXERCISE 6   Writing *To Be*

Write both the correct full form of the verb to be *and its contraction with an appropriate pronoun in each of these sentences.*

1. He _*is*___ (_*he's*___) talking to Mr. Williams.

2. I _____ (_____) intelligent, rich, and extremely modest.

3. School _____ (_____) a pleasure and a joy for me.

4. My dog _____ (_____) smarter than my brother.

5. We _____ (_____) happy to meet you.

6. You _____ (_____) in the right room.

7. They _____ (_____) going to be late.

EXERCISE 7   Correcting Errors with *To Be*

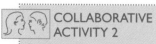
COLLABORATIVE ACTIVITY 2

Discussing Your Editing
Compare your answers to Exercise 7. Were any errors especially difficult to detect? Report your results to the class.

The following passage omits to be *in some sentences and substitutes sound-alike or look-alike words for the contractions of* to be. *Find these errors and write your corrections above the lines.*

More Facts About Leopards

(1) A leopard ^(is) a very versatile hunter. (2) When its hunting in the grassland of Africa, the big cat kills adult impalas, wildebeests, kudus, waterbucks, and gazelles. (3) In the forest areas, there also small mammals such as hares, monkeys, and squirrels, as well as reptiles such as frogs and fish. (4) Its typical for a female leopard to give birth to one to three cubs. (5) There kept in isolated areas, like bushes or small caves. (6) Their much darker than adults, which are usually spotted. (7) Female leopards very concerned mothers who leave their infants only when they slept. (8) When the cubs are about two years old, they leave their mother and go out on their own.

To Do

If Your First Language Is Not English

When *do* is the helping verb in questions or negatives, it needs to agree with the subject. The main verb following *do* is the same form no matter what the subject.

Do you play . . . ? You *don't* work.

Does he play . . . ? He *doesn't* work.

The verb *to do* (*do, does*) serves as a helping verb in most present-tense questions and negative statements:

> *Do* you play the guitar?
> He *doesn't* work on Sundays.

Here are the present-tense forms of *to do:*

Subject	Verb	Negative verb	Negative contractions
I, we, you, they	do	do not	don't
he, she, it	does	does not	doesn't

The negative forms of *do/does* create the most problems. Many people say and write, "He don't," instead of "He doesn't"—a common but very serious grammatical error. Remember that *does* is the correct form with *he, she,* and *it.*

E X E R C I S E   8   Writing Negative Statements with *To Do*

Write the appropriate negative contraction of to do *(doesn't or don't) in each sentence. You'll first need to determine whether the subject is singular or plural.*

Facts About Lions

1. Lions may attack other animals, but they usually *don't*_____ bother each other.

2. They're actually rather social animals. A lion _____ live alone but in a group of two to forty others called a *pride*.

3. However, one male rules the pride, and the rest of the animals certainly _____ share equal rights with him.

4. He is first in mating, and other lions _____ eat until he's had his portion.

5. Lionesses are chiefly responsible for hunting for food. The females _____ receive this assignment because the male is lazy. His big mane is simply too easy for prey to recognize.

6. In the wild, a 350-pound lion will eat 45 pounds of food daily. However, a lion _____ eat nearly as much in captivity—usually only 10 to 15 pounds a day.

7. The biggest threat to lions _____ come from other animals; it comes from human hunters and poachers.

To Have

You use *to have* as a simple verb:

> I *have* homework to do.
> In his self-portrait, the artist Vincent Van Gogh *has* only one ear.

And you use it as a helping verb:

> I *have worked* on my lab report for a week.
> Alfred *hasn't* ever *failed* an examination.

Here are its present-tense forms:

Subject	Verb	Contractions	Negative contractions
I, we, you, they	have	*I've, we've, you've*	*haven't*
		they've	or *don't have*
he, she, it	has	*he's, she's, it's*	*hasn't* or *doesn't have*

Don't confuse *have* and *has* with *had*—the past-tense form of the verb.

EXERCISE 9   Writing *To Have*

Write the appropriate present-tense form of to have—*affirmative or negative—in each of the following sentences.*

Facts About Baboons

1. Baboons *have* _____ their homes in African forests and mountains.

2. A typical baboon colony _____ *has* _____ 40 to 50 members.

3. At night a baboon climbs up a tree or cliff, where it _____ *has* _____ a place to sleep.

4. Baboons often travel as much as six miles from their spots, but they usually _____ *have* _____ several sleeping spots within their territory.

5. Baboons (negative) _____ *don't have* _____ much protection from their predators, especially leopards—and humans.

6. Therefore, each baboon _____ *has* _____ to be very careful.

7. If a predator approaches, the baboon (negative) _____ *doesn't have* _____ any time to lose as it runs to hide.

8. It _____ *has* _____ to climb a tree, but if there aren't any trees nearby, the male baboons will gather together, scream loudly to scare away their foes, and fight fiercely if necessary.

9. Baboons _____ *have* _____ a very strong social organization.

SPECIAL PROBLEMS WITH SUBJECT-VERB AGREEMENT

Subject-verb agreement is more difficult with certain kinds of sentences or words. We'll examine those tricky situations in this section.

Questions

The subject normally comes before the verb in a sentence, alerting you to the form of the verb that follows. But in questions, the verb comes first. This can lead to errors in agreement, especially with plural subjects. Here's an example:

Incorrect: Does Susan and Orlando want to go with us?

You may think that the verb agrees with *Susan,* the word that immediately follows. But then poor Orlando is left without a verb. The sentence needs to be rewritten:

Correct: Do Susan and Orlando want to go with us?

As you edit, look closely at the subject following the verb in a question. Make sure they agree.

EXERCISE 10   Writing Verbs in Questions

Fill in the proper present-tense form of to do *or* to be *in each of the following sentences.*

1. _*Are*_____ Luis and Lulu practicing for the pizza eating contest?

2. _*Are*_____ seven children, three dogs, four cats, and a slightly confused goat too much to take care of?

3. _*Do*_____ you love me now that I can dance?

4. _*Are*_____ Mrs. Barry and Dr. Graip coming to the Orange Bowl?

5. _*does*_____ a woman with triplets have three times the fun?

6. _*Aren't*_____ n't these sentences a pleasure to write?

Sentences That Begin with *There*

Expressions that begin with *there* also place the verb before the subject. (See Chapter 16 for ways to eliminate *there is* and *there are* from sentences.) Use *there is* or *there are*, depending on the subject, or subjects, that follow. These sentences are correct:

> *There's a man* lying on our kitchen table.
> *There are two men* lying on our dining room table. [Not *there's two men . . .*]
> *There are no places* left for us to sleep on.

EXERCISE 11   Writing Verbs with *There*

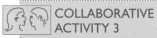
COLLABORATIVE ACTIVITY 3

Writing the Forms of To Be
Write six sentences—three questions and three statements—beginning with *there*. Leave the verbs blank. Use a variety of singular and plural subjects. Then, exchange papers and fill in the blanks with present-tense forms of *to be*. Discuss your answers.

Write the proper present-tense form of to be *in each sentence.*

1. There *are*_____ many people who want to win the lottery.

2. There _____ a band on that rickety old stage playing "Lean on Me."

3. There _____ two things that you need to know: be smart and be careful.

4. There _____ a football jersey, a can of deodorant, and a copy of *War and Peace* in the back seat of the car.

5. There _____ a few rules that no one can break.

6. There _____ no more sentences to complete in this exercise.

Collective Nouns

A **collective noun** represents a collection of two or more persons, things, or ideas:

class	orchestra	Longman Publishers
committee	faculty	the French

Most collective nouns are singular:

The *class is hearing* a lecture on economics.
The *baseball team wins* most of its games.

A few collective nouns are always plural:

The words *police, faculty,* and *staff:* The police patrol this area often.
Team names that end in *–s:* The New York Giants actually play their games in New Jersey.
All nationalities: The French are ecstatic about winning the World Cup.

E X E R C I S E   1 2   Writing Sentences with Collective Nouns

Write present-tense sentences in which the collective-noun subject agrees with the verb.

1. The collaborative group usually reviews the material before moving on to the next subject.

2. My family _____

3. The New York Yankees _____

4. The police _____

5. The British _____

6. Wal-Mart_____

Indefinite Pronouns

Indefinite pronouns (pronouns that don't refer to a definite person, place, or thing) are always singular. There are four categories of indefinite pronouns:

Some	Every	Any	No
somebody	everybody	anybody	nobody
someone	everyone	anyone	no one
something	everything	anything	nothing

EXERCISE 13   Writing Sentences with Indefinite Pronouns

Complete each of the following sentences, using a present-tense verb.

1. Everybody <u>has a fielder's mitt, a pair of baseball cleats, a uniform, and</u>
   <u>Ace bandages.</u>

2. Someone _____

3. Anyone _____

4. Somebody _____

5. Nobody _____

6. There _____ no one who_____

Phrases Between the Subject and the Verb

A **prepositional phrase** sometimes comes between the subject and the verb. Don't let it confuse you. For example, which verbs should you use in the following sentences?

> The woman with seventeen children (need/needs) a little help.
> The shape and size of the ring (is/are) unusual.

Be sure you're not misled by nouns or pronouns in prepositional phrases. The choice of the correct form will be clear when you draw a line through the prepositional phrase:

> That woman ~~with seventeen children~~ needs a little help.
> The shape and size ~~of the ring~~ are unusual.

Check these troublesome prepositional phrases as you edit.

EXERCISE 14   Creating Correct Subject-Verb Agreement

Cross out the prepositional phrase between the subject and the verb and then write the appropriate present-tense verb form.

1. The reason ~~for all the papers, cans, and other garbage in the park~~ (be)

   <u>is</u>_____ not difficult to determine.

2. A person with eleven cats (be) _____ not pussy-footing around.

3. The rules of this social club (do) _____ permit wiping watermelon

   juice from one's mouth with one's shirt tail.

4. The hard work of the engineers, drafters, contractors, and subcontractors (have) _____ all contributed to creating a beautiful new campus.

5. An enormous box of pizzas, french fries, garlic bread, onion rings, and nachos usually (disappear) _____ about fifteen minutes after Mario and his friends see it.

6. The cause of most deaths from fires (be) _____ smoke inhalation.

Relative Clauses

In relative clauses, the pronouns *who, which,* and *that* relate to a word or words immediately before them. That means the verb in the relative clause has to agree with the same word or words:

> I want to introduce you to *the man who owns* this palace.
> Be sure to see *The Killers of Elephants, which* is playing at the Center Cinema.
> Please pick up the *banana peels, apple cores, and hamburger buns that are* rotting on your bedroom floor.

However, *whom, which,* and *that* can also function as the object in a relative clause. In this case, the the verb agrees with the subject of the relative clause:

>   O   S   V
> This is the 300-pound man *whom you are* about to wrestle. [That is, you are about to wrestle *him*.]
>
>   O   S   V
> You'll love the specialty of the house, *which Chef Alberto makes* from freshly cut grass and hay. [That is, Chef Alberto makes *it*.]

EXERCISE 15   Writing Verbs in Relative Clauses

Complete each of the following sentences with a present-tense verb.

1. I want a car that _looks like a million dollars but costs about a thousand._

2. Ludmilla is looking for a man who_____

3. These are my new friends, who_____

4. I need a dog that _____

5. Mrs. Vanderbucks has a new eight-carat diamond, which _____

_____

6. To eat Ralph's stew, you need a set of teeth that _____

_____

IN SUMMARY   Present-Tense Subject-Verb Agreement

1. Almost all plural nouns end in –s, but the verbs that agree with them do not; almost all singular nouns do not end in –s, but the verbs that agree with them do.

2. The pronouns *he, she,* and *it* and all singular nouns agree with verbs ending in –s.

3. All other subject pronouns (*I, we, you,* and *they*) and all plural nouns agree with verbs that do not end in –s.

4. All compound subjects (two or more subjects joined by *and*) are plural and agree with verbs that do not end in –s.

5. In questions and sentences beginning with *there*, the subject follows the verb and determines agreement.

6. All indefinite pronouns are singular.

7. Most—but not all—collective nouns are singular.

8. The word or words preceding subject pronouns *who, which,* or *that* in relative clauses determine the verb agreement. But when *whom, which,* or *that* functions as an object, the subject follows them and determines verb agreement.

EDITING FOR MASTERY

Mastery Exercise 1

Correcting Noun and Verb Errors

The following passage contains fifteen errors in subject-verb agreement, noun plurals, missing verbs, and incorrect contractions with to be, *excluding the first error, which has been corrected for you. Correct the remaining errors by writing above the lines.*

COLLABORATIVE ACTIVITY 5

Comparing and Discussing Answers

Appoint someone to read the passage aloud so you can hear where errors occur. Correct the errors, discuss them, and report your findings to the class.

Some Facts about Cats

                        s

(1) Ever since the Egyptian^ made cats their pets 4,000 years ago, cats always been important to humans as rodent killers. (2) Today some cat still earn their living as rat exterminators, and a few others works in TV commercials. (3) However, the main job of cats these days are to be good companions—and kind owners—of their pet humans.

(4) A cat is very smart, but it don't learn the way a dog does. (5) Some tests of intelligence shows that the cat is brighter than a dog. (6) However, a cat won't allow itself to be trained. (7) As everyone know, a cat will obey its owner only when it's in the mood.

(8) There's thirty-six different breeds of cats, but all the breeds has basically the same physical make-up. (9) Their the only animals—other than camels and giraffes—that walks by moving their front and hind legs on one side, then the other. (10) And even though humans are fifteen times larger than cats, people have only 206 bones, while cats have 230.

(11) A cat is a very clean animal, and it have a strong sense of balance. (12) The cat's eyesight (especially at night) is its strongest sense, but a cat also hears well. (13) It's the only animal that purrs.

(14) How much like people is the female cat and male cat? (15) A mother cat is tender to her young, but, unlike a person, she can give birth several times a year. (16) A tom cat (male cat) is like a rolling stone. (17) No matter how many kittens the mother has, he don't stick around to take care of them. (18) Maybe he's just too catty.

Scorecard: Number of errors found and corrected _____

Mastery Exercise 2

Correcting Noun and Verb Errors

The following passage contains fifteen errors in subject-verb agreement, noun plurals, missing verbs, and incorrect contractions with to be, *excluding the first error, which has been corrected for you. Correct the remaining errors by writing above the lines.*

Animal Tricks and Traps

(1) Most animals are afraid of other creature^s. (2) Therefore, many creatures protects themselves from attack by imitating frightening beasts. (3) As a result, their predators think twice before eating them. (4) Certain animals that lives in burrows (like some birds) has the ability to hiss like snakes. (5) A group of the hissing bees in the hive make a bear wonder if taking their honey is a good idea.

(6) Other animals scare their enemies. (7) Theirs a type of frog that shrieks so loudly that a predator drop it out of shock. (8) Texas horned lizards inflate themselves like balloon. (9) They also explodes the walls between sinuses and eye sockets, squirting out jets of blood from their eyes. (10) An animal that wants to eat the lizards don't find their appearance too appetizing.

(11) Many creatures fool their foes by changing shape. (12) A hawkmoth caterpillar can inflate one end of its body into a "snake head" that sways back and forth. (13) A peacock butterfly combine strategies. (14) When its threatened by a bird, the butterfly spreads its wings and exposes large spots that look like eyes. (15) At the same time, it hisses like a snake.

(16) On the other side of the coin is those animals that use tricks to get their prey. (17) A snapping turtle has a piece of flesh inside its mouth that look like a worm, which makes catching dinner easy. (18) One kind of insect called a praying mantis resembles the petals of an orchid, and insects that land on it get a big surprise. (19) And here a final—and rather disgusting trick. (20) Certain beetles look just like bird droppings; they attract flies, which expect a tasty snack but instead become one.

Scorecard: Number of errors found and corrected _____

Using the Past Tense
and the Past Participle

You often write about the past, especially if you discuss your own experiences—actions you've done, seen, or heard. In these cases, you use past-tense verbs and their close relation, the past participle. These verb forms can be tricky, partly because they come in many varieties, and partly because they combine with other verbs in a variety of ways. This chapter will show you how to check all the verb forms as you edit. You'll learn about

- varieties of the past tense
- the verb forms to select in talking about the past
- other uses of these verb forms

THE PAST TENSE IN ITS USUAL FORMS

Like verbs in the present tense, past-tense verbs have a long history, and some of their forms changed over many centuries. Most verbs in the past tense share the original past-tense ending: *–ed.* However, more than one hundred verbs took irregular forms in ancient times, and they stubbornly refuse to give them up. We'll look at both regular and irregular forms in this chapter, starting with regular forms.

Regular Verbs

Here are some past-tense sentences:

Subject	Verb	
Ms. Miller	*sailed*	for Bora Bora in a canoe last week.
I	*collected*	my lottery winnings yesterday.
Jill	*tumbled*	down the hill after Jack.

Notice that each verb ends in *–ed*, no matter what its subject. As you probably know, most verbs form the **past tense** in this way. That means they are **regular verbs:**

> walk + –ed = *walked*
> seem + –ed = *seemed*
> (or for verbs that already end in *–e*)
> like + *d* = *liked*
> smoke + *d* = *smoked*

E X E R C I S E   1   Identifying Past-Tense Verbs

Circle each verb and then identify its tense. Write Pr for each present-tense verb and P for each past-tense verb.

1. Harold bowled a perfect game. ___*P*___

2. I build houses in my spare time. _____

3. They talk for hours every day. _____

4. He stayed home. _____

5. The turtle burped. _____

6. The exercise ends with this sentence. _____

E X E R C I S E   2   Transforming Verb Tenses

The following passage is written in the present tense. Change the passage to the past tense by writing the proper verb form above the line.

The Origins of the Wedding Cake

(1) Originally, the bride never ^*dined* ~~dine~~ on the wedding cake; the wedding guests ^*tossed* ~~toss~~ it at her. (2) According to custom, everyone expects children to come after marriage like night after day—and almost as often. (3) People in ancient times therefore shower the new bride with wheat, a symbol of fertility and wealth, while unmarried young women rush to pick up the grain to guarantee their own weddings. (4) Roman bakers later change the tradition. (5) Around 100 B.C. they start baking the wheat into small, sweet cakes—to be eaten, not thrown. (6) However, wedding guests continue to shower the bride with the cakes. (7) Then a new custom develops in which people crumble the wheat cakes over a bride's head. (8) And as a further guarantee of fertility, the couple consume some of the crumbs, a custom known as "eating together."

(9) The practice of eating the crumbs of small wedding cakes spreads throughout Western Europe. (10) The English wash down the crumbs with a special ale. (11) They call the brew itself "bride's ale," which changes into the word "bridal." (12) The cake-eating custom also shifts during hard times in the early Middle Ages. (13) Wedding guests bake plain biscuits to bring to the ceremony, and poor people receive the leftovers. (14) According to legend, another custom develops. (15) The guests pile the baked goods into one enormous heap. (16) The couple kiss each other over this mound of biscuits that often tumble down around them. (17) In the 1660s, a French chef visits London, watches this ceremony, and considers the practice uncivilized. (18) He therefore decides to transform the mountain of ordinary biscuits into a fancy cake with many layers and icing. (19) At first the British criticize this French creation but later adopt the practice as well.

EXERCISE 3   Writing Past-Tense Verbs

Use one of the words in the following box to complete each of the following sentences with an appropriate past-tense verb. Don't use the same verb twice.

play, watch, seem, behave, try, agree, share, look, feel, walk, miss, stagger, like, receive

1. I *received* _____ the award for the best-dressed student in the weight-lifting class.

2. Your son _____ like a perfect gentleman throughout the ceremony.

3. We _____ the train, so we _____ six miles home.

4. Ms. Fussfingers _____ on fourteen different pairs of socks before finding a pair she _____.

5. The glasses _____ very dirty.

6. Mr. Crier and Ms. Smiley _____ the same reactions.

7. Annie Dextrous _____ the violin, the drums, the bagpipes, and the kazoo all at the same time.

To Be

The verb *to be* is irregular. In fact, it's the only past-tense verb that has subject-verb agreement. Remember that the subject of a sentence determines whether the verb is singular or plural. When the verb is *to be* and the tense is past, the verb forms must agree with their subjects. You'll need to master those forms because they occur so often.

Subject	Verb
singular nouns	
I he she it	*was* or *wasn't*
plural nouns	
we you they	*were* or *weren't*

Notice that the past tense of *to be* acts much like a present-tense verb. The verb takes an *−s* ending (*was*) to agree with *he, she, it,* and singular nouns, as well as with *I.*

EXERCISE 4   Writing *To Be* in the Past Tense

Write the appropriate past-tense form of to be *in each blank space.*

The Elvis Estate

1. The eighty-two-page inventory of Elvis Presley's estate, which <u>was</u>
   worth $10 million at the time of his death, <u>was</u> filled with information
   about his mansion, Graceland.

2. The house _____ piled high with statues of tigers, lions, elephants,
   dogs, birds, a ram, a whale, an eagle, and a dolphin.

3. In the garages and throughout the grounds _____ the many trans-
   portation vehicles of the King of Rock 'n' Roll.

4. There _____ two Stutz Blackhawks, which _____
   worth at least $100,000 each.

5. His collection of other vehicles _____ quite a sight: a Ferrari, a
   Cadillac, an International Harvester Scout, a Jeep, a Ford Bronco, a custom-built
   Chevy pickup, three tractors, seven motorcycles, seven golf carts, three mobile
   homes, and six horses.

6. In the house itself, there _____ eighteen TV sets, including two
   seventeen-inch color sets in the ceiling above his nine-foot-square bed.

7. His wardrobe _____ rather simple.

8. There _____ a hundred pairs of pants, twenty-one capes, three
   cartons of shoes, and three jewel-studded vests.

9. Among his musical instruments _____ seven guitars; one
   _____ inlaid with his name in mother-of-pearl.

TIPS

For Hearing *–ed* **Endings**

Past-tense endings may be spelled *–ed*, but they often are difficult to hear because they're pro-nounced three ways:

–t When the last sound before the final *–ed* does not require the use of the vocal cords (sounds such as *s, ch, k, p, th, sh, f,* and *h*), the final *–ed* is pronounced like *t*:

	Pronounced
leaped	(leapt)
hiked	(hikt)
reached	(reacht)
raced	(ract)
wished	(wisht)
worked	(workt)

–d When the last sound before the final *–ed* requires the use of the vocal cords (sounds such as *b, g, m, n, r, v, w,* and *z*), the final *–ed* is pronounced like *d*:

	Pronounced
robbed	(robbd)
purred	(purrd)
begged	(beggd)
heaved	(heavd)
hummed	(hummd)
sewed	(sewd)

–ed When a *t* or *d* sound precedes the final *–ed*, the *–ed* is pronounced as a full syllable:

wanted	waited
pleaded	hated
needed	nodded

Could and *Would*

Can and *will* are verbs that frequently appear in your writing as you discuss the present or future. But you use them to discuss ideas in the past, too, although these verbs take different forms. The past tense of *can* is *could*, which discusses ability in the past. Compare these sentences:

You *can* kill a man, but you *can't* kill an idea.

—Myrlie Evers, after the death of her husband Medgar, the civil rights leader, in 1963

No one believed that the *Titanic could* sink.

The past tense of *will* is *would,* which refers to the future from a point in the past. Compare these sentences:

> Whether you like it or not, history is on our side. We *will* bury you.
>
>   —Russian President Nikita Khrushchev speaking at the United Nations in 1956
>
> When you first met him, he appeared easygoing, full of humor, and nice talking. But if you stayed longer, you'd find he was merciless and *would* destroy anyone and anything blocking his ambition.
>
>   —The doctor who treated former Chinese dictator Chairman Mao Zedong

As you edit your work, check for *can/could* and *will/would.* Have you used one verb form when you intended the other? If so, change the verb to the correct tense.

EXERCISE 5   Transforming Verb Tenses

Rewrite the following sentences, changing their tense from the present to the past or vice versa.

Present tense	Past tense
1. I know that I can pass the test on Friday.	**1.** I _knew that I could_ pass the test on on Friday.
2. He says that he will be late today.	**2.** _____ the next day.
3. _____ _____	**3.** Bill wanted to know if he could borrow your car.

Present tense	Past tense
4. _____ today.	**4.** His car wouldn't start yesterday.
5. _____ _____	**5.** Jeannette thought that she would graduate in two years.
6. No one can answer my question.	**6.** _____ _____

THE PRESENT-PERFECT TENSE

Compare these two sentences:

> Igor lived in Transylvania in 1965.
> Igor has lived in Transylvania since 1965.

Put a check next to the sentence that tells you Igor still lives in Transylvania.

You should have identified the second sentence. It is an example of the **present-perfect tense,** which describes an action that began in the past but continues up to the present. You use this tense to relate the past to the present time.

Forming the Present-Perfect Tense

Circle the verbs in these present-perfect-tense sentences:

> Bruno Hamhands has played professional football since 1999.
> I have owned my collection of Porsches for quite a while.
> Ralph "Aroma" Reed hasn't bathed in a week.

You should have found two parts to the verb in each sentence: (1) the helping verb *has* or *have* and (2) a verb form called the **past participle,** which for regular verbs ends in *–ed,* just like the past-tense form. Notice that the helping verb—*has* or *have*—is present tense and changes to agree with its subject, but the past participle does not change:

$$
\left.\begin{array}{l} has \\ or \\ have \end{array}\right\} + \text{past participle (verb ending in } –ed) = \text{present-perfect tense}
$$

EXERCISE 6   Transforming Verb Tense

Change the following past-tense sentences into present-perfect-tense sentences.

1. You probably loved hamburgers all your life. _You have probably loved hamburgers all your life._

2. They never consisted of ham. _____

3. They remained a part of American culture since 1900, when Louis Lassen invented them. _____

_____

4. They rested inside buns since the St. Louis Exposition in 1904. _____

_____

5. The original home of hamburgers, Louis Lunch in New Haven, Connecticut, served hamburgers until the present day. _____

_____

Using the Present-Perfect Tense

The present-perfect tense conveys two meanings:

1. **To describe an action that began in the past but continues into the present.**

Often such expressions include *since,* which signals the start of the action, or *for,* which signals the length of the action:

> Rome has been the capital of Italy only *since 1870.*
> California has prepared for a major earthquake *for many years.*

2. **To describe an action in the indefinite past (without mentioning a specific time) that relates to the present.**

When you discuss the past in relationship to the present, you usually use the present-perfect tense.

Present perfect	*Present*
Many people *have searched* for the Fountain of Youth,	but its location still *remains* a mystery.
The *Titantic has lain* at the bottom of the ocean since 1912,	and no one can raise its hull.

EXERCISE 7   Writing Verbs

Supply the appropriate past-tense or present-perfect form of the verb in parentheses.

1. In the 1870s three men (inform) __informed__ a German named Jake Waltzer about a gold mine in a mountain that was sacred to the Apache Native Americans of Arizona.

2. Waltzer promptly (kill) _____ the men, taking the mine for himself.

3. He (protect) _____ its location until he died in 1891, leaving a map to his mistress, although she never found the mine.

4. Since then, people (call) _____ it the Lost Dutchman Mine after the "Dutchman" Waltzer.

5. For a century, at least 1,000 fortune hunters (search) _____ Arizona's Superstition Mountains looking for the sacred gold mine, but they (discover) _____ nothing.

6. To date, twenty people (die) _____ as a result of accidents or murders while seeking the gold, creating the legend that the Native Americans (curse) _____ all who might try to desecrate their mountain.

7. Others say that pygmies or an old prospector (guard) _____ the entrance to the mine, shooting anyone approaching it.

THE PAST-PERFECT TENSE

Compare these three sentences:

> Igor lived in Transylvania in 1965.
> Igor has lived in Transylvania since 1965.
> Igor had lived in Transylvania before 1965.

Put a check next to the sentence that means Igor took up residence in Transylvania before 1965.

You should have picked the third sentence. It's an example of the **past-perfect tense,** which we're about to examine.

COLLABORATIVE
ACTIVITY I

Switching Tenses
Write five sentences in the
present tense. Then
exchange papers. Change
each sentence into a
past-tense sentence, then
a present-perfect-tense
sentence, and finally into a
past-perfect-tense sentence.
Discuss your answers.

Forming the Past-Perfect Tense

Like the present-perfect tense, the past-perfect tense is formed with a past participle and *had*, the past tense of *to have*.

had + past participle = past-perfect tense

Using the Past-Perfect Tense

Unlike the present-perfect tense, the past-perfect tense is purely a *past tense*. It describes an action that occurred before a later time in the past:

earlier   later
Columbus had traveled to America before Amerigo Vespucci did.

later   earlier
A German geographer said that Vespucci *had arrived* first. So the geographer decided to call the New World *America*.

EXERCISE 8   Writing More Verbs

In each of the following sentences, write the present-perfect tense or the past-perfect tense, using been *(the past participle of* to be*).*

1. Matthew __had been_____ absent a lot, but then his attendance improved.

2. I _____ just _____ watching the basketball team.

3. We _____n't _____ home to see our parents this year.

4. Anna _____ active in three or four different clubs until she became ill.

5. Working and going to school this semester _____n't _____ easy.

IRREGULAR VERBS

TIPS

**For Keeping the
Past-Perfect and
Present-Perfect Tenses
Straight**

The present-perfect and
the past-perfect tenses
are similar, so they are
easy to confuse. Remember these differences:

1. The present-perfect
   tense relates the past to
   the present. Its helping
   verbs are *has* and *have*.

2. The past-perfect tense
   relates an earlier past action to a more recent one.
   Its helping verb is *had*.

English is full of **irregular verbs.** More than one hundred verbs don't form their past tense or past participles by simply adding –*ed*. They're presented below in seven categories. You'll find you already know many of the verbs. But study all the categories and make a list of the verbs you don't know.

Category 1: –*d* to –*t*

In these verbs, the final –*d* in the present tense changes to –*t* in the past tense and past participle.

Present tense	Past tense	Past participle
bend	bent	bent
build	built	built
lend	lent	lent
send	sent	sent
spend	spent	spent

E X E R C I S E 9   Writing Irregular Verbs

Write the proper past-tense or past-perfect tense of the verb in parentheses.

James Buchanan "Diamond Jim" Brady (1856–1917): The World's Greatest Eater

1. James Buchanan Brady (build) _built_____ himself a reputation that no one has ever (be) _been_____ able to match: he (be) _____ the greatest eater of all time.

2. Of course, Brady (spend) _____ huge sums of money in earning the title, for no one (can) _____ eat like him on a poor person's income.

3. Born to Irish working-class parents in New York, he first (work) _____ as a baggage-handler at a railroad station. Then, a few years later, he accepted an offer to sell railroad equipment, and this job (send) _____ his fortunes flying.

4. By putting together a series of multimillion-dollar railroad deals, he later (build) _____ up a large fortune.

Diamond Jim Brady

Category 2: −d and Possible Vowel Change

In these verbs, the final consonant becomes −d.
Some have no vowel change before the final consonant.

Present tense	Past tense	Past participle
have	had	had
make	made	made

However, some do have a vowel change before the final consonant.

Present tense	Past tense	Past participle
flee	fled	fled
hear	heard	heard
lay	laid	laid
pay	paid	paid
say	said	said
sell	sold	sold
tell	told	told

EXERCISE 10   Writing Irregular Verbs

As in the previous exercise, write the proper past-tense or past-perfect tense of the verb in parentheses.

1. Jim Brady (make) *made* _____ millions of dollars when he (sell)

   sold _____ railroad equipment to major firms throughout the country.

2. He went on to use his wealth for a display of bad taste that no one (can)

   _____ ever challenge.

3. He (lay) _____ in a supply of two hundred custom-made suits and

   fifty silk hats.

4. He further decked himself out in a collection of jewelry that (have)

   _____ a net worth of at least $2 million.

5. For a single set of shirt studs, vest studs, and cuff links, Jim (pay)

   _____ $87,315.

6. People (say) _____ that his diamond rings (be) _____

   the biggest ever seen in New York, and among his more than thirty famous timepieces,

   he (have) _____ a single watch worth $17,500.

7. No one ever (hear) _____ Brady apologize for his flashy jewelry, and

   he took pride in his nickname, "Diamond Jim."

Category 3: –t and Possible Vowel Change

In these verbs, a final –t is added, and there is usually a vowel change before the final consonant.

Present tense	Past tense	Past participle
creep	crept	crept
feel	felt	felt
keep	kept	kept
leave	left	left
lose	lost	lost
mean	meant	meant
sleep	slept	slept
sweep	swept	swept

Some verbs show an additional vowel change and add –ght at the end of the word.

Present tense	Past tense	Past participle
bring	brought	brought
buy	bought	bought
catch	caught	caught
seek	sought	sought
teach	taught	taught
think	thought	thought

EXERCISE 11   Writing Irregular Verbs

Again, write the proper past-tense or past-perfect tense of the verb in parentheses.

1. Brady (leave) _left_____ none of his possessions alone but added expensive jewelry to them all.

2. He (keep) _____ twelve gold-plated bicycles with diamonds and rubies in the handlebars for his outings in Central Park.

3. For his girlfriend, the 200-pound singer Lillian Russell, Brady (buy) _____ a special bicycle with mother-of-pearl handlebars and emeralds and sapphires on the spokes of each wheel.

4. Every Sunday, Miss Russell (catch) _____ the attention of newspaper photographers when, dressed in white, she (bring) _____ this famous machine to the park for a ride.

5. However, although Diamond Jim liked women, he (feel) _____ his strongest passion for another matter: food.

6. It was in this endeavor that Brady's achievements reached such amazing heights; they (sweep) _____ away all competition for greatness.

Lillian Russell

7. The man never (lose) _____ an opportunity to eat, and stories of his

accomplishments (teach) _____ the world what true dedication to a

task really (mean) _____.

Category 4: Single Vowel Change

In these verbs, only the vowel changes, and the past tense and the past participle are the same.

Present tense	Past tense	Past participle
bind	bound	bound
bleed	bled	bled
breed	bred	bred
dig	dug	dug
feed	fed	fed
find	found	found
fight	fought	fought
grind	ground	ground
hang	hung	hung
hold	held	held
lead	led	led
meet	met	met
shine	shone	shone
	(or shined)	
shoot	shot	shot
sit	sat	sat
slide	slid	slid
speed	sped	sped
spin	spun	spun
stand	stood	stood

stick	stuck	stuck
strike	struck	struck
swing	swung	swung
win	won	won
wind	wound	wound
wring	wrung	wrung

In a few cases, the past participle is the same as the present tense.

Present tense	Past tense	Past participle
become	became	become
come	came	come
run	ran	run

EXERCISE 12   Writing Irregular Verbs

Once again, write the proper past-tense or past-perfect tense of the verb in parentheses.

1. For a typical breakfast, Brady (feed) _fed_____ himself hominy grits, eggs, corn bread, muffins, flapjacks, chops, fried potatoes, a beefsteak, and a full gallon of orange juice.

2. This "golden nectar" (win) _____ Brady's love when he was younger, and he never (find) _____ any pleasure in drinking liquor.

3. Diamond Jim (become) _____ hungry during the midmorning, so this (lead) _____ to a little snack of two or three dozen clams and oysters.

4. He (sit) _____ down to a real lunch at 12:30, when he (swing) _____ into action by downing additional clams and oysters, a platter of boiled lobsters, three deviled crabs, a joint of beef, and several kinds of pie.

5. He (fight) _____ off his hunger until afternoon tea, when he (find) _____ time for a platter of seafood washed down with another of his favorite drinks, lemon soda.

6. After that, Jim (hold) _____ his appetite until the evening, when it (come) _____ time for his major meal of the day.

7. He often (wind) _____ up at Charlie Rector's—a fancy New York restaurant—where the owner bragged that Brady (be) _____ "the best twenty-five customers" he (have) _____.

8. Diamond Jim started the meal when he (slide) _____ two or three dozen Maryland oysters down his throat.

9. Crabs (come) _____ next—six of them—and then at least two

   bowls of green turtle soup.

10. Then Brady (dig) _____ into the main courses: six or seven lobsters,

    two whole ducks, two portions of turtle meat, a sirloin steak, and vegetables—followed

    by an entire platter of pastries for dessert.

11. As the meal (wind) _____ down, he usually (have)

    _____ a two-pound box of chocolate as an after-dinner treat.

12. Crowds of people (stand) _____ around the table to cheer on his

    progress—and to make bets on whether he (will) _____ drop dead

    before dessert.

Category 5: Double Vowel Change

In these verbs, the vowel changes in each form.

Present tense	Past tense	Past participle
begin	began	begun
drink	drank	drunk
ring	rang	rung
sink	sank (or sunk)	sunk
spring	sprang (or sprung)	sprung
swim	swam	swum

EXERCISE 13   Writing Irregular Verbs

Once more, write the proper past-tense or past-perfect tense of the verb in parentheses.

1. Although Jim never (drink) _drank_____ any alcohol, his love for sweets

   (spring) _Sprang_____ as much from a desire for quality as for quantity.

2. For example, once when visiting Boston, Brady (hear) _____ about a

   local factory that (make) _____ fine chocolates.

3. He was impressed when sampling a five-pound box of bonbons, chocolate creams,

   and glazed walnuts. "Best darn candy I ever ate," his voice (ring)

   _____ out.

4. As he (begin) _____ to order several hundred boxes of candy for

   friends and acquaintances, he was told that the merchandise was in short supply.

5. "Heck," said Brady, taking out his checkbook, "tell them to build a candy factory with

   twice their capacity. Here's the money." The owner of the place nearly (sink)

   _____ to his knees when Brady (hand) _____ him a

   check for $150,000 to be paid back in candy.

Category 6: No Change

These verbs end in *–t* or *–d* and do not change for the past tense or the past participle.

Present tense	Past tense	Past participle
bet	bet	bet
burst	burst	burst
cast	cast	cast
cut	cut	cut
fit	fit (or fitted)	fit (or fitted)
hit	hit	hit
hurt	hurt	hurt
let	let	let
put	put	put
quit	quit	quit
read	read	read (the sound changes to "red")
rid	rid	rid
set	set	set
shed	shed	shed
shut	shut	shut
slit	slit	slit
spread	spread	spread
thrust	thrust	thrust

EXERCISE 14   Writing Irregular Verbs

You know the drill. Write the proper past-tense or past-perfect tense of the verb in parentheses.

1. Brady was at Rector's when a member of his party (burst) _burst_____ into

praise for a special sauce for fish prepared from a secret recipe at a restaurant in Paris.

2. Jim (let) _____ Charlie Rector know that the owner (have)

_____ to serve the dish at his restaurant or Brady (will)

_____ take his business elsewhere.

3. The next day, Rector pulled his son George out of college and (put)

_____ the young man on a boat to Paris.

4. Using an assumed name, the young Rector washed pots in the kitchen of the French

restaurant until he (fit) _____ in well enough to learn the secret of the

fabulous sauce.

5. After more than two years, George (quit) _____ the job in Paris and

returned home.

6. As soon as George stepped off the boat, Brady (thrust) _____

   himself forward and demanded, "Have you got the sauce?"

7. That night, as Jim (cut) _____ into the last of his nine portions of fish,

   he (spread) _____ some sauce on a piece of bread and (shut)

   _____ his eyes in pleasure.

8. Going back to the kitchen to congratulate George, Brady (set) _____

   the record straight: "If you poured some of the sauce over a Turkish towel, I believe

   I (can) _____ eat all of it."

Category 7: –n or –en and Possible Vowel Change

In these verbs, the past participle is formed by adding –n or –en. Sometimes there are vowel changes as well.

COLLABORATIVE ACTIVITY 2

Learning Verbs

Make a list of the verbs in Categories 1 through 7 that you don't know. With others, compile a single list and then quiz each other on the problem verbs.

TIPS

For Checking Irregular Verbs

If you aren't sure you've used the correct past-tense or past-participle form of a verb, look it up in a dictionary. The entry appears in the present tense, and the past tense and past participle are listed after it. So, for example, if you want to see if *swum* is the correct past participle, look under *swim*. You'll find all of its forms:

swim vb./swam/swum/ swimming

Good spellers are often bad spellers who know how to use a dictionary.

Present tense	Past tense	Past participle
beat	beat	beaten
bite	bit	bitten
blow	blew	blown
break	broke	broken
choose	chose	chosen
do	did	done
draw	drew	drawn
drive	drove	driven
eat	ate	eaten
fall	fell	fallen
fly	flew	flown
forget	forgot	forgotten
forgive	forgave	forgiven
freeze	froze	frozen
get	got	gotten
give	gave	given
go	went	gone
grow	grew	grown
hide	hid	hidden
know	knew	known
lie	lay	lain
ride	rode	ridden
rise	rose	risen
see	saw	seen
shake	shook	shaken
slay	slew	slain
speak	spoke	spoken
steal	stole	stolen

strive	strove	striven
swear	swore	sworn
take	took	taken
tear	tore	torn
throw	threw	thrown
wake	woke	woken
wear	wore	worn
weave	wove	woven
write	wrote	written

EXERCISE 15   Writing Irregular Verbs

COLLABORATIVE ACTIVITY 3

Changing Verb Forms
Write seven present-tense sentences, using one verb from each of the seven categories. Exchange papers. Turn each sentence into a past-tense sentence, a present-perfect-tense sentence, and a past-perfect-tense sentence. Then exchange papers again so a third student checks your work. Discuss your answers.

One more time, write the proper past-tense or past-perfect tense of the verb in parentheses.

1. For years, the 250-pound Brady (go) _went_ on defying the medical experts, who (give) _gave_ him only a short time to live if he (take) _took_ such poor care of his health.

2. Every time a doctor (speak) _____ to him about changing his eating habits, Jim quickly (forget) _____ the advice.

3. However, when his fifty-seventh birthday (draw) _____ near, Diamond Jim (fall) _____ victim to serious stomach trouble.

4. Until then, Diamond Jim (beat) _____ the odds of dying young, but he now (know) _____ he (have) _____ to listen to the doctors.

5. Therefore, he (break) _____ his old habits, (swear) _____ off rich food, and never again (overeat) _____.

6. His body eventually (wear) _____ down, and five years later the stomach illness (take) _____ his life.

7. After doctors (do) _____ an autopsy of his body, they (write) _____ up their findings, revealing that, over the years, Brady's stomach (grow) _____ five times larger than a normal person's.

8. In his will, Jim (give) _____ much of his fortune to the James Brady Urological Clinic, which he (begin) _____ at Johns Hopkins Hospital in Baltimore before his death.

EXERCISE 16   Writing Sentences

Choose five past-tense forms of the verbs in Category 7 and write a sentence using each form. Then rewrite each of these sentences in the present-perfect tense, rewording the sentence if necessary.

OTHER USES OF THE PAST PARTICIPLE

The past participle has many uses for expressing ideas. In addition to serving as the main verb in the present-perfect and past-perfect tenses, the past participle can appear in a variety of other places.

In Three-Word Verb Phrases

Many three-word verb phrases contain *have* plus the past participle to speculate about the past:

Helping verb	+	*have*	+	past participle
could		have		done
may		have		seen
should		have		gone
might		have		taken
must		have		been
would		have		thought

EXERCISE 17   Writing Verb Phrases

Complete each of the following sentences, using have *and an appropriate past participle.*

1. I didn't do well on the examination. *I should have done better.* _____

2. Yesterday was a holiday, and we could _____

    _____

3. If I had listened to your advice, I would _____

    _____

4. Mr. Fong wasn't at work yesterday. He must _____

    _____

5. I don't know if Dmitri wants to have lunch with us. He may _____

    _____ already.

6. Many people thought that they saw a flying saucer, but they might _____

    _____

In the Passive Voice

In some instances, you use the past participle after a form of *to be*, as in the following example:

This watch *was given* to me by my grandfather.

Notice that the sentence's subject, *the watch*, did nothing, for the grandfather did the giving. In other words, the subject is *passive*; it does not act but is acted upon. This form of expression is therefore called the **passive voice.** The passive voice always takes this pattern:

Subject + *to be* + past participle

Here are more examples of the passive voice in three different tenses:

Present tense: The awards *are* always *presented* by President Gray.
Future tense: Your grades *will be mailed* to you.
Past tense: My wallet *was stolen*.

The passive voice often sounds awkward, so don't overuse it. Use it only (1) when the action is more important than the person who performs it; or (2) when we don't know or care who performs the action. Otherwise, use the **active voice,** in which the subject performs the action:

Passive voice: Three home runs were hit by Smith. (This sounds awkward.)
Active voice: Smith hit three home runs. (This sounds much better.)

As an Adjective

Sometimes a past participle doesn't express an action. It functions instead as an adjective describing a noun. For example, a past participle often follows a linking verb (for example, *is, seem, become,* or *sound*) and describes the subject of the sentence:

Subject	Linking verb	Past participle
I	feel	*tired.*
The eggs	seem	*done.*
The blender	was	*broken.*

Write a word ending in *–ed* to describe the subject of the following sentence:

Yolanda looked _____ when she heard the news.

Did you write *surprised, startled, excited,* or *annoyed*? These words are past participles.

A past participle can also begin an adjective phrase that follows and describes a noun:

	phrase
A woman	*named Melinda* just asked to see you.
I've always liked books	*written by Hemingway.*

Finally, past participles can also be adjectives before nouns:

> A *frightened* dog hid under the table.
> He's a *well-known* actor.

Look carefully at the words before or after nouns when you edit. An incorrect past-participle form can be confusing and distracting, as in this sentence:

> There's a tire man resting on the couch.

Does the sentence say that the man sells tires or that the man is tired? It probably means the latter, but we can't be sure.

EXERCISE 18   Writing Sentences

Using the verbs provided, write two sentences that imitate the pattern of each example. Each uses a past participle.

1. We *were amazed* at the skill of the hibachi cook.

(impress) _I was impressed with the service at the restaurant._____

(annoy) _____

2. The Screaming Eagle ride is perfectly safe, so please *don't be frightened*.

(scare) _____

_____

(bore) _____

_____

3. I *am accustomed* to getting up at 5:00 A.M.

(use) _____

_____

(commit) _____

_____

4. He *seems interested* in our book group.

(involve in) _____

_____

(impress with) _____

_____

EXERCISE 19   Writing Past Participles

Write an appropriate past participle in each of the following sentences.

1. He sells _____ cars.

2. Do you know a man _____ Harry Leggs?

3. The police caught the man selling _____ goods.

4. When Grubbs caught the ball, 60,000 _____ fans leaped to their feet.

5. Several players were hurt during the game: Lopez had a _____

   nose; Johnson suffered a _____ leg muscle; and Hansen limped off

   with a _____ ankle.

6. You will see the new dishes _____ on the table.

7. Try not to go to places _____ by too many tourists.

8. Don't taste food _____ by Thumbs Thompson.

IN SUMMARY   Past-Tense Verbs

1. Denote events that occurred before the present.
2. Normally end in *–ed* but include more than a hundred irregular forms.
3. Include *was/were* for *be* and *could/would* for *can/will*.

Past Participles

1. Normally end in *–ed* but include more than a hundred irregular forms—
   which may be different from the irregular past-tense forms.
2. Appear in perfect tenses, which discuss events that occurred prior to a
   later time. The present-perfect tense uses *have/has* as the helping verb; the
   past-perfect tense uses *had*.
3. Appear after *have* in three-word verbs beginning with *could, should, may,
   might*, etc., and that speculate about the past.
4. Appear after *be* in the passive voice, in which the subject receives the
   action and doesn't perform it.
5. Function as adjectives after linking verbs or before or after nouns.

EDITING FOR MASTERY

Mastery Exercise 1   ***Correcting Verb Errors***

*The following passage contains fifteen errors in past-tense and past-participle forms,
excluding the two examples that have been corrected for you.*

The Fountain of Youth Industry

(1) Long before Walt Disney ^had ~~has~~ even thought of opening a park in Orlando, people
^were ~~was~~ paying to see Florida's longest-running tourist attraction: the Fountain of Youth.

(2) Supposedly, Juan Ponce de Leon discover Florida while searching for the fountain back in 1512. (3) But that story was just a myth.

(4) In 1512, Ponce was out of work. (5) The king of Spain has removed him as governor of Puerto Rico. (6) As a consolation prize, the king let him explore new lands in exchange for 10 percent of all the gold he can find. (7) The king didn't mentioned anything about a fountain of youth, and neither did Ponce. (8) In fact, he was not the kind of guy who looked for magical fountains. (9) In earlier voyages, he had seeked gold and slaves and developed a reputation as a ruthless character.

(10) In 1535, a Spanish historian claimed without proof that Ponce had went looking for the fountain. (11) That story reappeared in 1868, when a historian said that Ponce was searching for a fountain to restore youth to his aging body. (12) This was just a theory, but other historians accepted it, added details, and located the fountain in various areas in Florida.

(13) In 1870, a real-estate broker in St. Augustine, Florida, named a pond on his property Ponce de Leon Spring. (14) The attraction drawed a few visitors who drank its water. (15) Then in 1908, Louella McConnell tolded an amazing story about her property in St. Augustine. (16) She seen a large stone cross Ponce de Leon had put under a tree to mark a freshwater spring. (17) She also produced a map of Ponce's from a box bury near the tree. (18) When other people challenged her evidence, the map became too faded to read. (19) Then McConnell began to act crazy. (20) She wrote about conspiracies to kill women, was arrested for firing a gun, and told the judge that a police officer was trying to feed her poison apples.

(21) Meanwhile, a millionaire name Henry Flagler was building fancy hotels in St. Augustine and encouraging his wealthy friends to visit. (22) They usually wandered over to see the Fountain of Youth, where McConnell charge admission and sold bottled water and postcards. (23) McConnell sold her land to a Massachusetts developer in 1919, but then changed her mind and sued. (24) Even though the developer won the suit, it give up its plans for the property.

(25) After McConnell's death in an automobile accident in 1923, the property eventually passed to Walter Fraser, who make the Fountain of Youth into a leading tourist attraction. (26) An early Christian cemetery was discover on the property in 1934, indicating that the first Spanish town in the New World was probably located there—but this had nothing to do with Ponce de Leon.

(27) Today, Fraser's son, John, runs the park. (28) It contains a fountain (where visitors can have a drink), a Native American burial site, and a gift shop.

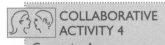

COLLABORATIVE ACTIVITY 4

Comparing Answers
Appoint someone to read the passage aloud so you can hear where errors occur. Make your corrections, discuss them, and report your findings to the class.

Scorecard: Number of errors found and corrected _____

Mastery Exercise 2

Correcting Verb Errors

The following passage contains fifteen errors in past-tense and past-participle verb forms, excluding one example that has been corrected for you. Write your corrections of these errors above the lines.

The Dolphin Pilot

helped

(1) He was a fourteen-foot dolphin, who, for more than two decades, ^help steamships avoid being shipwrecked off New Zealand. (2) He was the first dolphin in history whose life was protected by a special government law. (3) Pelorus Jack, name for Pelorus Sound, become famous in 1888 when he guided steamships through a six-mile stretch of rough, swirling water in Cook Strait, New Zealand. (4) He was love by both sailors and passengers who watched him playfully leaping above the waves toward their ships. (5) He will often scratch his back against the ship's hull and then swiftly glide out in front to guide a steamer along. (6) After getting one ship safely through, the dolphin would immediately leave to wait for another vessel.

(7) Passengers aboard ships described him as silvery white, with eyes that looked "almost human." (8) He always traveled alone and cutted through the waves with the greatest of ease. (9) When two ships needed his services at the same time, Pelorus Jack always choose the faster steamship.

(10) In 1903, a drunken sailor on the *SS Penguin* shooted at Pelorus Jack with a rifle. (11) Luckily, the shot missed. (12) Jack didn't showed up again for two weeks, but then he came back. (13) However, he never again accompanied the *Penguin*, which was wreck in 1909 in Cook Strait, killing seventy-five people. (14) In September 1904, the government of New Zealand passed a law to protect Pelorus Jack, for he had became an international celebrity. (15) A movie was make about him. (16) There was postcards that featured his picture. (17) There were many songs wrote about him. (18) A chocolate bar was named after him. (19) Sightseers, including Mark Twain, came great distances to see him, and when they seen him leaping toward them, someone would always shout, "Here comes Pelorus Jack!"

(20) In 1912, Pelorus Jack disappeared. (21) A local newspaper printed a tentative obituary, concluding, "If he is dead, more's the pity; if he has been slaughtered, more's the shame." (22) Pelorus Jack never appear again.

(23) Incidentally, no one will ever know, but he may have been a she.

Scorecard: Number of errors found and corrected _____

CHAPTER 12

Using Pronouns

The word *pronoun* literally means "for a noun," and **pronouns** are in fact substitutes for nouns. They're valuable substitutes, too. They help you avoid repetition, create unity, add emphasis, and combine sentences gracefully. You really couldn't write well without pronouns, so checking them as you edit is important. We'll take a look at a variety of ways to use them

- to replace nouns
- to make comparisons
- to establish clarity and unity
- to create emphasis

SELECTING THE RIGHT PRONOUN

Like nouns, pronouns serve a variety of functions in a sentence. Let's take a look at the pronouns and the functions they serve.

Personal Pronouns as Subjects and Objects

Unlike nouns, pronouns take different forms according to the role—or **case**—they fulfill in a sentence. Here are the **personal pronouns** that represent persons as subjects or objects:

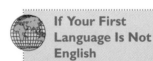

If Your First Language Is Not English

In many languages, the pronoun is included in the verb, but not in English. In Spanish, for example, the verb *está* means "it is." But English requires the pronoun.

Therefore, while editing your work, make sure you haven't omitted a pronoun in a clause and created a fragment.

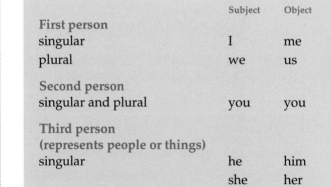

	Subject	Object
First person		
singular	I	me
plural	we	us
Second person		
singular and plural	you	you
Third person (represents people or things)		
singular	he	him
	she	her
	it	it
plural	they	them

Subject pronouns, like all subjects, usually come before verbs. Object pronouns follow verbs, words formed from verbs, or prepositions. Here are examples of object case pronouns.

As objects:	You helped *them*.
	I gave *them* the present.
As an object of an –ing *word*:	I wrote to Ms. Sanchez before meeting *her*.
As an object of an infinitive:	You must memorize the names to know *them* well.
As an object of a preposition:	between *you* and *me* from *him* to *her*

In clauses with just one subject or object, choosing the right pronoun case is usually no problem. For example, the pronouns in these sentences are obviously in the wrong case:

Me want a banana!
Nancy talked to *I*.

But determining pronoun case is trickier in clauses with more than one subject or object:

Me and her had a great time.
People have been very kind to *my friend and I*.

One way to determine if the pronouns are correct is to remove—but only temporarily—the nouns and leave only the pronouns. Or, if the clause contains only pronouns, remove one, then the other.

Incorrect
Me . . . had a great time.
. . . very kind to . . . *I*.

With the words removed, it is easier to see whether the pronouns are correct. In the first sentence, a subject case pronoun is needed. In the second sentence, an object case pronoun is needed.

She and I had a great time.
People have been very kind to my friend and me.

Choosing the correct pronoun case can also be confusing when *we* or *us* appears before a noun. Note these pronoun errors:

Before the lake became polluted, *us kids* always swam in it.
For *we folks*, nothing is too good.

Again, you can check the pronoun case by temporarily removing the noun:

Incorrect	Correct
. . . *us* . . . always swam in it.	*we* . . . always swam in it. [. . . *we kids* always swam in it.]
For we . . . , nothing is too good.	For *us* . . . , nothing is too good. [For *us folks*, nothing is too good.]

EXERCISE 1   Using Correct Pronoun Case

Some, but not all, of the following sentences contain errors in pronoun case. Write the correct forms above the lines. If a sentence is already correct, make no further changes.

1. *She and I*
   ^~~Her and me~~ have always said that for ^~~she and I~~ *her and me* nothing is too good.

2. Can you keep a secret between you and I?

3. Only four other students and him scored above 90 on the test.

4. Our pet boa constrictor is very close to LaVelle and I.

5. Me and him shared a pizza, a milk shake, and a diet cream pie.

6. Just send your money orders to her and me, but make them out to "Cash."

7. Some people feel that them are the best kind.

Personal Pronouns in Comparisons

Choosing the right pronoun can be difficult when you make comparisons. Notice in the following comparisons that a subject pronoun and a verb come after *than* or *as*:

> Harvey is a better swimmer *than I am*.
> But I dive as well *as he does*.

You can often leave out the verbs, but you should keep the same subject pronouns:

> Harvey is a better swimmer than *I (am)*.
> But I dive as well as *he (does)*.

If you compare objects instead of subjects, an object pronoun follows *than* or *as*:

> Ms. Blake treats him as well *as (she treats) me*.

Note carefully how the idea of this sentence changes if the pronoun is in the subject case.

> Ms. Blake treats him as well as *I (do)*.
> Now *I* treat him well, but who knows how Ms. Blake treats *me!*

If the meaning of the comparison is unclear with words omitted, don't omit them.

COLLABORATIVE ACTIVITY 1

Comparing Your Comparisons
Write ten sentences using pronouns, but for each pronoun slot, offer three choices—one of which is right. Be sure to include some comparisons. Exchange papers and then select the correct pronouns. Pass your completed paper to a third student to check your answers. Discuss any difficulties or debatable choices.

EXERCISE 2   Combining Sentences to Make Comparisons

Write a sentence making a comparison based on the information provided. Use than *or* as *in the sentence.*

1. Guy is 200 pounds, but she is 112 pounds. *Guy is heavier than she (is).*

2. Gloria is very pretty. Her mother is also very pretty. _____

   _____

3. Sam works hard. We don't work too hard. _____

   _____

4. Mr. Williams has three part-time jobs. She has only one job. _____

_____

5. The counselor talks to you quite often. She hardly ever talks to me. _____

_____

6. Albert ate fourteen hamburgers for lunch. I ate two. _____

_____

AVOIDING PRONOUN CONFUSION AND BIAS

✓ **TIPS**

For Distinguishing Between Contractions and Possessives

Whenever you aren't sure about using an apostrophe with a pronoun, look at the meaning you're trying to express. Remember

1. *possessives* don't use apostrophes: That is *your* hat. The dog hurt *its* leg.

2. *contractions* need apostrophes. *You're* in good shape. *It's* a nice day.

Because a pronoun often replaces—or refers back to—a noun, your readers need to know which noun. The word or words a pronoun refers back to are called **antecedents.** Here are some examples of antecedents and the pronouns that go with them:

Antecedent	Pronoun	Possessive before noun	Possessive
the team	it	its game	its
a person	he or she; him or her	his or her book	his or hers
John and I	we	our car	ours
John and me	us	our car	ours
John and she	they	their party	theirs
John and her	them	their party	theirs

Agreement in Number

To be clear and consistent, personal pronouns should agree in **number** with their antecedents. That is, a singular pronoun must have a singular antecedent, and a plural pronoun must have a plural antecedent. The following sentence, for example, may be confusing because the antecedent and pronoun don't agree:

        plural antecedent   singular pronoun
I stay away from *drugs* because *it's* nothing but trouble.

Rewrite the sentence to avoid the confusion: _____

_____

Did you change *it's* to *they're*? If not, note this carefully:

Singular: one drug = it
Plural: drugs = they

But suppose a pronoun could have more than one antecedent. The pronoun's reference may be unclear. For example, what does *he* refer to in the following sentence?

Roberto told his father that *he* had been wrong.

The answer can be either *Roberto* or *his father*, so the sentence needs to be revised. Here are two possibilities:

> Roberto told his father, "I was wrong."
> Roberto accused his father of being wrong.

Pronouns Without Antecedents

If a pronoun doesn't have an antecedent, the meaning of the pronoun may also be unclear. What does *he* refer to in this sentence?

> After I honked my horn at the cab that was blocking my way, *he* just honked back and refused to move.

The writer apparently means the *cab driver* but doesn't mention one, so the sentence needs to be revised to include the specific noun:

> . . . *the cab driver* just honked back and refused to move.

Here's a third common problem. In speaking, people sometimes use *they* or *we* without an antecedent:

> At work, *they* are receiving double-time pay.

Readers expect meanings to be more exact because writing is more literal than speech. So the sentence needs to be revised:

> At work, *the employees* are receiving double-time pay.

EXERCISE 3   Correcting Pronoun Agreement

Some—but not all—of the items contain an error in agreement between pronoun and antecedent. Circle the antecedent and underline the pronoun that refers to the antecedent. Then correct any errors you find.

1. The first bubble gum was invented by Frank Fleer in 1906, but ^it ~~they~~ never ^was ~~were~~ sold.

2. The gum was so sticky that only hard scrubbing with turpentine would remove them.

3. Fleer spent more than twenty years until they could fix the problem.

4. In 1928, stores everywhere began selling a "new, improved" gum named Dubble Bubble gum. They were pink because Fleer had only pink food coloring available in the factory.

5. None of the other penny candies could compete with Dubble Bubble, which outsold it all.

6. Other manufacturers copied Dubble Bubble, including its color.

7. Now pink bubble gum is everywhere; it's the industry's standard color.

E X E R C I S E   4   Clarifying Sentences

Insert nouns in place of pronouns whose antecedents are unclear or completely missing in the following sentences.

1. In the last twenty years, the microelectronics industry has made better and less
   expensive products. ^*Companies* ~~They~~ manufacture cellular phones, digital watches, computers,
   video games, CD-ROM players, DVD players, and minidisc players.

2. Pocket calculators used to cost $50 to $100, but now they sell them for $5.

3. Nowadays they don't repair calculators and many watches; they just throw them
   away.

4. Twenty years ago, nobody would have thought that computers would be in so many
   homes, but they are so inexpensive now that many families own them.

5. The electronics industry is changing so fast that you have to wonder: What will they
   think of next?

E X E R C I S E   5   Clarifying Sentences with Multiple Antecedents

Pronouns in the following sentences can refer to more than one antecedent. Underline each problem pronoun and substitute a noun that will clarify the sentence's meaning.

Odds and Ends About Famous People

1. At the beginning of the century, George Eastman wanted to make inexpensive
   cameras for children. He called ^*these cameras* ~~them~~ Brownies and sold them for a dollar.

2. Six-shot rolls of film sold for fifteen cents, but Eastman made hardly any profit from
   the cameras. They were the real money makers.

3. Because the king of Bavaria from 1886 to 1913 liked to shoot poor people for sport,
   his attendants purposely deceived him. One attendant dressed as a peasant, and
   the other gave a rifle filled with blank bullets to the king. He then strolled into view
   and fell dead at the sound of a gunshot.

4. Hans Christian Andersen, the famous writer of fairy tales, was terrified that he would
   pass out and be found by a policeman. Then he would bury him alive.

5. Andersen almost always carried a note in his pocket telling anyone who might
   discover him unconscious that he must not assume that he was dead.

6. King Charles II, the ruler of Great Britain from 1660 to 1685, sometimes took powder
   from the mummies of Egyptian kings and, in hopes of acquiring "ancient greatness,"
   would rub it on himself.

 **COLLABORATIVE ACTIVITY 2**

Discussing Pronouns
Review with others your answers to Exercises 3, 4, and 5. Report areas of disagreement to the class and try to reach some conclusions on the best ways to avoid pronoun confusion.

TIPS

For Identifying Singular Indefinite Pronouns

Here's a handy way to remind yourself that indefinite pronouns are singular. Look at the root words that most contain— *one* and *body*. It's simple arithmetic: *one* = one and *a body* = one body. If you're writing in the present tense, look at the verb, which should also be singular:

Everybody *has* . . . , no one *does* . . . , someone *is* . . . , and so on.

Pronouns Referring to Pronouns

Some pronouns don't refer to a specific person, place, or thing. So these are called **indefinite pronouns.** Here's a list of indefinite pronouns for people.

everyone	someone	each
everybody	somebody	every
anyone	no one	either
anybody	nobody	neither

All these indefinite pronouns are singular, so they present a special challenge. For example, which word (*their, his,* or *her*) should refer to *everyone* in the following sentence?

> Everyone in the class has done _____ homework.

Did you answer *their*? This plural word is a common choice, but it creates some problems. Remember that *everyone* is grammatically singular (its verb is *does*), even though it seems like a plural. (See Chapter 10 for more discussion of subject-verb agreement.)

Another choice for agreement with *everyone* might be *his.* It's certainly singular, but seems to leave the women out of the discussion. Of course, *his* works fine when an indefinite pronoun represents only males, and *her* would likewise be correct to represent females:

> Everybody in the men's gym class has done *his* exercises.
> Each of the women on the tennis team must practice *her* backhand.

As you can see, when an indefinite pronoun represents both sexes, there's no easy choice. Some people use *their,* but not in formal writing. Some people use *his* because they believe its meaning is neuter—neither male nor female—in this situation. Other people use *his or her,* as in "Everyone in the class has done his or her homework." Still others use the female pronoun, as in "Everyone in the class has done her homework." And others tend to rewrite the sentence with a plural subject:

> All of the students in the class have done their homework.

This last solution is probably the best, but it won't work in every situation. As you revise, pay special attention to pronouns. If they suggest a sexual bias you don't intend, change them or rework the sentence until it says what you mean.

Pronouns Referring to Collective Nouns

Like pronouns referring to pronouns, pronouns referring to collective nouns can give you trouble. A **collective noun**—a team, a band, an audience—represents a group of people or things, and almost all collective nouns are singular. Make sure the verb form you choose agrees in number.

> The *class has* met for half the term.
> The *band* at the football game *is* loud but not very good.

And any pronouns you use should be singular, too.

> The *orchestra* reaches *its* greatest heights when Rudolfo Parachuti conducts *it*.
> The *team* has already won more games than *it* (not *they*) won all last year.

EXERCISE 6   Removing Sexual Bias

Rewrite the sexually biased sentences by changing the male singular pronouns to plurals or use he *or* she, *or find another solution. Adjust the remainder of the sentence to reflect your changes. Replace pronouns with nouns, if necessary.*

1. It's a common superstition that when a person breaks a mirror, he will have seven years of bad luck. *It's a common superstition that when people break mirrors, the people will have seven years of bad luck.*

   (Note that, for consistency, the word *mirror* also becomes plural.)

2. However, the belief goes back to a time before someone even had a glass mirror that he could break. _____

   _____

3. The superstition about bad luck started in the sixth century B.C., when a person would gaze at his image and see his future in a shallow glass bowl filled with water.

   _____

   _____

4. A "mirror seer" would predict the future from the reflection of anyone who held the bowl in his hands. _____

   _____

5. If someone dropped and broke the bowl, that meant he would soon die, and the gods were sparing him the view of his horrifying future. _____

   _____

   _____

6. The modern superstition developed in the first century, when the Romans began to use a bowl called a *miratorium*. A person could predict his future by looking at his reflection in it. _____

   _____

7. They believed that a person's health changed every seven years and that he could determine his condition from the mirror. _____

   _____

8. Thus, seven years of bad health and bad luck came to the man who broke a mirror.

   _____

   _____

COLLABORATIVE ACTIVITY 3

Working with Pronouns
Write ten sentences—five with indefinite pronouns as subjects and five with collective nouns as subjects. Make the sentences complex enough to require pronouns that refer to the subjects, but leave the pronoun spaces blank. Exchange papers and then complete the sentences. Pay attention to case, number, and potential sexual bias. Exchange papers again and correct—or entirely rewrite—any sentences that have problems. Discuss the problems and solutions.

EXERCISE 7   Writing Collective Nouns

The subjects are supplied in these partial sentences. Complete each sentence, referring back to the subject with an appropriate pronoun.

1. The band *plays its best when Elvis Bernstein is the conductor.*

2. The jury _____

_____

3. A good department store _____

_____

4. The police _____

_____

5. The team _____

_____

6. The class _____

_____

SPECIAL PRONOUNS

Pronouns do more than simply replace nouns. They can emphasize your ideas and help you be specific. In this section, we'll look at three additional types of pronouns: reflexive pronouns, demonstrative pronouns, and relative pronouns.

Reflexive Pronouns

Sometimes the same person or thing is both the subject and the object in a sentence:

I admired *myself* in the mirror.
He loves *himself*, because nobody else does.

The object pronouns in these sentences are special kinds, called **reflexive pronouns,** because they reflect back to their subjects like mirrors. Here's a full list of these pronouns:

	Singular	Plural
First person	myself	ourselves
Second person	yourself	yourselves
Third person	himself (not hisself)	themselves (not theirselves)
	herself	
	itself	

Notice that the singular pronouns end in *–self,* while the plural pronouns end in *–selves.*

A reflexive pronoun can also repeat (but not replace) a subject or object for emphasis:

Albert ate seven whole pizzas, but I *myself* had only three.

However, people sometimes incorrectly use reflexive pronouns as subjects, especially when a sentence contains more than one subject:

Incorrect: John and myself are grateful for your help.
Incorrect: . . . myself am grateful for your help.
Correct: John and I are grateful for your help.

Again, the best way to determine the correct case is to remove the other subjects or objects temporarily. The correct form will then be clear.

EXERCISE 8   Writing Reflexive Pronouns

Write a pronoun in each sentence. Not every sentence requires a reflexive pronoun.

1. I like to carry on intelligent conversations with *myself*_____.

2. Brian has taught _____ several languages just by listening to the student

conversations between classes.

3. You folks should help _____ to some food.

4. We like to spend some time by _____ once in a while.

5. Shorty thinks very highly of _____.

6. Many students support _____ while going to school.

7. My brother, my sister, four cats, three dogs, and _____ still live at home.

Demonstrative Pronouns

The pronouns *this/that* and *these/those* actually make nouns more specific. They're called *demonstrative* words because they demonstrate what you're discussing. They serve as **demonstrative adjectives** before nouns (*this woman, that story, these women, those stories*) and as **demonstrative pronouns** by themselves (*this* is a nice place, but *that* is not).

Demonstratives have both singular and plural forms:

Singular	Plural
this	these
that	those

In general, use *this* or *these* to refer to things physically close and *that* or *those* to refer to things farther away—whether they're subjects or objects.

These cookies (close by) look fresh, but *those* (over there) don't look as appetizing. So I'll take *this one*—and on second thought, I'll take *that* one, too.

✔**TIPS**

For Handling Demonstratives

Don't use demonstrative pronouns as subjects of sentences. They almost never have clear antecedents.

EXERCISE 9   Writing Sentences with Demonstratives

Using the words supplied, write two sentences with demonstrative pronouns that imitate the pattern of each of the following sentences.

1. *These women* lost their handbags on the bus.

   (people) _These people found a young child in the park._

   (gorillas) _____

2. Do you want any of *these desserts* to take home?

   (compact discs) _____

   (hundred-dollar bills) _____

3. I'll take some of *this pasta* and a little of *that sauce.*

   (rice/sushi) _____

   (fruit/vegetables) _____

Relative Pronouns

COLLABORATIVE ACTIVITY 4

Writing Special Pronouns
Working in pairs, write two sentences that need reflexive pronouns, two that need demonstrative words, and two each that need *who* or *whom*—but leave the pronoun spaces blank. Then present your sentences to others and ask them to supply the correct words. Be sure that everyone agrees and understands. Report disagreements to the class.

When you use **relative pronouns,** which begin relative clauses, to refer to people, there are two choices: *who* and *whom.* The first choice, *who* serves as the subject:

> relative clause
> Please return this snake to the person *who* lent it to you.

> relative clause
> The man *who lent the snake to me* took my skunk in exchange.

In formal writing, many people insist that *whom* serves as the object. But you can usually drop *whom* from a clause, unless the pronoun directly follows a preposition:

> object subject verb
> Mr. Slither was the man *(whom)* you borrowed the snake from.
>
> but
>
> preposition + object
> Mr. Slither was the man *from whom* you borrowed the snake.

EXERCISE 10   Combining Sentences with Relative Pronouns

Combine each pair of sentences into one sentence, using who, whom, *or no relative pronoun.*

1. The identity of the person is unknown. The person created the first bagel. _The identity of the person who created the first bagel is unknown._

2. Somebody probably created the bagel by accident. The person dropped a piece of dough into hot water. _____

   _____

3. However, we do know the identity of the man. He first called a bagel a "bagel."

_____

_____

4. And, believe it or not, the person wasn't even Jewish! We give this person credit for inventing the word._____

_____

5. In 1683, the first coffeehouse in Vienna was opened by a Polish man. He introduced a new bread called the *beugel*._____

_____

6. Americans changed the name of the round bun to *bagel*. The foreign word was too difficult for them to pronounce. (*Hint*: Begin the clause with *for* or *because*.)_____

_____

_____

IN SUMMARY   To Use Pronouns Correctly

1. Choose subject case personal pronouns for subjects, object case personal pronouns for objects.
2. Make sure pronouns agree with their antecedents.
3. Correct pronouns that do not agree with antecedents or have no antecedents.
4. Rewrite pronouns that show sexual bias.
5. Use *this* and *that* before singular nouns, *these* and *those* before plural nouns.
6. Use *–self* for singular reflexive pronouns, *–selves* for plurals; do not use reflexive pronouns as subjects.
7. Use *who* as a subject, *whom* as an object.

EDITING FOR MASTERY

Mastery Exercise 1

Correcting Pronoun Errors

The following passage contains ten errors related to pronoun use, excluding the first error, which has been corrected as an example. Correct these errors by making your changes above the line.

Thomas Alva Edison (1847–1931): An Unlikely Genius

(1) People all over the world find^ themselves ~~themself~~ living better lives because of the inventions of one man, Thomas Alva Edison. (2) This man started three large laboratories where it invented and patented 1,097 different products—including the electric light

bulb, the phonograph, and the motion picture camera and projector. (3) However, there never was a more unlikely genius.

(4) When Edison was in first grade, his teacher told him to drop out of school because he was hopelessly stupid. (5) Edison soon did leave school, and at the age of twelve he was working full-time selling candy and newspapers on passenger trains. (6) Scarlet fever had already harmed his hearing, and when someone playfully lifted him by the ears, they made his hearing worse. (7) Although he didn't have much formal education, Edison began educating hisself by experimenting with new inventions. (8) Unfortunately, one of this experiments set a train on fire, and they fired him.

(9) Soon afterward, he saved the life of a stationmaster's son, and the stationmaster gave Edison a job as a telegraph operator. (10) His first invention, in 1868, was a business failure, but Edison soon quit his job as a telegraph operator and devoted his time to inventing. (11) In 1871, he built a machine shop in Newark, New Jersey, that eventually became the General Electric Company. (12) In the next few years, Western Union and Automatic Telegraph paid him $70,000 for the rights to inventions that his assistants and himself had perfected. (13) Soon another of his inventions—the phonograph—were earning him national fame. (14) Everyone was buying one for themselves. (15) With this sudden changes in his fortunes, Edison built another laboratory in Menlo Park, New Jersey. (16) There he invented most of his most important products, including the electric light bulb. (17) In Menlo Park, many more of Edison's dreams became reality—for he and the rest of the world.

Scorecard: Number of errors found and corrected _____

COLLABORATIVE ACTIVITY 5

Comparing Answers
Appoint someone to read the passage aloud so you can hear where errors occur. Make your changes, discuss them, and report your findings to the class.

Mastery Exercise 2

Correcting Pronoun Errors

The following passage contains ten errors related to pronoun use, excluding the first error, which has been corrected as an example. Correct these errors by making your changes above the lines.

Edison's Electric Light

(1) For years, Edison never stopped working, until ^he ~~him~~ and his family finally took a vacation in the summer of 1878. (2) They traveled to Wyoming to view a total eclipse of the sun, but it was hardly relaxing. (3) He spent the entire time talking with a traveling companion about electrically generated light. (4) When Edison returned to his laboratory, they put aside all their other projects and began working on a practical and dependable light bulb.

(5) Edison needed money to pay for the project, so he went to New York. (6) There on Wall Street, an important conversation took place between he and the banker J. P. Morgan. (7) Edison told him that the company could produce a reliable electric light in six weeks.

(8) As a result, Morgan talked other bankers into forming the Edison Electric Light Company. (9) They issued 3,000 shares, but they did not sell. (10) Therefore, to stimulate business, Edison lied to the newspapers, saying that they had already perfected the invention. (11) Everyone quickly bought stock for theirselves, and Morgan gave Edison $50,000 to conduct his research.

(12) For the next year, Edison's five assistants and himself worked twenty hours a day. (13) One of the most difficult problems was that the filament (the part that glowed) inside the bulb always burned up or melted after only a few minutes. (14) Edison tried to solve it by putting the filament in a glass bulb and creating a vacuum inside of it. (15) They also tested a variety of materials as filaments, including several types of bamboo.

(16) Finally, Edison manufactured cotton threads that were coated with carbon and used them as filaments. (17) This kinds of filaments worked, and Edison switched on his light bulb on October 21, 1879. (18) It glowed with a reddish light for over forty hours and quit only when Edison increased the voltage to test the filament's strength. (19) That small piece of thread in Menlo Park, New Jersey, turned night into day throughout the world.

Scorecard: Number of errors found and corrected _____

CHAPTER 13

Using Modifiers

Modifiers—adjectives and adverbs—are important tools. They add variety, liveliness, and specific information to your writing. They're also versatile tools, for they can describe more than one idea in a sentence. They therefore need to be placed correctly, next to the idea you want them to describe. This chapter will show you how to check your modifiers as you edit. It explains

- how to identify modifiers
- how to know where they belong
- how to avoid misplacing or misusing them

WHAT ARE MODIFIERS?

A **modifier** is a descriptive word, phrase, or clause that makes another word or phrase specific. In a sense, a modifier sets limits. For example, the modifier *large* before *sofa* rules out small or medium sofas. And the modifier *hastily* after *ate* rules out eating at any other speed.

Modifiers can be **adjectives,** which describe nouns. Adjectives also can be placed in a variety of positions. Single-word adjectives precede nouns such as *vase:*

> a *red* vase
> an *interesting red* vase

Adjective phrases come after a noun:

> a vase *with red flowers*
> a vase *broken into many pieces*
> a vase *sitting on the table*
> a vase *to hold the roses*

Or, as you may recall from Chapter 8, adjective (or relative) clauses also follow a noun:

> a vase *that we received as a wedding present*
> a vase, *which holds a great many flowers,*

Modifiers can also be **adverbs.** They describe verbs or words formed from verbs, such as *–ing* words or past participles, explaining *when, where, why, how,* or *how often* an action occurs or occurred. Like adjectives, they can appear in many places. For example, single-word adverbs, which usually end in *–ly*, can come before or follow a verb:

> I ran *quickly.*
> I ran *quickly today.*
> *Today,* I ran *quickly.*

Adverb phrases can also come before or can follow a verb:

> I ran *for thirty minutes.*
> I ran *accompanied by my friend Juanita.*
> *Trying to build up my endurance,* I ran *for thirty minutes.*
> I ran *to try to build up my endurance.*

And so can adverb clauses:

> *Because I wanted to build up my endurance,* I ran *three times a week.*
> I ran *before I had eaten breakfast.*

Notice that adjective and adverb phrases are a lot alike. Both types can begin with any of these:

- a preposition (*with* red flowers, *for* thirty minutes)
- an *–ing* word (*sitting* on the table, *trying* to build up my endurance)
- a past participle (*broken* into many pieces, *accompanied* by my friend Juanita), or
- an infinitive (*to hold* the roses, *to try to build* up my endurance)

Notice, too, that adjective clauses can begin with words such as *that, which, who,* or *whose,* while adverb clauses begin with such words as *before, if,* and *because.*

EXERCISE 1   Writing Adjectives and Adverbs

Change the adjectives in the left-hand column into adverbs in the right-hand column.

1. The train is slow.	**1.** The train moves _slowly_____.
2. The motor sounds quiet.	**2.** The motor runs _____.
3. The sea looks peaceful.	**3.** The waves roll in _____.
4. The towels are very neat.	**4.** The towels are folded _____.
5. She has bad eyesight.	**5.** She sees _____.
6. The band is very loud.	**6.** The band plays _____.

EXERCISE 2   Identifying Prepositional Modifiers

Underline each prepositional phrase and draw an arrow to the word(s) the phrase describes.

John Chapman (1774–1845): Johnny Appleseed

1. Young John Chapman had a lifelong love for <u>flowering plants and trees</u>—especially apple trees.

2. Chapman planted apple seeds throughout the Midwest, and he walked barefoot through his orchards.

3. This man in simple clothes was also deeply religious, so he preached from the Bible as he traveled.

4. He supposedly wore a tin pan on his head for protection against sun and rain and for use as a cooking pot.

5. Settlers on the frontier began calling him Johnny Appleseed in a spirit of humor or ridicule.

6. Native Americans, however, respected Chapman for his ability to cure their illnesses with herbs.

7. He is buried today in Johnny Appleseed Park, near Fort Wayne, Indiana.

EXERCISE 3   Identifying –ing Modifiers

Underline the –ing phrase modifiers in each of these sentences and then draw an arrow to the word or phrase the modifiers describe.

1. Benjamin Franklin performed the first successful electrocution, <u>killing</u> several <u>chickens and a ten-pound turkey with electric shocks in 1773.</u>

2. Up until 1785 in New England, engaged couples wearing clothes could share the same bed if they were separated by a board.

3. Guests to the White House were often amazed to be greeted by President Thomas Jefferson wearing plain working clothes—a shabby brown coat, corduroy pants, and old slippers.

4. Dropping the *u's* in words like *colour* and *labour,* Noah Webster's *American Spelling Book* in 1783 "Americanized" the spelling of many English words.

5. In 1791, when carpenters in Philadelphia went on strike, they formed their own organization, offering their services for *25 percent less* than their employers had charged.

6. In 1821, Emma Hart Willard opened the Troy Female Seminary, the first institution in the United States offering a high school education for girls.

EXERCISE 4   Identifying Past-Participle and Infinitive Modifiers

Underline each past participle or infinitive and draw an arrow to the word or phrase it describes.

1. Many people believe that the Liberty Bell was rung for the first time on July 4, 1776, to celebrate the colonists' Declaration of Independence.

2. We also know that the bell has a long crack, caused by its ringing on that fateful day.

3. The cause of the crack is a wonderful story, but it's a myth, invented by writer George Lippard in his 1847 book *Legends of the American Revolution*.

4. The actual bell was installed in 1753, twenty-two years before the American Revolution, and it rang many times to awaken people, call them to church, and so on.

5. Its nickname, "Liberty Bell," was coined in 1839 to refer to the hoped-for end of slavery in America.

EXERCISE 5   Identifying Clause Modifiers

COLLABORATIVE ACTIVITY 1

Checking Your Answers
Review your answers to Exercises 1 through 5. Has everyone determined the word or words each modifier describes? Which modifiers function as adjectives, describing nouns? Which function as adverbs, describing verbs, or words formed from verbs? Discuss your areas of disagreement with the class.

Underline each adjective clause and draw an arrow to the noun it describes.

1. "Yankee Doodle" is a Revolutionary War song that inspired General Washington's troops.

2. However, its composer was a British Army surgeon who wanted to make fun of the Americans.

3. Dr. Richard Shuckburgh, who wrote the first version of "Yankee Doodle," was camped with some British and American troops during the French and Indian War.

4. The Americans, who wore all sorts of clothes but no uniforms, looked sloppy compared to the uniformed British troops.

5. Shuckburgh wrote a crude song that made fun of the colonials' appearance.

6. The song insulted the Americans, who decided to change its lyrics and make it their own defiant song.

PLACING MODIFIERS CORRECTLY

Although modifiers can appear in many positions, their correct placement is very important.

Misplaced Modifiers

A misplaced modifier can't do its job. Notice, for example, how the meaning of the following sentence changes when you move the word *only*:

I *only* want to give Biggie Schnozzle a nose job.
Only I want to give Biggie Schnozzle a nose job.

> I want *only* to give Biggie Schnozzle a nose job.
> I want to give *only* Biggie Schnozzle a nose job.
> I want to give Biggie Schnozzle *only* a nose job.

Because so many meanings are possible, you must place *only* exactly where it expresses the right meaning. It usually—but not always—belongs directly before or after the word it describes.

Placing longer modifiers also affects meanings. Look at how incorrectly placed modifiers say something different from what you might mean.

> *Poor:*   The passengers were safe from the sharks in the boat. (What were the sharks doing in the boat?)
>
> *Better:*   The passengers in the boat were safe from the sharks.
>
> *Poor:*   Ralph gave a puppy to his girlfriend with brown spots and white whiskers. (What did Ralph give to his other girlfriend, who doesn't have these skin problems?)
>
> *Better:*   Ralph gave his girlfriend a puppy with brown spots and white whiskers.

EXERCISE 6   Placing Modifiers Correctly

Indicate where each modifier most logically belongs in the following sentences by drawing an arrow to that location.

The Real Uncle Sam

1. (modifier) in striped pants and top hat

   (sentence) The man who symbolizes the United States Government is based on a meat packer and politician from upstate New York who came to be known as Uncle Sam.

2. (modifier) now known as Arlington

   (sentence) Uncle Sam was Samuel Wilson, who was born in Massachusetts, on September 13, 1766, in the town of Menotomy.

3. (modifier) at the age of eight

   (sentence) Sam Wilson served as a drummer boy and was on duty the April morning in 1775 when Paul Revere made his famous ride.

4. (modifier) by banging the drum at the sight of the redcoats

   (sentence) In fact, young Sam alerted local patriots, who prevented the British from entering Menotomy.

5. (modifier) with the Treaty of Paris in 1783

   (sentence) After independence had finally been settled, Sam moved to Troy, New York, and opened a meat-packing company.

 **COLLABORATIVE ACTIVITY 2**

Composing Sentences
Rewrite the following sentences, attaching as many modifiers as you can—prepositional phrases, –ing phrases, past participles, infinitives, relative clauses, and *before/if/because* clauses.
   The cowboy rode his horse.
   The woman twirled her lasso.
Then share your sentences with others, who may suggest ways to place the modifiers more effectively.

6. (modifier) with great affection

   (sentence) People in the town called him Uncle Sam because of his cheerful manner and complete honesty.

7. (modifier) which was also fought against Britain

   (sentence) Another war caused Sam Wilson's nickname to be heard around the world.

8. (modifier) stamped with the abbreviation "U.S." for "United States"

   (sentence) During the War of 1812, Sam Wilson won a military contract to provide beef and pork to soldiers.

9. (modifier) when asked by government inspectors what the "U.S." stood for

   (sentence) One day, a meat packer joked that it represented the initials of his employer, Uncle Sam.

EXERCISE 7   Eliminating Misplaced Modifiers

Each of the following sentences contains a misplaced modifying phrase or clause. Underline the problem phrase, and then draw an arrow to the spot where it belongs.

1. The second president of the United States, <u>after living to be ninety,</u> John Adams, died at home in Braintree, Massachusetts.

2. This lifelong hypochondriac lived longer than any other president, who always feared an early death.

3. Adams complained to everyone at the age of thirty-five that his health was poor.

4. During the eighty-ninth year of his life, his son John Quincy Adams's inauguration as our sixth president gave John Adams great pleasure.

5. Ironically, John Adams died on the fiftieth anniversary of the signing of the Declaration of Independence, which he helped write at 6:00 in the evening.

6. Earlier that same day, July 4, 1826, the other author of the Declaration of Independence, Thomas Jefferson, unknown to Adams, had died.

Dangling Modifiers

Sometimes a modifier describes nothing at all. It dangles unattached because the word it should describe is not in the sentence:

> *Walking down the street on a windy day,* my hat blew off. (Who was walking down the street? It wasn't your hat—which is the only noun the phrase could describe in this sentence.)
>
> *Talking to Mr. Smith,* he said that the problem was serious. (Who talked to Mr. Smith? The sentence suggests that he talked to himself.)

✓ TIPS

For Testing Modifier Placement

If a sentence starts with an *–ing* word, examine it carefully. Draw an arrow from the *–ing* word to the subject. If the *–ing* word does not express an action that the subject performs, then the *–ing* word is probably dangling or misplaced. Rewrite the sentence.

Since the modifier doesn't describe anything in the sentence, moving a dangling modifier won't eliminate the problem. Instead, you must rewrite the sentence and add the word the modifier describes:

> *As I was walking down the street on a windy day,* my hat blew off.
> Mr. Smith *told me* that the problem was serious.

EXERCISE 8   Eliminating Dangling Modifiers

Each of the following sentences contains a dangling modifier. Underline the problem phrase and then rewrite the sentence. If necessary, you may change a phrase to a dependent clause.

More Facts About John Adams

1. After graduating from Harvard University at the age of nineteen, a job of teaching at a school became available. *After John Adams had graduated from Harvard University at the age of nineteen, a job of teaching at a school became available to him.*

2. After teaching for a few years, his parents thought that a career as a minister would be more appealing. _____

3. Unhappy with both teaching and the clergy, the law became his true love. _____

4. With a sharp mind and total honesty, the law practice became very successful. _____

5. His reputation could have been damaged by defending the British soldiers who shot some Massachusetts citizens in the Boston Massacre. _____

6. By proving that the British soldiers had fired in self-defense, the citizens of Boston greatly respected his courage and integrity. _____

EXERCISE 9   Combining Sentences

Combine each of the following groups of sentences, changing full clauses into modifying phrases. Use both coordinating conjunctions (for, and, nor, but, or, yet, so), and subordinating conjunctions (although, because, when, after, and so on) as needed. Check your combined sentences for misplaced or dangling modifiers.

1. Noah Webster saw something.

   There was a need.

If Your First Language Is Not English

1. Word order is crucial to meaning in English. But many other languages use a different word order than English uses. In Spanish, for example, an object often comes *before* a verb, while in English an object always comes *after* a verb. This verb-object combination usually cannot be separated by a modifier. Compare these sentences:

   Incorrect: I found in my book the answer.

   Correct: I found the answer in my book.

2. A similar problem occurs when two objects follow a verb. The first object receives the action of the verb and the second (in a prepositional phrase) receives the first object. The prepositional phrase cannot separate the verb from its object:

   Incorrect: Tom lent to me the book.

   Correct: Tom lent the book to me.

The need was for a dictionary.

The dictionary was for the American language.

He saw this need for a long time.

Then he began working on one.

Noah Webster saw the need for a dictionary of the American language long before he began working on one.

2. He began his work.

Americans were independent of the British.

English-language dictionaries ignored American words.

The dictionaries used English spellings.

The dictionaries used English pronunciations.

There were very few exceptions.

_____

_____

3. He was a brilliant young man.

He was also very patriotic.

He was sure of something.

A national language would unify the country.

He began his research.

He started in 1803.

_____

_____

4. Webster put in a great deal of effort.

He worked for three years.

He published *A Compendious Dictionary of the American Language.*

_____

_____

5. Webster then began to work again.

He worked on a dictionary.

It was much longer.

He finished his work.

It was two decades later.

_____

_____

6. He published the *American Dictionary of the English Language.*

The year was 1828.

The dictionary was in two volumes.

COLLABORATIVE ACTIVITY 3

Playing with Modifiers
Write three sentences that deliberately contain misplaced or dangling modifiers. (It's hard to do!) Then exchange papers. Rewrite the sentences to correct the problems. Exchange papers again so a third student can check your work. Discuss any problem sentences.

It had 70,000 words.

_____

_____

7. Webster died.

He died in 1843.

George and Charles Merriam bought something.

It was the rights to Webster's dictionary.

_____

_____

8. They continued his work.

They updated his work.

They did these things over many years.

They published *The Merriam-Webster Unabridged Dictionary.*

They published *The First International Dictionary.*

They published *The First Collegiate Dictionary.*

_____

_____

IN SUMMARY   To Eliminate Misplaced or Dangling Modifiers

1. Locate each modifier: adjectives, adverbs, prepositional phrases, *–ing* phrases, past participles, infinitives, relative clauses, and adverb clauses.
2. See if the modifier comes directly before or after the word or phrase it describes.
3. Move the modifier to another place in the sentence if necessary.
4. Rewrite the sentence entirely if necessary.

EDITING FOR MASTERY

Mastery Exercise 1

Eliminating Errors with Modifiers

Eight sentences in the following passage contain misplaced or dangling modifiers, aside from the first sentence, which has been corrected as an example. Find and revise the sentences with the errors.

More About Uncle Sam

1. At first, when thinking of Uncle Sam, only a name came to mind, until illustrations first

appeared in New England newspapers in 1820. *At first when people thought*

of Uncle Sam, only a name came to their minds, until illustrations first appeared
in New England newspapers in 1820.

2. Wearing a solid black hat and topcoat, the first pictures of the old gent showed a man without a beard. _____

_____

_____

3. Because of the work of many illustrators over more than a century, today we recognize a familiar image of Uncle Sam. _____

_____

_____

4. The first pictures of him were introduced in a red hat in the 1830s. _____

_____

_____

5. The flowing beard appeared during Abraham Lincoln's presidency, which was inspired by the president's own chin whiskers. _____

_____

_____

6. Uncle Sam was such a popular figure that cartoonists decided he should appear more patriotically dressed in the late nineteenth century. _____

_____

_____

7. His red pants were decorated with stripes, and his top hat with both stars and stripes, making him a sort of living American flag. _____

_____

_____

8. Pictures of a tall, thin man came from the pen of Thomas Nast, the famous cartoonist from the Civil War period, resembling the original Uncle Sam, Sam Wilson.

_____

_____

9. However, the most famous portrait of Uncle Sam was painted in this century by James Montgomery Flagg, the one most often reprinted and most widely recognized. _____

_____

_____

COLLABORATIVE ACTIVITY 4

Checking Your Answers
Appoint someone to read the sentences aloud so you can hear where errors occur. Make your changes, discuss them, and report your findings to the class.

10. With a serious face and a finger pointing directly at the viewer on World War I posters, this figure said, "I Want You for the U.S. Army." _____

_____

_____

11. The poster sold four million copies during the war, and more than half a million during the Second World War that showed Uncle Sam dressed in his full flag costume.

_____

_____

12. Flagg's Uncle Sam, however, is not a copy of Abraham Lincoln's face, but is a self-portrait of the artist, contrary to popular belief. _____

_____

_____

Scorecard: Number of errors found and corrected _____

Mastery Exercise 2

Eliminating Errors with Modifiers

Eight sentences in the following passage contain misplaced or dangling modifiers, aside from the first sentence, which has been corrected as an example. Find and revise the sentences with the errors.

The Real Dr. Jekyll and Mr. Hyde

1. A real man named William Brodie, who lived in Edinburgh, Scotland, became the inspiration for the fictional Dr. Jekyll and Mr. Hyde between 1741 and 1788. *A real man named William Brodie, who lived in Edinburgh, Scotland, between 1741 and 1788, became the inspiration for the fictional Dr. Jekyll and Mr. Hyde.*

2. Robert Louis Stevenson wrote *The Strange Case of Dr. Jekyll and Mr. Hyde,* using Brodie as his model, in a three-day period in 1885. _____

_____

_____

3. Brodie inherited a large estate and a profitable business from his father, who then became a member of the town council. _____

_____

_____

4. However, at night Brodie was the opposite of a respectable citizen with a few beers in his belly. _____

_____

_____

5. He kept company with thieves and gamblers, and he supported two mistresses and their children. _____

_____

_____

6. After running up huge debts from gambling losses and supporting three households, money became an obsession for Brodie. _____

_____

_____

7. Hanging inside their doors on a hook, Brodie's shopkeeper friends usually left their keys. _____

_____

_____

8. He copied these keys and burglarized the shops, and several times he was almost caught by the police. _____

_____

_____

9. In July 1786, after several small break-ins, the plans for committing bigger robberies entered his thoughts. _____

_____

_____

10. He robbed several stores along with a gang of three convicts. _____

_____

_____

11. After one of his partners confessed to the police hoping to escape, Brodie left the city. _____

_____

_____

12. Found hiding in a cupboard in Amsterdam, the police brought him back to Scotland for trial, where he was convicted and hanged. _____

_____

_____

Scorecard: Number of errors found and corrected _____

CHAPTER 14

Making Comparisons

Whenever you compare people or things, you use words like *taller, tallest*, or *more gracefully, most gracefully* to describe them. The forms of these expressions show the comparisons, but sometimes the forms can be tricky. This chapter will help you check for correct use of comparative forms as you edit. You'll examine

- ways to compare people and things that are alike
- ways to compare people and things that are different
- special forms of comparative words

COMPARING WITH ADJECTIVES AND ADVERBS

One way to compare people or things is with **adjectives.** You'll recall that adjectives describe nouns, and that one-word adjectives usually go before the nouns they describe:

> a *silly* mistake
> a *delicious* cake

One-word adjectives may also come after linking verbs and describe the subjects of those verbs:

> Mr. Gottbucks is *generous.*
> Your plan to save the universe sounds *interesting.*

Another way to make comparisons is with **adverbs,** which, as the name suggests, usually describe verbs. One-word adverbs usually end in *–ly.*

> Bruno dresses *casually.*
> Professor Tedium talked *slowly.*

Adverbs can also describe adjectives or other adverbs, usually to explain *how much* or *how often:*

> a *really* cool day
> a *slightly* crooked nose
> Silvia Shout talks *very* loudly.

Now let's look at these adjectives and adverbs as they actually work in comparisons.

ADJECTIVE FORMS

There are several methods for making comparisons with adjectives: in their simple form, comparative form, or superlative form.

The Simple Form

In one type of comparison, you explain that two people or things are the same in some way. Here are two examples:

> Stubby is *as short as* Tina [is].
> Billy Bob is *as strong as* an ox [is].

Note that this type of comparison uses *as . . . as*, and the adjective shows up in its usual form.

The Comparative Forms

When you want to explain that two people or things are different in some way, you can do so by adding *–er* to the end of an adjective, or by placing *more* or *less* before it. This is the **comparative form.** Here are some examples:

> Tomas is *smarter* than his dog [is].
> Walter is *thinner* than a cracker [is].
> My new Rolls Royce is *more expensive than* the last car I bought. The Honda was *less expensive.*

The following rules describe when to use *–er, more,* or *less:*

 Add *–er* to one-syllable adjectives (or *–r* to adjectives ending in silent *e*).

Simple	Comparative
bright	brighter
cute	cuter

 If the adjective ends in a single vowel plus a consonant, you usually double the consonant before adding *–er.*

Simple	Comparative
thin	thinner
big	bigger

 Add *–er* to two-syllable adjectives ending in *–y* or *–ow.*

Simple	Comparative
pretty	prettier
narrow	narrower

▶ Place *more* before most other two-syllable adjectives and all adjectives of three or more syllables.

Simple	Comparative
awful	more awful
beautiful	more beautiful
interesting	more interesting

▶ Place *less* before any adjective, no matter what its spelling or number of syllables.

less tall	less intelligent
less thin	less pretty

With every comparative form, you usually need to complete the statement with *than*:

After cleaning the basement, the barn, and the pig pen, Bill is dirtier *than a mud wrestler.*

EXERCISE I   Writing Comparisons

 COLLABORATIVE ACTIVITY I

Looking at Comparative Forms
Divide a sheet of paper into three columns. Then with a classmate list as many adjectives in the first column as you can think of. Try for thirty. (Just think of words before these nouns: *person* and *car*—as in *tall person, beautiful person, new car,* and *red car.*) Then, next to each adjective on your list, write the comparative form in the second column. Show which adjectives add *-er* and which need *more*. Leave the third column blank for the moment.

Fill in the correct form of each adjective in parentheses.

1. In Australia, sheep are five times (numerous) __more numerous__ than humans.

2. Grandma Moses began painting at an (old) _____ age than any other person in history; she was one hundred.

3. A block of cheddar cheese made in 1995 by a dairy cooperative in Quebec, Canada, was (large) _____ than any other block ever created; it weighed 28½ tons and measured 6 feet high, 32 feet long, and 4½ feet wide.

4. Thomas Wedders, who worked in a circus in the eighteenth century, had a (long) _____ nose than anyone else in recorded history. It measured 7½ inches.

5. John F. Kennedy was voted (popular) _____ than any other president.

6. Fifteen presidents in U.S. history were elected with (few) _____ than 50 percent of the popular vote—including Abraham Lincoln, who won with 39.8 percent.

EXERCISE 2   Writing More Comparisons

If Your First Language Is Not English

Some languages form all comparatives in only one way: by adding a word. (For example, *mas* in Spanish means *more*.) But in English, you cannot use *more* and *–er* with the same adjective:

Incorrect: Bill is more bigger than I am.

Correct: Bill is *bigger* than I am.

Compose five statements based on the information provided:

	Egbert Egghead	Bruno Masher
height	5'6"	6'6"
weight	140 pounds	330 pounds
age	45 years old	23 years old
education	Ph.D.	B.A.
job	college professor	pro football player
income	$50,000 yearly	$6 million yearly

1. Egbert Egghead is shorter than Bruno Masher. _____ (or)
   Egbert Egghead is less tall than Bruno Masher. _____

2. _____

3. _____

4. _____

5. _____

The Superlative Forms

When you compare three or more things, you usually use the **superlative form** of adjectives:

> Len Lanky is the *tallest* player on the basketball team.
> Jarrett is the *most articulate* person I have ever heard.

These superlative forms differ from comparative forms in three ways: the *–er* ending becomes *–est* in the superlative, *more* becomes *(the) most*, and *less* becomes *the least*. Note that *the* usually appears before the adjective:

Simple	Comparative	Superlative
long	longer	(the) longest
fat	fatter	(the) fattest
pretty	prettier	(the) prettiest
beautiful	more beautiful	(the) most beautiful
generous	less generous	(the) least generous

COLLABORATIVE ACTIVITY 2

Looking at Superlative Forms

Return to your list from Collaborative Activity 1 and write the superlative forms for each adjective in the third column.

EXERCISE 3   Writing Superlatives

Write the correct superlative form of the adjective in parentheses.

1. According to the American and Canadian Kennel Clubs, the border collie is (intelligent) _the most intelligent_ dog in the world.

2. On the other hand the basset hound (dumb) _____.

3. Although a female crocodile is a fierce predator, it is (gentle) _____ of mothers; she delicately picks up her newborn babies and carries them in a pouch inside her mouth.

4. The Loch Ness Monster, or "Nessie," is (mysterious) _____ animal in the world; it has been seen and even photographed many times, but no search party has ever proved its existence.

5. The city with (long) _____ name is probably Krung Thep Mahanakhon Borvorn Ratanakosin Mahintharayutthaya Mahadilok pop Noparatratchathani Burirom Udumratchanivetmahasathan Amornpiman Avatarnsathit Sakkathattiyavisnukarmprasit, which is the poetic, full name for the capital of Thailand. Foreigners call it Bangkok.

E X E R C I S E 4   Writing *Less* and *the Least*

Complete the following sentences, using less *or* the least.

1. Fred Fumbles is not very careful, but his brother is even *less careful* _____.

2. Professor Drab never gives a very interesting lecture, but today's was even _____ than it normally is.

3. Of all the artists in the world, Thumbs Thomas is probably _____.

4. I thought that *Halloween XXVII* was _____ than the first twenty-six movies.

5. Mrs. Twigg's older children hardly eat a thing, but little Tina eats even _____.

E X E R C I S E 5   Writing Statements of Comparison

Compose a statement using a superlative form of an adjective to describe one of each group in parentheses.

1. (three fish) _The salmon is the largest of the three fish._ _____

2. (three clowns) _____

3. (three birds) _____

4. (three suits) _____

5. (three watches) _____

6. (three witches) _____

ADVERB FORMS

TIPS

For Keeping Adjectives and Adverbs Straight

Don't confuse adjectives with adverbs. An adverb describes a verb, not a noun:

Incorrect: The road work is going slower (adjective) than planned.

Correct: The work is going more slowly (adverb) than planned.

Regular adverbs always end in *–ly* and do not change form in the comparative or superlative. Use the same patterns for comparing *–ly* adverbs that you use when comparing three- and four-syllable adjectives: *as . . . as, more than, and the most:*

The simple form
She dances *as gracefully* as a ballerina.

The comparative form
Prunilla did her work *more carefully* than Maria [did]. (Maria did her work *less carefully* than Prunilla did.)

The superlative form
Toni sang *the most beautifully* of all. (Terry sang *the least unpleasantly* of the group.)

EXERCISE 6   Comparing Adverbs

COLLABORATIVE ACTIVITY 3

Divide a sheet of paper into three columns. Then, with a classmate, list as many adverbs in the first column as you can think of. Try for twenty. Next to each adverb on your list, write the comparative form. In the third column, write the superlative form.

Supply the correct comparative or superlative form of the adverb in parentheses.

1. With more than 160 biographies published about him, William Shakespeare has been written about (extensively) *more extensively* than any other person.

2. Calamity Jane, with twelve husbands, was at the altar (frequently) _____ than Pancho Villa, with nine wives.

3. In the United States, the name Johnson appears (commonly) _____ than the name Jones.

4. People have bought the Bible (faithfully) _____ than they have bought any other book.

5. According to the FBI, a murder is (likely) _____ to happen between 6:00 P.M. and 6:00 A.M. than during the working hours of the day.

IRREGULAR ADJECTIVES AND ADVERBS

So far, you've seen the regular, comparative, and superlative forms of adjectives and adverbs—the forms that follow consistent rules. But several adjectives and adverbs don't follow these rules; they have irregular forms.

Adjectives and Adverbs That Are the Same

A few words can serve as both adjectives and adverbs. Here is a partial list:

early   hard   low   fast   late   straight

> The *early* bird arrives *early.*
> *Fast* Eddie runs really *fast.*

The comparative and superlative forms of these words are the same whether you use them as adjectives or adverbs:

Simple	Comparative	Superlative
early	earlier	(the) earliest
fast	faster	(the) fastest
hard	harder	(the) hardest

Note how they function as adjectives or adverbs:

>   adverb
> The first train *came earlier* than I thought, so I missed it and had to take *a*
>
> adjective
> *later train.*
>
> adjective
> My little brother is *the slowest eater I've ever seen.* Everyone *finishes dinner*
>
>   adverb
> *much faster* than he does.

Good and *Well, Bad* and *Badly*

Good is an adjective, and *well* is an adverb (or an adjective when it means "in good health").

Adjectives	Adverbs
Freddie did a *good* job.	Freddie did the job *well.*
The motor is in *good* shape.	The car runs *well.*
I feel *well.*	

However, the comparative and superlative forms of *good* and *well* are the same:

Simple	Comparative	Superlative
good	better	(the) best
well	better	(the) best

(adjectives) The salad is *good.* The soup is *better.* But the dessert is *the best* of all.

(adverbs) Juan sings *well.* Lourdes sings *better.* But Sixta sings *the best* of the three.

Likewise, *bad* is an adjective and *badly* is an adverb:

Adjectives	Adverbs
Frederico Falsini is a *bad* actor.	Frederico Falsini performs *badly*.
Toni felt *bad* about losing his teeth.	Toni took a *badly* needed vacation.

Bad and *badly* also share identical comparative and superlative forms:

Simple	Comparative	Superlative
bad	worse	(the) worst
badly	worse	(the) worst

(adjectives) The soup is *bad*. The salad tastes *worse*. And the fish tastes *the worst* of all.

(adverbs) Tom sings *badly*. His brother sings *worse*. But their father sings *the worst* of anyone in the whole family.

EXERCISE 7   Writing *Good/Well* and *Bad/Badly*

Circle the correct adjective or adverb in parentheses in the left-hand column. Then supply the correct comparative or superlative form of that word in the right-hand column.

1. Susan swims (good/well).

1. But Maria swims ___better___.

2. His painting looks (good/well).

2. But Renoir's painting looks _____ of all.

3. Nobody does it half as (good/well) as you.

3. Nobody does it _____.

4. I have seen some (good/well)-trained dogs.

4. But Prince is _____ -trained dog that I have ever seen.

5. The light in this room is (bad/badly).

5. In fact, of the light in all the rooms, it is _____.

6. The old schoolhouse looks (bad/badly).

6. But it looks _____ than it actually is.

7. He fell and broke his arm (bad/badly).

7. It was _____ -looking break that the doctor had seen in years.

LIVELY COMPARISONS

 **COLLABORATIVE ACTIVITY 4**

Using Adverbs as Similes
Return to the sentences you completed in Exercise 1 in Chapter 13. Rewrite them so that each contains a simile, such as, "The train moves as slowly as an elephant in mud." Then with others, brainstorm ways to make the sentences even more lively or humorous. Compile a list of the best ones and share them with the class.

Comparisons with adjectives and adverbs can enliven your writing, especially if you employ them creatively in similes. A **simile,** a common poetic device, is a comparison using *like* or *as*. Here are several examples with *as . . . as:*

> Otto is *as strong as a bull on steroids.*
> Albert eats *as sloppily as a hog in a barrel of mush.*
> At 3:00 A.M., Zeke sneaked into his room *as quietly as a cat in slippers.*

And here are a few similes with *like:*

> Otto walks *like a bull.*
> Albert eats *like a hog.*
> Zeke sneaked into his room *like a cat in slippers.*

IN SUMMARY   ## To Make Comparisons

With regular adjectives
1. Between equals (simple form): use *as (adjective) as.*
2. Between two unequal adjectives (comparative forms):
   a. Add *–er* to short adjectives and place *more* (or *less*) before long adjectives.
   b. Follow the adjective with *than* (not *then*).
3. Among three or more unequals (superlative forms):
   a. Add *–est* to short adjectives or place *most* (or *least*) before long adjectives.
   b. (Usually) place *the* before superlatives.

With regular adverbs
1. Between equals (simple form): use *as (adverb) as.*
2. Between unequals (comparative form): place *more* (or *less*) before the adverb and follow the adverb with *than.*
3. Among three or more unequals (superlative form): place *(the) most* (or *least*) before the adverb.

With irregular adjectives and adverbs
1. For *good/well:* use *better, (the) best.*
2. For *bad/badly:* use *worse, (the) worst.*

EDITING FOR MASTERY

Mastery Exercise 1   ***Correcting Adjective and Adverb Errors***

The following passage contains ten errors in the use of adjectives and adverbs, aside from the first error, which has been corrected for you.

The Passenger Pigeon's Rise and Fall

(1) One of the ^~~most sadest~~ *saddest* stories of modern times is the story of the extinction of the passenger pigeon in North America. (2) Never have so many animals disappeared so quick. (3) The story is filled with incredible statistics and eyewitness accounts that are even more harder to believe.

(4) Very few birds were as attractive and graceful as the passenger pigeon, with its light blue feathers and pink breast. (5) However, its greatest claim to fame was the giant size of its populations; there might have been more passenger pigeons than any other bird in history.

(6) The numbers are amazing. (7) One expert on birds watched for two days as one 150-mile-long flock passed over his home. (8) The famous naturalist John James Audubon said 300 million birds blotted out the sun for three days as they flew overhead. (9) Another flock of perhaps 2 billion birds caused a completer solar eclipse than the moon could achieve. (10) A single rifle shot into a flock could supposedly kill at least 200 birds.

(11) For centuries the passenger pigeon lived happy and created no problems to humans. (12) In fact, the bird saved the Pilgrims from starvation when a terrible winter hurt their crops bad in 1648. (13) And the bird became one of the mostest important parts of the diet of the settlers. (14) The pigeon tasted about the same like chicken but was a little more tough.

(15) During the 1700s and early 1800s, hunters found clever ways of killing the birds. (16) One method involved waiting until a flock of pigeons roosted in tree branches for the night. (17) The men set the grass on fire, and its dense smoke suffocated the pigeons. (18) Another device that worked good was to attract the birds through a decoy—a live passenger pigeon whose eyes had been sewn shut. (19) When it was placed on a perch called a stool, the bird called very loud and attracted an enormous flock, which the hunters then shot. (20) The term *stool pigeon*—for one person who sets up another—comes from this practice.

Scorecard: Number of errors found and corrected _____

<table>
<tr><td>

COLLABORATIVE ACTIVITY 5

Comparing Your Answers
Have someone read the passage aloud to help you hear errors. Make your corrections, discuss them, and report your findings to the class.

</td></tr>
</table>

Mastery Exercise 2

Correcting Adjective and Adverb Errors

The following passage contains ten errors in the use of adjectives and adverbs, aside from the first error, which has been corrected for you. Make your corrections above the line.

The Extinction of the Passenger Pigeon

(1) The ^~~mostest~~ *most* remarkable part of the disappearance of the passenger pigeon was how it happened. (2) A number of factors caused the extinction. (3) As the human population grew more large, the people cut down forests of trees and shrunk the pigeons'

food supply. (4) The railroad brought hunters to the West, and they killed the birds and sent them back east. (5) Passenger pigeons also became live targets in shooting galleries at city and county fairs. (6) By the 1880s, the baddest damage had been done. (7) There were no more passenger pigeons on either coast and only a few flocks in other places.

(8) The passenger pigeon's most big flock was in Michigan, where the lastest great pigeon hunt took place in 1878. (9) Hundreds of people began shooting as many as a billion pigeons in an area about five miles long by a mile wide. (10) Some pigeons flew away but then returned to the same trees, where the hunters killed them easy. (11) It took the hunters thirty days to wipe out the entire pigeon population. (12) Every day, they packed the birds into five railroad cars for shipment to Boston and New York.

(13) Although the hunters did their job good, the passenger pigeon was not yet extinct—but it was getting there quick. (14) On the morning of March 24, 1900, a teenager in Ohio shot the last passenger pigeon in that state. (15) Maine reported that its only remaining bird was shot by a hunter in 1904. (16) Arkansas recorded the end of the species in 1906.

(17) The pigeons that a hundred years more early had represented about 35 percent of birds in the United States were now reduced to a total of three, all in the Cincinnati Zoo. (18) When two of the birds in the zoo died, a pigeon named Martha was the only one left. (19) Martha lived to be real old—twenty-nine years—but died on September 1, 1914. (20) Its body was sent to the Smithsonian Institution in Washington, D.C., where it was stuffed and mounted. (21) It can be viewed today in the Smithsonian's collection of the most rarest birds.

Scorecard: Number of errors found and corrected _____

CHAPTER 15

Being Consistent

> As you read, you are annoyed if the writer confuses us.

Did that sentence seem confusing? It should have, for it contained an inconsistency. Here is the same sentence with the problem corrected:

> As you read, you are annoyed if the writer confuses you.

At best, inconsistencies are annoying; at worst, they're unclear and frustrating. But in either case you should edit to eliminate them. This chapter helps you correct inconsistencies

- in pronouns
- in verb tense
- in structures that build sentences

KEEPING PRONOUNS STRAIGHT

Consistency in **person** (first, second, or third) and in **number** (singular or plural) helps make writing clear and coherent. For example, here are the subject pronouns:

	Singular	Plural
First Person	I	we
Second Person	you	you
Third Person	he, she, it	they

As you edit, look for accidental shifts in person and number. A common shift is from first person *(I, we)* or third person *(he, she, it, or they)* to second person *(you)*. For example:

> *I* go to Sam's Sanitary Sandwich Shop because *you* always get a good meal there.

The sentence may be slightly confusing because it talks about two people: *I* and *you*. It should be revised:

> *I* go to Sam's Sanitary Sandwich Shop because *I* always get a good meal there.

This next sentence is not only confusing but unintentionally funny:

> There is such a wide selection of dresses at Wendy's Fashion Farm that *anyone* can find one that looks good on *you*.

Male readers will certainly appreciate the advice! The sentence should be revised:

> There is such a wide selection of dresses at Wendy's Fashion Farm that *any woman* can find one that looks good on *her*.

Here's another muddled sentence:

> *Any student* can make the dean's list if *they* study hard.

The subject shifts from singular (*any* is grammatically singular) to plural (*they*), *perhaps* to avoid the sexual bias problem, discussed in Chapter 12:

> Any student can make the dean's list if *he* studies hard.

This sentence, while technically correct, seems to ignore women. But what alternatives are available? One is to rewrite the sentence with plurals:

> *All students* can make the dean's list if *they* study hard.

A second alternative is to rewrite the sentence with both singular pronouns. And a third alternative is to use the female pronoun—and gently work against the male bias in language:

> *Any student* can make the dean's list if *he or she* studies hard.
> *Any student* can make the dean's list if *she* studies hard.

To be clear, be consistent. Choose the pronoun that makes the most sense in the writing—for example, *we*, *you*, or *everyone*—and stick with it throughout your paper, unless you have a logical reason to switch.

EXERCISE 1   Establishing Consistency in Person and Number

Replace the underlined word with the correct pronoun that maintains consistency. When you must use a third-person-singular pronoun, use a female pronoun, she *or* her.

Beyond Our Wildest Dreams

1. We spend nearly one-third of our lives sleeping, and now scientists are beginning to understand what happens when you (*we*) sleep.

2. A sleeping person's brain waves often increase in strength and speed, and with the increase, their (_____) eyes begin to move quickly behind the eyelids.

3. Our *rapid eye movement*, or *REM*, occurs about every ninety minutes and indicates that you (_____) are dreaming.

COLLABORATIVE ACTIVITY I

Rewriting Sentences

Write one sentence for each of the following subjects: *everyone, you,* and *people.* Refer back to the subject with an appropriate pronoun. Exchange papers. Correct errors in consistency if you find any. Then rewrite each sentence, changing its number or person. Exchange papers again and check for errors.

4. Experiments have shown that dreaming is important to mental health. If someone is awakened during REM, <u>they</u> (_____) will be short tempered the next morning.

5. But when the same person goes to sleep the following night, <u>their</u> (_____) dream activity will greatly increase.

6. If you take sleeping pills regularly, <u>it</u> (_____) may do more harm than good, for after a month or so, <u>our</u> (_____) REM activity will decrease and make <u>someone</u> (_____) irritable.

EXERCISE 2   Revising Sentences

Each of the following groups of sentences contains a shift in person. Cross out the inappropriate pronoun(s), and write in the appropriate one(s) above the line. Or, if necessary, rewrite the entire sentence.

1. I find psychology class fascinating. ^*I* ~~You~~ learn so much about ^*myself* ~~yourself~~.

2. I like to go to Frank's Finest Food Farm because you always find great bargains there.

3. People who like good food should try the Friendly Café. They serve great burgers and fries.

4. Everyone needs to learn to write if they want to enter a profession.

5. A person who wants to enjoy themselves should go to the new Sixteen Flags Over the Grand Canyon. They have the best and scariest rides.

6. One should be cautioned against trying to write in a formal style if you are unsure how to do so.

EXERCISE 3   Rewriting Sentences

Complete each of the following sentences, maintaining the same person and number. If the subject is third-person singular, use either the female pronoun (she, her) *or a combination of both male and female:* he or she, him or her, his or her.

1. When a teenager is at a party with people using drugs, *he or she will have to work hard to resist the peer pressure to try them.*

2. Every student should_____

   _____

3. Someone who wants to get a good job_____

   _____

4. The average billionaire_____

   _____

5. Most homeowners _____

_____

6. One should maintain consistency in a sentence or _____

_____

KEEPING TENSE CONSISTENT

TIPS

For Keeping Verb Tenses Straight

If you tend to omit verb tense endings or have trouble with consistency of tense, try this as you edit your work: Place a ruler under each line in your paper to focus your eyes on the verbs, underline each verb, and check the verbs for consistency.

Early in the writing process, you may accidentally shift from one tense to another—especially when you discuss literature, movies, or plays:

> The movie *Scream 16* **begins** just like the other ones, with actress Never Soupcan having to protect herself from a mad slasher. He **threatens** to attack her time after time. But as in the previous movies, Never **escaped** unharmed.

This passage begins in the present tense but ends in the past tense, a logical tense for storytelling, but not in this context. Here are some other examples of tense inconsistencies:

> I *was* positive that I *will* get an A. (This past-tense sentence should use *would*—the past tense of *will*.)
>
> Every day my mother *came* home and *would cook* dinner. (This past-tense sentence should use *cooked*.)

Look carefully at your verbs as you edit. Are their tenses consistent? If you've shifted tense, have you done so logically? And if you're not sure of the correct verb form, look it up in your dictionary or consult Chapter 12 of this book.

EXERCISE 4   Transforming Tenses

Change the following sentences from present to past action or from past to present action.

COLLABORATIVE ACTIVITY 2

Writing More Sentences

Working in pairs, compose a second sentence for each completed sentence in Exercise 4 that follows up on its idea. Write in the appropriate tense. Then examine and discuss the sentences.

Present time

1. He *can*_____ answer you.

2. It _____ fine.

3. He is supposed to come.

4. I _____ been there before.

5. I think it is all right.

6. I wonder if he will come to

work later.

7. I know they can do it.

Past time

1. He _____ answer you.

2. It seemed fine.

3. He _____ supposed to come.

4. I had been there before.

5. I _____ it _____ all right.

6. I _____ if he _____

come to work later.

7. I _____ they _____ do it.

EXERCISE 5   Writing in Consistent Verb Tenses

Complete each of the following sentences, using verbs in logically appropriate tenses.

1. When I was five years old, *I could ride a bicycle without training wheels.*

2. Every day when I do my homework, _____

_____

3. I told you that _____

_____

4. Willie smiled as _____

_____

5. You'll receive an award when _____

_____

6. You'd better be careful or _____

_____

EXERCISE 6   Editing for Consistent Verb Tense

The following passage contains eight illogical shifts in tense, excluding the first error, which has been corrected for you. Correct these errors above the lines.

If Your First Language Is Not English

1. Some languages don't use past-tense forms of *can, will,* and *is/are*—especially languages spoken in the Philippines and in parts of Africa. As a reminder, here are the forms:

   Present tense: **am, are, is; can; will**

   Past tense: **was, were; could; would**

2. Also, many Asian languages do not indicate time through verb tense, but only through adverbs. So someone might mistakenly write, "I am sick yesterday" instead of "I was sick yesterday."

Alexandra David-Neel (1868–1969): Explorer, Writer, and Adventurer

(1) Alexandra David, who was born in Paris in 1868, dreamed of traveling to faraway places, and she soon ^*left* ~~leaves~~ home as a young person to explore the world. (2) Although only five feet tall, Alexandra is physically tough and completely independent. (3) She traveled to Vietnam, Greece, and North Africa as an opera star, but she will eventually become a journalist to support herself. (4) However, she always kept in mind her goal of exploring Central Asia.

(5) In 1904, Alexandra married her distant cousin Philippe-Francois Neel. (6) Alexandra said that marriage and motherhood are threatening to her independence, so she never had children and didn't live with her husband. (7) But the couple always claimed to love one another, and Philippe Neel gave his wife money so she can explore Tibet without him for fourteen years.

(8) Alexandra became a Buddhist in 1911 and was the first European woman to meet privately with the spiritual ruler of Tibet, the Dalai Lama. (9) Afterward, Alexandra would become fluent in the Tibetan language. (10) A fifteen-year-old boy named Yongden aids her on many journeys through northern India, China, and Tibet. (11) He remained with her until he had died in France in 1955.

(12) Because Alexandra wanted passionately to learn more about the Tibetan way of life, she decides to undergo training as a Buddhist priest. (13) For two years, she lived as a hermit in a cave on top of a 13,000-foot mountain. (14) She loved the hardships of cold, hunger, and isolation. (15) The holy men of Tibet blessed her after she emerged from the cave in 1916.

KEEPING STRUCTURES PARALLEL

The following sentences will probably make you stop and puzzle for a moment:

> The movie star Barry Biceps is 6 feet 4 inches tall, weight 220 pounds, and piercing brown eyes.
> They loved telling stories, to dance, and sang.

The sentences wobble as if they have lost their balance. In fact, they are unbalanced; they join similar ideas but use different grammatical structures. The sentences would be clearer if they repeated the same structures:

> The movie star Barry Biceps is 6 feet 4 inches tall, *weighs* 220 pounds, and *has* piercing brown eyes. (three present-tense verbs)
> They loved *telling* stories, *dancing*, and *singing*. (three *–ing* words)

This repetition of grammatical structures is called **parallel construction,** or **parallelism.** You can use it to balance subjects with subjects, verbs with verbs, phrases with phrases, clauses with clauses—or any other grammatical structures. Notice how parallelism establishes clarity in the following sentences:

> We could have *gone* and *seen* it. (two past participles following *could have*)
> "It is true that you may *fool all the people some of the time; you can even fool some of the people all of the time; but you can't fool all of the people all of the time.*" (Abraham Lincoln)

EXERCISE 7   Identifying Parallel Structures

Underline the structure that is different from the others in each group.

1. shifting gears
avoid the accident
keeping control
swerving to the left

2. cooperation
admiring
teamwork
reliability

3. smart
clever
a good student
popular

4. works by night
plays by dawn
eats junk food
sleeps by day

5. exhausted

swollen feet

aching muscles

sore back

6. made by hand

decorated with ribbon

embroidered in red

an odd color

7. gone there

done it

ran back

been finished

EXERCISE 8   Using Parallel Structures

COLLABORATIVE ACTIVITY 3

Examining Parallelism
Compare the responses you prepared in Exercise 8. List the best ones and present them to the class.

Choose four groups of parallel phrases from Exercise 7 and write a sentence for each group. Be sure to keep all the phrases in a group parallel.

1. As the car began to skid, Ralph was able to avoid a collision by shifting gears, keeping control, and swerving to the left.

2. _____

_____

3. _____

_____

4. _____

_____

5. _____

_____

EXERCISE 9   Writing Parallel Structures

Complete each of the following sentences by maintaining the pattern it establishes.

1. The kids talked about hiking, sailing, and swimming. _____

2. She was spoiled by her mother, bored by school, and _____

_____

3. You could have called me, written me, or _____

_____

4. The movie has no story, only scenes. It has no believable characters, only _____

_____

5. We have been working hard, paying attention, and_____

_____

6. The food was too ordinary, the portions too small, the price_____

_____

EXERCISE 10   Editing for Parallel Structures

Each of the following contains an error in parallelism. Underline the section with the error and then rewrite it to make it parallel.

The Further Adventures of Alexandra David-Neel

1. Alexandra David-Neel set her sights on another accomplishment: <u>to journey through China,</u> climbing the Himalaya Mountains, and reaching the forbidden Tibetan city of Lhasa, which had never before been seen by a white woman.
   Rewritten: ,journeying through China_____

2. Over the next year, Alexandra and her companion, Yongden, traveled in disguise as a Tibetan peasant woman and his disguise was her Buddhist monk son.
   Rewritten: _____

3. They would have been killed if they were discovered. But they were saved time and again by Alexandra's complete knowledge of the Tibetan people, their language, and also the customs they had.
   Rewritten: _____

4. Along the way, they also faced deep piles of snow, bitter cold, and they had to deal with mountains 20,000 feet high.
   Rewritten: _____

5. Once, after struggling for nineteen hours along a snow-covered mountain pass, Yongden could not light a fire. He realized that they could not live through the night and calling on Alexandra to try an ancient Buddhist art of creating internal warmth through will power.
   Rewritten: _____

6. Alexandra refused to worry about warming herself, concentrated on drying out the materials, and a fire was started by her before Yongden had returned from his search for more wood.
   Rewritten: _____

7. After they finally reached Lhasa in 1923—Alexandra was fifty-five years old—the two remained in their disguises and undetected.
   Rewritten: _____

8. Several months later, she and Yongden journeyed first to India and then returning to Europe, where she stayed for the next ten years.

   Rewritten: _____

9. In the mid-1930s, her urge to travel made her return to Tibet and lived there until she had to flee on foot when the Japanese invaded in 1944. She was seventy-six years old.

   Rewritten: _____

10. Alexandra David-Neel then spent the rest of her life in France as a writer and famous. She died in 1969, just seven weeks shy of her 101st birthday.

    Rewritten: _____

IN SUMMARY	To Maintain Consistency

1. Check your pronouns—don't shift person or number illogically.
2. Check your verbs—don't shift tense illogically.
3. Check items in a series—don't lose parallelism.

EDITING FOR MASTERY

Mastery Exercise 1

Editing for Consistency

The following passage contains twelve errors in parallelism, shifts in person, and shifts in tense—aside from the first error, which has been corrected as an example.

The Eruption of Mount Vesuvius

(1) August 24, A.D. 79, began like any other day in the resort town of Pompeii, Italy: people opened their window shutters, shopkeepers ^got ~~would get~~ ready for business, and the townspeople discussed the upcoming elections. (2) However, at 1:00 P.M., you could hear a mighty roar and then a big explosion. (3) The volcano Mount Vesuvius is awakening from 1,500 years of sleep. (4) A black cloud rose to cover the sky and blotting out the sun. (5) Melted rock shot from the volcano's mouth, cooled quickly in the air, and then it would fall back into the volcano. (6) The volcano exploded a second time and raining stones all over the mountainside.

(7) A few people ran from the city, reached the sea, and had escaped in their boats. (8) He or she lived to tell about the disaster. (9) However, most people tried to find safety in their homes, temples, or they went to the public baths. (10) These people weren't as lucky as those who left by sea. (11) They died as hot stones piled on roofs, collapsed

COLLABORATIVE ACTIVITY 4

Comparing Answers
Compare your corrections with others and report the results to the class.

some roofs, and setting others on fire. (12) Poison gases killed many people, while thirty to fifty feet of volcanic ash buried the city, and the rest were suffocated.

(13) Within 24 hours, 30,000 people were dead. (14) Their bodies and homes will be preserved in the ash for almost 1,700 years. (15) At that point the city was excavated, and you could visit the city near the sleeping killer volcano.

Scorecard: Number of errors found and corrected _____

Mastery Exercise 2

Editing for Consistency

The following passage contains twelve errors in parallelism, shifts in person, and shifts in tense—aside from the first error, which has been corrected as an example. Correct these errors above the lines.

The Explosion of Krakatoa

(1) In 1883, a small, uninhabited island called Krakatoa was the scene of the most destructive volcano eruption in history. (2) Three volcanoes on the island ^had have slept for half a million years, but, early in the year, they showed signs of life. (3) People all around the world can hear the sound of the explosion.

(4) The first warning of the disaster occurred at 10:55 A.M. on Sunday, May 20, 1883. (5) A German ship sailed close to the island and its captain saw a large black cloud above it. (6) The cloud sent out flashes of lightning, exploding, and ash showers also came out of it. (7) It appeared again in June and July. (8) On Sunday, August 26, the three volcanoes blew their tops. (9) Black clouds shot seven miles into the sky. (10) Then, the ash from the volcanoes blacked out a 150-square-mile area and had turned day into night. (11) You would not see anything for the next three days. (12) The sea turned violent, dark, and it was frightening. (13) It rose and was falling in huge waves. (14) At 7:55 P.M., a violent earthquake shook the whole area, and rain and lightning were everywhere. (15) By midnight, the beaches of the other islands are buried in huge waves. (16) At 1:00 A.M., an entire village was washed away, and the waves almost reaching people on top of a 125-foot hill. (17) The next morning, a wave would pick up a ship at sea, carried it more than a mile inland, and killed all of the crew. (18) Still the eruptions continued, the earth would shake, and the waves took more lives. (19) Finally, at 10:02, three-quarters of Krakatoa disappeared into the sea.

(20) The explosion created winds that circled the globe seven times. (21) A wall of water flooded beaches, buried villages, and knocking down hilltops. (22) Gigantic tidal waves traveled as far south as the bottom of Africa and to the English Channel. (23) At least 36,417 people on nearby islands died, while 165 villages were completely destroyed and many more villages were badly damaged.

Scorecard: Number of errors found and corrected _____

CHAPTER 16

Writing Concretely and Concisely

Your writing should be direct and concise, putting each word to work. It should be specific, concrete, and lively. You should speak to readers in a strong voice, and you can add strength to your voice during revising and editing. This chapter looks at ways to strengthen your voice through

■ choosing strong verbs and adjectives

■ eliminating unnecessary words and meaningless expressions

CHOOSING WORDS THAT WORK

If Your First Language Is Not English

In most languages, only one verb expresses the different meanings of the English verbs *do* and *make*.

• **Make** means to create something in the physical world, in our imagination, or in our minds: make a dress, make a cake, make a decision

• **Do** means *to perform an action or a job:* do homework, do (wash) the laundry, do (the work on) a paper

Therefore: A teacher makes an assignment; the students do it.

We make the dishes dirty when we eat; then we do (clean) them.

Don't be content to limp along on flabby word choice after your first draft. Put a little muscle into your verbs and adjectives. We'll show you how.

Strong Verbs

Look carefully at **verbs**—the words that carry the action. Are they strong and lively? Commonly used (and overused) verbs such as *is/are/am, go, get, have, make, do, run, put, take, see, use,* and *talk* are weak, vague, lifeless. The verb *take,* for example, can express countless meanings:

> take medicine, or a powder
> take a nap, a walk, a shower, or a vacation
> take up, down, off, in, on, over, from, to, away, or back
> take your time, your pick, or your punishment

But let's take a break from these examples!

Obviously, you can't eliminate all common verbs, but don't overuse them. Replace them with more precise, interesting verbs whenever you can.

To strengthen your verbs:

• circle common and repeated verbs

• consider replacing them with less common verbs that more precisely express your meaning.

Original	Revision	
Black Bart *took* the money.	Black Bart	*accepted* *snatched* *ran off with* the money.

Look especially at the verb *have*. Does it simply express possession? If so, perhaps you can replace it with a **possessive** such as *my, his, her, their, our, your,* or *Ralph's.* You may then be able to combine the ideas from two sentences into a single sentence.

To eliminate unnecessary uses of *have:*

- circle *have, has,* or *had* when these words express possession
- substitute a possessive word if possible, and combine ideas

Original	Revision
I *have* an old car. It barely runs anymore.	*My old car* barely runs anymore.

EXERCISE 1   Choosing Strong Verbs

Replace each of the following common verbs with a strong and vivid verb. (Notice, incidentally, that you are replacing two words with one.)

1. get on <u>board</u>

2. get in _____

3. get on _____

4. get better _____

5. get out _____

6. give up _____

7. do again _____

8. get back _____

9. come back _____

EXERCISE 2   Finding Alternative Verbs

Write three or more different verbs or phrases that express each idea in parentheses, but don't rely on common verbs.

1. (fast movement) The big cat <u>shot, darted, raced, tore, scooted</u> into the room.

2. (talk angrily) The woman _____ at the

   salesperson.

3. (build) The workers _____ a garage in just a few hours.

4. (slow movement) The sheriff _____ through

   the saloon, staring at each man at the poker tables.

5. (remove) The man in the dark suit _____ the

   wallet from the shopper's backpack.

6. (give) Waldo _____ the stinking fish to (or at)

   the waiter.

EXERCISE 3   Revising Sentences

COLLABORATIVE
ACTIVITY I

Comparing Changes
Compare and discuss your
revisions to the sentences
in Exercises 1, 2, and 3, and
report your results to the
class.

Streamline each of the following sentences (if there are two, combine them) by eliminating the verb have.

1. I have a French poodle. She thinks she is queen of the house. *My French poodle thinks she is queen of the house.*

2. The university has natural science courses that are really interesting._____

3. I have a friend. He can balance spoons on his nose. _____

4. That dog has fleas. They are bigger than grapes. _____

5. I have a car. It belongs in the museum of ancient, worthless machines. _____

6. When I wake up in the morning, I have hair that looks as if it were caught in a tornado. _____

EXERCISE 4   Eliminating Common Verbs

COLLABORATIVE
ACTIVITY 2

Comparing Changes
Compare and discuss your
revisions in Exercise 4. Make
a list of the best ones and
report your results to the
class.

The following passage relies too much on the verbs do *and* get. *Rewrite it, supplying more exact and vivid verbs and making any other changes that will strengthen the passage. (Don't be afraid to rewrite a sentence completely.)*

When I get home from school each day, I have a lot of chores to do. I do the laundry and the housecleaning, I do the dishes from breakfast and lunch, and I get dinner ready for my family. We eat dinner at around 5:30, and after we get finished, I do the dishes again. I usually don't get any help from my children or spouse, so I have to do everything myself. I get the kids into bed around 9:00, which is when I can do my homework. I do my math assignments first because I can do problems while the TV is on. Then I do the rest of the assignments I've got for the next day. I usually get to bed around midnight so that I can get up at 6:00 the next morning.

Vivid Adjectives and Details

Examine your **adjectives** as you revise. If you find flat, imprecise, and too common adjectives such as *good, bad, nice, great, different,* or *happy,* consider replacing them. Think of more lively adjectives that more precisely express your meaning.

To strengthen your adjectives:

- circle overused and imprecise adjectives
- substitute more lively words or phrases
- or completely rewrite the sentence using more specific detail

Original	Revision	
The Stephen King novel was *very interesting*.	The Stephen King novel was	$\begin{cases} riveting. \\ fascinating. \\ terrifying. \end{cases}$

(*Or:* Some especially frightening parts of the Stephen King novel made the hair on my arms curl.)

EXERCISE 5   Choosing Fresh Adjectives

Circle the adjective in each of the following sentences and replace it with a more precise, animated word. Or, if you wish, rewrite the sentence to include much more specific detail. The first item contains four examples.

1. The view of the Grand Canyon is ^pretty. *breathtaking (astonishing, magnificent)* The jagged walls, deep and varied colors, and incredible size of the Grand Canyon create an overwhelmingly beautiful sight.

2. The movie *Die Hard 15* was interesting. _____

_____

3. Martin Luther King was a good leader. _____

_____

4. The tree is big. _____

_____

5. The afternoon talk shows on television are dumb. _____

_____

6. The dinner at Chez French Fry was nice. _____

_____

DISCARDING WORDS THAT DON'T CONTRIBUTE

Wordiness is easy to spot. Compare these sentences:

1. In the modern-day world of today, there are many important problems that concern each and every one of us, and one of the most important of these problems is the problem concerning the danger of biological and chemical warfare.
2. Everyone fears biological and chemical warfare.

You probably prefer the second sentence, which states its point in just six words. The first sentence, all forty words of it, is bloated with repetition. Let's examine it further:

1. In the modern-day world of today . . . (Isn't *today* a day, and isn't it modern? Why mention *the world* unless we expect a discussion of the moon instead?)
2. there are many important problems that concern each and every one of us . . . (Don't we know that? And what is the difference between *each* and *every*?)

In short, sentence 1 is filled with *deadwood:* lifeless and useless language. Don't worry about such language as you compose your first draft. But as you revise, try to prune the deadwood.

In fact, revising your sentences at this stage can be fun. You've already done the hard work of capturing your ideas in words. Now you can take pleasure in shaping those ideas more gracefully and powerfully.

Empty Sentence Starters

There is and *there are* often are merely sentence starters: empty words that add bulk without meaning. Eliminate these empty sentence starters by turning statements around. If the result is awkward, try another way to express your idea.

To eliminate *there is/are* (or *was/were, will be,* etc.):

- circle these expressions
- delete them from the sentence
- if possible, begin the sentence with the last words of the original

Original	Revision
1. <u>There are</u> two important facts that you must know.	You must know two important facts.
2. <u>There is</u> a man at the next table who is eating a sandwich with green meat.	A man at the next table is eating a sandwich with green meat.

EXERCISE 6   Cutting Empty Sentence Starters

Rewrite each of the following sentences, eliminating there is or there are.

1. There are three important rules that everyone should follow. <u>Everyone should follow</u> <u>three important rules.</u>

2. There was a man at the party who was wearing a purple hat. _____

_____

3. There were fourteen girls, fifteen guys, and a large turtle packed into my minivan.

_____

4. There are many people in the United States who were born in other countries.

_____

5. There will be a new musical that is opening on Broadway this month. _____

_____

6. There is one more sentence that ends this exercise. _____

_____

Vague Expressions

Vague, general words and expressions such as *things, ways, stuff, type of, methods,* and *factors* often add very little meaning to a statement.
To replace these expressions:

• find and circle them
• express the same ideas through more specific details or information

Original	Revision
Everybody likes Susan because of *all the funny things she does.*	Susan makes everyone laugh when she says, "This test will be no problem," and then fakes a heart attack.

EXERCISE 7   Increasing Clarity and Liveliness

Rewrite each of the following sentences in more vivid and exact language.

1. Tom's behavior is annoying. <u>When Tom borrows my clothes and returns them dirty,</u>
<u>eats half a gallon of ice cream from my freezer without asking, or calls me at</u>
<u>2:00 A.M. to find out the next day's homework assignment, I seriously consider</u>
<u>turning him over to the proper authorities for prosecution and imprisonment.</u>

2. What the acrobat did was interesting. _____

_____

_____

3. Pedro has a nice personality. _____

_____

_____

4. My friend sometimes does odd things. _____

_____

_____

5. The dog acts really silly. _____

_____

_____

6. The rock concert was great. _____

_____

_____

Repetition

A word or sound accidentally repeated, even in a different form or with a different meaning, can be annoying, confusing, or dull.

To avoid weak repetition:

- read your work aloud, listening for words or sounds accidentally repeated
- circle repeated words or sounds, including those used in different forms or with different meanings
- rewrite the passage, substituting for or eliminating the weak repetition

Original	Revision
Ball State *University* is a *university* that provides a complete program of undergraduate and graduate study.	Ball State University provides a complete program of undergraduate and graduate study.
He had a *reasonably* good *reason* to be absent.	His absence was justifiable.
I just read a fascinating *book*. The *book* was about the U.S. space program.	I just read a fascinating book about the U.S. space program.

Not all repetition is weak, however. Sometimes writers intentionally repeat words or sounds to build to a climax or tie ideas together:

[Climax] Each day Brian *studies* the sports section, *studies* the movie listings, and occasionally even *studies* his assignments.

[Coherence] We waited for an explanation, an excuse, or any kind of answer, but *no answer* ever came.

✓ **TIPS**

For Testing Repetition

A simple way to distinguish between weak and strong repetition is the "oops and ah" test. If, when reading a repeated word or idea you react with "Oops, I didn't mean that," the repetition is weak. If you react with "Ah, that sounds good," feel proud of yourself!

EXERCISE 8   Cutting Repetition

Rewrite each of the following sentences to eliminate unnecessary repetition. In some cases you may combine sentences.

1. Some of the algebra problems gave me problems. *Some of the algebra problems were difficult.*

2. Our new house is a beautiful house. _____

_____

3. Bus fare is fairly high in this city. _____

_____

4. Jill's teacher is not like my teacher. My teacher is very understanding. _____

_____

5. Stretch Everest, the center on our basketball team, is always the center of attention

when he comes on the floor. _____

_____

6. I always read the directions on an examination first. After I read the directions, I know

exactly what is expected of me. _____

_____

_____

Wordiness

Good writing is clear, simple, and direct. Why say in ten words what you can say in four or five? Moreover, bad writing is not only tiresome but may needlessly explain what is already implied. Why state, "My mother is a woman who" unless we have reason to believe your mother is a man? Even the best writers create wordy early drafts, so tighten your language as you revise and edit.

To tighten your sentences:

- circle words whose meanings are already included in other words
- circle vague words and expressions such as *thing, type of, kind of, way, area,* and *method*
- eliminate these unnecessary words
- or rewrite a statement to express its idea more directly

Original	Revision
1. *As far as looks are concerned*, Maria is very pretty.	Maria is beautiful.
2. I can't talk to you *at this point in time*.	I can't talk to you now.
3. He *has the ability to* swim.	He can swim.
4. She shouted at him *in a very loud voice.*	She screamed at him.
5. Calculus *is a branch of mathematics that presents different types of challenges* to students.	Calculus challenges many students.
6. *The reason why* hip hop music is so popular *is because* it appeals to the rebel in all of us.	Hip hop music appeals to the rebel in all of us.

EXERCISE 9   Tightening Sentences

Rewrite and tighten each of the following sentences.

1. The pie had an unusual taste to it. *The pie tasted unusual.* _____

2. Celia Gonzalez is the kind of student who studies hard and gets good grades. _____

_____

_____

3. The reason why I like art is because it allows me to be creative. _____

_____

4. The car was large in size and blue in color. _____

_____

5. Anita seems to have a lot of self-confidence in herself. _____

_____

6. When my instructor returned back my paper to me today, I saw that it had several

different types of errors that were mistakes that came from being careless. _____

_____

_____

EXERCISE 10   Combining Sentences

*Find the weak repetition and unnecessary words in each of the following groups of
sentences. Then combine each group into one graceful sentence. Omit repeated words
or ideas whenever possible.*

The Origin of the Teddy Bear

1. It was November 1902. Theodore (Teddy) Roosevelt was president. The president
   visited the South. He went to settle an argument. The argument was between
   Mississippi and another state. The name of the state was Louisiana. *In November
   1902, President Theodore (Teddy) Roosevelt visited the South to settle an
   argument between Mississippi and Louisiana.*

2. Roosevelt had an official duty. His duty was to "draw the line" between the states.
   He took time off from his duty. He went bear hunting. _____

   _____

   _____

3. His host showed him an easy target. The target was a baby bear. A baby bear is
   also called a cub. The president refused to shoot it. _____

   _____

   _____

4. A cartoonist drew a picture. The picture was of the president. The president was
   refusing to kill the cub. The picture had a caption. The caption was underneath the
   picture. The caption said, "Drawing the line."_____

   _____

   _____

   _____

5. Morris Michtom was the owner of a toy store. The toy store was in Brooklyn, New York. He was inspired by the cartoon. He and his wife made a bear. The bear was soft. The bear was brown. _____

_____

_____

_____

6. They put the bear in the window. They put a copy of the cartoon in the window. They put a sign in the window. The sign said "Teddy's Bear."_____

_____

_____

_____

7. The bear sold quickly. Then many more bears sold quickly. A fad developed. The fad became very popular. _____

_____

_____

8. Michtom wrote to the president. He wanted to use the president's name. His purpose was to sell stuffed animals. He wanted to sell them all across the country. ____

_____

_____

_____

9. The president sent a note to Michtom. The note was handwritten. It granted the permission._____

_____

_____

10. Many imitators of Teddy's bear appeared. They came from manufacturers. The manufacturers were all across America. The manufacturers were also from Europe. They created an extremely popular toy. _____

_____

_____

_____

Tired Expressions

In your first rush to put words on paper, you may find yourself using familiar expressions such as "last but not least." These expressions—called **clichés**—are often *too* familiar. They're so overused and tired that they've lost both power and meaning. Here are a few examples:

one in a million	over and done with
as cold as ice	selling like hotcakes
stick like glue	bored to tears
barely scratches the surface	tried and true
easier said than done	up at the crack of dawn
few and far between	it goes without saying

Expect to write clichés in early drafts—everyone does. But when you revise, try to substitute fresher expressions.

To avoid clichés:

- circle tired expressions as you revise
- substitute fresh, original language

Original	Revision
It was *raining cats and dogs*.	The rain covered the streets and flooded basements.
I opened my umbrella *as quick as a wink*.	I instantly opened my umbrella.
Jamie's mind is *as sharp as a tack*.	Jamie's mind is sharp as a laser cutter.

EXERCISE 11   Eliminating Clichés

 COLLABORATIVE ACTIVITY 3

Listing Clichés
With others, brainstorm and list as many clichés as you can. Then add to the list throughout the term. Share your lists with the class. The lists will help make you aware of expressions to avoid.

Find the clichés in each of the following sentences. Then replace each cliché with a fresh expression.

1. The Moving Violations' new album is selling like hotcakes. *The Moving Violations' new album is extremely popular.*

2. He was as happy as a lark. _____

_____

3. Getting rid of every cliché is easier said than done. _____

_____

4. The day of the exam I was up at the crack of dawn so I'd be good and ready. _____

_____

_____

5. In this day and age, honest politicians are few and far between. _____

_____

6. This exercise barely scratches the surface of eliminating clichés; you must work like a horse to get rid of them in your writing. _____

_____

IN SUMMARY   To Eliminate Weak or Unnecessary Words

1. Identify overused common verbs such as *do, get, make, put, go,* and *have;* then replace them with more specific and stronger verbs.
2. Identify and replace common and imprecise adjectives.
3. Identify and eliminate any unnecessary uses of *there is* and *there are.*
4. Identify and replace vague and tired expressions with more specific and vivid language.
5. Identify and eliminate unnecessary repetition.
6. Identify wordiness and revise wordy passages with more concise expressions.
7. Identify and eliminate any clichés.

EDITING FOR MASTERY

Mastery Exercise 1

Writing Concretely and Concisely

Each of the items in the following passage contains empty language, unnecessary repetition, and weak verbs or adjectives. Rewrite the items to eliminate the problems.

A Desperate Situation in World War I

1. It was on October 4, 1918, when a division of American soldiers was fighting the Germans in the Argonne Forest that was in France. *On October 4, 1918, a division of American soldiers was fighting the Germans in the Argonne Forest in France.*

2. The thing that the Germans did was surround the Americans and attack them. _____

3. Another bad thing was that the American division also was getting "friendly fire" from their own army. _____

4. The division had a commander. His name was Major Charles W. Whittlesey. He knew that many of his men had been killed or hurt, and they had almost run out of rations and medical supplies. _____

5. There was more "friendly fire" that was coming at the division. To stop this friendly fire from coming, Whittlesey decided to do something. He wrote a note to his

superiors at division headquarters at Rampont. _____

_____

_____

_____

6. He asked them to do something. They had to stop bombing the division. _____

_____

_____

7. There was only one way to get the message to headquarters. The location of the
headquarters was twenty-five miles away. It was to send the message by carrier
pigeon. _____

_____

_____

8. Whittlesey had five pigeons that he sent up with the message. But German marksmen killed each and every one of them in the blink of an eye. _____

_____

_____

9. There was only one pigeon left. His name was Cher Ami, which means "dear
friend" in French, and the message was put inside a capsule, and the capsule was
attached to his leg. _____

_____

_____

10. Cher Ami made a short flight, and as quick as a wink he landed on the branch of a
tree that was nearby. Cher Ami decided that the thing to do was to start grooming
his feathers. _____

_____

_____

COLLABORATIVE
ACTIVITY 4
Comparing and Discussing
Answers
Compare and discuss the
change you made to each
item in Mastery Exercise 1.
Report your findings to
the class.

11. Major Whittlesey knew that this was a situation that was bad, so he had to do
something. What he decided to do was make the bird fly. _____

_____

_____

_____

Scorecard: Number of errors found and corrected _____

Mastery Exercise 2

Writing Concretely and Concisely

*Each of the items in the following passage contains empty language, unnecessary repe-
tition, and weak verbs or adjectives. Rewrite the items to eliminate the problems.*

The Pigeon Hero

1. Major Whittlesey and the unit's pigeon handler, who was named Sergeant Richards, tried to get Cher Ami to take off. What they did was shout and wave their hands.

   Major Whittlesey and the unit's pigeon handler, Sergeant Richards, tried to get Cher Ami to take off by shouting and waving their hands.

2. They even tossed stones at the pigeon, but there was nothing that worked. Because nothing else worked, Richards got the idea that he would climb up in the tree where the pigeon was and then he would shake the branch that that pigeon was on. _____

   _____

   _____

3. The action that Richards did made Cher Ami finally get off of the tree and fly. As soon as Cher Ami began to get into the air, he was shot and fell to the ground. _____

   _____

   _____

4. The pigeon stayed on the ground for a few minutes. What he did next was to start to fly again. As quick as a wink, he was shot, but even though he was shot, he continued to his way "home" to Rampont. _____

   _____

   _____

   _____

5. When all was said and done, Cher Ami made it to Rampont. What had happened to the bird before he made it there was that he had lost one eye and he had also lost one leg, and he had been shot in the breast. _____

   _____

   _____

   _____

6. It was good that he still had the message in the capsule that was put on his leg.

   _____

   _____

7. The soldiers at Rampont made the decision to stop the bombing right then and there, and when they did that, the division that belonged to Major Whittlesey was saved.

   _____

   _____

8. The United States had a medal that was called the Distinguished Service Medal that they gave to heroes, and it was Cher Ami that received it. He also got a medal from France. _____

_____

_____

9. The pigeon spent a lot of time getting well, and after he got well, he took a trip to Washington, D.C. When he got there, the United States Signal Corps took good care of him. _____

_____

10. The thing that happened to Cher Ami was that he became famous, and the other thing that happened to him was that he lived for another year. _____

_____

_____

11. It was in 1919 that the pigeon died, and after he died, the government decided that the best thing to do was to put him on display at the Smithsonian Institution. That is where the famous pigeon is at today. _____

_____

_____

_____

WHERE TO PUT THE –S

With subject-verb agreement (see pp. 116–120)

Singular noun or third-person pronoun	*Singular verb* ← *s*
The boy, he, she, it	goe**S**, play**S**, walk**S**, know**S**

Plural noun ← *s*	*Plural verb*
The boy**S**	go, play, walk, know

But not with irregular plurals
  (children, men, women, etc.)

With possessives (see pp. 334–335)

Singular noun	*Plural noun*
the boy'**S** room	the two boy**S**' room

With contractions (see p. 157)
  he is = he'**S**
  she is = she'**S**
  it is, it has = it'**S**

But not with possessive pronouns
  his car
  its tires

WHAT TO MAKE AGREE

Subjects and verbs in number (see pp. 118–121)

Pronouns and antecedents in person and number (see pp. 157–160)

WHAT FORMS ARE IRREGULAR

Plural nouns not ending in –s (see pp. 118–119)

Verbs that form past tense and past participles without –ed (see pp. 138–157)

Adjectives and adverbs that form comparisons with word changes (see pp. 181–187)

WHERE TO PUT THE –ED

On regular verbs (see pp. 131–134, 138–151)	*Past tense*	*Past participle*
work, play, want	work**ed**, play**ed**, want**ed**	has work**ed**, has play**ed**, has want**ed**

But not on irregular verbs (see pp. 138–151)		
bend, build	ben**t**, buil**t**	has ben**t**, buil**t**
pay, has	pai**d**, ha**d**	has pai**d**, ha**d**
feel, lose, bring	fel**t**, los**t**, brou**ght**	has fel**t**, los**t**, brou**ght**
find, sit, stand	f**ou**nd, s**a**t, st**oo**d	has f**ou**nd, s**a**t, st**oo**d
become, come, run	bec**a**me, c**a**me, r**a**n	has bec**o**me, has c**o**me, has r**u**n
begin, drink, swim	beg**a**n, dr**a**nk, sw**a**m	has beg**u**n, has dr**u**nk, has sw**u**m
bet, cut, read	be**t**, cu**t**, rea**d**	has be**t**, cu**t**, rea**d**
break, eat, see	br**o**ke, **a**te, s**a**w	has br**o**ken, eat**en**, see**n**

Or Be (see p. 133)		
I am, he is	I, he **was**	I have **been**, he has **been**
they are	they **were**	they have **been**

WHAT WORDS TO CUT OUT
(see pp. 201–206)

Overused verbs
have, go, get, put, make, do, etc.

Overused adjectives
nice, interesting, etc.

Vague and tired expressions
tried and true, last but not least, etc.

Empty sentence starters
there is, there are, it is

WHICH PRONOUNS TO USE
(see pp. 154–157, 163–164)

Subject
I, we, you, he, she, it, they saw John.

Object
John saw me, us, you, him, her, it, them.

Possessive
My, our, your, his, her, its, their house.

Demonstrative
this house   these houses
that house   those houses

WHERE TO PUT THE MODIFIERS (see pp. 171–176)

Before the noun
Without new tires, ← the car is dangerous to drive.

After the noun
I can't drive **the car** → *without new tires.*

WAYS COMPARISONS WORK (see pp. 180–188)

Comparative forms	*Superlative forms*
stronger	strongest
more athletic	most athletic
better	the best

WHAT VERB TENSES TO USE (see pp. 131–138)

Present	I *study*
Past	I *studied*
Present-perfect	I *have studied*
Past-perfect	I *had studied*
Future	I *will study*

Writing Types of Paragraphs: Shaping the Structure

The chapters of Unit I introduced you to the writing process and applied that process to composing both paragraphs and essays. You saw that you write for many different purposes and audiences. You explored and practiced the six steps in the writing process and learned to develop your ideas clearly and convincingly.

Unit IV looks at the writing process in more detail. It introduces and examines a variety ways to apply the process to different purposes, using different organizational structures. You'll learn how to work with description, narration, report writing, process analysis, cause and effect analysis, classification, comparison and contrast, definition, and summary and response. Each type of writing lays a foundation on which to build more complex structures. Each can shape a paragraph or whole essay, but you will often combine several types of writing in order to achieve your goal. ■

CHAPTER 17

Describing a Scene

Description is a useful tool in many kinds of writing. In narration or storytelling, it creates a sense of realism. In reports or explanations, it clarifies and makes ideas more specific. You can describe many things, including people, but in this chapter we'll practice with one kind of description—of a scene.

A clear and lively description depends on close observation. You must pay attention to what you see and hear, and to specific word choice that will make those observations vivid for your readers. Description also demands that you pay attention to the whole writing process. You will work on that process in this chapter, by

- examining a model of description

- analyzing what makes description effective

- thinking through ways to organize a paragraph of description

- writing a description of a scene

A MODEL PARAGRAPH: DESCRIBING A SCENE

A **description** of a scene must concentrate on specific details, use several of the five senses, and arrange the details in some logical way. Some scenes are views of nature, but most scenes involve the actions of people, animals, or things. You should therefore first describe the physical setting and then tell what goes on within the setting. Make it easy for readers to locate things by arranging the details in **spatial order.** That involves first providing an overall picture of the scene, then locating each important part in a consistent arrangement from top to bottom, right to left, or nearest to farthest.

A blueprint of a typical descriptive paragraph might include most or all of these elements:

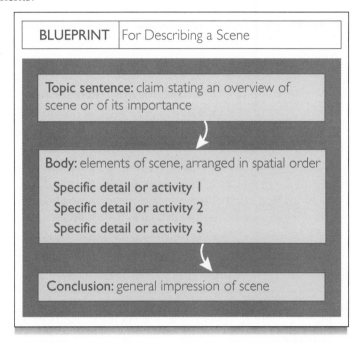

BLUEPRINT | For Describing a Scene

Topic sentence: claim stating an overview of scene or of its importance

Body: elements of scene, arranged in spatial order
  Specific detail or activity 1
  Specific detail or activity 2
  Specific detail or activity 3

Conclusion: general impression of scene

Not every description includes all these elements. Some descriptions include people or animals and therefore have a great deal of activity. Other descriptions include almost no activity. Here's an example:

This passage from a novel by Tracy Chevalier is almost pure physical description. Here's the situation: The narrator, a young woman, has just become a maid in the house of the famous painter Johannes Vermeer (1632–1675), who lived his entire life in the Dutch city of Delft. She is in his studio for the first time to sweep and dust, but she has been warned not to move or disturb anything. After standing on a chair to look outside, she now focuses her attention on the room itself, taking in the layout and the placement of the furnishings.

As you read the passage, note how the body sentences of each paragraph support the claim of the first sentence. Note, too, how the passage moves from a general outline of the room to the arrangement of the furniture and then to the peacefulness of the room.

Excerpt from *Girl with a Pearl Earring*
Tracy Chevalier

* * * *

Now that I had a moment I surveyed the room. It was a large, square space, not as long as the great hall downstairs. With the windows open it was bright and airy, with white-washed walls, and grey and white marble tiles on the floor, the darker tiles set in a pattern of square crosses. A row of Delft tiles painted with cupids lined the bottom of the walls to protect the whitewash from our mops. . . .

Though it was a big room, it held little furniture. There was the easel and chair set in front of the middle window, and the table placed in front of the window in the right corner. Besides the chair I had stood on there was another by the table, of plain leather nailed on with brass studs and two lion heads carved into the tops of the posts. Against the far wall, behind the chairs and easel, was a small cupboard, its drawers closed, several brushes and a knife with a diamond-shaped blade arranged on top next to clean palettes. Beside the cupboard was a desk on which were papers and books and prints. Two more lion-head chairs had been set against the wall near the doorway.

It was an orderly room, empty of the clutter of everyday life. It felt different from the rest of the house, almost as if it were in another house altogether. When the door was closed it would be difficult to hear the shouts of the children, the jangle of Catharina's keys, the sweeping of our brooms.

Questions for Analysis

1. What is the function of the first paragraph of the description?

2. The topic sentence of the second paragraph claims that the room had little furniture but goes on to describe furniture. Does this topic sentence work or not? Why?

3. The narrator begins her observations of the furniture by noting the objects close to the windows. Why? What is the location of the objects she observes next? Underline the transitional words that establish the locations.

4. Vermeer was a painter. How does this fact relate to the narrator's observations of how the room feels in the third paragraph?

WRITING ASSIGNMENT FOR DESCRIBING A SCENE

Write a one-paragraph advertising brochure whose central claim would interest students in enrolling at your college. Describe one area—an attractive, unusual, or lively gathering place, the library, the weight room in the gym, the student center, the counseling center, the cafeteria, the quadrangle, or any other place you find attractive—and the typical activity that goes on there.

Gathering, Generating, and Arranging the Materials

The best way to gather material for the paragraph is to visit the place for about half an hour and take notes on what you see and hear—and even smell. Record as much information as possible. Although you probably won't use it all, it's better to have more than you need than not enough when you compose the first draft.

Then arrange the details in some consistent spatial order. A brainstorming list or clustering diagram may help as you generate details and decide how to arrange them.

The following questions should guide your note taking:

1. Where is the location? (And what is its name?)
2. What are its dimensions and most important features? Where is each feature—on the right, in the middle, above something else, close, or far away?
3. How large or small are the objects you see? How are they shaped? What are their colors?
4. How many people are in the scene, and where are they? What do they look like? What are they doing?
5. What are the names of things and important people? Use them.

Here is an example of the kind of brainstorming notes you might gather in a half-hour visit to the student center.

one-story building, modern, lots of glass

hundreds of students inside

built in 1990

square building, with large central entrance and four rooms, each on one
     side of building

located on Wright Avenue in center of campus

large TV room on south end, with 60-inch HD plasma TV, and 50 chairs,
     busy during soap operas

table tennis room on east end with six tables

skills of players range from poor to tournament quality

pool room on west end, with six tables

cost $1.50 to play each game

large study and music room on north end, with many tables, carrels,
     upholstered chairs and sofas

music playing softly

two or three couples on sofas, arms around each other, one couple kissing

students at circular tables talking about an assignment

students at other tables, playing cards

a lot of coming and going throughout the center

These notes would probably fill more than one paragraph, so you need to narrow the focus. Select the details that are most important, and that directly support the central claim of your paragraph. You can accomplish this task in one of two ways—or both of them:

1. Write a topic sentence and select the details that support its claim.
2. Select and arrange the material through additional brainstorming, clustering, freewriting, or an informal outline. Then write the topic sentence.

The final draft of the topic sentence might look like this, making three broad claims that the remainder of the paragraph supports.

At almost any time of day, you'll find the Student Center a comfortable
place to enjoy yourself, relax, and study in pleasant surroundings.

The body of the paragraph would probably be organized as follows:

1. A general description of the setting
2. Specific descriptive details arranged in spatial order
3. Transitional sentences or phrases that locate things spatially or introduce activities
4. A description of the main activities, that take place in the study and music room.

Here's an informal outline of the body (note that it omits a number of unnecessary details from the original brainstormed notes):

> overall view of the center
> modern, one-story square building on Wright Avenue in the center of campus
> large central entrance and four rooms, each on one side of building
> hundreds of students coming and going
> four rooms around the center of the building
>   east end, table tennis room with six tables
>   west end, pool room with six tables
>   south end, room with 60-in. high-definition plasma TV, with 50 chairs,
>   busy during soap opera time
>   north end, music room—where the most activity occurs
>   a lot of tables, upholstered chairs, and sofas
>   students reading, talking, eating doughnuts, drinking sodas
>   card games at several tables
>   students at table near windows talking about an assignment
>   two or three couples on the sofas talking, holding hands, even kissing

Composing the Paragraph

After arranging your material, write a first draft. Don't assume that your arrangement is final. You'll probably shift around details each time you revise.

Relax and let the words flow. Say your sentences aloud so you can hear what sounds natural and clear. After finishing the draft, put it aside for a while unless you immediately think of ways to rearrange, restate, or further develop your ideas.

TEMPLATES FOR DESCRIPTION

In writing a description, you need to help your reader see what you see. You can point out where things are and when things happen by supplying transitions. Here are some templates (that is, guides in which you fill in the blanks) for transitional sentences and phrases that you might use or adapt, taken directly from Tuyet-Ahn Van's "The Happiest Place of My Life" at the end of this chapter:

These templates are useful for locations:

1. In front of _____ was _____ where _____.

2. Not far from there was _____.

3. At the corner of _____, there was _____ where

   _____.

4. From _____ nearby, a _____.

These templates are useful for times:

5. In the afternoon, _____ I used to _____.

6. I sometimes _____.

7. Every morning, _____ . . . and now and then _____.

And here are other transitional expressions for location:

On the north side
A hundred yards to the west
Near the main building
In the middle
Farther down, . . . and still farther
Next to the trees

Revising Your First Draft

Don't revise your first draft immediately. Let it sit for a few hours or even days. Then you can view it with a clear mind and probably with better judgment. Look at the arrangement of details. Is it consistent and clear? And have you used transitional phrases, such as the ones in the templates, to show the spatial relationship of the details to each other? If you see problems, then consider ways to rearrange the details and places where the templates for transitions might be helpful.

Let the following checklist guide you in revising your paragraph. Answer the questions yourself—or work with one or more of your classmates. If you or your classmates answer "no" to any question, revise the paragraph to correct the problem. First, make changes above the lines or in the margins. Then rewrite the paragraph.

REVISION CHECKLIST FOR DESCRIPTION

	YES	NO
1. Does the paragraph include a clear topic sentence that states a claim, or main idea?	☐	☐
2. Is the paragraph unified, with all the details contributing to the main idea?	☐	☐
3. Is the organization consistent, moving from front to back, left to right, top to bottom, or some other way?	☐	☐
4. Do transitions show the locations of objects and activities within the scene?	☐	☐
5. If people are engaged in activities, is there a clear transition between the description of the place and the people's activities?	☐	☐
6. Are there enough—or too many—supporting details?	☐	☐
7. Are the nouns and verbs specific?	☐	☐

Take notes of these responses and let them guide your revision. Rewrite the paper later when you can examine it with fresh eyes and a clear head.

Further Revising and Editing

Return to your paragraph and revise it again, this time paying special attention to specific details and strong word choice. Make sure you haven't overused adjectives and adverbs, which will make your writing sound flowery and unnatural. Then edit and proofread your paper, checking for misspelled words, words accidentally left out (or left in—especially if you've composed and revised your paper on a computer), and any other errors you notice. Hand in a clean copy of your work.

ADDITIONAL WRITING ASSIGNMENT

Assume you're writing a brochure for visitors to an exhibit at an art museum. Write a description of the picture that follows, making clear why visitors should stop to see this picture. For example, your topic sentence might say that the picture shows a shocking or humorous scene. Compose, revise, and edit the paragraph following the advice provided throughout this chapter.

William Hogarth, *The Enraged Musician,* **1741, British Museum**

A STUDENT MODEL PARAGRAPH

The paragraph that follows was written by Tuyet-Ahn Van, a Vietnamese student now living in Chattanooga, Tennessee. The scene begins with a general discussion of the larger setting, moves to a specific location, and then describes places and activities within it.

The Happiest Place of My Life
Tuyet-Ahn Van

* * * *

The place that I love the most is in the small country where I was born and spent my childhood. It was a small village in the middle of a rather large area surrounded with green bamboo hedges. In front of the village was my house with a yard where wet clothes were dried and which was also storage for the rice crop in harvest-time. Not far from there was a beautiful garden full of pretty flowers and fruit trees. It was my favorite place. In the afternoon, I used to run merrily along its flower-bordered walks, chasing gorgeous butterflies or catching shining beetles. In doing so, I sometimes trod on a flowering plant, and I was scolded by my mother for being so careless. At the corner of the garden, there was a small arbor with a seat where I spent much time reading some fairytales or doing my homework. Every morning, I also watched the farmers go by with their horses on their way to the fields. Now and then, their merry laughter broke the momentary silence of the countryside. From some cottages nearby, a slender thread of smoke curled upward, announcing the first activities of the hamlet. Certainly, my home was only a humble village, but I still love it very much. It was the place where I had the happiest memories of my life.

Questions for Analysis

1. What is the topic sentence of the paragraph? What words establish its claim? What general details about the village does Tuyet-Ahn provide? What place within the village does she focus on most specifically?

2. What words and phrases establish the location of things? What words or phrases establish the times of activities?

3. Aside from visual description, does Tuyet-Ahn call on any of the other five senses, either directly or indirectly? If so, where?

4. What main impression does the writer wish you to take from her description?

FINAL WRITING ASSIGNMENT

Think about a place that you loved or hated when you were younger, or visit a place that you love or dread now. Describe it so your classmates can experience the feelings it creates in you: excitement, affection, fear, disgust, calmness—or whatever. Make that point clear in your topic sentence and support the point with relevant physical details and actions.

CHAPTER 18

Developing Through Exemplification

How many times in daily conversations have you asked, "Can you give me an example?" You ask because examples are a natural way to support and clarify general ideas. Indeed, examples are among a writer's most important tools. If you claim, "I really was nervous before the big test," a few examples—the temptation to have a cigarette after vowing to quit, the chewed-up eraser you almost swallowed, and the first, second, and third trips to the washroom just before you entered the classroom—will make the point vividly. Using examples well will help strengthen description and narration and every other kind of writing you do.

This chapter will help you write an effective paragraph developed through examples by

- examining a model
- analyzing types of examples
- considering ways to organize a paper developed through examples
- writing a paper that supports its claims through examples

MODELS OF EXEMPLIFICATION

As you know, the body sentences of a paragraph support its central claim. And one of the most common and effective forms of support is **exemplification,** or the use of examples. Suppose you claim that your one-hour commute to campus this morning was horrible. Your reader may understand your claim, but won't know why or even care to know. Examples put the meat on the bones of the claim, and flavor it as well. No matter what organizational pattern you use in developing an idea—description, cause-and-effect, comparison–contrast, or any other pattern you see in the chapters in this unit—examples will play a large role in that development.

Examples can be any length, from a few words to a sentence, to a whole paragraph, or even longer.

The Short Example

Some examples can be as short as a few words. If, for instance, you wish to clarify the word *amphibian,* you might cite examples such as frog, toad, salamander, and your four-year-old daughter, who seems to be able to live in the water at the beach (well—that's not exactly an example, but you get the point).

The Sentence Example

Other times, a few words won't be enough to illustrate or clarify a claim. So you may need to write a sentence or two that specifically illustrate or clarify the claim. Suppose, for example, that you say the ride to school today was horrible. You could follow that statement by adding that you stood in the heat and rain for fifteen minutes until the bus arrived, boarded it soaked and sweaty, had to stand the whole way while carrying a backpack filled with thirty pounds of books, and arrived ten minutes late for your first class.

The Long—or Extended—Example

This is an example that occupies the whole body of a paragraph, or several paragraphs. Typically, it can be a story that illustrates a point, or a complex idea that requires explanation.

A blueprint of a typical paragraph of exemplification might look like this:

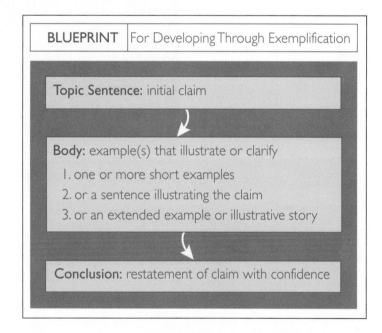

| BLUEPRINT | For Developing Through Exemplification |

Topic Sentence: initial claim

Body: example(s) that illustrate or clarify
1. one or more short examples
2. or a sentence illustrating the claim
3. or an extended example or illustrative story

Conclusion: restatement of claim with confidence

As you read the following paragraph, note how it develops an extended example. Note also how specific details are organized spatially.

A Giant of a Dwarf

* * * *

Although the royal family in seventeenth-century Spain treated dwarfs cruelly, Diego Velázquez portrayed them with great dignity in his paintings. A perfect example is the portrait of Sebastian de Morra. In it, a handsome man sits on the ground, staring directly at the viewer. His face is striking, with its square jaw, neatly trimmed black hair, sideburns, full goatee, and handlebar mustache. His deep-set eyes gaze darkly beneath arched eyebrows as if he is studying us with great intelligence. He wears elegant clothing: for instance, a green jacket that skirts out at the waist, with a delicate white fabric at the sleeves and wide collar. A long, heavy orange cape covers the front and back of his shoulders but not his fists, which are clenched as if preparing for a confrontation. Only the man's tiny legs, pointing directly at us, reveal that de Morra is a dwarf. This is a perfect example of a portrait of a nobleman, not a ridiculous figure, and it is a tribute to the heart and talent of the artist.

Diego Velázquez, *Sebastian de Morra,* **1643–44, Museo del Prado**

Questions for Analysis

1. What is the topic sentence—the sentence that states the central claim of the paragraph?

2. As the second sentence indicates, the description of Sebastian de Morra functions as an extended example of the central claim. But there are two other claims in the paragraph. What are those claims, and what shorter examples support them?

3. The examples are all descriptive. How are they arranged spatially? Why do you think the writer chooses this arrangement? Why doesn't the writer use phrases like "at the top" or "on the left" to help you locate what is being described?

4. An effective description also reveals something about a person's character. What details show the dignity of Sebastian de Morra?

5. The writer establishes the contrast between the royal family's treatment of dwarfs and the treatment by Velázquez. Why?

WRITING ASSIGNMENT FOR DEVELOPING THROUGH EXEMPLIFICATION

Select one of the following photographs by Walker Evans, who worked during the Great Depression of the 1930s. Evans wasn't merely taking photographs; he was trying to convey a message about people in the midst of poverty.

South Street, New York

Roadside Stand Near Birmingham

Closely examine the photograph you've chosen, and make a claim about what you believe Evans was trying to convey. Then support the claim through exemplification, in this case, details from the photograph. As in the description of Sebastian de Morra, you may write an extended example by focusing on the

Bud Fields and his family, Hale County, Alabama, Summer 1936

whole scene. Or you may cite several short examples involving specific people or other details in the photograph. Use what you learned from Chapter 17 about writing description.

Gathering, Generating, and Arranging the Materials

Begin by jotting down a preliminary reaction about what you think Evans seems to be "saying." It might take a form like this:

> The famous photographer Walker Evans wanted to _____
> in his photography, and _____ conveys that idea. For
> example, _____ shows _____.

Then follow these steps in planning the paragraph:

1. Take notes on the details you observe in the photograph. What do the clothes, faces, and postures of the subjects suggest? How do the people seem to feel, and how do you know? What do the buildings or surroundings suggest?
2. Using brainstorming or clustering, capture and structure your ideas on paper. Here is part of the clustering diagram for the description of Sebastian de Morra you just read:

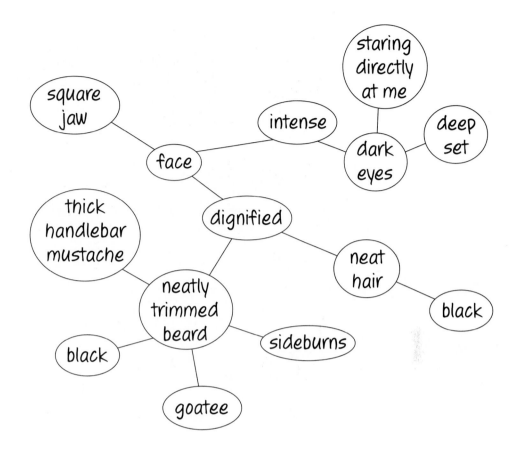

3. Now consider if the examples support—or change—your reaction to the photograph. Does that first reaction still hold up, or should you revise it? Would further examples support that reaction? Are any details unimportant or off the topic?

4. Then organize your materials in an informal outline. Here, for example, is an outline for the description of Sebastian de Morra, revised several times until the arrangement of details is clear:

Central Claim: Velázquez paints dwarfs with great dignity

   Example: portrait of Sebastian de Morra

   Claim: handsome man

    face

    neat black hair, beard, sideburns, mustache

    eyes-deep-set, intense

   Claim: elegant clothes

     jacket, green with white collar and sleeves long, skirted at waist

    cloak over shoulders

    fists clenched at waist

   Short legs only real clue that he is a dwarf

Conclusion: perfect example of portrait of a nobleman

Composing the Paragraph

Now, after looking at the outline, revise the beginning of the paragraph if necessary so the opening claim leads logically into the examples. Then write the first draft. Relax and let the words flow. Say your sentences aloud so you can hear what sounds natural and clear. After finishing the draft, put it aside for a while unless you immediately think of ways to rearrange, restate, or further develop your ideas.

TEMPLATES FOR EXEMPLIFICATION

You can introduce examples in a number of ways. Here, for instance, are some templates you might use or adapt.

1. A _n excellent_ example of _____ is _____, which _____.

2. For instance, the person wearing _____ seems _____. He _____.

3. If the people were, for example, _____, then they _____.

4. Suppose that _____. Then they (or he, she, or it) _____ would _____.

Revising Your First Draft

Let the following checklist guide you in revising your paragraph. Answer the questions yourself—or work with one or more of your classmates. If you or your classmates answer "no" to any question, revise the paragraph to correct the problem. Make changes above the lines first or in the margins. Then rewrite the paragraph.

REVISION CHECKLIST FOR EXEMPLIFICATION

	YES	NO
1. Does the paragraph include a clear topic sentence that states a claim, or main idea?	☐	☐
2. Are the examples concrete and specific?	☐	☐
3. Are there enough supporting examples?	☐	☐
4. Are the examples clearly introduced?	☐	☐
5. Are extended examples developed in detail?	☐	☐
6. Do transitions show the locations of objects, people, and activities within the scene?	☐	☐
7. Are the nouns and verbs specific?	☐	☐
8. Is the language clear at every point?	☐	☐

Take notes of these responses to guide your revision. Rewrite the paper when your mind is clear and you can attend to word choice, clarity, and conciseness.

Further Revising and Editing

Now edit and proofread your paper, checking for misspelled words, words accidentally left out (or left in—especially if you've composed and revised your paper on a computer), and any other errors you notice. Hand in a clean copy of your work.

ADDITIONAL WRITING ASSIGNMENT

Describe a person you know well so your classmates can see the person's most important character traits and perhaps your attitude toward the person. Make the central claim about the person in the topic sentence and then support it with revealing physical details.

A LONGER MODEL OF EXEMPLIFICATION

Natalie Goldberg (born 1948) is a painter, poet, and teacher of creative writing, and author of a number of books on the relationship between writing and Zen meditation. A resident of northern New Mexico, she has written a number of books on the process of writing, including this chapter from Writing Down the Bones: Freeing the Writer Within, *published in 1986. The following essay is excerpted from that book. The footnotes are the author's.*

As you read the essay, note the variety of specific examples that support her claims: single words, full sentences, and extended examples. Before you begin, though, look up the word "hone."

Be Specific
Natalie Goldberg

* * * *

1   Be specific. Don't say "fruit." Tell what kind of fruit—"It is a pomegranate." Give things the dignity of their names. Just as with human beings, it is rude to say, "Hey, girl, get in line." That "girl" has a name. (As a matter of fact, if she's at least twenty years old, she's a woman, not a "girl" at all.) Things, too, have names. It is much better to say "the geranium in the window" than "the flower in the window." "Geranium"—that one word gives us a much more specific picture. It penetrates more deeply into the beingness of that flower. It immediately gives us the scene by the window—red petals, green circular leaves, all straining toward sunlight.

2   About ten years ago I decided I had to learn the names of plants and flowers in my environment. I bought a book on them and walked down the tree-lined streets of Boulder [Colorado], examining leaf, bark, and seed, trying to match them up with their descriptions and names in the book. Maple, elm, oak, locust. I usually tried to cheat by asking people working in their yards the names of the flowers and trees growing there. I was amazed how few people had any idea of the names of the live beings inhabiting their little plot of land.

3   When we know the name of something, it brings us closer to the ground. It takes the blur out of our mind; it connects us to the earth. If I walk down the street and see "dogwood," "forsythia," I feel more friendly toward the environment. I am noticing what is around me and can name it. It makes me more awake.

4   If you read the poems of William Carlos Williams,* you will see how specific he is about plants, trees, flowers—chicory, daisy, locust, poplar, quince, primrose, black-eyed

---

*William Carlos Williams, "Daisy," in *The Collected Earlier Poems* (New York: New Directions, 1938).

Susan, lilacs—each has its own integrity. Williams says, "Write what's in front of your nose." It's good for us to know what is in front of our nose. Not just "daisy," but how the flower is in the season we are looking at it—"The days eye hugging the earth/in August . . . brownedged,/green and pointed scales/armor his yellow." Continue to hone your awareness: to the name, to the month, to the day, and finally to the moment.

5   Williams also says: "No idea, but in things." Study what is "in front of your nose." By saying "geranium" instead of "flower," you are penetrating more deeply into the present and being there. The closer we can get to what's in front of our nose, the more it can teach us everything. "To see the World in a Grain of Sand, and a heaven in a Wild Flower. . . ."**

6   In writing groups and classes too, it is good to quickly learn the names of all the other group members. It helps to ground you in the group and make you more attentive to each other's work. Learn the names of everything: birds, cheese, tractors, cars, buildings. A writer is all at once everything—an architect, French cook, farmer—and at the same time, a writer is none of these things.

Questions for Analysis

1. Who is the audience for this essay? How do you know?

2. Where does Goldberg use single-word examples? Where does she use full sentences?

3. In the first paragraph, Goldberg claims that naming things gives them dignity, as if they were human. Later in paragraph she refers to the "beingness" of a geranium. What assumptions lie behind these statements?

4. Aside from listing specific names to exemplify her claims, she also cites a personal experience about how she learned names. What purpose does that experience serve?

5. In a second extended example, Goldberg quotes William Carlos Williams: "No idea, but in things." What do you think Williams means?

6. She concludes by claiming that a writer "is all at once everything . . . and at the same time . . . none of these things." What is her point, and how does it relate to claims she has made earlier in the essay?

FINAL WRITING ASSIGNMENT

Like Natalie Goldberg, give specific advice to a particular audience about how to succeed, for example, in a job interview, in getting the best seats at a concert, in studying for a test, in waiting (or bussing) tables, or in any other activity that comes from your experience. Tell the audience how the advice will be useful to them, and back up your claims with specific examples. Be sure to explain how the examples reinforce the claims.

**William Blake, "The Auguries of Innocence."

CHAPTER 19

Writing Narration

Narration is one of the most powerful ways of communicating with others. A well-written story lets your readers respond to some event in your life as if it were their own. They not only understand the event, but they can almost *feel* it. The action, details, and dialogue put the readers in the scene and make it happen for them.

Moreover, because narration often engages readers' emotions so powerfully, it can play a large role in other types of writing. A strong narrative paragraph can support a persuasive argument or illustrate an explanation or report. It gives life to your ideas.

This chapter will help you to write a strong narrative by

- examining a model of narration
- analyzing what makes a narration effective
- thinking through ways to organize a narration
- writing a narration

A MODEL OF NARRATION

Narration is telling a story. And to be interesting, a good story must have interesting content. It should tell about an event your audience would want to read. You might even think of your narrative as a movie in which readers see people in action and hear them speak. Therefore, it should be detailed and clear, with events arranged in the order in which they happened or in some other effective way. You should aim for a narrative that achieves all of the following goals:

1. It's unified, with all the action developing a central idea.
2. It's interesting; it draws the readers into the action and makes them feel as if they're observing and listening to the events.
3. It introduces the **four Ws** of a setting—*who, what, where,* and *when*—within the context of the action.
4. It's coherent, with transitions indicating changes in time, location, and characters.
5. It begins at the beginning and ends at the end. That is, the narrative follows a **chronological order**—with events happening in a time sequence.
6. It builds toward a **climax.** This is the moment of most tension or surprise—a time when the ending is revealed, or the importance of events becomes clear.

A blueprint of such a paragraph of narration might look something like this:

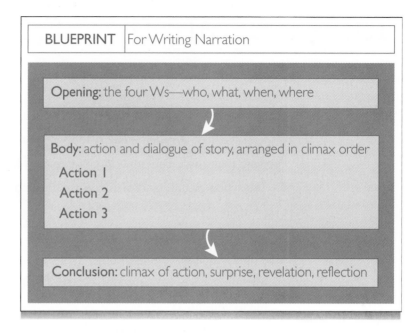

The following narration was written by Victor Ciurte, a student at Truman College in Chicago and immigrant from Romania. As you read the story, notice how it starts in the middle of the action and introduces the four Ws of setting as the action continues. Notice the specific detail and the use of dialogue. And notice how details at the beginning of the story relate to the end.

The Toughest Man
Victor Ciurte

* * * *

1   "Victor, wake up! It's time to go!" my grandma's voice woke me up at six A.M.

2   I was so happy to hear her voice. Normally being awake at such an early hour would not make me happy. But now all my worries were left behind in the big city. Even though we were about to go do some manly work in the Hungarian fields and mountains, I didn't mind because I was anxious to smell the fresh mountain air. I was anxious to walk the five miles to the field, anxious to work all day long, anxious for sweat to drip down my body, anxious to go back to the origins and live a simple life.

3   That morning my grandfather and I left the house to go cut the grass on one of the fields they owned. My grandfather and I didn't exchange a word on the way. He was always quiet, a man of few words. He never expressed his feelings and always played the part of a tough guy. His actions spoke louder than words. I was trying to find a subtle way of asking about his doctor appointment. I was afraid I would hurt his feelings and I was hoping he would mention it. He was never sick. Actually, I think it was the first time he saw a doctor. He didn't say anything to anybody. The questions were zooming through my head and, in hope of finding the best approach, I said "What did he say?"

4   "Who?" he replied.

5   "The doctor."

6   "Aaahh! Nothing." He continued walking faster than before.

7   Once we reached our destination, we both kept to ourselves. I was left to the mercy of my own thoughts. I remembered that when I was just a little kid I hated staying for a week or two with grandparents. I would miss my neighbors I used to play with all day long. That was a long time ago. Nowadays, I think of it as my escape from all the worries and troubles. I find myself at the top of the mountain very often.

8   I woke up from dreaming when, out of nowhere, my uncle showed up. He had a puzzled look on his face. Since he drove from another village, we realized he had something important to tell us. I had won the emigration lottery that I had been awaiting for a long time. I was one of the few lucky ones who was on the way to the United Sates.

9   I left in a hurry. I kissed and hugged my grandparents. I could see this was very hard for my grandfather. He was trying as always not to show his emotions. His voice was breaking as he said, "Take care and make me proud." As I stole one last glance at my grandfather, I saw a tear in his eye.

10   Four days later a friend of mine picked me up from O'Hare Airport. As we drove away, my friend asked questions about Romania. That is when I realized that I left not only my country behind but my family and everything I held dear.

11   It took me just a couple of days to find an apartment and get a job. Having done this, I picked up the phone and called my parents. I wanted to share everything and show that I was capable of living on my own. I guess that stubborn streak I liked so much in my grandfather was something we had in common. Since there was no answer at my parents' house, I decided to call my grandparents instead. My mother answered the phone. It was strange. It was Tuesday and my mother was there. She always works weekdays. That made me suspicious, and she did not sound like herself. Her voice was trembling. I could feel something was wrong and she was trying her hardest to tell me something. Finally, she told me, "Your grandfather passed away. We just returned from his funeral."

12   I was devastated. I was trying to go back in time and find clues, but there were not any. In my eyes he was a rock, someone who is never supposed to get sick, let alone leave us so suddenly.

13   This rock's name was Victor Ciurte.

Questions for Analysis

1. At the beginning of the story, what is the physical setting for most of the action? Where, apparently, does Victor live?

2. What are the other three Ws of the story—who, what, and when?

3. Think of the story as a movie with scenes. What are the scene divisions, and what transitions—of time, location, or participants in the action—introduce the scenes? (Notice that some transitions are long phrases or whole sentences.)

4. Although the action of the story is chronological, Victor Ciurte shifts back and forth in time in paragraph 7. What transitions signal these shifts? Underline them twice. What does he mean in the last sentence?

5. What is the point of the story, and why isn't it stated at the beginning? What is the climax of the story, when the point becomes clear, and what details earlier in the story hint at the point?

6. What does the author mean, in the last sentence of paragraph 7, when he says he finds himself "at the top of the mountain"?

7. Who is "the toughest man"? How does Victor resemble his namesake?

WRITING ASSIGNMENT FOR NARRATION

Even if we think our own lives have not been dramatic, tragic, or fun-filled, all of us still have personal stories worth telling. Write a paragraph (or more than one paragraph) about one event that affected you greatly and would probably interest your classmates. Your main purpose will be to entertain, but you may also wish to make a larger point about a lesson in life. "Firsts" often serve as excellent subjects for such narratives: your first day at school, your first date, your first job, the first time you drove a car, or the birth of your first child.

Gathering, Generating, and Arranging the Materials

Specific details create the realism and drama of a story. But if you choose too large a topic to discuss, one of two problems might result.

1. You will find yourself writing a book.
2. You will write a short paragraph filled with generalizations because you can't possibly develop each one.

You should begin, therefore, by choosing a subject that is small enough for you to explore. List three or four topics to write about and record any details that occur to you about each one. If possible, consider the point your story might make. That will help you decide which details to include. For example, don't describe your uncle and aunt's little store if that information doesn't develop the point of the story. But if you want to emphasize the great loss your uncle and aunt suffered when the building burned down, then take your readers on a short tour of the store.

Specific details create the realism and drama of a story. And often the best details include dialogue. The words people speak in a story often create more of a sense of realism than their actions. So consider whether to quote the speech of someone and the response that follows.

Explore your topic through freewriting, brainstorming, or clustering, and then arrange your ideas chronologically. A revised brainstorming list about a first day at school, arranged in chronological order, might look like this:

Arrived at school, holding Mom's hand

Met lady who said she was my teacher

Cried when Mom told me good-bye

Ran after her, but teacher stopped me

Told me that I would meet all sorts of new friends

Led me into a classroom filled with toys, bright posters, and assorted treasures

Became interested in all this new stuff

Maybe school wouldn't be too bad

Composing the Paragraph or Essay

Now compose a first draft of the paragraph or essay. The story should include these elements:

1. The point of the narrative should be clear. The point could be stated at the beginning or omitted altogether if revealing the main idea at the beginning will destroy the climax.
2. Information to establish the setting: *who, what, where,* and *when*
3. Enough detail to develop the topic idea convincingly and clearly
4. An arrangement of the details in chronological order
5. A progression to a climax or dramatic conclusion

If the first draft of your paragraph turns out to be only five to seven sentences long, you're probably summarizing events rather than developing them specifically. Try one or more of the following procedures to generate more details:

1. Look for the verbs *used to* or *would.* Look also for expressions such as *always, usually, often,* and *sometimes.* These verbs and expressions introduce habitual actions—that is, generalizations. Omit them if you can. Then compose sentences beginning with expressions such as *once, one day, one evening,* or a specific hour or day. These sentences should lead you through a sequence of more specific actions.
2. Close your eyes and put yourself back into the experience. What did you do first, next, and then next? What did other people do, and how did they respond to each other's actions? As events enter your mind, write them down quickly so that you capture them. When you revise later, you can eliminate the unnecessary details and smooth out your language.

TEMPLATES FOR NARRATION

In addition to the templates for transitions in time and place useful for description (Chapter 17, pp. 224), here are templates to signal oppositions and contrasts that create interest or tension. They are partially based on the story by Victor Ciurte.

1. Normally, I _____, but today _____
   _____.

2. When I was younger, I didn't _____, but now _____
   _____.

3. I realized that not only had I _____ but also _____
   _____.

4. Although it was _____, I didn't _____
   _____.

The following templates, based on the story by Bozena Budżyńska later in this chapter, signal the use of quotations.

5. "_____," Lisa said.

6. " _____!" she screamed.

7. She said, " _____."

8. " _____," I thought, realizing that _____.

9. " _____." He was trying to be funny.

And here are some verbs to use in speaker tags:

said, told me, replied, answered, asked, inquired, claimed, muttered, murmured, whispered, sighed, mentioned, groaned, yelled, screamed, shouted, shrieked, admitted, responded, demanded, commanded, insisted, protested, agreed

Revising Your First Draft

Return to the paragraph after a few hours or days and revise it further, clarifying your point, adding (or removing) details, and checking for coherence.

Check and improve your use of dialogue. These are the general rules.

1. Begin and end each quotation with **quotation marks** (" "), whether the quotation is a single word, a sentence, or several sentences.
2. Capitalize the first word of the quotation.
3. Use a **speaker tag** such as *he said* or *she asked* after the quotation ends. If the speaker tag follows a statement, end the statement with a comma. If the speaker tag follows a question, end the question with a question mark. But place the end punctuation inside the quotation mark, like this:
   ," he said.
   ?" she asked.
4. Change paragraphs each time you change speakers.

Let the following questions guide you in revising your draft. Answer them yourself or collaborate with a group of three or four classmates. As usual, photocopy your paper, or read it aloud twice. If you, or your classmates, answer "no" to any question, revise to eliminate the problem.

REVISION CHECKLIST FOR NARRATION

	YES	NO
1. Is the point of the story clear?	☐	☐
2. Are the four Ws established?	☐	☐
3. Is there enough detail?	☐	☐
4. Do all the details contribute to the point?	☐	☐
5. Is the organization arranged chronologically, or, if not, in a way that is easy to follow?	☐	☐
6. Are the transitions clear?	☐	☐

7. Does the action lead to a climax?	☐	☐
8. If dialogue is included, is the paragraphing and the use of speaker tags correct?	☐	☐
9. Is the language clear throughout?	☐	☐

Take notes of these responses to guide your revision. Rewrite the paper later when you can examine it with fresh eyes and a clear head. Pay special attention to word choice, clarity, and conciseness.

Further Revising and Editing

Review and revise your paragraph again. Then edit and proofread, checking for misspelled words, words accidentally left out (or left in—especially if you've composed and revised your paper on a computer), and any other errors you notice. Hand in a clean copy of your work.

ADDITIONAL WRITING ASSIGNMENT

When many families get together on holidays or special occasions, they hear the same stories year after year. Write an account of one of the legends from your family. (You may wish to write a story of perhaps four or five paragraphs in length.)

Assume that your audience is a group of people who don't know you, and shape the story so it reveals something important about your family or one of its members. If you can't recall a family legend, write a story about a pleasant event from your childhood, perhaps one that you'll pass on as a legend to the next generation. Assume again that your primary purpose is to entertain. At the beginning or end of the story, make its significance clear.

A STUDENT MODEL ESSAY

Bozena Budżyńska was born and educated in Poland (and elsewhere, as you'll see) before becoming a student at Truman College in Chicago. As you read her story, notice the opening sentence, which serves as the thesis statement; it hints at what is going to happen without revealing the specific events. Notice how the story introduces information about the setting (who, what, where, and when) as the action unfolds. Notice, too, how dialogue carries much of the narrative. And notice how small details near the beginning of the story become important at the end.

The Time of Living Dangerously
Bozena Budżyńska

* * * *

1   The love of photography can be a dangerous affair. So I found out one beautiful day in the tiny West African village.

2   Visiting Ghana as a college exchange student, I met, among other international students, Lisa from Norway. We liked each other instantly and became friends. I enjoyed her wicked sense of humor, adventurous nature, and easygoing personality.

We shared a room at the Accra campus and many days full of local delights as well as evenings full of laughter. We also shared an interest in photography. She had her always-working Canon; I had my temperamental Zenith, a Russian camera, which became the theme of many jokes.

3   One day, encouraged after an interesting and relatively trouble-free trip to Togo, we decided to hitchhike through Ghana. Our backpacks ready, cameras loaded, and spirits excited, we said good-bye to our fellow students. Two weeks and many beautiful memories later, we arrived at our destination, a small village in North Ghana just a couple of miles away from Burkina Faso.

4   It was supposed to be our last evening before heading back, when we met two teenage boys who told us how easy it is to cross the border to Burkina Faso even without visas. Wanting to experience yet another African country and maybe to impress the students back in Accra, we decided to take the risk.

5   "We will just take a couple of photos, look around, and go back the same day," Lisa said, her voice full of excitement.

6   "You will have to take the pictures since my camera is having a bad day," was my response, as if that was the only problem we should worry about.

7   The warm sunshine coming through the window screen woke us up that morning. Aromas of the street-cooked breakfast wafted in. Delicious grilled plantain never tasted so good. All we needed was a drink of coconut juice. We were ready for the day.

8   The road to the border led through woods. The mild wind tingled our bare arms and faces. The ever so colorful African earth painted our shoes red with each step.

9   Two sleepy border patrol guards smiled as we crossed the border and greeted the little boy who followed us from the village on his yellow bike.

10   "I don't even know what language they speak in this country," Lisa said.

11   "We don't even have the right currency of this country," I added, realizing that this was not a well-planned affair.

12   Just then we came upon a tiny village with men dressed in long embroidered shirts and women in colorful skirts.

13   "Oh my, have you ever seen anything like it?" exclaimed Lisa, pointing to an enormous flag posted in the middle of the village square. It was indeed extraordinary in its design and bright patterns.

14   She reached for her camera and started shooting.

15   Suddenly, a tall man with a hat grabbed Lisa's hand and said in English, "Taking pictures is not allowed here!" His voice was harsh and angry.

16   "Let go!" she screamed.

17   "Give me your camera!" he shouted.

18   "Leave me alone!" Lisa yelled louder.

19   They were both wrestling with the camera.

20   Meanwhile, more people gathered around us, their voices and their faces clearly showing us that we were not welcome there.

21   "They come here to take pictures and later to laugh at us," someone said loudly.

22   "Take the camera away!"

23   "Destroy the film!"

24   I don't like crowds, let alone angry ones, and the situation was getting worse by the minute. "This is dangerous," I thought, realizing that we were no longer in our beloved Ghana with its friendly people. The stories of kidnapped foreigners flashed through my mind. The villagers must have had a bad experience with foreigners to react in such a resentful way.

25   "Just give them the film," I murmured to Lisa.

26   "Over my dead body!"

27   "That might just be, Lisa. Don't be silly."

28   "This is the film with the crocodiles. Don't you understand!"

29   Ah, she mentioned the crocodiles, yet another of our brilliant ideas! We had a local guard let us see the crocodiles up close and feed them chicken. We barely escaped

before too many of them came out of the swamp. Lisa snapped a couple of pictures before we had to run.

30   "We will visit them again on our way home and you will take the whole roll," I was trying to be funny.

31   Just then the crowd parted and a serious looking village official approached us. Everyone was trying to explain what was happening.

32   "You must give me the film or I will take you to prison,"he demanded.

33   "I am not giving you my film!!!"

34   Prison was more like a mud hut; nevertheless, there we ended up. We could hear the angry crowd outside.

35   "Give me your passports!" the one with the hat demanded.

36   "How do you like your crocodiles now?" I whispered.

37   Suddenly there was some commotion outside and voices raised in a local dialect. The Ghanian guards we met earlier that day burst in.

38   "You are coming with us!"

39   Lisa looked at me and winked. Outside, next to the soldiers' motorbikes stood the little boy and his yellow bike.

40   Safely across the border, and after the lecture from the guards, we kissed the little boy's cheeks and showered him with treats.

41   And no, I don't have the photograph of the crocodiles on my wall. Lisa's camera and the film were stolen on our way back to the campus. My Zenith, though, is one of my cherished possessions.

Questions for Analysis

1. What is the function of the first two paragraphs of the story? What is the function of the third paragraph?

2. What transitions in the story signal the passage of time or change in location? Underline them.

3. Much of the action and humor of the story is revealed through the dialogue. Look at how the dialogue is handled mechanically: its punctuation, placement of quotation marks, use of capitalization, the paragraphing of dialogue, and the identification of the speakers.

4. Notice that in some dialogue, the speakers are not identified. How do you know who is speaking?

5. Much of the enjoyment and tension in a story also comes from oppositions—conflicts, surprises, and contrasts. List some of the most important oppositions.

6. What do the main characters—Bozena and her friend—have in common? But, more important, how are they different, and how do those differences contribute to your enjoyment of the story?

FINAL WRITING ASSIGNMENT

Write about a time when you found yourself in a surprising, unpleasant, or even dangerous situation. Perhaps you had an adventure that would be fun to write about. Establish the circumstances (*who, what, where,* and *when*) at or near the beginning, and then let the action unfold. You may wish to include a bit of dialogue as Bozena Budżyńska did.

Although your narrative may not be as long as Bozena's, you will probably find that it will need more than a single paragraph.

Writing a Report

In college and beyond, the results of meetings, discussions, laboratory experiments, and research need to be communicated clearly and accurately. Managers, teachers, scientists, students, businesspeople, and community leaders want to know these results so they can evaluate and act upon them. These people are often busy, however, so they want a brief report that summarizes what happened, how it happened, and perhaps why.

This chapter will show you how to write several types of reports by

- examining a model report
- analyzing what makes reports effective
- thinking through ways to organize reports
- writing reports

A MODEL PARAGRAPH: A REPORT

A **report** is an organized summary of information; it clearly and accurately relates the decisions, actions, or conclusions involved in an event, an activity, or an investigation.

There are many kinds of reports: formal reports (called *minutes*) on discussions and votes taken in a meeting, reports on the main ideas of a lecture or presentation, reports on the results of an experiment or some research. Each kind follows its own format, but all reports have some things in common.

A report typically begins with a statement of its purpose, its central idea or claim, or its conclusions. Then it presents the supporting information, usually in chronological order or in categories. However, as you will soon see, the supporting information includes only the main ideas or actions. Reports have fewer explanations, details, or examples than other kinds of writing.

Many reports are entirely **objective:** they don't include any opinions of the writer. But some reports also make recommendations based on the information they present. We'll look at both types of reports in this chapter, beginning with the objective report.

A blueprint of a typical informational report looks like this:

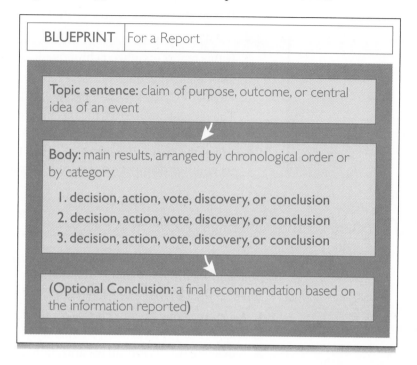

The following is an informational report appearing in a newsletter addressed to the residents of a small suburban city. As you read it, notice that the writer summarizes the facts objectively, offering no opinions or interpretations

Budget Challenges

1   The City Council has taken a number of steps in its attempt to solve the city's $2 million budget deficit. On July 12, the Council held a public meeting to hear suggestions from residents. A number of residents offered opinions on possible cuts in services identified in the survey conducted the previous month. However, many residents objected to any cuts in services. Instead, the residents suggested ways that the city could increase revenues. Those suggestions included raising the sales tax from 8.5 percent to 8.75 percent or creating new taxes, such as a tax on hotel rooms.

2   Following the open meeting, the City Council discussed the issues at its Financial Review Meeting on July 31. Members of the Council explored ways to save money by cutting or reducing services. Among the possibilities were a cutback in garbage collection from three times a week to twice a week, and a reduction in the number of days scheduled for picking up the leaves during the fall.

3   After a lengthy debate, the Council agreed not to make any immediate changes in services at this time and to explore the effects of new taxes suggested by the residents at the July 12 meeting. One member of the Council estimated that an increase in the sales tax would result in an additional $1.5 million in revenue. However, residents would have to vote on this increase in a general election, which could not be scheduled until November 7.

4   The Council instructed members of its staff to investigate the possible results of any cuts in services, tax increases, or new taxes and to report its findings to the Council at the August 5 meeting. No further action will be taken until then.

Questions for Analysis

1. Which sentence states the central claim? Underline it.
2. What is the purpose of the report?
3. Is this report organized chronologically or by category?
4. How many meetings does the report discuss? What words or phrases identify those meeting times and purposes? Circle these words or phrases.
5. The report summarizes the meetings and doesn't mention the names of any participants. Why?
6. When the staff reports its findings to the City Council in August, how will its report probably be organized—chronologically or in categories?

WRITING ASSIGNMENT FOR A REPORT

Attend, participate in, or observe some event. Take notes on what you see and hear, and then write a report summarizing your observations for someone who wasn't there. Here are some possible events to report on:

1. A lecture in one of your classes
2. A lecture or presentation you attend
3. A meeting (for a club, an organization, a committee, or even a gathering of friends)
4. A television show that presents important or interesting information
5. An experiment in a laboratory course
6. A celebration, holiday gathering, or other joyous event you participate in or witness

Bring along a notebook or laptop computer to record your notes. Don't worry about writing complete sentences. No one will read the notes but you.

Gathering, Generating, and Arranging the Materials

Remember that a report is a **summary:** a discussion of only the main ideas or most important information, arranged in a way that makes the information easy for the reader to grasp. (See Chapter 26 for more discussion of summaries.) Because the report is a summary, it omits almost all the specific details. A report on a meeting, for example, includes the decisions agreed to, the votes taken, or the activities completed. It doesn't include what each person said at the meeting, but only the outcomes of the discussion. It doesn't include every fact, but only those facts that lead to decisions, votes, activities, or actions. Therefore, as you take notes of the event, focus only on the central activities or ideas.

Consider these guidelines when taking notes:

1. Record the time and date, the place, and the names of the important participants.
2. Record everything that happens in very brief notes, which needn't be complete sentences. Omit small details unless they make the main ideas clearer.
3. As the event progresses, you'll see the results of a discussion, the outcome of votes, the decisions agreed to, or the central ideas emerging. Highlight those in your notes by underlining, or by drawing arrows or stars in the margins.

After the event, rewrite your notes, limiting them to a summary of the essential information. Think of the summary as a series of topic sentences. Focus on the main actions, results, or conclusions. Omit supporting details, unless they're

TIPS

For Distinguishing Between a Narration and a Report

Most narratives lead up to a climax, with the most important information at the end. You can visualize a narrative as a triangle:

Narration

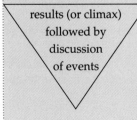

events
leading to
climax

A report, however, reveals the result at the beginning of the first paragraph. The details leading up to that result follow. You can visualize the report as an upside-down triangle:

Report

results (or climax)
followed by
discussion
of events

TIPS

For Organizing a Report

If there is a printed (or spoken) outline of a lecture or printed agenda of a meeting, be sure to get a copy of it. The outline will guide you toward the main points.

necessary to explain the central claim. Omit names of the participants unless they're important (for example, the name of the instructor delivering a lecture). If you've recorded any statistics, cite only those that give totals, not those that contribute to the totals. The information you select may be only one-tenth of what you recorded in your original notes, but it should be sufficient for your readers to understand what happened.

Then organize your notes. The following questions should serve as guidelines:

1. What was the purpose of the event?
2. What was the outcome (or what were the outcomes) of the event?
3. What main ideas were expressed? Or what important decisions were made?
4. What supporting details are needed to explain or illustrate those ideas or decisions?

Then arrange the material. Here's an informal chronological outline of the report you've seen earlier:

> July 12 meeting
>   Service cuts suggested
>   Objections to service cuts
>   Suggestion for increasing sales tax
>   Suggestion for hotel tax
> July 31 meeting of City Council
>   Reducing garbage pickup
>   Reducing leaf pickup days
>   Increase in sales tax
>   Decision to consider increase in sales tax
>   Requiring vote by the residents
> Staff to investigate and report at August 5 meeting

Composing the Report

Now write a draft of the report. State the result or central claim first, followed by the most important supporting ideas, actions, and details.

Remember that the information you include must be **objective:** you cannot state opinions or interpret events. Compare the following statements. The first directly expresses an opinion, while the second presents a conclusion without interpreting it:

Not objective:	The committee made a good decision. (The writer has interpreted the decision to be good.)
	The group argued over the issue. (The writer has interpreted the discussion as an argument.)
Objective:	The committee decided to delay the vote until the following meeting.
	Members of the group expressed different views of the issue.

TEMPLATES FOR A REPORT

The following templates may be useful in stating the central idea or claim at the opening of a report.

1. At the meeting on _____ at _____ , the _____ decided to _____ .

2. The _____ committee passed the following resolution at its meeting on _____ at _____ .

3. After a long debate at the _____ meeting, the _____ committee _____ agreed to _____ .

4. By a vote of _____ to _____ , the _____ decided that _____ .

5. The _____ group has agreed to _____ ; the policy will take effect on _____ .

Revising Your First Draft

Let the following questions guide your revision of the paragraph. You may answer them yourself or collaborate with three or four classmates who'll discuss them. If the answer to any question is "no," revise to eliminate the problem.

REVISION CHECKLIST FOR A REPORT

	YES	NO
1. Is the purpose of the event clear?	☐	☐
2. Is the central idea or claim clearly stated at the beginning?	☐	☐
3. Are the outcomes clearly summarized?	☐	☐
4. Are the main results presented in a clear and consistent organization?	☐	☐
5. Do all the details contribute to the point?	☐	☐
6. Is the level of detail appropriate?	☐	☐
7. Is the report objective?	☐	☐
8. Is the language clear throughout?	☐	☐

Take notes of these responses to guide your revision. Rewrite the paper later, and attend to word choice, clarity, and conciseness.

Further Revising and Editing

Return to the report and revise it again. Edit and proofread your work, checking for misspelled words, words accidentally left out or left in, and any other errors you notice. Hand in a clean copy of your work.

ADDITIONAL WRITING ASSIGNMENT

Write a report of a discussion you were involved in that led to a simple decision. It could have taken place within your family, among your friends, at work, in a club, or in a class. Limit the topic to something you can examine specifically in one paragraph. Begin by stating the decision you reached, and then explain how you reached it. Be sure to include who was involved (although you don't have to use everyone's name), and when and where the decision was made.

A STUDENT MODEL REPORT

The following report was written some time ago by Veronica Fleeton, a former member of the armed forces and a student at Truman College. The purpose of the report is to recommend improvements in the cleanliness of the washrooms of the college. As you read the report, notice that it summarizes the results of a plan the students themselves devised. Notice that it explains how the plan was carried out, as well as what each part of the plan revealed. Notice, too, that it concludes with a call to action, which—in this case—was actually accepted.

Let's Keep It Clean
Veronica Fleeton

* * * *

1   A student committee has examined the washrooms throughout the college over the semester. We have concluded that there is very little evidence that they are being cleaned often enough. During several visits to various washrooms on different floors this semester, members of the committee found the doors propped open, the maid carts in the washrooms, but no one actually cleaning the rooms. At other times, we have checked the trashcans, sinks, commodes, floors, corners, and soap and towel dispensers. We found that trashcans were overflowing and the towel and soap dispensers were empty. As a further test, we intentionally planted objects in conspicuous areas such as corners or stall areas. We revisited the washrooms the next day to see if they had been removed. In most cases, they were right where we had planted them.

2   We recommend that this situation be immediately addressed. The college has a large population, and the washrooms are constantly being used. Since they are receiving heavy usage, they should be cleaned at least twice a day to accommodate students in both day and night classes.

Questions for Analysis

1. Who is the probable audience for this report?

2. What is the topic sentence of the first paragraph—the sentence whose claim summarizes the conclusions of the report? Underline it.

3. According to the report, what specific problems were found in the washrooms?

4. What did the group of students do to uncover these problems? Specify each action the students took. (Notice that the report is organized by categories of action.)

5. Although the report is not arranged in chronological order, some transitions make references to time. Circle them.

6. Read the conclusion. Restate the recommendation in your own words.

FINAL WRITING ASSIGNMENT

Make a simple plan to observe and evaluate a facility in your school or surrounding community. Does it function well or badly? Would you recommend any improvements? You might evaluate the cafeteria or parking facilities at your school (if the school has them). You might evaluate the service and food at a local restaurant, the facilities in a recreation center or health club, or even a childcare center for small children. You don't have to uncover a scandal or file a complaint. In fact, your report may discuss how well the facility operates. You may wish to collaborate with other students on this report, especially if it involves observations happening at different times. Divide the visits among the members of the collaborative group.

Your plan shouldn't require frequent visits, and you shouldn't disturb the people in the facility. But while you're there, take notes of your findings.

If you collaborate, each person in the group may write a separate report, or the group may collaborate on a single report. The audience for the report should be the person or persons who would find it most useful. End the report with praise of the facility, or recommendations for improvements, if either seems appropriate.

CHAPTER 21

Describing a Process

Describing a process—explaining how to do something or how something works—is useful for communicating because it tells readers something they want or need to know. A recipe in a cookbook tells how to perform a process. Instructions for operating MP3 players and appliances describe processes. So do descriptions of how an egg develops into a mature chicken or how an automobile's motor mixes gasoline with air. This chapter will help you describe a process by

- examining a model description of a process
- analyzing what makes a such a description effective
- thinking through ways to organize a description of a process
- describing a process

A MODEL PARAGRAPH: PROCESS ANALYSIS

A **process analysis** explains how something works or how to do something. When it explains how something works, it *observes* the process and describes it in the third person. ("The egg begins to hatch in a week.") When it explains how to do something, it *instructs* the reader in sentences that tell what he or she is to do. ("Mix the eggs, flour, and milk in a large bowl.")

In either case, your explanation or instructions must be clear. You must consider what readers already know and what they need to know. You must define technical terms. You must present the information completely and logically—breaking down the process into a series of steps. And you must label those steps clearly with transitional expressions.

The organization of a process analysis typically includes two parts:

1. an introduction of the process and a list of the materials (tools, parts, or ingredients) that the process requires
2. an explanation of each step in the process, presented in **sequential order**—that is, moving consecutively from first to last—so readers can visualize the process or perform it themselves

A blueprint of such a paragraph would look like this:

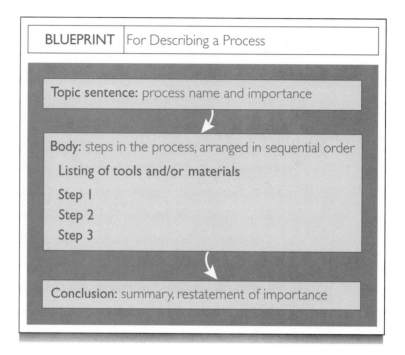

| BLUEPRINT | For Describing a Process |

Topic sentence: process name and importance

Body: steps in the process, arranged in sequential order

Listing of tools and/or materials

Step 1

Step 2

Step 3

Conclusion: summary, restatement of importance

The following example of a process analysis is taken from an article in the "Hers" Column of the New York Times *in 1984 by Sue Hubbell. Ms. Hubbell, a graduate of Swarthmore College, moved to the Ozark Mountains of Missouri, where she kept bees for 25 years. The example describes her experiences in teaching a young man how to tolerate bee stings. Her goal is to help readers understand the process, not perform it.*

The Beekeeper
Sue Hubbell

* * * *

1   The time to harvest honey is summer's end, when it is hot. The temper of the bees requires that we wear protective clothing: a full set of overalls, a zippered bee veil and leather gloves. Even a very strong young man works up a sweat wrapped in a bee suit in the heat, hustling 60-pound supers while harassed by angry bees. It is a hard job, harder even than haying, but the jobs are scarce here and I've always been able to hire help.

2   This year David, the son of a friend of mine, is working for me. He is big and strong and used to labor, but he was nervous about bees. After we had made the job arrangement, I set about desensitizing him to bee stings. I put a piece of ice on his arm to numb it and then, holding a bee carefully by its head, I put it on the numbed spot and let it sting him. A bee stinger is barbed and stays in the flesh, pulling loose from the body of the bee as it struggles to free itself. The bulbous poison sac at the top of the stinger continues to pulsate after the bee has left, pumping the venom and forcing the stinger deeper into the flesh.

3   That first day I wanted David to have only a partial dose of venom, so after a minute I scraped the stinger out. A few people are seriously sensitive to bee venom; each sting they receive can cause a more severe reaction than the one before—reactions ranging from hives, to breathing difficulties, accelerated heart beat and choking to anaphylactic shock and death. I didn't think David would be allergic that way, but I wanted to make sure.

4   We sat down and had a cup of coffee and I watched him. The spot where the stinger went in grew red and began to swell. That was a normal reaction, and so was the itching that he felt later on.

5   The next day I coaxed a bee into stinging him again, repeating the procedure, but I left the stinger in place for 10 minutes, until the venom sac was empty. Again the spot was red, swollen and itchy, but had disappeared in 24 hours. By that time David was ready to catch a bee himself and administer his own sting. He also decided that the ice cube was a bother and gave it up. I told him to keep to one sting a day until he had no redness or swelling and then to increase to two stings. He was ready for them the next day. The great amount of venom caused redness and swelling for a few days, but soon his body could tolerate it without reaction and he increased the number of stings once again.

6   Today he told me he was up to six stings. His arms look as though they have track marks on them, but the fresh stings are having little effect. I'll keep him at it until he can tolerate ten a day with no reaction and then I'll not worry about taking him out to the bee yard.

Questions for Analysis

1. What tools or clothing are needed to perform this process? Why is the process difficult?

2. What is the first main step in the process of desensitizing David to stings? What actions are involved in this step? Why are those actions necessary?

3. What is the second step, and which parts of the actions are different from the ones in the first step? What leads to the next step in the process?

4. At what point does David take over the process? Why?

5. What does Hubbell assume the reader doesn't know about the effects of bee stings? What does she therefore explain?

6. Hubbell does not define technical terms. If there are any you don't understand, look them up in a dictionary.

WRITING ASSIGNMENT FOR DESCRIBING A PROCESS

Write an entertaining description of the steps you, a friend, or a relative goes through in performing some daily, weekly, or less frequent ritual. Keep the topic simple so you can describe it in one paragraph. For example, you could describe dressing for a date or formal event, getting ready to write a paper, doing stretching and warm-up exercises, studying for a big examination, combing hair over a bald spot, or straightening up the mess in a bedroom. Assume your readers are adults who might find your article in a popular magazine.

Gathering, Generating, and Arranging the Materials

After choosing a topic, brainstorm or cluster several lists of details to include in the paragraph. Add to these lists as more ideas occur to you. Include the following:

1. All the materials needed to perform the task (for example, shampoo, conditioner, towel, blow-dryer, comb, brush, hair spray, curlers, curling iron, wall mirror, handheld mirror, and chewing gum)

2. Any terms that need to be defined and explained (such as *mousse*, *gel*, or *tantrum*)

3. All the steps in the process (for instance, washing, drying, setting, combing out, teasing, further combing, primping, crying—and then resetting, combing out, and so on)

Now make an outline in which you list all the steps in the order you will present them. Include explanations of each step. The outline might look like this:

   I. Introduction and topic sentence
     a. What the process is
     b. Why the process is worth knowing about
  II. Preliminary information
     a. Tools needed
     b. Definitions of terms
 III. Steps in the process
     a. Step one
     b. Step two
     c. Step three, and so on
 IV. Conclusion

Composing the Paragraph

Now compose a first draft of the paragraph that includes all of these elements:

1. A topic sentence that identifies the process and suggests or outlines the steps, such as "My teenage son goes through an elaborate ritual in preparing his hair for a date."
2. One or more sentences that list the materials used in the process and define any specialized terms.
3. A step-by-step description of the process, arranged in sequential order.

TEMPLATES FOR PROCESS ANALYSIS

The following templates may be useful in introducing and identifying the steps in a process analysis.

1. You can perform _____ by following this simple procedure.

2. The process of _____ involves several steps.

3. To perform _____ , you need to do _____

    _____.

4. The operation of _____ takes place in _____ stages.

5. The first step in the process involves _____.

6. Second (third, fourth), you must _____.

7. After completing this step, _____.

8. Next, be sure to _____.

9. At the same time, _____.

10. Finally, place the _____ on the _____.

Revising Your First Draft

The following questions should help you in revising the paragraph. You may answer them yourself or collaborate with three or four classmates. If the answer to any question is "no," revise the paragraph to correct the problem.

REVISION CHECKLIST FOR PROCESS ANALYSIS

	YES	NO
1. Does a topic sentence identify the process and introduce, outline, or suggest the steps involved?	☐	☐
2. Is the goal of the explanation—either to understand the process or perform it—clear?	☐	☐
3. Does the paragraph identify the tools or materials needed to perform the process?	☐	☐
4. Does the explanation define any new or specialized terms?	☐	☐
5. Is the explanation logically organized in sequential order?	☐	☐
6. Are all the steps included and clearly explained?	☐	☐
7. Are the transitions between steps clear?	☐	☐
8. Is the language clear throughout?	☐	☐

Take notes of these responses to guide your revision. Rewrite the paper when your mind is clear and you can attend to word choice, clarity, and conciseness.

Further Revising and Editing

Return to the paragraph and revise it again. Edit and proofread it before handing in a clean, proofread copy of your work.

ADDITIONAL WRITING ASSIGNMENT

Write instructions that accompany the following diagram to explain and clarify the process it illustrates. Assume that your purpose is to inform readers who want to understand the process. They will be looking at the diagram as they read your instructions.

Begin by studying the diagram and outlining the steps. Then write a full description of the process, explaining each step or series of related short steps. Revise the paper until it clearly follows a logical format such as the following:

1. An opening sentence that introduces the subject, summarizes the process, and mentions the materials or parts involved.
2. A middle section (7–10 sentences) that describes each step in the process.
3. A final sentence that summarizes the process and ends gracefully.

Be sure to include appropriate transitional words to show the movement between steps. Revise and edit your paper and hand in a clean final draft.

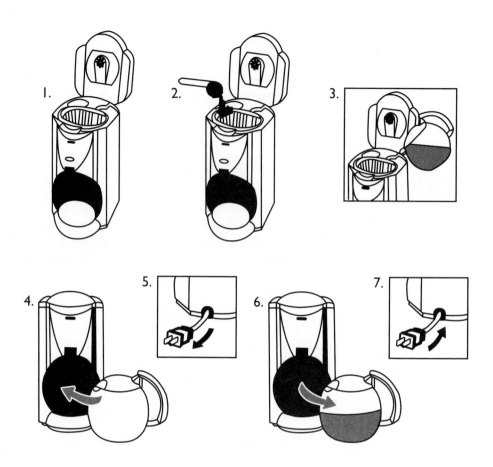

A STUDENT MODEL ESSAY

Here's a process analysis by Erica Teal, a student at Truman College in Chicago. As you read it, notice her goal in writing the essay—that is, what she wants readers to do with the information. Pay special attention to the first paragraph, noting why she feels the process she describes is important and how she introduces the three major steps of the routine.

Stretching for the Long Run
Erica Teal

* * * *

1 I never thought warming up and stretching were important before and after a long run, until I pulled a muscle in my thigh, and that was just part of the pain. Isn't running supposed to be good for you? I was having too much fun to worry about such details. Warming up and stretching might possibly be the most crucial part of your workout, so don't skip it. To get the best out of running from both performance and enjoyment, adopt a routine that includes an effective warm-up, stretching, and cooldown.

2 Warming up is often overlooked, but should be part of your injury prevention routine. After my injuries, I decided to warm up five minutes each day before my run. The benefits of a warm-up before running include increasing your body temperature and getting your blood flowing. The increased blood flow in the muscles gives you flexibility, which reduces the likelihood of injury. To warm up, you could pedal for a few minutes on a stationary bike or jump rope a few turns.

3   After you have warmed up, you are ready to stretch. Stretching gives flexibility, and without it, you are an injury waiting to happen. Stretching is not the same as warming up. A good stretching routine will enhance your performance through elasticity. When you stretch, move slowly and gradually into each position and hold it for ten seconds before relaxing again. Repeat each stretch several times. After stretching, your muscles are warmer and more elastic. Never stretch a muscle to the point of pain. Pain indicates that you are stretching too hard or that you have an injury that needs some attention—a doctor's attention, that is.

4   Cooling down is just as important as warming up. After a run, it's important to recover gently. A cooldown brings your muscles back to a resting state and decreases the likelihood of your getting hurt. A cool-down period is at least three minutes long and is followed by stretching the muscles to avoid soreness and, once again, injury.

5   A good warm-up, stretching, and cooldown are especially important before and after a run. The more you prepare for a run, the more you will enjoy yourself. You'll be injury free and happier in the long run.

Questions for Analysis

1. Which sentences in Erica Teal's first paragraph serve as the introduction? Underline them. Which sentence states the thesis? Circle it.

2. What three steps in the process does Erica list in the first paragraph?

3. Underline the topic sentences in the three body paragraphs.

4. Briefly summarize the benefits of each step in the process.

5. What words in the conclusion restate (but vary) the main points of the body paragraphs?

FINAL WRITING ASSIGNMENT

As Erica Teal does, write a paragraph of advice to people your age about the process involved in succeeding in some task. Your audience should be people who want or need to know this advice.

The subject matter could relate to a job, to schoolwork, or to family or social life. You might, for example, discuss how to prepare for a job interview. You might discuss how to share responsibilities at home or how to resolve a typical conflict between siblings or roommates. In any case, choose a process you know well and feel confident explaining.

Your instructor may ask you to make an oral presentation, followed by a question-and-answer period, to your collaborative group (or the whole class) prior to submitting your final draft of the paragraph. Explaining the process aloud and hearing responses or questions from others often reveal steps or instruction that need clarification.

Writing About Causes and Effects

Much of our thinking focuses on analysis: why something happened or is happening. Why won't my car start? Why do I have a sore throat? Likewise, we need to know the results of some action or event. If I have the car repaired, how much will it cost? If a take a new antibiotic, will it cure my sore throat?

Writing about causes or effects is an important part of academic and professional life. In science courses—and in scientific professions—you may investigate the causes of a chemical reaction or the effects of a new chemical. In a nursing course, you need to know the causes of a fever and the results of a treatment. In a history course, you may need to know the causes—and results—of a war. In a business course—and in actual businesses—you may examine the effects of a new method of accounting or of advertising.

This chapter will show you how to write a paragraph on causes or effects by

■ examining a model paragraph of causal analysis

■ analyzing what makes an effective paragraph on causes or effects

■ thinking through ways to organize the paragraph

■ writing a cause or effect paragraph

A MODEL PARAGRAPH: CAUSAL ANALYSIS

A **cause** is the reason an event happens, while an **effect** is the result of the cause. So, for instance, the cause of passing a course may be studying hard, while the effect of passing the course may be earning a degree. A **causal analysis** examines the cause of an event or the results of an event, or both.

Many things, however, have more than one cause. For example, a person may become ill from lack of sleep, too much stress, poor nutrition, and exposure to a virus. Likewise, many things can have more than one effect. A violent storm may destroy trees, flood streets, blow down power lines, and even tear the roofs off of houses.

If you trace several causes or effects in your paragraph, you may organize it in the same way as narration or process analysis. You can tell a story of why something happened in **chronological order.** You were late this morning because the alarm didn't go off, you missed your bus, and the traffic was much slower than normal. Or you can explain the causes in a series of steps arranged in **climax order**—moving from the weakest to the strongest reason. The restaurant is popular because the location is good, the prices are low, the service is fast, and the food is terrific.

Blueprints of a paragraph discussing causes and a paragraph discussing effects might, therefore, look like these:

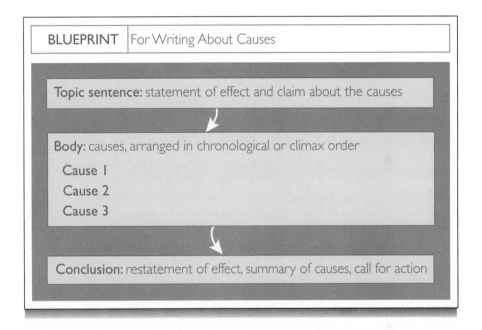

BLUEPRINT | For Writing About Causes

Topic sentence: statement of effect and claim about the causes

Body: causes, arranged in chronological or climax order
    Cause 1
    Cause 2
    Cause 3

Conclusion: restatement of effect, summary of causes, call for action

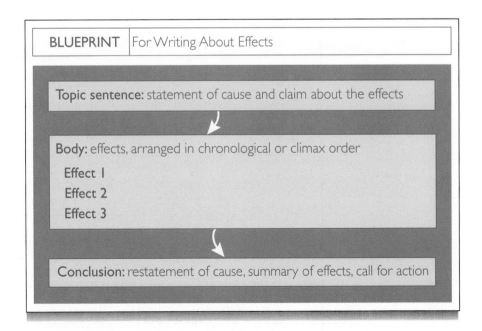

BLUEPRINT | For Writing About Effects

Topic sentence: statement of cause and claim about the effects

Body: effects, arranged in chronological or climax order
    Effect 1
    Effect 2
    Effect 3

Conclusion: restatement of cause, summary of effects, call for action

Here's an example of a short essay that explains the probable causes of an effect. Because the causes need to be explained in detail, the essay devotes an entire paragraph to each. As you read the essay, notice that the first paragraph introduces the effect—the result of the causes—while the body paragraphs of the essay explore those possible causes of—or reasons for—the effect. Note that the conclusion summarizes the causes.

The Mystery of Custer's Last Stand

* * * *

1   Probably no single battle in U.S. history has created more controversy than the Battle of Little Bighorn River. On June 25, 1876, General George Armstrong Custer made his famous last stand against members of the Great Sioux Nation. After dividing the 700 troops of the Seventh Cavalry into three groups that would surround and attack a Native American village, he took command of one group and rushed them into the battle alone. As a result, 3,000 Sioux, led by their chief, Sitting Bull, killed Custer and every one of his 250 men. No one will ever know why Custer ordered his men into such a one-sided fight in which they had no chance for survival. No one will ever know why he didn't retreat once the battle had begun. No one will know the answers because no one from Custer's side lived to tell the story. However, some information about the battle, gathered from scouts, messengers, and the members of the other two groups, suggest four reasons.

2   First, Custer ignored the orders of his commanding officer. He was supposed to bring his troops to the valley of the Little Bighorn River and wait there until one of the other two divisions could join him. Custer decided to attack alone. He rode his troops all night and well past dawn, and his men and horses were exhausted when they entered the valley.

3   Second, Custer apparently ignored the advice of his own Native American scouts. The two men, Mitch Bouyer and Bloody Knife, warned him that there were too many Sioux warriors to be captured even by all of the soldiers in the three divisions. Custer probably thought that his Seventh Cavalry could whip any Native American party and didn't take the warnings of the scouts seriously.

4   Third, Custer probably misinterpreted the movements of the Sioux. After one of the three divisions, led by Major Marcus Reno, charged the village, a messenger told Custer that it contained far more warriors than they had expected. Custer apparently assumed that the number of Sioux didn't matter because they were fleeing. He and his men therefore rushed to the far end of the campsite to cut off the escape. He rode hard and fast, further wearing down his men and their horses.

5   Fourth, after the three groups of Custer's men had separated, they probably soon lost communication with each other. Major Reno attacked the campsite, expecting Custer to follow him from the rear. But Custer was trapped at the far end of the camp. Reno finally retreated to the woods near the village, where he was forced to make a stand. His Native American opponents not only outnumbered him, but they had better weapons. By the time the third division of the Seventh Cavalry arrived, many of Reno's men were dead, and this last division was trapped as well. Meanwhile, Custer and every single one of his men were being slaughtered.

6   To this day, when people think of Custer, they think of headstrong behavior and stupidity. Although no one knows exactly why Custer and his men lost their lives, that headstrong behavior and that stupidity are the likely reasons.

Questions for Analysis

1. Why doesn't this essay give definite causes (reasons) for Custer's defeat and the deaths of his soldiers?

2. How many causes does the essay suggest? What in the organization makes these causes easy to locate?

3. What is the function of the first paragraph of the essay? Which sentence makes its central claim? What specific details do you learn from it? What is the function of the last paragraph?

4. What words and phrases show a lack of certainty? Why are they necessary?

5. When does the essay depart from past-tense explanation? Why?

6. Is the final paragraph a logical conclusion, based on the evidence presented? Why or why not?

WRITING ASSIGNMENT FOR CAUSAL ANALYSIS

Write a paragraph analyzing the reasons behind an important decision you've recently made: for example, to major in a particular field, to work part time, to move, or to buy a car. Assume you're writing to explain your decision to an academic advisor, your parents, or a friend.

Gathering, Generating, and Arranging the Materials

Explore your ideas by clustering or brainstorming a list of the causes. Then choose at least three reasons for your decision—the most important, most distinct reasons—to develop in your paragraph. List the reasons either (1) chronologically if they happened in a time sequence, or (2) from the least to most important if they happened at or near the same time. This method, called **climax order,** builds to the strongest point:

> "Finally, and most importantly, I realized . . ."
> "But these reasons alone wouldn't have been enough. The strongest reason came . . ."

Using a simple chart may help you organize ideas:

Possible Causes (or Possible Effects)

1. _____

Example: _____

2. _____

Example: _____

3. _____

Example: _____

Composing the Paragraph

As you begin work on your first draft, write a topic sentence that establishes your claim, and introduces or summarizes the causes you'll discuss:

> "After careful consideration, I decided to major in computer sciences *for several reasons.*"
> "I decided to major in computer sciences *because of my interest in business, my good grades in computer classes, and the great job opportunities in this field.*"

Explore your reasons in the body of the paragraph, but don't just list them. Explain them, and, if you can, support them with specific examples.

TEMPLATES FOR CAUSES AND EFFECTS

The following templates may be useful in introducing and identifying causes:

1. The first cause of _____ is _____.

2. One source of _____ may be _____.

3. A second reason for _____ probably _____
   _____

4. _____ could have happened _____ because _____
   _____.

5. _____ might have resulted from _____.

These templates may be useful in introducing and identifying effects:

6. One effect of _____ is that _____.

7. A third result of _____ is _____.

8. Consequently, _____ occurred when _____
   _____.

9. As a result, _____ the _____ happened.

10. _____ may have led to (caused) _____.

Revising Your First Draft

The following questions should help you in revising the paragraph. You may answer them yourself or collaborate with three or four classmates. As usual, if the answer to any question is "no," revise the paper to correct the problem.

REVISION CHECKLIST FOR CAUSES AND EFFECTS

	YES	NO
1. Does a topic sentence state the effect (the decision) and clearly introduce or summarize the causes?	☐	☐
2. After reading the topic sentence, stop to predict what will follow. Does the body of the paragraph fulfill reasonable predictions?	☐	☐
3. Is the organization logical and easy to follow?	☐	☐
4. Are examples needed at any point?	☐	☐
5. Are the transitions between causes graceful and clear?	☐	☐
6. Are the transitions between steps clear?	☐	☐
7. Is the language clear throughout?	☐	☐

Take notes of these responses to guide your revision. Rewrite the paper when your mind is clear and you can attend to word choice, clarity, and conciseness.

Further Revising and Editing

Revise the paragraph again. Edit and proofread it, and, as always, hand in a clean, proofread copy.

ADDITIONAL WRITING ASSIGNMENT

Choose another important event in your life, one resulting in three or more important effects—changes in your living conditions, changes in your behavior, or changes in your attitudes. Here are a few examples:

gaining a younger sibling

losing a loved one or caregiver

losing a job

being involved in an accident

moving to a new neighborhood, city, or country

Assume that your audience is a group of people who know you now but didn't know you at the time of the event. Your purpose should therefore be to let these people understand you better. If you prefer not to write about yourself, choose an event in the life of someone you know well.

List at least three effects of the experience, perhaps by brainstorming, and then arrange them from weakest to strongest. Consider examples of each. Freewriting may be useful here. Explain and illustrate each effect.

A STUDENT MODEL PARAGRAPH

The following paragraph was written by Sara Sebring at Chattanooga State Community College. In this paragraph, she describes an allergic reaction to a medicine—in other words, the effects of a cause. As you read it, notice first the cause (or reason she took the drug), the immediate results of taking it, and then the longer-term results.

A Reaction to Medicine
Sara Sebring

* * * *

Some people can take medicines without having a problem. Others react mildly to some medicines. However, I had one terrible reaction to an antibiotic, one that taught me that I would never take it again. I went to the doctor to get treatment for my right eye, which had been swollen shut for the previous two days. He told me my eye was infected and gave me a prescription for Duricef and Polymeral. I then left the doctor's office, had the prescription filled, and went home to take the medicine. I took the Polymeral and had no problems; however, after taking the Duricef, I experienced an allergic reaction. First I fell asleep and slept for fourteen hours. When I finally woke up, my speech was slurred; I couldn't catch my breath; my neck broke out in a rash; and my face was swollen all over. In addition, I kept running into walls because my balance was off. As a result, I called the doctor's office and reported my condition to the nurse, who said the doctor would return my call in two minutes. Four hours later, the doctor returned my call and said he would phone the drug store and order a new prescription to stop my swelling. To my dismay, the new prescription was never called in, and three days later my symptoms were still present. Finally, after four days of misery, the symptoms disappeared, and I found out that Duricef was a type of penicillin to which I have an allergic reaction. From this entire episode, not only did I learn that I cannot take Duricef, but I also learned that some doctors do not respond quickly enough to their patients' medical needs. This was truly the worst experience I have ever had.

Questions for Analysis

1. What is the topic sentence of this paragraph? Underline it.

2. What was Sara Sebring's first reaction to the medicine? Following that, what symptoms did she exhibit? What was the last allergic reaction she mentions, and what transition introduces it?

3. The allergic reaction caused her to take additional actions. What were they? What results did they bring?

4. What transitional expressions show time relationships? How much time passed between Sara's initial infection and her recovery from the allergic reaction?

5. Two changes in Sara Sebring's attitude and behavior occurred as results of this experience. What were they? What transition introduces them? How—and why—do these changes relate to the topic sentence?

FINAL WRITING ASSIGNMENT

Like Sara Sebring, you or someone you know has probably suffered from an illness or had a medical emergency. Write a paragraph in which you describe what happened—the causes—and the results of the illness or emergency—the effects. Your subject matter will determine which part receives the most development. For example, if the illness or emergency resulted in important changes in health, behavior, or attitude, you may wish to stress those changes.

CHAPTER 23

Classifying Information

Classification helps us make sense of our world. Each day we place or identify things in categories: busy streets and quiet streets, expensive and inexpensive purchases, important mail and junk mail. In business transactions, we organize computer databases into categories: accounts paid, accounts unpaid, and new customers. In our coursework, we study information in categories. Biology, for example, classifies life-forms as reptiles, mammals, and amphibians. Thus, classification is a type of thinking and writing you use in college coursework—in reports and examinations. Classification can also support description, definition, and causal analysis.

This chapter will show you how to write a classification paragraph by

- examining a model paragraph of classification
- analyzing what makes a classification effective
- thinking through ways of organizing a classification
- writing a classification paragraph

A MODEL PARAGRAPH: CLASSIFICATION

Classification is a way of dividing a group of people, objects, or ideas into categories based on some **criterion,** or standard for judging them. In fact, you've already seen an example of a paragraph that places people into categories. The model paragraph in Chapter 2 is a classification of pizza customers.

You could classify a group in many ways. You could divide cars into categories based on size: full-size cars, midsize cars, compact cars, and subcompacts. But you could just as easily classify cars by cost, gas mileage, or color. You could classify college students into four categories according to the number of credit hours they've completed: first-year students, sophomores, juniors, and seniors. But you could just as easily classify students by age, grade-point average, or religion.

Therefore, once you've chosen a topic for a paragraph on classification, follow these guidelines for creating clear and consistent categories:

1. *Use only one criterion for classifying.* You can group people according to their income, intelligence, or ambition—but not according to income *and* intelligence or intelligence *and* ambition. Otherwise, you might discover that a person fits into more than one category. A rich student can also be bright; a bright student can be either lazy or hardworking. Besides, if the classification gets too complicated, you'll never be able to discuss it fully in a single paragraph.

2. *Create categories that allow room for everyone or everything you are classifying.* Suppose, for example, that you're grouping your classmates according to age. If the youngest category includes people between the ages of eighteen and twenty, it excludes a

classmate who is only seventeen. A better category might be students seventeen to twenty years old or students twenty years old and younger.

3. *Illustrate the categories through examples.* The categories will be clearer, and more interesting, if you provide specific examples. Show a hardworking waitperson scooting from table to table, balancing four trays on one hand while pouring water in cups with the other.

Above all, don't oversimplify, or you might be guilty of stereotyping people. There are too many negative and misleading stereotypes in the world already, and they tend to create and reinforce prejudices.

A blueprint of a typical paragraph of classification might look like this:

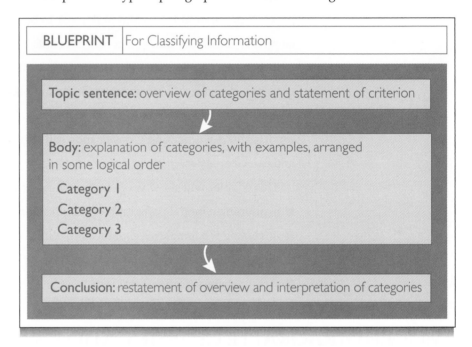

BLUEPRINT | For Classifying Information

Topic sentence: overview of categories and statement of criterion

Body: explanation of categories, with examples, arranged in some logical order

Category 1
Category 2
Category 3

Conclusion: restatement of overview and interpretation of categories

Here's an example of a paragraph that classifies people into three categories. As you read it, notice the criterion for determining the categories. Notice the explanations of each category. And notice the examples that support each explanation.

Every Body Has a Place

* * * *

If you are looking for ways to describe fat, muscular, and wiry bodies, William H. Sheldon has created a handy vocabulary for doing so. In 1940, he invented a system of classifying body types that corresponds to the three layers of cells in an unborn child: endoderm—the inner layer, which later becomes the stomach and intestines; mesoderm—the middle layer, which forms the skeleton, muscles, and veins; and ectoderm—the outer layer, which develops into the skin, hair, nails, and nervous system. He believed that these layers emerge differently in each adult. In some people, the layers are evenly balanced, but in many people, one layer dominates the others and forms one of Sheldon's three main body types. The first is the *endomorph*, a person with a soft body and many bulges. He or she may have strong muscles, but they are hard to find beneath the body fat. Famous endomorphs include the late comedians John Belushi and Chris Farley, and other examples are easy to spot at any ice cream or pizza parlor. The second body type is the *mesomorph*, a person with big bones and rock-hard neck, shoulders, chest, stomach, buttocks, arms, and legs. You often see mesomorph body types in ads for health clubs or as action heroes like, for instance, the movie star, former Mr. Universe, and Governor of California (elected in 2003), Arnold Schwarzenegger. The third type is the *ectomorph*, a person with a wiry body, small bones, thin chest, a flat stomach, and small buttocks. An ectomorph tends to have long arms and legs, and is generally very active. Just about any marathon runner is a typical ectomorph. Although Sheldon's classifications aren't perfect, they provide a useful way to describe the hulks, hunks, and scarecrows who populate the planet and compete in the rings and on the fields, courts, and tracks of the world.

Questions for Analysis

1. Which sentence introduces Sheldon's classifications of body types? Why isn't it the first sentence in the paragraph?
2. What criterion determines the classifications?
3. What is the stated purpose for classifying body types?
4. Does the paragraph include any examples? If so, what words or phrases identify them as such?
5. Examine the conclusion. What attitude toward Sheldon's classifications does it express?

WRITING ASSIGNMENT FOR CLASSIFICATION

For a popular magazine that specializes in entertainment and humor, write a paragraph of classification on one of these topics. They'll be familiar to your audience (your classmates), so have some fun and try to be entertaining.

1. types of people on a crowded bus, in a library, or in a department store during a blowout sale, or at a party
2. types of people at movie theaters or concerts
3. types of grandparents
4. types of customers you serve
5. types of pets (or dogs)

Gathering, Generating, and Arranging the Materials

Begin by thinking of a single criterion for classification—such as the amount of noise that fans at a sporting event make—and then brainstorm or cluster at least three categories, along with examples that fit within each. If you can't think of a criterion, start by generating categories, see what criterion holds them together, and eliminate or reshape the categories that don't fit the criterion.

Organize your ideas into a chart like the following one. Notice that the main categories, on the left, are arranged from most to least noisy. The examples of each type haven't yet been placed in any order.

Types of fans at a sports event

Criterion:	Amount of noise they make

Category	Example
Loudmouth	The "expert" commentator, the insulter, the screamer, and the person who talks about everything but the game
Semi-talker	The occasional cheerer, the groaner, and the question-asker
Quiet mouth	The watcher, the silent scorekeeper, and the sleeper

Composing the Paragraph

Write a first draft of the paragraph. Discuss the examples in some detail so your paragraph is lively and entertaining, and not merely a list. Then put your paper aside.

TEMPLATES FOR CLASSIFICATION

The following templates may be useful in introducing classifications:

1. The _____ can be classified into _____ categories.

2. There are _____ types of _____, determined by the level (size, length, degree) of _____.

3. _____ can be divided into _____ main groups (categories) according to their _____.

4. We have several levels of _____.

These templates may be useful in introducing the specific categories:

5. One category is _____.

6. The first group is the _____.

7. Second, _____ form the largest group of _____.

8. A major classification is the _____, which _____ _____.

9. Finally come the group known as _____, who _____ _____.

Revising Your First Draft

The following questions should help you in revising the paragraph. You may answer them yourself or collaborate with three or four classmates. As usual, if the answer to any question is "no," revise to eliminate the problem.

REVISION CHECKLIST FOR CLASSIFICATION

	YES	NO
1. Does the opening introduce the classification clearly?	☐	☐
2. Are the categories divided according to a single criterion?	☐	☐
3. Is the organization logical and easy to follow—moving from least to most, most to least, or some other consistent order?	☐	☐
4. Does the paragraph explain and illustrate each category?	☐	☐
5. Are there clear transitions to introduce each category?	☐	☐
6. Is the language clear throughout?	☐	☐

Take notes of these responses to guide your revision. Rewrite the paper when your mind is clear and you can attend to word choice, clarity, and conciseness.

Further Revising and Editing

Return to the paragraph and revise it again. Edit and proofread it before handing in a clean, proofread copy of your work.

ADDITIONAL WRITING ASSIGNMENT

Write a classification of any of the following:

1. favorite places at your college
2. types of movies
3. types of music (or concerts)
4. nightclubs, restaurants, or other gathering places

No matter what subject you choose, assume again that you're writing for a popular magazine, that your audience is already somewhat familiar with your topic, and that your purpose is mainly to entertain.

Be sure to use only one criterion for classifying and create at least three different categories within the classification. Include at least one interesting or humorous example for each category.

A STUDENT MODEL ESSAY

Jane Smith is a student at Danville Community College in Danville, Virginia. As you read her essay, notice that the first paragraph introduces three categories and that each category is discussed in a separate paragraph in the body of the essay. Notice, too, how her concluding paragraph summarizes the discussion and ends on a positive note.

Chamber Volunteers
Jane Smith

* * * *

1   My first volunteer experience was when I joined the Burnes County Junior Women's Club twenty-five years ago. Since that time I have become so involved in this activity that a group of my friends has dubbed me a professional volunteer. According to my husband John, this is defined as any job that offers no pay, demands lots of time, and requires the donation of supplies from our office. Over the years, I have learned a great deal about the different types of people who work in volunteer organizations. Although most organizations consist of similar types of members, as president of the Burnes County Chamber of Commerce, I have observed that the chamber has a unique membership because these people are representing their businesses, industries, and professions. Therefore, they have distinct motives for offering their time and talents. The majority of these volunteers can be divided into three main categories: the bossy executives, the glory seekers, and the backbones.

2   The bossy executives are always right. If you don't believe it, just ask them! They have grand ideas and are very willing to tell you how to carry them out. The problem is they expect everyone else to do all the work. When someone else comes up with a different idea, the bossy executives will discuss only its negative aspects even if the idea is much better than theirs. If the committee decides to proceed with the new idea, the executives will still do it their way. No matter what the outcome of a project is, you can be sure of one thing: if anything goes wrong, it is not the bossy executives' faults because they are always right.

3   Unlike the bossy executives who like to be heard and obeyed, the glory seekers participate so that they can be seen. They are the first ones to volunteer for a project that is high profile and involves a lot of free publicity. If they happen to think of a good idea, everyone will know because they will be sure to take all of the credit. However, if anything goes wrong, they react like the bossy executives and are never at fault. When the time comes to begin working, they somehow feel that their presence is not necessary. They leave all of the planning and activities to the third type of volunteers, the backbones.

4   In any committee, if you can have at least one backbone, you can be sure that the work will be done because the backbones believe that actions speak louder than words. Whether these backbones are chairing committees or are members of the team, you know that they will follow through with their responsibilities and pitch in to complete the unfinished tasks of the bossy executives and the glory seekers. Their only motivation is the satisfaction they receive from supporting the organization, and their aim is to follow through and complete every project. When the cameras are flashing and the credits are given, the backbones are content to take the pictures and give the credits to the other team members.

5   Even though the backbones are the ideal chamber members, the bossy executives and the glory seekers do contribute in their own special ways to the goal of the Burnes County Chamber of Commerce. That goal is to deal with issues that affect the economic well-being of our community, and, through the unified efforts of everyone, this goal continues to be achieved.

Questions for Analysis

1. Jane Smith begins the first paragraph by discussing her experience in volunteer organizations and her role as president of a local chamber of commerce. How do those experiences qualify her to classify volunteers?

2. What are three categories of volunteers introduced in the first paragraph? Underline them. What words identify and repeat categories in the three body paragraphs? Underline them, too. How is the language similar? How is it different?

3. Examine the first sentence of the third paragraph, beginning with "Unlike the bossy executives." Why does Jane Smith make this contrast? What role does it have in unifying the essay?

4. How are the first two categories similar? How are they different? Which of the three categories does Jane Smith respect the most?

5. Jane Smith doesn't say which category she belongs to. Which one is the most likely? Why?

6. How does the structure of this essay resemble the structure of a single paragraph? How is the structure different? Why wouldn't this essay work as only one paragraph?

FINAL WRITING ASSIGNMENT

Like Jane Smith, classify people in an organization into three types—saving the best type for last. You can discuss types of students in a class, members of a club, or players on a team. Arrange the categories so the best appears at the end. According to the directions of your instructor, you may write a single paragraph or an essay.

CHAPTER 24

Writing Comparisons and Contrasts

Each day you make comparisons or contrasts: this lesson was easier than the last one; traffic this morning ran as smoothly as traffic the day before; the test in biology was the hardest yet. Comparisons and contrasts examine the similarities and differences among people, ideas, or things.

Comparisons and contrasts play an important role in writing. For example, you use them to evaluate: that is, to argue that something is better, more valuable, or more useful. Or you use them to clarify: that is, to explain an unfamiliar idea by comparing or contrasting it to a familiar one.

This chapter will show you how to write a comparison or contrast paragraph by

- examining a model paragraph of comparison and contrast
- analyzing what makes a comparison and contrast effective
- thinking through ways to organize a comparison–contrast paragraph
- writing a comparison–contrast paragraph

A MODEL PARAGRAPH: COMPARISON–CONTRAST

A **comparison** shows how people or things are similar. A **contrast** shows how they are different, usually when evaluating them. And a **comparison–contrast** paragraph discusses both similarities and differences. To do so, it must also organize, explain, and illustrate the similarities and differences in ways that make sense.

There are two main strategies for organizing the comparisons and contrasts:

1. **Whole-to-whole.** In this organization, you describe Movie X completely, and then Movie Y completely. You draw the comparisons and contrasts while describing Movie Y, or after describing Movie Y.
2. **Part-to-part.** In this organization, you describe one part of Movie X, such as its plot, and then compare it to the plot of Movie Y. Then you return to Movie X to describe its acting, followed by a comparison to the acting in Movie Y. You continue in this way until you have drawn all the comparisons between the two movies. If you discuss point A about one subject, then your readers must see its relationship to point A about the other.

Keep these additional guidelines in mind as you compose and revise the paragraph:

1. *Don't oversimplify.* Very few issues are as simple as black versus white or good versus evil. So be careful as you evaluate—deciding if something is better than something else. It's fine to say that Movie X is better than Movie Y, but don't automatically assume Movie Y is a waste of time. Movie Y may be entertaining, but not as entertaining as Movie X.

2. *Don't use circular reasoning.* When explaining why Movie X is better than Movie Y, give specific reasons to support your claim. Don't say that Movie X was better because it was better. For example, the statement, "Movie X was interesting because it held my attention" is circular reasoning because "interesting" and "held my attention" mean the same thing. Say instead, "Movie X was interesting because it was fast-moving, full of surprises, and well acted."

3. *Be consistent in your organization.* Make your comparisons and contrasts easy for your readers to understand. If you discuss the acting, directing, photography, and editing of Movie X, you must discuss all these matters for Movie Y. You should also present the points in the same order for both movies.

A blueprint of a paragraph using the whole-to-whole organization might look like this:

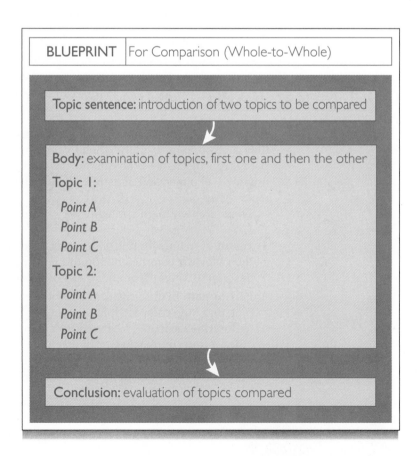

| BLUEPRINT | For Comparison (Whole-to-Whole) |

Topic sentence: introduction of two topics to be compared

Body: examination of topics, first one and then the other

Topic 1:

 Point A
 Point B
 Point C

Topic 2:

 Point A
 Point B
 Point C

Conclusion: evaluation of topics compared

And a blueprint of a paragraph using part-to-part organization might look like this:

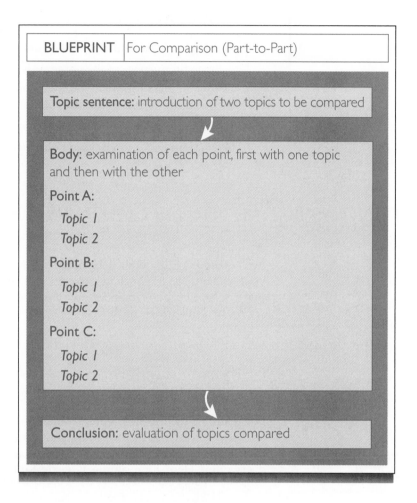

BLUEPRINT | For Comparison (Part-to-Part)

Topic sentence: introduction of two topics to be compared

Body: examination of each point, first with one topic and then with the other

Point A:

Topic 1
Topic 2

Point B:

Topic 1
Topic 2

Point C:

Topic 1
Topic 2

Conclusion: evaluation of topics compared

The following paragraph compares and contrasts two subjects. As you read it, notice that it begins with a comparison of white and dark meat. Then notice that it's followed by a comparison between two types of birds.

The Light and the Dark of It

* * * *

Why do chickens and turkeys have both dark and light meat, while most other birds we eat (such as quail, duck, or pigeon) have dark meat only? The reason is that there are two types of fibers in the muscles of birds: red and white. The red fibers contain a muscle protein that makes animals able to work for much longer periods than do white fibers, which are designed for short, powerful bursts of activity. You can therefore guess which birds have the most red-fibered muscles—and the most dark meat. They are the creatures that must fly long distances to migrate or to find food—the geese, ducks, and quails. But chickens and turkeys live a less strenuous life. They move around by walking or running, so only their legs and thighs contain dark red fibers. These land birds don't use their wings and breasts very much, so these parts contain light white fibers. In fact, the absence of red fiber in wings and breasts is an advantage. When chickens and turkeys are threatened, their wings and upper bodies must deliver a lot of power quickly but for only a short time. The next time you pay an extra 50 cents for an order of all-white-meat chicken, remember that these parts of birds racked up fewer trips in the air than you may have taken in an airplane.

Questions for Analysis

1. What is the topic sentence of the paragraph?
2. Is the main purpose of the paragraph to inform, persuade, or entertain?
3. List the points of comparisons and contrasts in the paragraph. Which does the paragraph mainly discuss—similarities or differences?
4. Which words show similarities? Which words show differences?
5. Is this primarily a whole-to-whole or a part-to-part comparison?

WRITING ASSIGNMENT FOR COMPARISON–CONTRAST

Write a paragraph for a feature section of a newspaper or magazine. Compare two subjects you know well. Conclude by recommending one or both of them to your readers. You might choose two movies, two popular music groups (or songs), two books, two performances, two types of sports (or two games in the same sport), two celebrities, or two cars.

Gathering, Generating, and Arranging the Materials

Use a simple grid to help you generate and organize the points of comparison and contrast. As you list one point about the first subject, you must consider the corresponding point about the second subject. Continue until your grid covers every point. Here, for example, is a grid for two movies:

	Beach Blanket Bozos	Crash and Burn
Type	comedy	action
Actors	no-name actors	major stars
Plot	not much plot	suspense leading to a climax
Contents	slapstick humor and silly dialogue	action more important than clever dialogue
Rating	R	R
Length	90 minutes	two hours
Cost	low budget, no unusual locations, and hardly any special effects	high budget, with plane crashes, car chases, and many special effects
Audience	appeals to teenagers	appeals to teenagers

After you've completed the grid, construct a second grid with the items grouped according to similarities and differences:

Beach Blanket Bozos		Crash and Burn
Similarities		
Rating	R	R
Audience	teenagers	teenagers
Dialogue	weak	weak
Differences		
Type	comedy	action picture
Actors	no-name actors	major stars
Plot	not much plot	suspense leading to a climax
Contents	slapstick humor	action
Length	90 minutes	two hours
Cost	low budget, no unusual locations, and hardly any special effects	high budget, with plane crashes, and many special effects

Then decide on the type of organization to use in your comparison. Read down both columns of the grid for a whole-to-whole approach. Read across the columns for a part-to-part. As you continue planning, select examples of each point of comparison or contrast, and consider what explanations to provide.

Composing the Paragraph

Now compose a first draft. Write a topic sentence that states the central claim of the paragraph. Use either the whole-to-whole or part-to-part organization. If the organization you choose doesn't work well when you compose the draft, switch to the other organization. Add transitions to introduce the points of comparison and to emphasize the similarities and differences. Try to conclude with a statement that sums up the main points of the paragraph, or that packs a punch.

TEMPLATES FOR COMPARISONS AND CONTRASTS

The following templates may be useful in introducing comparisons:

1. _____ and _____ are similar in a number of ways.

2. There are several ways in which _____ is like _____ _____.

3. Likewise, _____ also resembles _____ in the way they both _____.

4. Just like _____ , the _____ , too.

These templates may be useful in introducing contrasts:

5. There are several differences between _____ and _____.

6. _____ is different from _____ because _____.

7. Unlike the _____ , a _____ doesn't _____ , but instead will _____ .

8. One important distinction between _____ and _____ is that _____.

9. On the other hand _____ will not _____.

Revising Your First Draft

As usual, the following questions should help you in revising the paragraph. You may answer them yourself or collaborate with three or four classmates. If the answer to any question is "no," revise to eliminate the problem.

REVISION CHECKLIST FOR COMPARISONS AND CONTRASTS

	YES	NO
1. Does the topic sentence clearly establish the comparison or contrast?	☐	☐
2. Is the purpose of the comparison or contrast clear?	☐	☐
3. Does the organization follow a consistent pattern—whole-to-whole or part-to-part?	☐	☐
4. Do any of the comparisons or contrasts need further explanation or illustration?	☐	☐
5. Are there clear transitions between the comparisons or contrasts?	☐	☐
6. Does the conclusion follow logically from the points of comparison or contrast?	☐	☐
7. Is the language clear throughout?	☐	☐

Take notes of these responses to guide your revision. Rewrite the paper when your mind is clear and you can attend to word choice, clarity, and conciseness.

Further Revising and Editing

Return to the paragraph and revise it again. Edit and proofread it before handing in a clean, proofread copy of your work.

ADDITIONAL WRITING ASSIGNMENT

Assume you're a newspaper or magazine columnist who often expresses opinions on matters of interest to you and your readers. Write a paragraph of comparison and contrast on one of the following topics:

1. small or large families
2. studying liberal arts or studying business administration
3. marrying young or marrying later in life
4. working part time to pay for college or borrowing the money
5. doing high-impact activities such as running or low-impact activities such as walking

Choose a subject you know well. If you used whole-to-whole organization in the earlier assignment in this chapter, then use part-to-part here—or vice versa. Explain any ideas that are unfamiliar to your readers. Tell little stories or cite examples to support your main points if possible. Recommend or suggest which of the two things you're comparing is best—or perhaps best for some people, while the other thing is best for other people.

A STUDENT MODEL ESSAY

Here's an essay written by Mirham Mahmutagic, a student at Truman College who grew up in Bosnia. It compares how Bosnians and Americans think about how to use their time. As you read it, notice how Mirham makes a part-to-part comparison between time spent in school in the two countries and then, later, between time spent with families.

Examining the Differences: Old Tradition vs. New World
Mirham Mahmutagic
* * * *

1   When I first came to the United States, I remember wondering why Americans have fast-food restaurants, or why they spend so much time eating out, instead of cooking their meals at home, the way we did in Bosnia. Well, after spending six years here in Chicago, I have learned that besides food, everything else also seems to be "on the go," here in the States. That, simply said, is the biggest difference between the "old world" of tradition and history, where I came from, and this "new world" of high rises and big money.

2   In the United States, time, or should I better say the lack of it, has a direct impact on people and their decision on how to use that time throughout the entire course of their lives. People in the States spend a lot of time in their schools, starting as early as the first grade of elementary school. On the average, children here attend eight to nine hours of school every day, five days a week, while children in Bosnia, on the average attend five to six hours of school every day. After graduating from high school, American youth will face five to eight years of schooling toward their professional degrees, while in Bosnia that translates into four to five years of college. Finally, at the

age of twenty-three, a young doctor starts practicing medicine in Bosnia, while at the same age of twenty-three the American future physician is finishing the first year of medical school and heading toward the next three. Ironically, the American doctor will spend the rest of his or her life chasing that time "lost" in school by working endless hours and 48-hour shifts year after year, while the doctor in Bosnia will work forty to fifty hours a week, enjoying most Saturdays and Sundays off.

3   This seemingly simple time grid suggests that children in Bosnia do have more time, outside of school, to spend with their families and their friends while children in the States don't. Accordingly, children in Bosnia do grow up closer to their families, and as adults they adjust their lives so that they can spend more time in their homes and less time at work. On the other hand, children in America probably grow up with a different set of values, where their career and work will come first and the time for their families and friends will come second. As a result of their dedication to their careers and their work, young Americans appear to be more independent, ambitious, efficient, and prosperous compared to youth in Bosnia. As adults, they seem to have much stronger work ethics than Bosnians do, which ultimately leads to the current immeasurable economic difference between the two countries. Today, those Americans are able to give their children modern toys and video games, expensive cars, and the latest technological inventions, which is something most of the children in Bosnia grow up without.

4   I can still remember just how beautiful my childhood was growing up in Bosnia. My friends, with whom I have spent endless hours playing games like tag, riding a bike or playing ball, constantly surrounded me. Unlike many fathers in the States, my father always had time to play with me, help me with the homework, and simply be around whenever I needed him. Now that I think about how important his presence in my life was, I keep wondering if I will have enough time to spend with my child to be able to show him how important the family is, just like my parent showed to me.

Questions for Analysis

1. What sentence or sentences in the first paragraph introduce the comparison? Underline the sentence(s). What are the topic sentences in the remaining paragraphs? Underline them as well.

2. How many comparisons does Mirham make in the second paragraph? Number them, and circle the words that serve as transitions between comparisons.

3. In the third paragraph, and then later in the final paragraph, Mirham begins to discuss how the two cultures he compares seem to have differing values. What differences does he see? Do you agree with his observations? Which values, in your opinion, are most important?

4. How does the conclusion relate to ideas earlier in the essay?

5. Construct a grid of the comparisons or contrasts Mirham makes in his essay. Are they consistent and complete?

FINAL WRITING ASSIGNMENT

Like Mirham Mahmutagic, write a paragraph (or an essay) in which you contrast one set of values you have learned with another set that other people seem to think are important. You might consider any one of the following issues: the relationship between parent and child, neatness, study habits, manners, behavior in school, behavior at parties, showing off, the use of language (including slang or profanity), or the importance of money or material possessions.

CHAPTER 25

Defining Terms

No matter what type of writing you do—whether you're explaining a process, comparing objects or ideas, or writing a report—you may use a term that your audience doesn't understand. In these cases, you need to define, or explain what you mean by, the term. Sometimes defining can be done in a few words. But sometimes defining is not so simple. A word may have several meanings, or you may want to define the word in a special way. Your definition may therefore require a full paragraph in which you discuss and illustrate exactly the meaning you intend—or don't intend.

This chapter will show you how to write a paragraph of definition by

- examining a model definition
- analyzing what makes a definition effective
- thinking through ways to organize a definition
- writing a definition

A MODEL OF DEFINITION

As you predict your audience's response to your writing, you must think about the times they might ask, "What do you mean?" Suppose, for example, that in a letter suggesting changes in the curriculum to your local school board, you use the term "good students." The board members might wonder whether you mean quiet students or talkative students, competitive students or cooperative students, students who can recite what they learn or students who can apply it. You need a **definition**—an explanation of how you're using the term.

A definition often begins with a sentence that restates the definition. Then a fuller explanation of its meaning follows. That explanation might include examples that ground the definition specifically or contrast it with other terms that clarify the meaning.

You can state the definition in one of two ways:

- You can express it simply by using a **synonym**—a word with virtually the same meaning as another word. Here are examples of definitions by synonym:

A CRT is computer terminology for a *monitor* or *television screen*.
The *aardvark*—or *anteater*—is found in southern Africa.
To eschew means to *avoid*.

The synonym must be the same part of speech as the word it defines: noun and noun, infinitive and infinitive, adjective and adjective. In this way, one term can substitute for another.

- You can express it in a **formal statement of definition,** the method most often used in dictionaries. The statement begins by placing the term into a larger category, or class:

Word	Category or class
A psychiatrist	is a medical doctor . . .

Then the statement adds **criteria**—or standards for judging the definition and distinguishing it from other things in the category or class:

Word	Category or class	Distinguishing characteristics
A psychiatrist	is a medical doctor	who specializes in the study, diagnosis, treatment, and prevention of mental illnesses.

You may be able to quote the formal statement of definition from a dictionary or textbook—if that definition fits your meaning and you cite your source. (See Chapter 27, which discusses the use of quotation marks and italics with definitions.) But writers sometimes define a term in a way that doesn't fit the standard dictionary definition. You'll see an example shortly.

Once you've defined the term, you can then explain and illustrate exactly the meaning you intend—or do not intend—in the remainder of the paragraph. That definition may therefore include comparisons, contrasts, a classification, and examples.

Here's a blueprint of one way a definition paragraph might be organized, assuming that the definition includes three important points. Note that it arranges the points in **climax order**—going from the least important to the most.

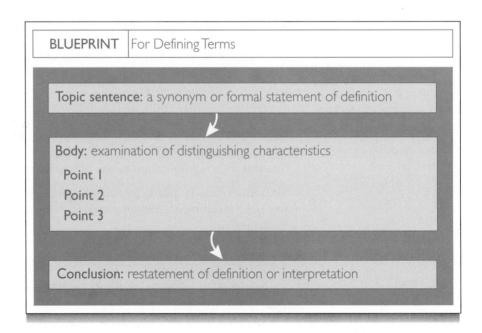

| BLUEPRINT | For Defining Terms |

Topic sentence: a synonym or formal statement of definition

Body: examination of distinguishing characteristics

    Point 1

    Point 2

    Point 3

Conclusion: restatement of definition or interpretation

The following definition, from an article in the September 22, 2003, issue of Newsweek, *discusses the growing epidemic of allergies among young people. As you read it, note the formal definition of* allergy *in the first sentence. The author then describes how a foreign substance enters the body and how the body reacts to it.*

What Is an Allergy?
Jerry Adler

* * * *

1   An allergy is an overreaction by the immune system to a foreign substance, which can enter the body through a variety of routes. It can be inhaled, like pollen or dander, the tiny flakes of skin shed by domestic animals. It can be injected, like insect venom or penicillin, or merely touch the skin, like the latex in medical gloves. Or it can be ingested. According to the Food Allergy & Anaphylaxis Network, almost any food can trigger an allergy, although eight categories account for 90 percent of all reactions: milk, eggs, peanuts (technically, a legume), tree nuts, finfish, shellfish, soy, and wheat. (Allergies have nothing to do with the condition known as food intolerance; people who lack an enzyme for digesting dairy products, for instance, may suffer intestinal problems, but they are not allergic to milk.)

2   For reasons not fully understood, in some people these otherwise harmless substances provoke the same reactions by which the body attempts to rid itself of dangerous pathogens. These may include sneezing, vomiting, and the all-purpose localized immune-system arousal known as inflammation. The lungs may be affected; allergies are a leading trigger for asthma attacks. In extreme cases, the reaction involves virtually all organ systems and leads to anaphylaxis, a dramatic drop in blood pressure accompanied by extreme respiratory distress that may be fatal without prompt treatment.

Questions for Analysis

1. Where is the term allergy defined? Put a star next to the definition.

2. How many ways may foreign substances enter the body? What words help you identify the number of ways?

3. What examples are given for each of the ways? Underline them. Which of the ways has the most examples? Why?

4. Underline the sentence that draws a contrast. Why was that sentence included?

5. What is the topic sentence of the second paragraph that makes its central claim? Underline it twice.

6. Is the second paragraph arranged in sequential order or climax order? What effect does this arrangement create?

7. The definition of allergy also includes definitions of additional terms. Circle the words defined. Why are those definitions included?

8. This definition includes a description of two processes. What are they? How does understanding these processes increase your understanding of the word *allergy*?

WRITING ASSIGNMENT FOR A DEFINITION

Assume you are writing a short definition of a term for your classmates. Your choice of a term to define can come from your coursework in school (for example, *mitosis* in biology, *html* in computer science, *socialism* or *capitalism* in social science, *ethics* in philosophy, *thesis statement* in composition, the *Middle Ages* in world history, *counterpoint* in music, *impressionism* in art, and so on). It can come from your job experiences. Or it can come from your experiences living in another country or in different parts of the United States.

Gathering, Generating, and Arranging the Materials

Brainstorm a list, or make a clustering diagram, of the most important or easily noticed characteristics of the term you are defining. You should mention at least three characteristics. Consider examples you can cite for each characteristic.

Here's a clustering diagram for the definition of *allergy*. It starts with the term and its formal definition in the center. Each branch explores a different characteristic. Further branches list the examples.

After you've brainstormed or clustered your ideas, select at least three of the most important characteristics to develop further. Make sure each is supported by examples. Include contrasts. Notice, in the clustering diagram, that *allergy* is partially defined by what it is not—it is not a food intolerance.

You may wish to outline your paragraph of definition before you start writing, using the blueprint as your guide.

Composing the Paragraph

Look over your outline. Then write a preliminary topic sentence that makes a claim that includes a general definition. Continue with sentences that state each of the characteristics you've chosen. Follow each characteristic with an example. You may want to expand on one example if it works especially well to illustrate the meaning of the word you are defining. Conclude with a restatement or interpretation.

TEMPLATES FOR DEFINITIONS

The following templates may be useful in stating definitions:

1. _____can be defined as a _____, which can be characterized by _____.

2. A/an _____ is a type of _____, often including a _____.

3. According to _____, a (n) _____ is "_____ _____."

4. _Webster's Collegiate Dictionary_ defines _____ as _____. However, I would define the term somewhat differently, as _____.

These templates may be useful in introducing the distinguishing characteristics:

5. It may be _____. It may also be _____. And finally it may be _____.

6. It includes _____, but does not include _____ _____.

7. It differs from _____ in several ways. For example, it _____.

8. Unlike _____, it is _____ and _____.

Revising Your First Draft

Once again, the following questions should help you in revising the paragraph. You may answer them yourself or collaborate with three or four classmates. If the answer to any question is "no," revise to eliminate the problem.

REVISION CHECKLIST FOR DEFINITIONS

	YES	NO
1. Is there a clear statement of definition, either through a formal statement or a synonym, or both?	☐	☐
2. Is the purpose of the paragraph clear?	☐	☐
3. Do the distinguishing characteristics fit within the definition?	☐	☐
4. Are these characteristics supported by examples?	☐	☐
5. Does the paragraph include a strong extended example?	☐	☐
6. Is the organization of the paragraph clear?	☐	☐
7. Does the conclusion bring the paragraph to a graceful or powerful end?	☐	☐
8. Is the language clear throughout?	☐	☐

Take notes of these responses to guide your revision. Rewrite the paper when your mind is clear and you can attend to word choice, clarity, and conciseness.

Further Revising and Editing

After waiting a few hours or days, return to the paragraph and revise it again. Edit your work, and hand in a clean, proofread copy.

ADDITIONAL WRITING ASSIGNMENT

Define an abstract term such as *love, friendship, maturity, beauty,* or *success.* Establish your criteria for the definition and use one person as an extended example that defines your term. Narration may help you explain what this person did to show love or friendship. You may want to introduce contrasts—what this person chose not to do, or what other people often do. The full definition may require only one paragraph or be several paragraphs.

A STUDENT MODEL ESSAY

Amra Skocic, a student at Truman College who came from Bosnia, wrote the following definition essay. In it, she defines the term courageous act *by examining the behavior of one person. Note that she begins by citing a formal definition of the term in the first paragraph. Then, in the body of the essay, she gives the definition substance by examining specific criteria and characteristics and providing examples of each. Her final paragraph summarizes the key points.*

True Courage
Amra Skocic

* * * *

1   It is not very often that we hear about, read about, or experience a truly courageous act. Indeed, do we really even understand what a courageous act is? According to *Webster's Dictionary, courage* is defined as "the ability to control fear when facing danger or pain." But there is much more involved. A courageous act is an unselfish gesture taken on a voluntary basis which involves some risk. An example is Oscar Schindler, the real-life hero of the movie *Schindler's List*, who performs a courageous act by saving thousands of Jewish lives during the Second World War.

2   Oscar Schindler is a German factory owner who employs Jewish people and later rescues them from death in the concentration camps. In the beginning, he is primarily motivated by the opportunity to start production and earn a high profit using forced labor. As time goes by, Schindler's motivation changes from greed to selflessness. As he witnesses the mass execution and torture of the Jews in Poland, he realizes that he has the ability to save innocent lives. Gradually this realization overcomes his desire for money. Led by unselfish motivation, his action meets the first criterion for courage.

3   A courageous act must be voluntary, meaning that the person performing the act must have the full opportunity to walk away and avoid risk. Schindler understands his choices, but the one that he makes is to employ Jewish people. He could just as well have employed German workers or used other options without taking any risk. The voluntary nature of employing Jewish people in his factory meets the second criterion for courage.

4   A courageous act involves risk and sacrifice. How much the goal is worth determines the price of risk. From the moment Oscar Schindler decides to save those innocent lives, he is aware of the danger to his own life. If discovered by the Nazis, he will inevitably be killed. This risk completes the third and the final criterion for a courageous act.

5   Is there anything worth risking our own lives for? For most of us, probably not, but for a courageous person like Oscar Schindler, obviously there is. This points out the great difficulty of true courage, which the world rarely sees. Today it is more common for people to act out of selfishness, to avoid any danger, and to let others volunteer. Schindler sets himself apart when he accepts a great risk without potential reward, and without hesitation. Schindler stands as a beacon of courage in a world that still has many dark corners. We would all do well to emulate the courage of Schindler.

Questions for Analysis

1. Amra Skocic includes a dictionary definition in her first paragraph. Why? What sentence in the first paragraph introduces the three main criteria she uses to shape her essay?

2. Underline the sentence in the first paragraph twice that introduces the three distinguishing characteristics of courage that will shape the essay. Number them.

3. In the second, third, and fourth paragraphs, the topic sentence makes a claim introducing each of the three criteria of the definition. Underline them. Where does she place these sentences and why?

4. Amra provides some contrasts in her extended examples. Underline them twice. Why does she provide them?

5. Would the definition be strengthened if she had discussed the actions of more than one person? Why or why not?

6. What ideas are repeated in the summary paragraph? Circle them.

FINAL WRITING ASSIGNMENT

Write your own personal definition of a good or bad manager, advisor, friend, teacher, or leader. Use an extended example of an individual. Include several characteristics in the definition. Introduce each one with a clear transitional expression, and illustrate each one. Your examples supporting the main points of the definition can come from your own experiences or the experiences of people you know, or they can be hypothetical.

CHAPTER 26

Summarizing and Responding

Summaries and responses play an important role in college writing. In essay examinations and papers, you demonstrate your understanding of a reading by briefly summarizing its main ideas and explaining them in a condensed form. But you often go beyond merely summarizing; you also respond to the reading. You analyze it, compare or contrast it with other material you've studied, agree or disagree with its ideas, or expand on them further.

This chapter offers you advice and practice summarizing and responding by

- examining a model summary
- analyzing what makes a summary effective
- taking you through the process of writing a summary
- then repeating the process with a response

A STUDENT MODEL: A SUMMARY

Before you can respond to something you've read, you need to summarize it so your readers (1) know the subject of the summary (such as the author and title of the reading if they're given); (2) understand the ideas you're responding to; and (3) know that you understand the ideas as well. If your summary of the material isn't accurate, your response may be inaccurate as well.

As Chapter 20 explains, a **summary** is a shorter version of a longer piece of information; it presents the main idea and the most important supporting information. A summary is also **objective:** it reports what you have read—with no opinions or interpretations. Therefore, a summary should never include the personal pronouns *I* or *me*. You'll state your interpretations and opinions in the response, which follows the summary.

Summaries vary in length from just a few sentences to several paragraphs, depending on the complexity of the information, the familiarity of the readers with the subject matter, and the length readers expect the summary to be.

A blueprint of a typical summary might look like this:

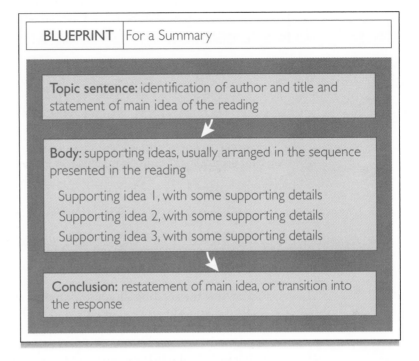

| BLUEPRINT | For a Summary |

Topic sentence: identification of author and title and statement of main idea of the reading

Body: supporting ideas, usually arranged in the sequence presented in the reading

Supporting idea 1, with some supporting details
Supporting idea 2, with some supporting details
Supporting idea 3, with some supporting details

Conclusion: restatement of main idea, or transition into the response

The following is a summary of Amra Skocic's essay found on pp. 286–287. Note that it identifies the author and title, includes only the main ideas of the original, and quotes a partial sentence from the original. It also establishes a context for the response, which you will see later in this chapter.

What Is Courage?

In "True Courage," Amra Skocic defines courage as "an unselfish gesture . . . which involves some risk." The gesture must also be voluntary and involve some personal sacrifice. She cites Oscar Schindler from the movie <u>Schindler's List</u> as an example. Schindler is a real factory owner who lives in Nazi Germany during World War II. Schindler acts unselfishly in employing Jewish workers in his factory and protecting them from harm. He voluntarily chooses to protect them and has nothing to gain personally from his action. Furthermore, Schindler risks his own life by protecting the Jews, for he knows that if the Nazis discover what he is doing, they will kill him. Therefore, Skocic argues, he fulfills all the criteria of the definition.

Questions for Analysis

1. Look at the first sentence of the summary. What factual information does it include?

2. How many criteria must be met to satisfy the definition of courage? List them.

3. Compare the summary to the original. What supporting details are omitted?

4. Is the summary objective? Does it include any opinions or interpretations?

5. Look at the phrase quoted from the original source. How is it integrated into a sentence in the summary? How is it punctuated? How does the writer show that he has left out some words from the original source?

6. Circle the verbs of the summary. What tense are they?

WRITING ASSIGNMENT FOR A SUMMARY

Summarize one of the student models of writing from any Chapter from 17 to 25. Your summary should be much shorter than the original.

Gathering, Generating, and Arranging the Materials

An accurate summary must be based on a clear understanding of its subject matter. Therefore, in gathering and generating your materials, the first step is to read the original and read it more than once. Here's how:

1. **Preview the reading.** If you're summarizing a chapter of a book or a long article, you can locate main ideas in the headings within a chapter, in the topic sentences of paragraphs, and perhaps in stated summaries at the end of the chapter or article. For shorter readings, look at the opening paragraph, the first sentences of body paragraphs, and the first sentence of the conclusion. These will probably help you identify the main and supporting points when you begin to read.

2. **Read the selection carefully.** Highlight or underline the main ideas and important supporting details. Go over the selection more than once until you're confident you understand it.

3. **Be thinking about your response.** As you plan the summary, you'll probably consider ideas you want to include in your response. Make notes to remind you of those ideas.

Now you can select the information to include in your summary. Here's how:

1. **Take notes and plan.** Look over the parts of the reading that you've highlighted or underlined. Then write notes—in your own words—of the ideas you want to include.

2. **Organize your ideas logically.** In most cases, this means following the organization of the original. Begin by outlining the main points until your arrangement is clear and consistent.

Here's an informal outline of the summary paragraph you read earlier in the chapter:

Definition of courage
  Unselfish
  Involves some risk
  Voluntary
  Involves personal sacrifice

Example from _Schindler's List_
  Unselfish in employing Jewish workers in Nazi Germany
  Protects them voluntarily
  Risks losing his own life, a great personal sacrifice

Composing the Summary

Now look over your notes and write the first draft. Begin with a **topic sentence** that states the central claim of the reading and names its author and title.

Write the summary in the present tense since you're explaining what the material says _now_—as you read it—not what the author wrote in the past. Don't copy sentences or parts of sentences from the original. **Paraphrase** the material, using your own vocabulary and sentence structure. Don't imitate the sentence structure of the original, substituting synonyms for a few words. Otherwise, the summary will be awkward and perhaps ungrammatical, and it won't demonstrate to your reader that you truly understand the material.

It's okay to use short phrases from the original, but you must **quote** those phrases exactly and integrate them within the paraphrase. Place the quoted material in **quotation marks.** If you leave out words from the original, you can use **ellipsis marks** (. . .) to show where they're omitted. (You'll see an example of a quote with ellipsis marks in the example of a summary on p. 289. And you'll find more advice on using quotations in Chapter 27.)

TEMPLATES FOR A SUMMARY

The following templates may be useful in introducing summaries:

1. In "_____ ," the author _____ argues that _____.

2. In chapter five of _Title_, _____ maintains that _____.

3. The U.S. Department of Labor reports that _____

   and_____.

Additionally, here are some verbs to use when introducing summaries:

claims, contends, suggests, maintains, believes, indicates, insists, proposes, recommends, advocates, is in favor of, opposes, defines, examines.

Note that this list does not include "talks about," which is so vague that it means almost nothing.

Revising Your First Draft

You'll probably revise both your summary and response at the same time. But we'll focus on the revision of the summary first.

Begin the revision by rereading the original material and comparing it to the summary. Then use the following guidelines in revising. You may answer the questions yourself or collaborate with three or four classmates who'll discuss them. If the answer to any question is "no," revise to eliminate the problem.

REVISION CHECKLIST FOR A SUMMARY

	YES	NO
1. Does the topic sentence clearly introduce the summary, including the name of the author and the title of the work?	☐	☐
2. Does the topic sentence employ a strong verb, such as those listed in the templates?	☐	☐
3. Is the summary complete?	☐	☐
4. Does the summary include the right amount of detail?	☐	☐
5. Is the organization of the summary coherent, avoiding the mere listing of ideas?	☐	☐

Further Revising and Editing

After waiting a few hours or days, return to the summary and revise it again. Or wait until you have written a draft of both the summary and response. Then revise them both.

WRITING ASSIGNMENT FOR A RESPONSE, WITH A STUDENT MODEL

After completing the first or second draft of the summary, you can write your response. A response is **subjective;** it expresses your interpretations, opinions, and arguments.

You may, for example, evaluate how well the writer has achieved his or her goals. You may agree or disagree with one or more points the writer makes. You may expand on the main ideas of the original material, comparing it to other materials you've studied in the course. You may relate your own experiences to the material. And because these responses are subjective, you may use the personal pronouns *I* or *me*.

A blueprint of a response might look like this:

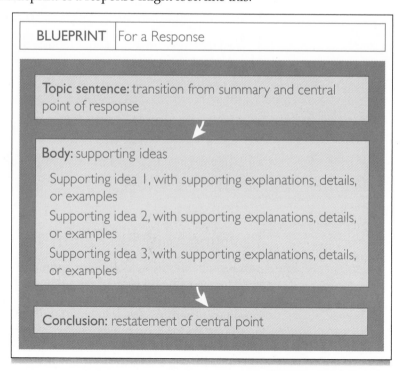

BLUEPRINT | For a Response

Topic sentence: transition from summary and central point of response

Body: supporting ideas

Supporting idea 1, with supporting explanations, details, or examples

Supporting idea 2, with supporting explanations, details, or examples

Supporting idea 3, with supporting explanations, details, or examples

Conclusion: restatement of central point

Here's the response that follows the summary of Amra Skocic's essay. Note that the first sentence establishes a transition from the summary and states the central point of the response. Note that the second paragraph introduces a second, and contrasting, point.

1   I agree with Amra Skocic's definition of heroism, and with her selection of Oscar Schindler to illustrate the definition. His actions are especially heroic because of the circumstances in which he chooses to act. When a person risks his or her life to save the lives of others, we surely admire that person's heroism. We applaud the actions of firefighters, police, or ordinary citizens that involve risks to save lives. We call these actions heroic because they fit within our society's shared sense of morality. We know that these people have done the right thing.

2   But, like Skocic, I think Schindler's heroism is different from and more admirable than the heroism of firefighters and the police. He risks his life within a society that opposes and condemns his actions. The official policy of Nazi Germany is to murder Jews, not to save their lives. Therefore, according to the Nazis, anyone who tries to protect them is acting immorally and illegally. He is a traitor to his country. Yet Schindler acts according to his belief in a higher moral authority, one that rises above the accepted morality of his society. The example of Oscar Schindler therefore seems to argue for an expanded definition of heroism. There are perhaps two kinds of heroism: one that corresponds to the society's moral sense and laws, and a second—and greater—kind that corresponds to a higher form of morality and may directly violate the society's laws. This kind of heroism is rare, but is the kind we tend to admire the most. It is the heroism of Joan of Arc, Mahatma Gandhi, and Martin Luther King.

Questions for Analysis

1. What is the topic sentence of the first paragraph? Underline it.
2. The writer partially disagrees with Amra Skocic. Does he think that Skocic is incorrect? Explain.
3. The writer develops the response through a contrast. What two ideas is he contrasting?
4. What examples does the writer cite to support the two contrasting ideas?
5. What words or phrases demonstrate that the response is subjective? Circle them.
6. Much of the unity of the paragraphs is achieved through repetition of words and sentence structure. Circle the repetition that most clearly establishes that unity.

Gathering, Generating, and Arranging the Materials

Review the original reading—or the notes you've already made about possible responses. Consider a central point to develop in your response and write it in a preliminary topic sentence. List any supporting ideas or examples. Then develop an organizational plan.

Composing the Response

Now draft a response, beginning with a transition from the summary and a statement of your central point. Address your response to the main ideas in the summary. Remember that you're discussing the material you read, not telling your own story!

Here's the beginning of another response to Amra Skocic's essay. Notice its transition from the summary and statement of its point, which leads immediately into an explanation and a comparison. The writer can then develop and illustrate the comparison.

> Amra Skocic defines courageous action well, but this definition doesn't have to be limited to actions involving physical risk. A courageous action can also involve risks to a person's reputation or standing in the community. Both involve potential harm to oneself while benefiting others.

A complete blueprint of the summary and response might look like this:

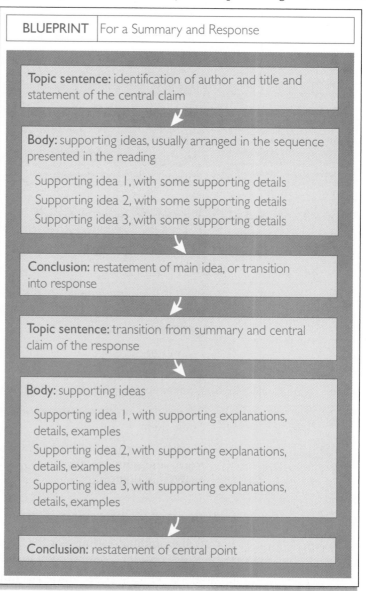

BLUEPRINT For a Summary and Response

Topic sentence: identification of author and title and statement of the central claim

Body: supporting ideas, usually arranged in the sequence presented in the reading

   Supporting idea 1, with some supporting details
   Supporting idea 2, with some supporting details
   Supporting idea 3, with some supporting details

Conclusion: restatement of main idea, or transition into response

Topic sentence: transition from summary and central claim of the response

Body: supporting ideas

   Supporting idea 1, with supporting explanations, details, examples
   Supporting idea 2, with supporting explanations, details, examples
   Supporting idea 3, with supporting explanations, details, examples

Conclusion: restatement of central point

TEMPLATES FOR A RESPONSE

These templates may be useful in introducing responses:

1. Although the author's argument is persuasive, I do not agree that _____ because he tends to overlook one important point.

2. I agree with _____ because of my own experience.

3. I have differing views on this subject. On the one hand, I feel that _____. On the other hand, I am not sure that _____.

4. _____ is only partially correct, for he ignores the _____ _____, which proves that _____.

5. The author's position on this issue is extremely biased. He distorts the facts when he claims that _____.

Revising Your First Draft

Now revise the response according to the following guidelines. You may answer the questions in the guidelines yourself or collaborate with three or four classmates who'll discuss them. If the answer to any question is "no," revise to eliminate the problem.

REVISION CHECKLIST FOR A RESPONSE

	YES	NO
1. Is the transition into the response clear?	☐	☐
2. Does the response make its central claim clear?	☐	☐
3. Is the response supported with clear explanations and specific references to the original material being summarized?	☐	☐

Take notes of the answers to these questions, and those from the Revision Checklist for a Summary, to guide your revision. Rewrite the paper when your mind is clear and you can attend to word choice, clarity, and conciseness.

Further Revising and Editing

After waiting a few hours or days, return to both the summary and response to revise them again. Make sure they tie together neatly.

FINAL WRITING ASSIGNMENT

Summarize and respond to one of the additional readings at the end of this book.

Types of paragraphs

- description
- exemplification
- narration
- report
- process analysis

- cause and effect
- classification
- comparison and contrast
- definition
- summary and response

What to include in introductions
(see pp. 21, 40)

attention getter

overview or preview

topic sentence (or thesis statement) that makes a claim

What conclusions might include
(see pp. 21, 40)

general summary or impression

recommendations or call for action

interpretation or evaluation

climax: surprise, revelation, reflection

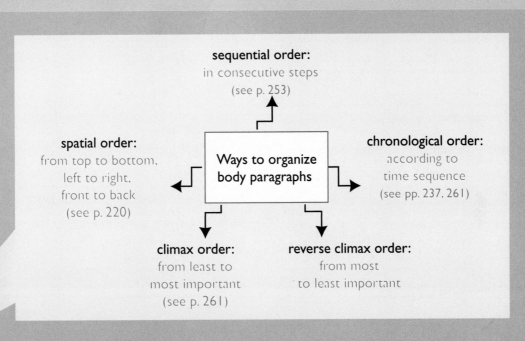

sequential order:
in consecutive steps
(see p. 253)

spatial order:
from top to bottom,
left to right,
front to back
(see p. 220)

Ways to organize
body paragraphs

chronological order:
according to
time sequence
(see pp. 237, 261)

climax order:
from least to
most important
(see p. 261)

reverse climax order:
from most
to least important

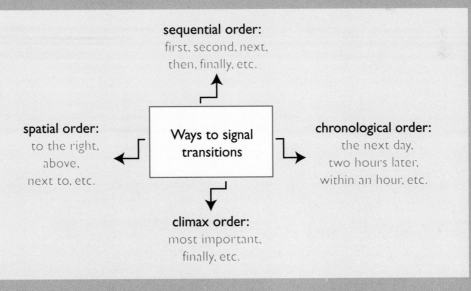

sequential order:
first, second, next,
then, finally, etc.

spatial order:
to the right,
above,
next to, etc.

Ways to signal
transitions

chronological order:
the next day,
two hours later,
within an hour, etc.

climax order:
most important,
finally, etc.

Editing for Grammar and Mechanics: Finishing the Job

Previous units of this book have discussed the writing process as well as ways of organizing, developing, and strengthening paragraphs. This final unit offers you additional help in editing for grammar, punctuation, and the mechanics of written presentation. Some parts of this unit—especially Chapters 30 and 31—may be particularly helpful if your first language is not English. You may want to study the whole unit, some chapters in the unit, or only the parts of the chapters that address your individual concerns. You may even wish to use the unit as a reference as particular issues arise.

Specifically, the chapters discuss the following topics:

1. punctuation—including the rules for all the punctuation marks
2. spelling and matters related to spelling
3. look-alike and sound-alike words
4. verbs and the arrangement of words that accompany verbs
5. articles and prepositions

Take what you need from the unit so your work will exhibit the polish and clarity that call forth confidence. ■

Punctuating Sentences

As you've seen in Chapters 5 to 9, punctuation marks—commas, periods, semicolons—are signals that help readers understand your sentences and avoid confusion. Incorrect punctuation can announce the end of a sentence that hasn't ended, join ideas that shouldn't be joined, or separate ideas that shouldn't be separated.

To punctuate correctly, you must know the rules. This chapter will help you

- identify where punctuation is needed
- know which punctuation marks to select: commas, periods, question marks, exclamation points, semicolons, colons, dashes, parentheses, or quotation marks

THE COMMA [,]

If you tend to place a comma wherever you hear a pause, be careful. You might be mispunctuating. **Commas** have six specific uses—some to separate ideas and others to enclose them.

Items in a Series

Separate three or more items with commas.

A **coordinating conjunction**—usually *and*—ends the series. A comma before the conjunction is optional; you can include the comma or not. But be consistent; include it or omit it each time:

Subjects:	Anna, Maurice, *and* I
Verbs:	They came late to the party, threw their coats on the bed, *and* made a dash for the refreshments.
Adjectives:	The field was wet, muddy, *and* slippery.
Phrases:	They looked on top of the dresser, in the drawers, behind the nightstand, *and* under the bed.

EXERCISE 1   Editing for Comma Use

In each sentence, place commas between items in a series. Add and *before the last item.*

1. Benjamin Franklin was a printer^writer^philosopher^inventor^scientist^politician^ *, and* diplomat.

2. Franklin was so successful that he was able to retire at the age of forty-four. He had started a newspaper begun a club for tradespeople founded the first American subscription library become clerk to the Pennsylvania legislature established the first fire company become postmaster of Philadelphia begun the American Philosophical Society begun his famous *Poor Richard's Almanac*—a collection of wit wisdom financial advice he continued for twenty-five years.

3. King Henry VIII of England (1491–1547) had six wives: Catherine of Aragon Anne Boleyn Jane Seymour Anne of Cleves Catherine Howard Catherine Parr.

4. He divorced the first Catherine beheaded Anne lost Jane in a childbirth death canceled his marriage to Anne executed the second Catherine stayed married to the last Catherine.

Independent Clauses

 Place a comma before the coordinating conjunction joining two independent clauses.

> The Cherokee Indians were an agricultural people, *and* they lived in villages in the southern part of the United States.
> Their homes at first were made of mud, *but* later the Cherokees built themselves log cabins.
> They established their own courts and schools in the early 1800s, *and* they had a higher standard of living than their white neighbors.

Only the coordinating conjunction joining two independent clauses requires a comma. Don't use a comma between two nouns or verbs.

> Incorrect: The Cherokees also had a written constitution, and published their own newspaper.
>
> Correct: The Cherokees also had a written constitution and published their own newspaper.

EXERCISE 2   Editing for Comma Use

Place commas where they're needed before coordinating conjunctions that join independent clauses. There are seven missing commas in the passage; the first has been corrected as an example.

TIPS

For Using the Coordinating Conjunctions

To help you recall the coordinating conjunctions, think of the phrase FAN BOYS.

For	But
And	Or
Nor	Yet
	So

Sequoyah (c. 1770–1843): Inventor of an Alphabet

(1) Young Sequoyah called the white people's books "the talking leaves"ˌ^ and he and his fellow Cherokees of Tennessee were fascinated with their mysterious power. (2) They had seen the white settlers reading books and writing messages on paper. (3) Sequoyah's friends said that the Great Spirit had given this magic to whites but hadn't given it to the Indian peoples. (4) Sequoyah thought their arguments were nonsense for the white man had himself invented "the talking leaves."

(5) Sequoyah came from the Native American village of Taskigi (later Tuskegee) and his mother was a member of the emperor's family. (6) As he grew older, he became a master silversmith, a talented storyteller, and a skilled participant in dances, foot races, and ball games. (7) He was illiterate like everyone else in his tribe.

(8) A hunting accident left Sequoyah slightly handicapped or his life might have taken a different path. (9) After the injury, he had more free time and more chances to think about how his people might also come to get "the talking leaves." (10) He began wandering off into the woods and there he spent hours alone, avoiding everyone, playing like a child with pieces of wood, or making odd little marks with one stone or another. (11) His wife and friends encouraged and sympathized with him for they were sure that he was either going mad or communicating with spirits. (12) Months became years and the sympathy turned to ridicule and disrespect. (13) Nevertheless, Sequoyah was overpowered with his dream.

Scorecard: Number of errors found and corrected _____

Interrupters

▶ Place two commas around words, phrases, or clauses that interrupt a sentence. These interrupters can be temporarily removed without changing the basic meaning of a sentence, as in these examples:

With interrupter:	A Cherokee newspaper, *the Phoenix*, began publication in 1828.
Interrupter removed:	A Cherokee newspaper began publication in 1828.
With interrupter:	Many Cherokee, who live in Oklahoma and North Carolina today, originally lived in what is now Tennessee.
Interrupter removed:	Many Cherokee originally lived in what is now Tennessee.

Think of the interrupter as something you'd place in parentheses. Although commas and parentheses are not the same, the two commas enclose the interrupter like parentheses. (You'll see how to use parentheses on p. 313.)

> The main branches of the Cherokee (who live in Oklahoma and North Carolina today) trace their ancestors back to what is now Tennessee.
> The main branches of the Cherokee, who live in Oklahoma and North Carolina today, trace their ancestors back to what is now Tennessee.

One sentence interrupter is called an **appositive,** a word or phrase that renames a noun. Appositives after proper (that is, capitalized) nouns usually need commas, but appositives after common (uncapitalized) nouns do not:

> Will Rogers, *a famous actor,* was a Cherokee Indian.
> The famous actor Will Rogers was a Cherokee Indian.

Be sure to enclose an interrupter in two commas, even if you think you hear just one pause. Otherwise, the sentence may be confusing:

> *Incorrect:*   Sequoyah, whose name many people know was a famous leader of the Cherokee. (This looks like a sentence fragment.)
> *Correct:*   Sequoyah, whose name many people know, was a famous leader of the Cherokee.

Remember, too, that commas enclose **relative clauses** (*who, whom, whose, that, which* clauses) only when they are **nonrestrictive**—that is, they don't provide essential information. The clause in the previous example is nonrestrictive. A **restrictive relative clause** provides information essential to understanding the idea, so it isn't enclosed in commas. You may wish to review the discussion of these clauses in Chapter 8.

Introductory or Concluding Expressions

Place a comma after most introductory phrases or clauses.

Long introductory (or transitional) phrases require a comma, but many short phrases don't:

> *For many centuries,* the Cherokee lived in the hills of Tennessee.
> *Perhaps* the first European contact with the Cherokee happened in 1540.

An introductory dependent clause requires a comma:

> *When Fernando de Soto came from Spain to the New World in search of gold,* he had many conflicts with the Cherokee.

A sentence can also end with a transitional word or phrase:

> He never found gold, *however.*
> He died instead, *having searched throughout Florida and along the Mississippi River for three years.*

You can usually hear when no comma is needed:

> De Soto's body was sunk in the Mississippi *to prevent the Cherokee from mutilating it.*
> His companions floated down the river to the Gulf of Mexico, *from where they returned to Spain.*

EXERCISE 3   Incorporating Transitional Expressions

Add the transitional expressions in parentheses to the sentences that follow. Decide if the expressions belong at the beginning or the end. Punctuate the sentences with commas when necessary.

Sequoyah's Attempt at Developing an Alphabet

1. (at first) Sequoyah tried to give every word of Cherokee its own separate character.

   At first, Sequoyah tried to give every word of Cherokee its own separate character.

2. (however) He eventually found that approach too difficult and decided to assign a character to each sound. _____

   _____

3. (when his friends and neighbors talked) He no longer heard what they were saying.

   _____

   _____

4. (instead) (trying to separate the sounds and identify new ones) He carefully listened to their sounds. _____

   _____

5. (with eighty-six characters representing all the sounds of spoken Cherokee) What he eventually achieved was not so much an alphabet as a *syllabary.*_____

   _____

6. (when combined) These characters produced a clear and remarkably effective written language._____

   _____

7. (in all) The task took Sequoyah twelve years. _____

   _____

EXERCISE 4   Punctuating Interrupters and Transitional Expressions

Punctuate the passage. You should add thirteen commas.

Sequoyah's Fame

(1) Many stories, true or false, have been told of how Sequoyah presented his "alphabet" to the Cherokee people. (2) According to one legend his little daughter read aloud what the chiefs had privately told him to write on a paper, instantly amazing and convincing everyone. (3) Sequoyah's alphabet was so simple that it could be learned in a few days. (4) Moreover those who learned it then taught it to others. (5) Within a few months a group of almost entirely illiterate people suddenly became literate. (6) Furthermore the odd little man who had been ridiculed by his people was now treated as almost a god.

(7) In 1828 Sequoyah and other Cherokees arrived in Washington, D.C., to settle a dispute over the federal government's failure to honor its treaties. (8) Because Sequoyah had already become famous he received a great deal of attention in the capital. (9) Charles Bird King a famous painter asked him to sit for a portrait, and many newspaper reporters asked for interviews.

(10) During their negotiations the Cherokees signed another treaty to exchange their lands for new ones in Oklahoma. (11) Although most Cherokees refused to leave Tennessee and Alabama Sequoyah's group from Arkansas moved westward to Oklahoma. (12) Sequoyah now over sixty years old built himself a new cabin, took care of his small farm, and traveled through the woods to the salt springs from time to time. (13) He lived there for days or weeks, filling his kettles, tending his fires, scooping out salt, and talking to anyone who came to see and speak with the famous Cherokee philosopher.

Scorecard: Number of commas added _____

Two or More Adjectives

 Place a comma between adjectives before a noun if *and* could go between the adjectives.

Sometimes you pile up several adjectives before a noun, to sharpen a description or make it more specific. If you join them with *and* or reverse their order, that means they're equal. You should separate them with a comma:

> an ugly, disgusting wart (a disgusting, ugly wart)
> a thick, juicy steak (a thick and juicy steak)

If you cannot reverse the adjectives, don't separate them by commas:

> a bright red rubber ball (not a rubber red bright ball)
> a large frozen pizza (not a frozen large pizza)

EXERCISE 5   Punctuating Adjectives

Place commas where they are needed in the following phrases.

1. a clever^, resourceful man
2. a beautiful large birthday cake
3. an old red wagon
4. a torn worn faded pair of jeans
5. an awkward tall basketball player
6. a skillful old worker

> ✓ **TIPS**
>
> **For Punctuating Adjectives**
>
> If both adjectives describe the *noun*, they're equal and need a comma to separate them. But if the *first* adjective describes the *second adjective*, then they're not equal. You cannot separate them with a comma: a shiny blue car (*shiny* describes *blue*, not *car*).

Dates, Places, and Addresses

Place a comma between parts of dates, places, and addresses.

Put commas after the day and year for full dates. Also put a comma between a city and state in a sentence—and after the state, too, if the sentence continues. When you address an envelope, however, don't put a comma between the abbreviation for the state and the zip code:

> On August 9, 2012, the building should be completed. (No comma separates the month and day, but a comma follows the year.)
>
> Brookline, Massachusetts, is a lovely town. (Note the comma after the state.)
>
> 324 W. Juneway Street, Brookline, MA 01506 (No comma comes before the zip code.)

EXERCISE 6   Punctuating Addresses

Place commas in the following dates or places.

1. (on envelope) 1522 E. Hartford Street^, Elizabethtown^, New York 12932
2. Have you been to Columbus Ohio before?
3. After December 5 2011 Kathy will be an attorney.
4. We expect 2011 to be a good year—after we pay our income taxes.
5. The Declaration of Independence was signed on July 4 1776 in Philadelphia Pennsylvania.

EXERCISE 7   Editing for Commas

Place commas where they're needed in the passage. You should add nineteen commas.

Sequoyah's Final Deeds

(1) Although Sequoyah lived in a peaceful forest around Lee's Creek^, Oklahoma^, the Great Spirit did not allow him to end his life that way. (2) The federal government which had

COLLABORATIVE ACTIVITY 1

Looking at Commas
Review your answers to Exercises 2, 3, 4, and 7. Discuss areas of disagreement with the class.

for so long wanted to grab the Cherokees' land in Tennessee and Alabama decided to remove them from the area. (3) Consequently a large battalion of well-armed hostile soldiers drove some 17,000 Cherokees from their homes. (4) The Native Americans began a long hard journey westward and suffered for many months. (5) About 4,000 Cherokees died before the Native Americans arrived in the Oklahoma Territory in the spring of 1839. (6) Because they greatly outnumbered the Cherokees who were already there problems immediately started. (7) The groups argued over the land over the members of local government and over many other matters.

(8) Sequoyah who wished to stop the conflict among his people persuaded them to be reasonable. (9) At a meeting of the entire tribe all the groups agreed to live in peace. (10) Consequently the Cherokees of Alabama Tennessee Arkansas and Oklahoma joined together to become the Cherokee Nation.

(11) However Sequoyah still could not rest. (12) He wanted to find a band of Cherokees who had come out west many years before. (13) Where were these lost Cherokees who did not know of his alphabet or the new Nation? (14) Sequoyah who was now an old man headed south with nine horsemen. (15) He supposedly found the lost Cherokees and died somewhere in Mexico. (16) Not long afterward in California, according to many sources, a type of redwood that included the largest trees in the world was named "sequoia" after the only man in history to invent an entire alphabet.

Scorecard: Number of commas added _____

COLLABORATIVE ACTIVITY 2

Correcting Comma Errors
Write ten sentences in which you deliberately omit necessary commas. Include at least one error representing each of the six rules in this chapter. Exchange papers, correct the errors, and then exchange papers again so a third student checks your work.

THE PERIOD [.]

Periods have two functions: to signal the end of sentences and to mark abbreviations.

Statements

▶ **End every complete statement with a period.**

Sentences that aren't statements need a different mark of final punctuation. End questions with a question mark, exclamations with an exclamation point:

> It looks like a nice day.
> *but*
> Do you think it will rain?
> Get out of here!

Abbreviations

► **Use periods for most abbreviations.**

The following abbreviations require periods:

> Mr., Ms., Mrs., Dr., Rev.
>
> A.M., P.M.
>
> etc., i.e., e.g.

Abbreviations require periods, but **acronyms** do not. Each letter of an acronym represents a word. Here are some common examples:

1. government agencies (*CIA*—the **C**entral **I**ntelligence **A**gency—and *FBI*—the **F**ederal **B**ureau of **I**nvestigation)
2. well-known organizations (Operation *PUSH*—**P**eople **U**nited to **S**ave **H**umanity)
3. television or radio stations (*WGN*—owned by the *Chicago Tribune*, which modestly calls itself the **W**orld's **G**reatest **N**ewspaper)
4. and words such as *scuba*—**s**elf-**c**ontained **u**nderwater **b**reathing **a**pparatus—which have become so well known that the acronym is now a word

Consult your dictionary when you aren't sure whether the word is an abbreviation or an acronym.

TIPS

For Using Abbreviations Correctly

Most words in compositions shouldn't be abbreviated, for example:

lb. (use *pound*)   w/ (use *with*)

& (use *and*)   Va. (use *Virginia*)

ft. (use *feet*)   hr. (use *hour*)

Feb. (use *February*)   yr. (use *year*)

St. (use *Street*)

EXERCISE 8   Including Periods

Place periods where they're needed in the following groups of words.

1. I don't care what you say^ I am not going to speak in front of all those people^
2. (on envelope) 121 W Third Ave, New York, N Y
3. N B C
4. Mr and Mrs Jones
5. The Environmental Protection Agency is called the E P A
6. Get your scuba gear we're going to dive off the coast

THE QUESTION MARK [?]

► **Place question marks only after direct questions.**

Question marks, like periods, end sentences—in this case, sentences that ask a question.

A **direct question** always ends with a question mark:

> *Direct questions:*   When was the Cherokee War?
>
> Who fought in the war?

But don't use a question mark with an **indirect question,** which is contained within a larger statement and uses the word order of a statement:

Indirect questions:	I asked when the Cherokee War occurred.
	Please tell me who fought in the war.

EXERCISE 9 Punctuating Direct and Indirect Questions

Place a period or a question mark at the end of each sentence.

1. When did Sequoyah die^?^

2. No one knows for sure where Sequoyah died

3. Sequoyah asked his people if they could live in peace with each other

4. I want to know how many letters are in Sequoyah's alphabet

5. How many Sequoyah trees are in the national forest

6. Where do the Cherokee live today

THE EXCLAMATION POINT [!]

COLLABORATIVE ACTIVITY 3

Using End Punctuation
Write ten sentences—simple statements, direct questions, statements with indirect questions, and exclamations. Omit all the end punctuation marks. Exchange papers and supply the missing punctuation marks. Revise as necessary.

Use exclamation points after expressions of strong emotion.

An **exclamation point** signals excitement, anger, fear, or other strong emotions, whether in a full sentence or simply in a partial sentence:

> This is the last time I'll tell you!
> Don't, please!
> Help! Police!

Don't overuse exclamation points! Too many of them will bombard your readers! (As do the sentences you have just read.)

EXERCISE 10 Supplying End Punctuation

Punctuate the sentences with a period or an exclamation point.

1. The Cherokee have survived terrible losses to their people^.^

2. In just a few years after de Soto arrived in 1540, European diseases wiped out at least 75 percent of the Cherokee population

3. During the Civil War, the Cherokee lost 25 percent of their population.

4. No other group of Americans suffered as much during the conflict

5. With as many as 370,000 persons, Cherokee are the largest Native American group in the United States today

6. Amazingly, at least 15,000 are full-blooded Cherokee

THE SEMICOLON [;]

A **semicolon** is a combination of a period and a comma. Like a period, it makes the reader stop. Like a comma, it urges the reader to go on. The semicolon has two uses: to join independent clauses and to separate items in a series containing internal punctuation.

Independent Clauses

 Join independent clauses with a semicolon.

A semicolon may join independent clauses whose ideas are closely related:

> The name Cherokee comes from a Creek Indian word; it means "people of a different speech."

Don't use a conjunction after the semicolon. But you may use a transitional word (a conjunctive adverb) after the semicolon. The transitional word is followed by a comma:

> Most Cherokee today accept this name; *however*, some call themselves *Tsalagi*, which comes from their own language.

EXERCISE 11   Using Semicolons

Insert semicolons and commas in each sentence. Be careful. One sentence doesn't require a semicolon.

1. The early Cherokee village had about sixty houses⌃ it also had a large council house.

2. A house looked like an upside-down basket it was made of branches and the outside was plastered with mud.

3. The houses where the Cherokee lived were sunken into the ground however their council house was usually located on a raised mound.

4. The Cherokee had settled on land used by earlier tribes therefore they did not build the mounds themselves.

5. Each council house was used for meetings and religious ceremonies each contained a sacred fire, which the Cherokee always kept burning.

6. Cherokee villages usually had their own governments, although the villages came together for ceremonies or war councils.

If Your First Language Is Not English

Spanish begins a question with an inverted question mark [¿] and an exclamation with an inverted exclamation point [¡]. English uses only the end punctuation. Don't confuse the different practices and check for errors in your editing.

Items in a Series

 Use semicolons to separate items with internal punctuation.

Remember that commas separate three or more items in a series. But if the items themselves contain commas, separate the items with semicolons:

> According to the census estimates for 2006, the only cities in the United States with a population of more than one million are New York, New York; Los Angeles, California; Chicago, Illinois; Houston, Texas; Phoenix, Arizona; Philadelphia, Pennsylvania; San Antonio, Texas; San Diego, California; and Dallas, Texas.

According to a list compiled by ten (male) members of an advisory board to the Modern Library in 1998, the five best novels in the English language are James Joyce, *Ulysses*; F. Scott Fitzgerald, *The Great Gatsby*; James Joyce, *A Portrait of the Artist as a Young Man*; Vladimir Nabokov, *Lolita*; and Aldous Huxley, *Brave New World*. Of the one hundred best novels, only eight were written by women.

EXERCISE 12   Punctuating Items in a Series

Place semicolons and commas where they are needed.

1. The novels you will read in the American literature course are Nathaniel Hawthorne *The Scarlet Letter* Mark Twain *Huckleberry Finn* Herman Melville *Moby-Dick* William Faulkner *The Sound and the Fury* F. Scott Fitzgerald *The Great Gatsby* and Ernest Hemingway *For Whom the Bell Tolls.*

2. The winners of the Academy Awards for 2007 were as follows: Best Picture *The Departed* Best Director Martin Scorsese for *The Departed* Best Actor Forest Whitaker in *The Last King of Scotland* Best Actress Helen Mirren in *The Queen* Best Supporting Actor Alan Arkin in *Little Miss Sunshine* and Best Supporting Actress Jennifer Hudson in *Dreamgirls.*

3. If you are going south on your vacation, be sure to visit Bear Wallow Kentucky Pewee Kentucky Bulls' Gap Tennessee Difficult Tennessee Hot House North Carolina Improve Mississippi Scratch Ankle Alabama and Dime Box Texas. (They are all on the map.)

4. Among the most important dates in World War II were September 1 1939 when Hitler invaded Poland December 7 1941 when the Japanese attacked Pearl Harbor Hawaii September 3 1943 when Italy agreed to suspend fighting May 7 1945 when Germany surrendered unconditionally and September 2 1945 when Japan signed formal terms of surrender.

THE COLON [:]

Colons are like equal signs. They indicate that the last words of a grammatically complete statement are equal to the words that follow the statement.

Use a colon after a complete introductory statement.

When you introduce a list or a long quotation, end the introduction with a colon:

Please bring the following items: a package of doughnuts, a case of soda pop, a picnic blanket, and a four-foot dueling sword.

Here is part of a letter written by James H. Harris, warden of the United States Jail, written on January 6, 1906: "This is to certify that Mr. Harry Houdini at the United States Jail today was stripped stark naked, thoroughly searched, and locked up in cell No. 2 of the South Wing—the cell in which Charles J. Guiteau, the assassinator of President Garfield, was confined during his incarceration, from the date of his commitment, July 2nd, 1881, until the day on which he was executed, June 30th, 1882. Mr. Houdini, in about two minutes, managed to escape from that cell and then broke into the cell in which his clothing was locked-up. He then proceeded to release from their cells all the prisoners on the ground floor."

Be sure to place a colon only after a complete statement:

Please bring a package of doughnuts, a case of soda pop, a picnic blanket, and a four-foot dueling sword. (*Please bring* is not a complete statement because the verb requires an object, so don't use a colon here.)

Never place a colon after any form of *to be:*

Incorrect: Albert's favorite foods are: tacos, enchiladas, and chop suey.
Correct: Albert's favorite foods are tacos, enchiladas, and chop suey.

EXERCISE 13   Using Colons

Place colons and commas where they are needed.

1. For our trip to Central America, we took only the essentials⌃ suntan lotion⌃ some light clothing⌃ and a great deal of money.

2. For any dance at which *The Moving Violations* play you need three important items comfortable shoes comfortable clothes and comfortable earplugs.

3. Sally's appearance follows all the latest fashions a neon T-shirt jeans torn at the knees orange and green spiked hair and seventeen pierces in her left ear.

4. The three winners of the contest were Rolando Rodriguez Lavelle Wilson and John Jacobs.

5. You can take one from column A two from column B and your choice of two from column C or D.

6. Don't forget to add mustard, mayonnaise, ketchup, tomatoes, pickles, peppers, garlic salt, relish, and onions to make a great hot dog, if you can still find it under all that stuff.

THE DASH [—]

Dashes separate—and enclose—items in a sentence. They usually come in pairs.

Enclose an emphasized sentence interrupter in two dashes.

Use dashes (—) in pairs, just like the two commas that enclose sentence interrupters. Unlike the commas, however, the dashes call attention to the interrupter:

Some—but not all—of the work was easy.
The answer—I think—is obvious.

Use only one dash for an interrupter at the end of a sentence.

Of course, when an interrupter comes at the end of a sentence, it needs only one dash:

> The answer is obvious—I think.

Dashes are especially useful to set off an interrupter that contains commas.

> Punctuation marks—commas, periods, semicolons, and the like—help readers understand your sentences.

PARENTHESES [( )]

COLLABORATIVE ACTIVITY 4

Using Punctuation
Write ten sentences that use semicolons, colons, dashes, or parentheses. But omit all these punctuation marks. Exchange papers and supply the missing punctuation marks. Then exchange again so a third student can check your work.

Parentheses enclose an item that isn't essential to a sentence's meaning. They always come in pairs.

Enclose a deemphasized sentence interrupter in parentheses.

Dashes call attention to a sentence interrupter; parentheses draw attention away from it. They enclose information that's merely incidental to a sentence (usually short explanations, definitions, or examples—such as the material you're reading right now). Think of parentheses as footnotes within a sentence; almost anything that can go into a footnote can go into parentheses:

> The wallaby (a small- or medium-sized kangaroo) is found only in Australia and New Zealand.
>
> George Washington Gale Ferris (1859–1896) built the Ferris wheel for the World's Columbian Exposition in Chicago in 1893.

The parentheses are part of the sentence in which they appear, so a period follows the second parenthesis (like this).

EXERCISE 14   Using Dashes and Parentheses

Punctuate each sentence interrupter with two dashes (or one dash) or with parentheses.

1. Sizzling hot meteors^some huge fireballs, others tiny specks^bombard the earth's atmosphere at the rate of one million per hour.

2. Five planets Mercury, Venus, Mars, Jupiter, and Saturn are visible to the naked eye.

3. Uranus the first planet beyond normal eyesight to be observed was discovered accidentally by William Herschel, who thought it was a comet.

4. The best candidate among the planets for having life other than Earth, of course is Mars.

5. Since the moon's gravity is too weak to hold atmosphere, there is no weather at all on the moon in fact, there is no wind, no sound, no life.

6. The surface temperature of the sun is approximately 6,000 degrees Kelvin 11,000 degrees Fahrenheit.

QUOTATION MARKS [" "]

In speaking, when you want to tell someone *exactly* what another person said, you gesture with your hands or imitate the other person's voice to emphasize that fact. **Quotation marks** function much like that gesture or change in voice. They come in pairs, enclosing and identifying the exact words of another speaker or writer.

Quotation marks can also identify the exact words that you've taken from other sources—including titles, words being defined, or words used in a special way. We'll begin with those uses.

Titles

Use quotation marks for titles of poems, songs, articles, and chapters.

Use quotation marks around the titles of short works or works contained within longer ones:

> "Coming of Age" (chapter title within a book)
> "Raging Fire Kills Three" (newspaper headline)
> "Michelle" (song title contained within an album)
> "Ode on a Grecian Urn" (poem contained within a book of poems)

Underline (or set in italics if you are using a computer) the titles of complete books, the names of magazines, the names of newspapers, and other longer works:

> *Time* (magazine)
> The *Chicago Tribune* (newspaper name)
> *The Simpsons* (television series)
> *Writing with Confidence* (book title)
> *Superbad* (movie)
> *Wicked* (play)

TIPS

For Quoting Titles

Don't put quotation marks around the titles of your own writing or writing assignments. But if, in another assignment, you refer to the title of another work (including another of yours), then place the title in quotation marks.

My Summer Vacation
  (title of assigned essay)

My Reaction to Being
  Asked to Write about
  "My Summer Vacation"
  (journal entry)

EXERCISE 15   Punctuating Titles

Use underlining or quotation marks where appropriate.

1. <u>Life</u> magazine

2. The New York Post (newspaper)

3. The Da Vinci Code (novel)

4. The Fight Against AIDS (title of article) in Newsweek (magazine)

5. High School Musical is a very popular Broadway production.

6. My favorite song from the album Rappin' with the Dudes is Gimmee Gimmee Some Heartburn.

Definitions

▶ **Underline (or italicize) words you define, and quote the definitions.**

Agnostic literally means "without knowledge" (of God), while *atheist* means "without belief in God."

Recalcitrant means "unwilling"; it comes from a Latin word, *recalcitrare*, which means "to kick back."

Words Used in a Special Way

▶ **Use quotation marks for words used in unusual ways.**

When you use a word or phrase in an original or unusual way, enclose it in quotation marks:

> When the famous temperance leader Carry Nation was smashing saloons and crusading against the use of liquor, Kansas was technically a "dry" state—that is, liquor was illegal.
> The world's most famous eater, "Diamond Jim" Brady, never touched a drop of alcohol but instead drank his "golden nectar," orange juice.

Don't overuse quotation marks, especially to quote slang words. If you feel you must excuse your word by placing it in quotes, use another word instead:

> *Poor:*   Sam is a real "loser."
> *Better:* Sam is always in trouble.

✔ **TIPS**

For Handling Definitions

Underlining and italicizing are interchangeable. But choose one or the other and then be consistent.

EXERCISE 16   Replacing Slang Words

Substitute another expression for each item in quotation marks or remove any unnecessary quotation marks.

1. I really "have a knack" for science. *I'm really good at science.*

_____

2. Prince Fielder "blasted" a home run into the third deck. _____

_____

3. Let's go and "boogie" tonight. _____

_____

4. I can't stand the "hassle" of registration. _____

_____

5. Thomas is always "putting down" the people he meets. _____

_____

6. Juan is "as cool as a cucumber" when he meets some "tough dudes." _____

_____

_____

Speech

Use quotation marks for the exact words a person says or writes.

Quotation marks signal a **direct quotation**—the exact words of a speaker or writer. Never use quotation marks with **reported speech**—a retelling in your own words of what the speaker or writer says or said:

Direct quotation:	Harry said, "I need to rest for a while."
Reported speech:	Harry said that he needed to rest for a while.
Direct quotation:	Patty asked, "Are you studying for the exam with anyone?"
Reported speech:	Patty asked if I was studying for the exam with anyone.

Note that the words *that* or *if* (or *whether*) introduce reported speech. Notice, too, that with direct quotes, the words identifying the speaker are not within the quotation marks.

EXERCISE 17   Writing Quotations and Reported Speech

Change each of the following direct quotations into reported speech or vice versa.

Direct quote

Reported speech

1. Tomas said, "I know what I am doing."

1. Tomas said that he knew what he was doing.

2. My mother always asks me, "What do you want for supper?"

2. _____

_____

3. _____

_____

3. Martha told me that she had been working late.

4. The doctor told me, "You can make an appointment for tomorrow."

4. _____

_____

5. Mr. Joseph asked, "Where is the registrar's office?"

5. _____

_____

6. The man asked us, "Have you seen a kangaroo carrying a pogo stick?"

6. _____

_____

Follow these rules when punctuating and capitalizing quotations:

a. Capitalize the first word of a complete quoted sentence, but don't capitalize the first word of a partially quoted sentence.

b. Place a comma after the introductory words that identify the speaker.

c. Place a comma, question mark, or exclamation point inside the end quotation mark, followed by the words identifying the speaker, which do not begin with a capital letter.

d. Enclose the entire quote—whether one word, one sentence, or more than one sentence—in a single set of quotation marks.

e. However, you may interrupt a quotation to identify the speaker and then resume the quotation.

Note these examples:

> In a letter to a friend, Thomas Jefferson asked, "What country before has ever existed a century and a half without a rebellion?" (A comma follows the identification of speaker; the quotation begins with a capital letter; and the question mark comes before the final quotation mark.)
>
> "Give me liberty," said Patrick Henry, "or give me death!" (The quotation ends to identify the speaker and then resumes without capitalization. The exclamation point is the end punctuation of the sentence and appears inside the quotation mark.)
>
> Carry Nation was famous for her crusades against alcohol. Once, after she had smashed tables, chairs, and the bar inside a saloon, a police officer came to arrest her for defacing property. She protested, "Defacing? I am defacing nothing! I am destroying!" (The three sentences are treated as a single quotation.)

When you write dialogue, begin a new paragraph each time you change speakers. Here's an example:

> When author Sam Clemens, alias Mark Twain, proposed marriage to Olivia Langdon, her upper-class father asked the young suitor for character references, which the latter provided. However, the letters Langdon received gave Clemens a unanimous and enthusiastic thumbs down. Two even predicted that the author would fill a drunkard's grave.
>
> "Haven't you a friend in the world?" Langdon asked.
>
> "Apparently not," Clemens replied.
>
> "I'll be your friend myself," Langdon said. "Take the girl. I know you better than they do."
>
> His instincts were correct, since Clemens proved a loyal and loving husband to Olivia.

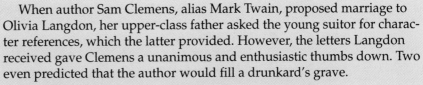
EXERCISE 18   Punctuating Quotations

Correctly punctuate and capitalize the quotations.

Famous Last Words

1. As Ethan Allen, the famous Revolutionary War soldier, lay dying, his doctor said to him^"General I fear the angels are waiting for you.^" ^"Âre they?^" he answered. ^"Waiting, are they? Well—let 'em wait!^"

2. It is very beautiful over there said Thomas Edison as he lay in a near-coma.

3. Well, I must arrange my pillows for another weary night murmured Washington Irving, the famous American author when will this end?

4. As Marie Antoinette, the French queen, was being led to her execution, she stepped on the executioner's foot. Monsieur she exclaimed I beg your pardon!

5. Marie Antoinette's husband, King Louis XVI, bravely asked his servants why do you weep? Did you think I was immortal?

6. I have a terrific headache complained Franklin D. Roosevelt.

7. Please mumbled Theodore Roosevelt put out the lights.

IN SUMMARY   To Punctuate Sentences

Using commas

1. Separate three or more items in a series with commas.
2. Separate two independent clauses joined by *and, but, or, for, so, nor,* or *yet* with a comma.
3. Enclose a sentence interrupter with commas.
4. Separate introductory words or phrases from the rest of the sentence with a comma.
5. Separate two or more adjectives preceding a noun with a comma if the adjectives could be reversed.
6. Separate elements in dates, places, or addresses with commas.

Using periods

1. Use periods after sentences that make a statement.
2. Use periods after abbreviated words, except those that stand for government and other well-known organizations, television and radio stations, and acronyms.

Using question marks

Question marks follow all direct questions but not indirect questions.

Using exclamation points

Use exclamation points after all sentences or sentence fragments expressing strong emotion.

Using semicolons

1. Semicolons join two independent clauses whose ideas are closely related but are not joined by *and, but, yet, or, nor, so,* or *for.*
2. Semicolons separate items in a series when the items have internal punctuation.

Using colons

Placed after a complete sentence, a colon introduces a list or a long quotation (but a colon never is placed after the verb *to be*).

Using dashes

Dashes enclose a sentence interrupter that you want to emphasize.

Using parentheses

Parentheses enclose incidental information in a sentence.

Using quotation marks

1. Put quotation marks around the titles of short works or works contained within longer works.

2. Use quotation marks around definitions.

3. Set off words with quotation marks that you use in a special way.

4. Use quotation marks around a speaker's exact words (but not reported speech).

   a. Capitalize the first word of a complete quoted sentence.

   b. Place a comma after words that introduce the quotation, including the words that identify the speaker.

   c. End quotations with a comma, a question mark, or an exclamation point. Place all periods and commas inside the final quotation mark. Place question marks and exclamation points inside the final quotation mark if they're part of the quotation, but outside the final quotation mark if they're not part of the quotation.

   d. Use quotation marks around the *entire* quotation, not each sentence in the quotation.

   e. Each time you quote a new speaker, begin a new paragraph.

EDITING FOR MASTERY

Mastery Exercise 1

Correcting Punctuation Errors

The following passage contains fifteen punctuation errors, aside from the first error, which has been corrected as an example. Some punctuation marks are missing, and others are incorrect. Write in your corrections.

Creation of the World: A Yakima Indian Legend

(1) In the beginning of the world, everything was water. (2) Whee-me-me-ow-ah, the Great Chief Above^ lived up in the sky all alone. (3) When he decided to make the world he went down to the shallow places in the water and began to throw up great handfuls of mud that became land.

(4) He piled some of the mud so high that it froze hard and made the mountains. (5) When the rain came, it turned into ice and snow on top of the high mountains. (6) Some of the mud was hardened into rocks. (7) Since that time the rocks have not changed, they have only become harder.

(8) The Great Chief Above made trees berries, and roots grow on the Earth. (9) He made a man out of a ball of mud, then he told the man to take fish from the waters, and deer and other game from the forests. (10) When the man said, "I am lonely", the Great Chief Above made a woman to be his companion and taught her how to dress skins, how to find bark and roots, and how to make baskets out of them. (11) He taught her which berries to gather for food and how to pick them and dry them. (12) He showed her how to cook the salmon; and the animals that the man brought home.

(13) When the woman prayed to the Great Chief. (14) She said, "Please answer my prayer." (15) I need help in having children." (16) He answered her prayer.

(17) But in spite of all the things the Great Chief Above did for them, the new people quarreled. (18) They argued so much that Mother Earth was angry, and she shook the mountains so hard that those hanging over the narrow part of Big River fell down. (19) The rocks, that fell into the water dammed the stream and also made rapids and waterfalls. (20) Many people and animals were killed and buried under the rocks, and mountains.

(21) Someday the Great Chief Above will overturn those mountains and release the spirits that once lived in the bones buried there. (22) Those spirits live in the tops of the mountains; watching their children on the Earth and waiting for the great change that is to come. (23) The voices of these spirits can be heard in the mountains at all times. (24) Mourners who cry for their dead hear spirit voices reply, therefore they know that their lost ones are always near.

(25) We did not know all this by ourselves. (26) We were told it by our fathers and grandfathers, who learned it from their fathers and grandfathers. (27) No one knows, when the Great Chief Above will overturn the mountains. (28) But we do know this: The spirits will return only to the people who kept the beliefs of their grandfathers.

Scorecard: Number of errors found and corrected _____

Mastery Exercise 2

Correcting Punctuation Errors

The following passage contains fifteen punctuation errors, aside from the first error, which has been corrected as an example. Some punctuation marks are missing, and others are incorrect. Write in your corrections.

COLLABORATIVE ACTIVITY 6

Comparing Answers
Appoint someone to read the passage aloud so you can hear where errors occur. Write your corrections above the lines. Compare your answers and report your findings to the class.

Grandmother Spider Steals the Sun: A Cherokee Indian Creation Legend

(1) In the beginning, there was only blackness, nobody could see anything. (2) Animals kept bumping into each other and moving blindly. (3) They said, "What this world needs is light." (4) Fox said that he knew that some people on the other side of the world had plenty of light, however, they were too greedy to share it with others. (5) Possum said that he would be glad to steal a little of it. (6) He added, "I have a bushy tail." I can hide the light inside all that fur. (7) Then he traveled to the other side of the world. (8) He found the sun hanging in a tree and lighting everything up. (9) He sneaked over to the sun, picked out a tiny piece of light, and stuffed it into his tail. (10) However; the light was hot and burned all the fur off. (11) The people discovered his theft and took back the light; and Possum's tail has been bald ever since then.

(12) "Let me try." said Buzzard. (13) "I know better than to hide a piece of stolen light in my tail. (14) I'll put it on my head. (15) He flew to the other side of the world and, diving straight into the sun grabbed it in his claws. (16) He put it on his head; but it burned his head feathers off. (17) The people took the sun away from him, and Buzzard's head has remained bald ever since that time.

(18) Then Grandmother Spider said, "Let me try!" (19) First, she made a thick pot out of clay, next, she spun a web reaching all the way to the other side of the world. (20) She was so small, that none of the people there noticed her coming. (21) Quickly, Grandmother Spider snatched up the sun, then she put it in the bowl of clay, and rushed back home along one of the pieces of her web. (22) Now her side of the world had light, and everyone was happy.

(23) Grandmother Spider brought the sun to the Cherokee; and she also brought fire with it. (24) Besides that, she taught the Cherokee people, the art of pottery making.

Scorecard: Number of errors found and corrected _____

28

Checking Spelling, Apostrophes, Hyphens, and Capitals

Spelling and related matters may seem to be trivial issues. But trivial issues can distract your readers from the important one: the content of your writing. You should therefore pay close attention to spelling, apostrophes, hyphens, and capitalization as you edit your work. This chapter will help you

■ learn the rules

■ give yourself practice in applying them

SPELLING

You can eliminate many spelling problems if you follow some simple practices:

1. *Develop a healthy mistrust for the way you spell words.* "Good" spellers are often bad ones who suspect errors and check them in the dictionary or on computer spell-checkers. If you compose by hand, circle words whose spelling you aren't sure of and then look them up as you edit. The dictionary will not only show you how to spell the words, but it will also show you how to pronounce them, where to separate them between syllables, and what their forms are in different tenses, as plurals, or as different parts of speech.

2. *Carefully pronounce words you aren't sure how to spell,* look them up in the dictionary, and learn the spellings that correspond to those pronunciations. But because English is a combination of several languages, each with its own spelling rules, a sound can be spelled in many ways. So keep that dictionary handy. And don't rely entirely on a computer spell-checker. It can give you the "correct" spelling of a word—but not the word you want to use.

3. *Look for root words in longer, more complex words.* For example, *member* is inside *remember* and *differ* is inside *different.* This advice is especially important in words with a silent letter or a hard-to-recognize vowel sound. For example, *finite* is in *definite* and *labor* is in *laboratory.*

4. *Don't confuse words that sound or look alike (their/there/they're, its/it's,* and so on). Check your dictionary repeatedly until you can clearly distinguish one word from the other.

5. *Use memory games to remind you of tricky spellings.* For example, everybody wants to eat two deSSerts, but nobody wants to be stranded in a deSert more than once. You'll find tips throughout this chapter to help you remember tricky spellings.

6. *Keep your own spelling list of problem words* (preferably on flash cards so that you can study each one separately) and write each word in a sentence. Underline or capitalize the troublesome part of the word: proBABly, choiCe, studYing. Consult Appendix D at the back of this book for additional help with many tricky spellings.

7. *Carefully proofread your papers,* whether you write them by hand or keyboard them into a computer. You should catch a number of careless errors in the process. Use computer spell-checking programs—but don't rely on them entirely. They can't think for you, and they won't catch every mistake.

The following rules should also help improve your spelling.

The Long and Short Vowel Sounds

Carefully pronouncing words will help you spell them only if you know which letters represent the various sounds. That's especially true with the **vowels,** which can have a number of sounds and spellings.

The Long Vowel Sounds.   When you say the names of the vowels, you're pronouncing the long vowel sounds. But most often when spelling these long vowel sounds, you must *combine two vowels,* either together or separated by a single **consonant.** Here are some examples:

Sound	Spelling	Example
long *a*	*ai*	main, lain, chain
	ay	hay, say, pay
	ei	sleigh, reign
	a consonant *e*	fate, hate, crate
long *e*	*ee*	seem, meet, three
	ea	beat, dream, league
	ie	believe, achieve, brownie
	(c)*ei*	receive, deceive, conceive
	final *y*	happy, ugly, unity
	e consonant *e*	precede, Chinese, complete
long *i*	*ie*	pie, tie, flies
	igh, ign	light, sigh, sign
	y	sky, fly, cry
	i consonant *e*	nice, cite, line
long *o*	*oa*	boat, coat, roam
	final *o*	piano, auto, potato
	old	sold, scold
	o consonant *e*	chrome, wrote, role
long *u*	*oo*	boot, shoot, food
	ui	fruit, juice
	ew	new, few, crew
	final *ue*	clue, argue, true
	u consonant *e*	cute, huge, refuse

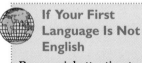
If Your First Language Is Not English

Pay special attention to vowel sounds, which can be confusing. Many languages don't have a short *i* sound, and pronounce English letters *i* and *e* as *e* and *a*. For example, *bit* in English is pronounced like *beat* in many languages. And *bet* in English is pronounced like *bait* in many languages. Proofread your work carefully.

TIPS

For Spelling Words with *ie* **or** *ei*

To keep these spellings straight, remember this rhyme:

I before *e*

Except after *c*

Or when sounded like *a*

As in *neighbor* or *weigh*.

1. *i* before *e*: believe, relief
2. except after *c*: receive, conceive
3. or when sounded like *a*: eighty, sleigh

Some exceptions: caffeine, either, their, foreign, protein, leisure, weird, seize.

The Short Vowel Sounds. A single vowel is usually pronounced as a short vowel sound. Compare these words:

Short vowel sounds	Long vowel sounds
hat	hate
bat	bait
man	main
bet	beat, beet
pet	Pete
bit	bite
quit (*u* always follows *q* and is not considered a vowel in this position)	quite
hop	hope
hot	hotel
lot	load
cut	cute
subtle	suit

Although nothing can provide an instant cure for misspelled long and short vowel sounds, the list should help. And each time you hear a vowel sound you aren't sure how to spell, check your dictionary. You'll learn more about spelling long and short vowel sounds later, when the chapter discusses doubling final consonants.

EXERCISE 1 Writing Long Vowels

Write two or three words using the vowels supplied. Don't use any of the words from the list already given.

1. long *a*

ai _claim, bait, train_   ay _____

ei _____   a consonant *e*_____

2. long *e*

ee _____   ea _____

final *y* _____

3. long *i*

ie _____   igh, ign_____

final *y* _____   i consonant *e*_____

4. long *o*

oa _____   final *o* _____

old_____   o consonant *e*_____

5. long *u*

oo_____   ui _____

ew_____   ue_____

u consonant *e*_____

EXERCISE 2   Choosing the Correct Spelling

Circle the correctly spelled word.

1. (brief)/ breif   **5.** chief / cheif

2. field / feild   **6.** reciept / receipt

3. conciet / conceit   **7.** decieve / deceive

4. frieght / freight   **8.** thier / their

Plurals of Nouns and Singulars of Verbs

Add *–s* or *–es* to make plural nouns and present-tense, third-person-singular verbs. Both nouns and verbs follow the same spelling rules for taking *–s* or *–es*.

▶ Add *–es* to nouns or verbs ending in *ss*, *ch*, *sh*, *z*, or *x*.

boss, wax, reach, wish = *bosses, waxes, reaches, wishes*

▶ Add *–es* to most nouns or verbs ending in *–o*.

tomato, potato, do = *tomatoes, potatoes, does*
Some exceptions: radios, pianos, stereos

▶ Change final *–y* to *–i* and add *–es* after a consonant.

study, try, sky = *studies, tries, skies*

▶ Do not change final *–y* after a vowel; merely add *–s*.

boy, play, buy = *boys, plays, buys*

▶ Change noun (but not verb) endings from *–f* or *–fe* to *–ve* before adding *–s*.

leaf, knife, wife = *leaves, knives, wives*
Some exceptions: beliefs, chiefs, safes, chefs

EXERCISE 3   Forming Plurals

Make the following nouns plural.

1. knife *knives*_____   **4.** hoof_____

2. half_____   **5.** shelf_____

3. self_____   **6.** chief_____

▶   Add –s to most other nouns and verbs.

> lamp, pie, make, walk = *lamps, pies, makes, walks*
> *Some exceptions:* child = *children,* man = *men*

EXERCISE 4   Adding Word Endings

Add –s or –es to these words, and change word endings when necessary.

1. ride *rides* _____

2. beach _____

3. beauty _____

4. rush _____

5. tax _____

6. flower _____

7. rose _____

8. witch _____

9. breath _____

10. key _____

Suffixes

A **suffix** is an ending attached to a **root word** to form a new word. Here are some examples:

Root word	Suffix	New word
agree	–ment	agreement
grace	–ful	graceful
sad	–ness	sadness

Note the rules for the spelling of words when suffixes are added:

▶   Change –y to –i if the letter before –y is a consonant.

Root word	Suffix	New word
busy	–ness	business
happy	–er	happier
pretty	–est	prettiest
angry	–ly	angrily
deny	–al	denial
beauty	–ful	beautiful

Note: Never change final *y* to *i* before the suffix *–ing:* denying, trying

▶   Don't change a –y that comes after a vowel.

Root word	Suffix	New word
play	–ed, –ing	played, playing
lay	–er	layer
employ	–ment	employment

EXERCISE 5   Adding Suffixes

Combine the following root words and suffixes, making whatever changes are necessary.

1. destroy + er *destroyer* _____

2. stay + ed _____

3. apply + cation _____

4. ugly + est _____

5. pay + ment _____   **8.** fly + ing_____

6. witty + cism_____   **9.** happy + ly_____

7. fly + er_____

▶ **Drop final *–e* when the suffix begins with a vowel.**

Root word	Suffix	New word
ridicule	*–ous*	ridiculous
argue	*–ing*	arguing
strangle	*–ing*	strangling
Some exceptions: hoeing, canoeing		

▶ **With most words ending in *–ce* or *–ge*, do not drop the final *–e*.**

courageous	noticeable

▶ **Keep final *–e* when the suffix begins with a consonant.**

Root word	Suffix	New word
hope	*–ful*	hopeful
complete	*–ly*	completely
time	*–less*	timeless
Some exceptions: acknowledgment, argument, judgment, truly, awful		

EXERCISE 6   Combining Root Words and Suffixes

Join the following root words and suffixes, making whatever changes are necessary.

1. hate + ful _hateful_____   **5.** fame + ous_____

2. awe + ful_____   **6.** amuse + ment_____

3. dance + ing_____   **7.** dine + ing_____

4. sincere + ly_____   **8.** admire + ation_____

▶ **The suffix *–ly* changes adjectives to adverbs without changing the spelling of the root word (except that final *–y* may become *–i*).**

This rule is especially important for root words ending in *–l* (making *–lly*) or root words ending in *–e* (making *–ely*):

Root word	New word
real	really
sure	surely
sincere	sincerely
careful	carefully
One exception: true = truly	

E X E R C I S E   7   Adding –ly to Root Words

Change the following adjectives to adverbs by adding –ly.

1. ideal _ideally_

2. bare _____

3. usual_____

4. sure_____

5. angry_____

6. necessary_____

7. real_____

8. true_____

 For short vowel sounds, double the final consonant.

As you saw earlier in the chapter, a combination of vowel-consonant-vowel (such as *–ate*, *–ine*, and *–ope*) usually creates a long vowel (which sounds the same as the name of the vowel):

> hate   Pete   bite   hope   cute

However, a combination of vowel-consonant-consonant creates a short vowel sound, as in the following examples:

hat	hatter
pet	petted
bit	bitten
hop	hopped
cut	cutting

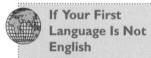

If Your First Language Is Not English

Speakers of Spanish need to be careful about doubling final consonants. Spanish doesn't double consonants, and all vowels have only a single sound. Proofread your work carefully.

 Doubling the consonant makes the vowel before it short.

If the vowel sound remains long, the consonant does not double. Contrast these words:

(to cause a scar)	scar	scarring, scarred
(to frighten)	scare	scaring, scared
(to get rid of)	rid	ridding
(to ride, as in a car)	ride	riding
(to hop, like a bunny)	hop	hopping, hopped
(to wish)	hope	hoping, hoped
(to slice)	cut	cutter
(attractive)	cute	cuter

E X E R C I S E   8   Adding Suffixes

Add suffixes to the root words, doubling the final consonant when necessary.

1. win + ing _winning_

2. tune + ing_____

3. write + ing_____

4. stop + ed_____

5. run + ing_____

6. hit + ing_____

7. heat + ing_____

8. stir + ing_____

▶ **Don't double all final consonants of words with more than one syllable.**

A root word can have more than one **syllable**—a grouping of letters containing a single vowel sound. With multisyllable root words, double the final consonant only if the accent falls on the syllable immediately before the suffix:

commit′ ted	occurr′ ed
begin′ ning	submit′ ted
preferr′ ed	expell′ ed
Exception:	offer off′ erred off′ erring

When the accent falls on another syllable, do not double the consonant:

hap′ pened	lis′ tened
an′ swered	coun′ selor
pref′ erence	trav′ eled

These rules also help in determining when to double consonants in other situations:

apple	*but*	ape
beggar	*but*	begin
rummage	*but*	union

EXERCISE 9   Doubling Final Consonants

Combine the following root words and suffixes, doubling the final consonant of the root word when necessary. Be careful to note where the accent falls.

1. defer + ed *deferred*

2. unravel + ing_____

3. parallel + ing_____

4. compel + ed_____

5. prefer + ence_____

6. occur + ed_____

EXERCISE 10   Recognizing Correct Spelling

Circle the correct spelling.

1. runing / (running)

2. diferent / different

3. stuborn / stubborn

4. refered / referred

5. writing / writting

6. gramar / grammar

7. occured / occurred

8. comming / coming

9. biten / bitten

10. sitting / siting

Prefixes

A **prefix**—an addition to the beginning of a root word—never affects the spelling of the root. No letters are dropped or doubled:

Prefix	Root word	New word
un-	natural	unnatural
dis-	integrate	disintegrate
mis-	spell	misspell
il-	logical	illogical
in-	accurate	inaccurate
im-	moral	immoral
co-	operate	cooperate

E X E R C I S E   1 1   Identifying Correctly Spelled Words

Circle the correct spellings.

1. (disinterested) / dissinterested
2. unnable / unable
3. inumerable / innumerable
4. unnerve / unerve
5. disatisfied / dissatisfied

6. ilegal / illegal
7. immaterial / imaterial
8. missapply / misapply
9. misstake / mistake
10. disagree / dissagree

E X E R C I S E   1 2   Correcting Misspellings

Correct each misspelled word. When the spelling rules won't help you, use a dictionary or look at the list of commonly misspelled words in Appendix D.

1. accross _across_
2. adress _____
3. alot _____
4. arguement _____
5. athelete _____
6. basicly _____
7. begining _____
8. beleive _____
9. brillient _____
10. buisness _____

11. carefuly _____
12. childrens _____
13. choosen _____
14. comming _____
15. competion _____
16. definate _____
17. delt _____
18. diffrent _____
19. dinning _____
20. disapoint _____

✔ TIPS

For Using Memory Devices

1. StationERy is papER.
2. Old AGE isn't a trAGEdy.
3. Bad gramMAR will MAR your writing.
4. The LLs are paraLLel in this word.
5. He is BUSY in his BUSIness.
6. The princiPAL is your PAL.
7. TOGETHER we went TO GET HER.
8. To write ALL RIGHT as one word would be ALL WRONG.
9. AFFECT is a verb that begins with A for ACTION.
10. Strange but true, there is a LIE in beLIEf and beLIEve.
11. Don't let the IR in theIR IRk you.
12. There is an ITCH in wITCH.
13. WhICH one has the sandWICH?
14. HERE is in tHERE and wHERE.
15. There is no word in English that begins with RECCO. Recommend means Re commend.
16. FULL loses an L at the end of a word: THANKFUL, GRATEFUL, HELPFUL, etc.

21. discribe _____
22. dosen't _____
23. eigth _____
24. entrence _____
25. enviroment _____
26. existance _____
27. explaination _____
28. extremly _____
29. finaly _____
30. freind _____
31. goverment _____
32. grammer _____
33. heigth _____
34. hisself _____
35. hopeing _____
36. imediately _____
37. interlectual _____
38. intresting _____
39. jewlry _____
40. knowlege _____
41. localy _____
42. lonly _____
43. mispell _____
44. necesary _____
45. ocasion _____

46. occurance _____
47. perfer _____
48. possble _____
49. potatoe _____
50. preceed _____
51. priviledge _____
52. probly _____
53. recieved _____
54. rember _____
55. sacrafice _____
56. sence _____
57. seperate _____
58. shinning _____
59. sincerly _____
60. studing _____
61. suceed _____
62. suprise _____
63. temperture _____
64. themselfs _____
65. tomatoe _____
66. truely _____
67. trys _____
68. usualy _____
69. writen _____
70. writting _____

THE APOSTROPHE [']

The rules for using apostrophes are actually rather simple. The **apostrophe**—a little hook above the line where a letter (or letters) would normally be—has only three functions: to form possessives of nouns, to form contractions, and to make letters plural.

Possessives

 Add 's to make a singular noun possessive.

When something belongs to someone, that person possesses it. There are several ways to express possession or ownership:

> the house that belongs to Jerry
> the car my neighbor owns
> the room of my brother

 **COLLABORATIVE ACTIVITY I**

Creating Memory Devices
Try your talents at creating memory devices for the following words. Report your results to the class.

1. piece
2. attendance
3. comparative
4. existence
5. friend
6. misspell
7. disappoint
8. capitol (building)
9. different
10. marriage

However, a simple apostrophe (') + s added to a noun signals possession in a shorter and more direct way:

> *Jerry's* house
> my *neighbor's* car
> my *brother's* room

This form of the noun is called the **possessive.**

Although a house, a car, and a room are concrete and material, a person can also possess abstract, nonmaterial things:

> the idea of my friend = my *friend's* idea
> the explanation made by the teacher = the *teacher's* explanation
> the ambition that Rafael has = *Rafael's* ambition

EXERCISE 13   Forming Possessives

Rewrite each of the following using apostrophe + –s.

1. the book that belongs to Tom _Tom's book_

2. the coat that Judy has _____

3. the work done by Willie _____

4. the personality of Karen _____

5. the apartment that belongs to Maria _____

6. the bicycle that the boy owns _____

7. the statement made by Mr. Johnson _____

 Add ' to make a plural noun ending in –s possessive.

As you know, most plural nouns end in –s:

| friends | boys | classes | the Smiths |
| teachers | students | parents | the Gonzalezes |

You make these plural words possessive by adding ' after the *–s*:

> the books that belong to more than one boy = the *boys'* books
> the car that belongs to my neighbors = my *neighbors'* car
> the attitude of my parents = my *parents'* attitude

The correct placement of the apostrophe is important; it tells the reader whether the possessive noun is singular or plural:

> the *boy's* house (singular—one boy)
> the *boys'* house (plural—more than one boy)

All singular nouns should add *'s*, even if they end in *s*.

> *Carlos's* smile
> the *boss's* desk

TIPS

For Keeping the Possessive Forms of Pronouns Straight

Personal pronouns already have their possessive forms built in; they do not take apostrophes:

Singular	Plural
my house	*our* house
your house	*your* house
his house	
her house	*their* house
its house	

EXERCISE 14   Making More Possessives

Rewrite each of the following expressions, using 's or '.

1. the lounge for women _the women's lounge_

2. the idea of my boss _____

3. the house that belongs to Ms. Jones_____

4. the room that belongs to the children_____

5. the day for every mother_____

6. the schedules of the professors_____

7. the laws of Texas_____

8. the best restaurant in the city_____

 Use *'s* or *'* to show possession with objects and time.

Objects can also possess things, as in these examples:

> the front tire of the bicycle = the *bicycle's* front tire
> the new stoplights of the streets = the *streets'* new stoplights

Even some time expressions use *'s* or *s'*. Notice that the phrases with apostrophes sound more graceful than the ones with *of*:

> the pay of a week = a *week's* pay
> the work of two years = two *years'* work

EXERCISE 15   Editing for Apostrophes

Insert the missing apostrophes in each of the following sentences.

1. I'm taking a week^'s vacation soon.

2. The rooms air conditioner needs to be repaired.

3. A few hours work should take care of the problem.

4. This years schedule allows more time off than last years schedule.

5. The cars front fenders were dented in two separate accidents.

6. I'll be off on New Years Day.

EXERCISE 16   Spelling Words Ending in –s

Circle the correct spelling in parentheses.

1. It was the (companies /(company's)) responsibility.

2. The Mets scored five (runs / run's) in the ninth.

3. He (runs / run's) a large business.

4. Four men were shot in the (movies / movie's) opening scene.

5. I ate at the (cities / city's) best restaurant.

6. She (lights / light's) the fire each night.

7. The trees have lost their (leaves / leaf's).

8. He (says / say's) that the coat doesn't fit.

TIPS

For Correcting Errors with Apostrophes

Some people want to put apostrophes before every final –s. Remember that apostrophes signal possession, not plurals or third-person-singular verbs.

Contractions

Use an apostrophe to replace the missing letter(s) in a contraction.

A **contraction** is a joining of two words that requires omitting a letter or several letters from the second word. An apostrophe occupies the spot of the missing letters:

> do not = *don't* (' replaces *o*)
> cannot = *can't* (' replaces *no*)
> it is = *it's* (' replaces *i*)
> they are = *they're* (' replaces *a*)
> they would = *they'd* (' replaces *woul*)

EXERCISE 17   Forming Contractions

Make the following pairs of words into contractions, placing apostrophes properly.

1. he is _he's_____

2. we will_____

3. it has _____

4. they are _____

5. we are _____

6. has not_____

7. you are _____

8. it is_____

9. does not_____

10. can not_____

E X E R C I S E   1 8   Editing for Apostrophes

Add apostrophes where necessary.

1. It^'s^cold today.

2. Were going to get it done.

3. Well have to see what she says.

4. What do you think hell do?

5. I dont know what youre asking me.

6. Its purpose is clear.

7. Whos there?

8. Theyre always getting into trouble.

COLLABORATIVE ACTIVITY 2

Correcting Apostrophe Errors

Write five sentences containing words that need apostrophes, but omit the apostrophes. Exchange papers and add the apostrophes. Exchange papers again so a third student can check the work.

Plurals of Letters

Add *'s* to form the plurals of letters used as letters.

When you need to make a letter or group of letters plural, add an apostrophe before the final *–s* so that your readers don't mistake the *–s* for one of the letters:

> Watch your *p's* and *q's*.
> Billy already knows his *ABC's*.
> Maria got all *A's*.

HYPHENS [-]

Hyphens always join. They join two or more words to make them one, or they keep words joined when you must break them at the end of a line.

Hyphens to Join Words

    Hyphenate two-word numbers.

In formal writing, use a hyphen to join all two-word numbers between twenty-one and ninety-nine, as well as all fractions:

> thirty-five   one hundred
> fifty-one   *but*   321 (Use numerals for numbers that require three or
> two-thirds   more words to write out.)

E X E R C I S E   1 9   Hyphenating Numbers

Hyphenate the following numbers if necessary.

1. twenty^-^one

2. three hundred

3. forty six

4. one thousand

5. three fourths

6. eighty two

▶ **Hyphenate between a prefix and a capitalized noun.**

> pro-American   anti-Chinese

▶ **Hyphenate between the prefixes *self–*, *all–*, and *ex–* (meaning "former") and all nouns.**

> self-confidence   ex-husband   all-world

▶ **Hyphenate words with *–in-law*.**

> mother-in-law   brothers-in-law (Note how the plural is formed.)

▶ **Hyphenate two or more words acting as a single adjective before a noun.**

> a three-piece suit   a four-star movie
> a good-for-nothing guy   a ten-foot pole

But don't hyphenate these groups of words when they don't precede nouns:

> That guy has always been good for nothing.
> The movie received four stars from many critics.

E X E R C I S E   2 0   Hyphenating Words

Hyphenate the following groups of words as necessary.

1. an ex‸officer of the group   **4.** a two man job

2. two sisters in law   **5.** a pro Russian speech

3. a self made millionaire   **6.** a hard to get out of bed morning

▶ **Check your dictionary about hyphenating compound words.**

A **compound word** is formed from two or more complete root words (like *background*). There are three different ways to write compounds:

1. As one word:

Root word	Root word	New word
horse	fly	horsefly
through	out	throughout
school	house	schoolhouse

Notice that these compound words do not drop any letters from their root words.

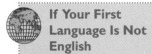

If Your First Language Is Not English

Unlike the practices in many languages, adjectives in English don't change to show the plural. Therefore, a hyphenated word before a noun (in the adjective position) always takes a singular form:

A two-*star* movie (not *stars*)

a five-*foot* ladder (not *feet*)

2. As hyphenated words:

Root word	Root word	New word
heavy	duty	heavy-duty
go	between	a go-between
give	(and) take	give-and-take

3. As two separate words (these are not really compound words):

monkey wrench   heat wave   grand piano

Use your dictionary when you're unsure about hyphenating or spelling a compound word.

EXERCISE 21   Writing Compound Words

Create a compound word by adding a second root word after each of the words below.

1. day _daylight_

2. run_____

3. bitten_____

4. house_____

5. news_____

6. ground_____

7. chair_____

8. maker_____

9. half_____

10. under_____

Syllables

Hyphenate words at the end of lines only between syllables.

A **syllable** is a complete sound that must include a vowel. For example, the word *understand* has three complete sounds: un der stand. When you must hyphenate a word at the end of a line, break the word only between syllables. You cannot hyphenate a one-syllable word such as *go, make,* and *seen*:

accu-rate		stra-ight (one syllable)
intel-lectual	*but not*	
com-munity		pict-ure (the syllable break is at *pic-ture*)

Here are some hints about breaking words into syllables.

1. Break syllables after complete root words:

transfer-able   spell-ing   play-er

2. Break syllables after prefixes or before suffixes:

un-interesting   sad-ly
trans-port   govern-ment

3. Break syllables between two consonants—unless the consonants form one sound, such as *-th, -sh, -sc,* or *-ch:*

cap-tain	south-ern
volun-tary *but*	
hus-band	reach-ing

Consult your dictionary if you are unsure of the syllable breaks.

4. Break already hyphenated words only at the hyphen.

Since two hyphens in one word will confuse your reader, break a hyphenated word only at its hyphen:

Poor: un-Amer-ican
Better: un-American

In fact, try not to break a hyphenated word between lines.

5. Don't hyphenate a contraction.

Incorrect: does-n't   is-n't

6. Don't leave only one letter at the end or beginning of a line.

Poor: a-live   cloud-y
Better: alive   cloudy

And don't trust a computer to hyphenate for you. It doesn't know the difference, for example, between *pre-sent* (verb) and *pres-ent* (noun) or *pro-ject* (verb) and *proj-ect* (noun).

EXERCISE 22   Hyphenating Between Syllables

Divide each word with a hyphen, unless the word cannot be divided.

1. unnecessary *unnec- essary*
2. repeat_____
3. stepped_____
4. waited_____
5. watered_____

6. seemed_____
7. ex-president_____
8. aren't_____
9. guardhouse_____
10. attention_____

CAPITALIZATION

Capitalize sentences, names, and titles according to the following rules.

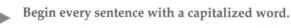 **Begin every sentence with a capitalized word.**

In the beginning, the book was slow reading.
He said that he felt fine.

▶ Capitalize the pronoun *I*.

> **I** *but* we he they his myself

▶ Capitalize names of people, places, courses, organizations, languages, and words formed from them.

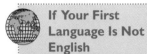

If Your First Language Is Not English

Nationalities and names of languages aren't capitalized in Spanish, but they are in English:

I speak Spanish.
He is French.

> Howard   Fleet Street
> the National Audubon Society   English
> New York   New Yorker
> Main High School (*but* high school)
> China
> Biology 111 (the name of a course) *but* biology (not a course name)

EXERCISE 23   Capitalizing Proper Nouns

Underline the letters that should be capitalized.

1. r̲ussian

2. george herman "babe" ruth

3. the corner of prairie road and central street

4. mathematics 101

5. mathematics

6. california wine

7. i, you, him

8. american civil liberties union

9. spanish

▶ Capitalize a person's title before his or her name.

> Mayor Juarez   *but*   He is the mayor.
> Professor Williams   *but*   Who is your English professor?
> President Bush   *but*   George W. Bush is president.
> Dr. Williams   *but*   She is a doctor.

▶ Capitalize names of areas or countries.

Don't capitalize these terms when they mean only a direction:

> The North won the Civil War.   She is from the West.
>   *but*   *but*
> We are traveling north.   Which way is east?

▶ Capitalize the names of days, months, and holidays.

Don't capitalize the seasons of the year:

> Tuesday   summer
> March   *but*   spring
> Independence Day   fall

Capitalize all major words in titles.

Don't capitalize little words—short prepositions, conjunctions, and articles—unless they're the first or last words in the title or subtitle:

> *For Whom the Bell Tolls*
> *The Godfather*
> "What Hurts the Most"
> *Journal of the American Medical Association*
> "What to Listen For"

E X E R C I S E   2 4   Capitalizing Nouns

Underline the letters that should be capitalized.

1. tuesday

2. winter

3. august

4. the wild west

5. a reverend

6. the reverend mr. haley

7. the wind is coming from the east.

8. webster's collegiate dictionary

IN SUMMARY   Spelling, Apostrophes, Hyphens, and Capitals

Adding final –s or –es

1. Add –es to words ending in s-like sounds or most words ending in o.
2. Change –y to –i after a consonant and add –es.
3. Change most nouns ending in –f or –fe to –ve before adding –s.

Adding a suffix

1. Change –y to –i after a consonant.
2. Keep final –e before a suffix beginning with a consonant.
3. Before a suffix beginning with a vowel, double the final consonant to make a short vowel sound. Don't double the final consonant to make a long vowel sound.

Using apostrophes

1. To show possession, add –'s to all singular nouns, but add just an apostrophe to plural nouns ending in –s.
2. To make a contraction, put the apostrophe in the place of the omitted letter(s).
3. To make letters plural, add –'s.

Using hyphens

1. Hyphenate two-word numbers from *twenty-one* to *ninety-nine* and all fractions.
2. Hyphenate a prefix and a capitalized noun.
3. Hyphenate the prefixes *self–*, *all–*, or *ex–* and a noun, and all words with *–in-law*.
4. Hyphenate two or more words acting as a single adjective before a noun.
5. If you break a word at the end of a line, hyphenate only between syllables.

Capitalizing

1. Capitalize the first word of every sentence or title.
2. Capitalize the pronoun *I*.
3. Capitalize names of people, places, organizations, courses, languages, and words formed from them.
4. Capitalize a person's title when it is used before the name.
5. Capitalize areas or countries (but not directions).
6. Capitalize names of days, months, and holidays (but not seasons of the year).
7. Capitalize words in titles, except short prepositions, conjunctions, and articles.

EDITING FOR MASTERY

Mastery Exercise 1

Correcting Spelling and Other Matters

The following passage contains twenty errors in spelling, apostrophe use, hyphenation, and capitalization, excluding the first error, which has been corrected as an example. Correct each error above the line.

The Origins of the "Happy Birthday" Song

(1) ^*Believe* ~~Beleive~~ it or not, the tune you have heard at countless birthday party's is copyrighted, and the copyright owners often recieve royalties when its sung. (2) The melody was writen by two sisters from Kentucky, Mildred and Patty Smith Hill, and was first published under the title "Good Morning to All" in 1893. (3) The song was never meant for birthday celebrations, but instead welcomed youngsters enterring a class room each morning. (4) It took a diffrent role as a result of a theft.

(5) Mildred Hill, who composed the melody, was a church organist, a concert pianist, and an authority on african-american spirituals. (6) She died in Chicago at the age of fifty seven. (7) Her sister Patty Smith Hill had writen the original lyric's for the song while she was principal of a kindergarten in Louisville, Kentucky, where Mildred also taught.

(8) The Hill sisters copyrighted their song on October 16, 1893. (9) However, on March 4, 1924, it apeared without thier approval in Robert H. Colemans songbook. (10) Although

the song still had its original title, Coleman changed part of the lyrics to say, "Happy birthday to you."

(11) The song was then published sevral times over the next ten years, often with small changes in the lyrics. (12) By 1933, everyone knew the song as "Happy Birthday to You." (13) A year later, when the birthday tune was sung every night in a Broadway Musical, another Hill sister, Jessica, took the case to court. (14) She was fed up with the theft of the song and the total absence of royalty's to her brothers and sisters. (15) She won her lawsuit. (16) The Hill family owned the rights to the melody and had to be payed every time the song was part of a commercial production.

(17) The results of the suit were immediate. (18) The Western Union company, which had deliverred a half-million singing birthday greetings, stoped using the piece. (19) It was dropped from two plays on Broadway. (20) And in another play entitled "Happy Birthday," it's star, Helen Hayes, spoke the lyrics so the producers could avoid paying royalties.

(21) Dr. Patty Smith Hill died at the age of seventy eight, aware that she and her sister had started an amazing birthday tradition.

Scorecard: Number of errors found and corrected _____

Mastery Exercise 2

Correcting Spelling and Other Matters

The following passage contains twenty errors in spelling, apostrophe use, hyphenation, and capitalization, excluding the first error, which has been corrected as an example. Correct each error above the line.

COLLABORATIVE
ACTIVITY 3
Checking Your Answers
Compare answers to
Mastery Exercise 1, and
report your results to
the class.

The Ghostly Rhyme (A Chinese Legend)

(1) Long ago, a wise man was sent to the jungle after he complained about dishonesty in the ^goverment. *government*. (2) He built a small hut near a stream among the cinnamon trees. (3) He brought the water for his tea in a bamboo diper and ate the fish he caught, the fruit he picked, and the vegtables he grew in a small patch. (4) But usualy he spent his day reading.

(5) When a friend asked him why he lived in such a lonly spot, he was supprised. (6) "But I'm not alone," he said. (7) "My books have told me all about these hills. (8) I have the spirits of the wood's for company." (9) Later, when he developed a cough, his friends tried to get him to come down to the city to see a doctor, but he refused. (10) "The smell of Pine is the best medicine," he said.

(11) One day, he picked up a book by his favorite poet, but worms had eatten away the outside edges of the pages. (12) He opened the book to read a poem and found that the last line was missing, which he could not rember. (13) He tryed to recall it by reciting

the next-to last line over and over: (14) "The sun on my old garden shine's . . ." (15) He soon forgot to eat and even sleep.

(16) One day, his friend's found him dead still inside his hut, with the book in his lap. (17) Saddly, they buried him with the book, but that night the sound of the wind shaking the leafs of the cinnamon trees sounded like someone sighing. (18) The raindrops fell like someone impatiently taping a finger.

(19) Then his ghost appeared, reading the poem aloud, but stopped just before the last line. (20) At first, people were frightened, but they realized that his ghost was harmless. (21) Eventually, though, he began to haunt the Main street and shout out the words of the poem. (22) People beged the old man to go away.

(23) At last, a poet went up to the hut in the woods, sat down, and waited for the wise man to come. (24) The ghost finaly appeared and read from the book. (25) The poet recognized the poem, and when the wise man ended before the last line, the poet asked him to continue. (26) Once again, he read but stopped at the same place. (27) "The sun on my old garden shines . . ."

(28) "But I am gone," the poet finished. "No flesh confines."

(29) The ghost smiled in releif and closed his book. (30) He dissapeared, and no one ever saw or heard him again.

Scorecard: Number of errors found and corrected _____

CHAPTER 29

Writing the Right Word

Words that look alike or sound alike cause even the most experienced writers to mistake one for the other. Computer spell-checkers aren't much help, either, for the words may be correctly spelled but incorrectly used. If you tend to confuse certain words, you can study them in this chapter. Whatever the case, try to focus on *one word* in a look-alike or sound-alike pairing—the one that occurs or confuses you most often. Prepare your own mental or written list of sound-alikes and look-alikes to watch out for as you revise.

This chapter will help you examine many of the most common look-alikes and sound-alikes by

- identifying the most common confusions among these words
- suggesting ways to keep them straight

THE MOST COMMON SOUND-ALIKES AND LOOK-ALIKES

The following four categories of errors are especially troublesome and therefore deserve special attention.

Contractions

The contractions of *is* or *are* function as both the subject and verb of a sentence or clause:

Contraction	Meaning	Example
it's	it is (or it has)	*It's* a nice day.
who's	who is (or who has)	*Who's* driving tonight?

Contraction	Meaning	Example
they're	they are	*They're* talking right now.
you're	you are	*You're* doing a good job.

People often confuse contractions with these possessive words:

Possessive word	Example
its	The dog has *its leash*.
whose	*Whose briefcase* is this?

> ✓ **TIPS**
> **For the Place Words**
> If you have trouble distinguishing between *their/there* and *we're/where*, simply remember that the place words both contain the word *here*: t**HERE** w**HERE**.

| their | The students all handed in *their* assignments. |
| your | *Your* finger may be broken. |

People also sometimes confuse *were*, a past-tense form of *to be*, with *we're*:

We *were* vacationing in Mexico.
We're planning to go there again next year.

One other source of confusion is the place words *there* and *where*. *There* looks like *they're* and *their*, and *where* looks like *we're* and *were*.

EXERCISE 1   Identifying Correct Word Choice

Underline the correct word in the parentheses.

1. Because (<u>we're</u>/were/where) all so accustomed to using aluminum foil, (it's/its) probably surprising to learn that the product wasn't invented until 1947.

2. (It's/Its) inventor, Richard S. Reynolds, first worked for his uncle, R. J. Reynolds, (whose/who's) company made cigarettes and loose tobacco that (we're/were/where) wrapped in thin sheets of tin and lead.

3. Reynolds later established his own business, the U.S. Foil Co., from (we're/were/where) he continued to wrap tobacco and candy.

4. He then quickly began to use a new wrapping material called aluminum when (its/it's) price began to drop in the late 1920s.

5. Reynolds soon offered people an impressive list of products for use in (there/their/they're) homes and hobbies: aluminum siding and windows; aluminum pots, pans, and kitchen utensils; and aluminum boats.

6. But (its/it's) another product, which Reynolds created in 1947, that is most responsible for introducing Americans to the benefits of this metal:
Reynolds' Wrap.

7. Today (your/you're) likely to use aluminum products in all sorts of ways.

COLLABORATIVE ACTIVITY 1

Writing Sentences
Write a sentence for each of the words highlighted in this chapter. Then exchange your sentences with another student and correct each other's work.

Too/Two/To

TIPS

For *Too*
This sentence should help you remember the meanings of *too* with two *oo*'s: The *zoo* was *too* crowded, *too*.

Here are three more frequently confused sound-alikes:
Too means *also* or *more than enough*:

We are coming, *too*. (also)
We have *too* many problems. (more than enough)
Two means the number 2.
To is used in all other cases.

EXERCISE 2   Identifying Correct Word Choice

Underline the correct word in the parentheses.

1. Back in 1886, John S. Pemberton used an iron pot (too/<u>to</u>/two) mix a batch of a drink, later (too/<u>to</u>/two) be called Coca-Cola.

2. Pemberton had returned (too/to/two) Atlanta, Georgia, after the Civil War (too/to/two) open a drugstore.

3. A friend named the drink after its (too/to/two) main ingredients: coca, the dried leaf of a plant, and cola, from the kola nut.

4. (Too/To/Two) years later, Pemberton died, and ownership of the soft drink was sold (too/to/two) a company for $2,300.

5. Soon the public began (too/to/two) call the drink *Coke,* which the company felt was (too/to/two) informal a name.

6. In 1920, the company gave in (too/to/two) the public's practice and registered the name *Coke* as a trademark.

The *of* Error

When you speak, you probably use the following contractions:

could've = could have	would've = would have
should've = should have	might've = might have

The *–'ve* ending in each contraction sounds like the preposition *of.* So many people write "could of" when they mean *could have* and so forth:

Incorrect:	He should of done it.
Correct:	He should have ('ve) done it.
Incorrect:	I might of gone.
Correct:	I might have ('ve) gone.

Remember that *of* cannot follow the words *could, should, would, might,* and other helping verbs.

EXERCISE 3   Identifying Correct Word Choice

Underline the correct word in the parentheses.

1. Ivory Soap's famous ability to float might never (of/<u>have</u>) happened if it hadn't been for a lucky accident.

2. In 1878, an employee of Procter & Gamble should (of/have) turned off the soap-mixing machine before he went to lunch.

3. Leaving the machine on so long could (of/have) been dangerous, but the result was that the machine created a different kind of soap.

4. The employee could easily have gotten rid (of/have) the soap, but he didn't.

5. He should (of/have) told his bosses about the error, but he packaged it like any other batch instead.

6. The lengthy mixing process must have added a lot (of/have) air to the soap, and as a result, it floated.

7. People loved it, so an employee who might otherwise (of/have) been fired was a company hero.

Three Words Ending in –*d*

Notice the –*d* endings on these words that precede *to:*

use*d* (to)   supposed (to)

The sounds of the letters *d* and *t* are almost identical. Many people therefore drop the final –*d* before *t* in *supposed to* or *used to*. That final –*d* is important, though, for it indicates a past-tense verb *(used)* or a past participle form *(supposed)*:

We *used* to vacation in Michigan.
We are *supposed* to call later.

Another word that creates problems is the past-participle verb form *prejudiced*, which also requires a final –*d:*

Incorrect: He is prejudice against me.
Correct: He is *prejudiced* against me.

Prejudice can be a noun that does not end in –*d:*

Racial *prejudice* makes me angry.

E X E R C I S E   4   Identifying Correct Word Choice

Underline the correct word in the parentheses.

1. In 1917, Edwin Cox (use/<u>used</u>) to go door to door, selling a new product, aluminum cookware.

2. Many homemakers were (prejudice/prejudiced) against such newfangled inventions, so Cox had a hard time even demonstrating his product.

3. He needed a gimmick he could (use/used) to overcome this (prejudice/prejudiced) and get him into people's kitchens.

4. He knew that people hated when food stuck to pans, so he (use/used) his imagination and developed a pad that combined steel wool with soap.

5. These little pads were extremely popular. Although he gave each homemaker a free sample, most women asked for more, and Cox soon became (accustom/accustomed) to questions about where to buy the product.

6. A few months later, Cox quit the door-to-door selling he (use/used) to do so he could manufacture his little pads—called "S.O.S." for "Save Our Saucepans."

COMMONLY CONFUSED WORDS

Aside from the errors you've just seen, a number of errors show up in sound-alikes and look-alikes. We'll examine a number of the most common ones throughout the rest of the chapter.

Accept/Except

Accept means "to receive":

> He *accepted* the reward.

Except means "excluding" or "but":

> Everyone *except* him is here.

✓ TIPS

For *Accept/Except*
Except—which means *excluding*—also begins with *ex–*.

E X E R C I S E   5   Identifying Correct Word Choice

Underline the correct word in the parentheses.

1. George Eastman's new camera had many good selling points, (accept/<u>except</u>) that it had no trademark.

2. He felt that a trademark must be short, strong, and unusual to be (accepted/excepted) by the general public.

3. He made up a nonsense word, Kodak, which he thought would be (acceptable/exceptable).

4. Today everyone knows the word, (accept/except), perhaps, creatures on Mars.

Advice/Advise

Advice is a noun:

> We got *advice*.

TIPS

For *Advice/Advise*
Advice is nice, but only the wise *advise*.

Advise is a verb:

> He *advised* us to be careful.

EXERCISE 6 Identifying Correct Word Choice

Underline the correct word in the parentheses.

If Your First Language Is Not English

You may have difficulty distinguishing between the first vowel sounds in *affect* and *effect*. You may also have difficulties with the *–c* (pronounced like "s") and *–s* (pronounced like "z") spellings in *advice* and *advise*.

1. At a fair in 1904, Abe Doumar overheard an ice-cream seller complain that he had run out of ice-cream dishes. Doumar (adviced/<u>advised</u>) him to make a cone from a waffle, fill it with ice cream, and double his price.

2. It was good (advice/advise). The seller made a good profit from this new dish, the ice-cream cone.

3. Two years later, Doumar followed his own (advice/advise) and set up an ice-cream stand on Coney Island and later in Norfolk, Virginia.

4. Many years after Doumar's death, his sons were still operating the same ice-cream stand. Perhaps the moral is that it is more blessed to take than to give (advice/advise).

Affect/Effect

Used as a verb, *affect* means "to influence" or "change":

> Old age *affected* his ability to walk.

Used as a noun, *effect* is the result of a cause:

> What will be the *effect* of the new law?

TIPS

For *Affect/Effect*
His *age affected* his actions. His actions had an *excellent effect*.

EXERCISE 7 Identifying Correct Word Choice

Underline the correct word in the parentheses.

1. From 626 to 582 B.C., when he died, the Hebrew prophet Jeremiah warned the Israelites to reform their ways or God would destroy their temple, but his warnings had little (affect/<u>effect</u>).

2. In fact, the only (affects/effects) of his predictions were to anger the king and create threats against Jeremiah's life.

3. Nothing (affected/effected) the prophet's courage, however, and while living in hiding, he dictated his prophecies to one of his followers.

4. One day, Jeremiah begged a woman to give up her sinful behavior, warning that Jerusalem would soon be attacked by people from the north. His pleas had no (affect/effect).

5. Realizing that he couldn't (affect/effect) human behavior, he said his famous words: "Can the leopard change his spots? Then may ye also do good, that are accustomed to evil."

An/And

An is the article used before a vowel sound:

> *an* egg, *an* opportunity, *an* hour

And is a joining word.

> He huffed, *and* he puffed, *and* he blew the house down.

TIPS

For *An/And*
An apple *and* a pear.

EXERCISE 8   Identifying Correct Word Choice

Underline the correct word in the parentheses.

1. The can—or tin canister, as it was first called—was developed in 1810 by a British man named Peter Durand (an/<u>and</u>) was used to supply food to the Royal Navy during the Napoleonic Wars.

2. But no one had ever developed a convenient way to open the can, (an/and) British soldiers had to tear open their rations with bayonets, pocket knives, or—when all else failed—rifle fire.

3. In fact, some historians claim that the bayonet, invented in the French town of Bayonne, was not intended to be (an/and) article for piercing bodies but for piercing cans.

4. Ezra J. Warner of Waterbury, Connecticut, patented the first practical can opener in 1858. It was (an/and) odd machine with a large blade that cut hands (an/and) fingers as often as it cut cans.

5. The modern-day can opener—with a cutting wheel that rolls around the can's rim—was patented by William W. Lyman in 1870. It was revolutionary in concept (an/and) design, (an/and) it was (an/and) immediate success.

Breath/Breathe

Breath is a noun:

> She caught her *breath*.

Breathe is a verb:

> She *breathed* deeply.

TIPS

For *Breath/Breathe*
If the vowel sound is long *e*, there is silent *–e* at the end.

EXERCISE 9   Identifying Correct Word Choice

Underline the correct word in the parentheses.

1. *Life Savers* were originally advertised as "Crane's Peppermint Life Savers—5¢—For That Stormy (<u>Breath</u>/Breathe)."

2. *Smith Brothers Cough Drops* have been a favorite since about 1850 with people who coughed or couldn't (breath/breathe) because of a cold.

3. The first submarine was invented in 1620 by a Dutchman named Cornelius J. Drebbel, who figured out a way to get oxygen to fifteen rowers so they could (breath/breathe) under water.

4. The men could stay under for fifteen hours—a long time to exist with no (breaths/breathes) of fresh air.

Buy/By

As a verb, *buy* means "to purchase":

> Where did you *buy* that hat?

✓ **TIPS**
For *Buy/By*
You should *buy* it *by* credit card.

By, a preposition, has several meanings, including "near to," "at," and "by means of":

> We placed the plants *by* the window. We were finished *by* 10:00 A.M.
> Bill paid for his college education *by* working every summer.

EXERCISE 10   Identifying Correct Word Choice

Underline the correct word in the parentheses.

1. William Collins Whitney (1841–1904), an American millionaire, would (<u>buy</u>/by) expensive things for the most trivial reasons.

2. Once, for example, in order to give an enormous ball for his friends, he decided to (buy/by) a brownstone building on Fifth Avenue in New York.

3. He then furnished it (buy/by) going on a four-year tour of Europe to (buy/by) antiques, stained-glass windows, and fireplaces.

4. (Buy/By) the end of his tour, however, he had made his most outrageous purchase, (buying/bying) an entire ballroom from a castle in France and shipping it back to New York (buy/by) boat.

5. The ball he gave for his 500 guests was an enormous hit, highlighted (buy/by) a fountain that gushed 1,200 bottles of champagne.

Clothes/Cloths

Clothes are what people wear. *Cloths* is the plural of *cloth*—a piece of fabric.

EXERCISE 11   Identifying Correct Word Choice

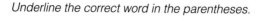

> **TIPS**
>
> For *Clothes/Cloths*
> *Clothes* sounds like *close*, which also contains an *–e*. *Cloths* has no *–e*.

Underline the correct word in the parentheses.

1. When we think of good (<u>clothes</u>/cloths), we don't usually consider underwear.

2. But three men did think about making high-quality (underclothes/undercloths).

3. Their names have not become household words associated with (clothes/cloths), but their product, B.V.D., has.

4. The initials represent the last names of the three men—Bradley, Voorhees, and Day—who turned millions of (clothes/cloths) into underpants and undershirts.

> **TIPS**
>
> For *Conscience/Conscious*
> *Science* is in *conscience*, and both teach you something.

Conscience/Conscious

Your *conscience* tells you that you are being bad or good. To be *conscious* means that you are awake and aware.

EXERCISE 12   Identifying Correct Word Choice

Underline the correct word in the parentheses.

1. In 1895, King C. Gillette, a traveling salesperson, (<u>consciously</u>/consciencely) decided to invent something that people would use a few times, throw away, and then pay to replace.

2. Apparently the idea of planned obsolescence did not bother Gillette's (conscious/conscience).

3. One day as he was shaving, he (unconsciously/unconsciencely) thought of the first disposable blade to be inserted into a razor. It became known as the Gillette blade.

–ence/–ent; –ance/–ant

–Ence and *–ance* are noun endings:

> The *difference* was amazing.
> The *significance* of the event was great.

–Ent and *–ant* are adjective endings:

> **TIPS**
>
> For Distinguishing Between Noun and Adjective Endings
> The *rent* is *different*. The *dance* had *elegance*.

> It has a *different* meaning.
> It has a *significant* meaning.

EXERCISE 13   Identifying Correct Word Choice

Underline the correct word in the parentheses.

1. In Cleveland in 1912, a candymaker named Clarence Crane decided to create something (difference/<u>different</u>): a mint he could sell in the summer.

2. Up to then, most mints were imported, but Crane figured he could cut the price by making them in the United States and not be (dependence/dependent) on European factories.

3. He came up with an (excellence/excellent) idea; he had a pill maker manufacture the mints.

4. But Crane was (ignorance/ignorant) of one (importance/important) problem: the machinery would work only if it punched a hole in the middle of each candy.

5. Crane had an (elegance/elegant) solution to the problem—he decided to call the mints *Life Savers.*

Fine/Find

Fine, as an adjective, means "acceptable" or "excellent." As a noun, it means "a penalty you must pay":

> You did a *fine* job on this assignment.
> If you get caught speeding, you must pay a *fine.*

Find means "to discover" or "locate":

> We never *find* a place to park near school.

TIPS
For *Find/Fine*
How can I *find* a *fine* job?

EXERCISE 14   Identifying Correct Word Choice

Underline the correct word in the parentheses.

1. You'll never (<u>find</u>/fine) a more influential book than Dale Carnegie's *How to Win Friends and Influence People.*

2. Although it was originally published in 1936, you can still (find/fine) the hardcover or paperback editions in just about any bookstore.

3. The book offers some (find/fine) advice. No one succeeds alone, so we must get along with and influence others to do what we want them to do.

4. Read the book, and you'll (find/fine) these words: "There is only one way under high heaven to get anybody to do anything. Did you ever stop to think of that? Yes, just one way. And that is by making the other person want to do it."

Know/No; Knew/New

Know means "to be familiar with" or "understand." Its past tense is *knew*:

> I *know* your brother, and I *knew* your sister in high school.

No is a negative word. And *new* is the opposite of old:

> Our old car has *no* radio, but we're buying a *new car* soon.

EXERCISE 15   Identifying Correct Word Choice

Underline the correct word in the parentheses.

1. You may not (<u>know</u>/no) the origin of the phrase, "Don't look a gift horse in the mouth."

2. Contrary to popular opinion, it has (know/no) relation to the gift of the Trojan horse but comes instead from St. Jerome in around A.D. 400.

3. The man (knew/new) that a gift should be appreciated for the thought and spirit behind it, not for its value.

4. Since a (knewborn/newborn) horse is worth more than an old one, people generally examined a horse's teeth to determine its age.

5. Therefore, Jerome, who accepted (know/no) payment for his writing, advised people with this phrase: "Never inspect the teeth of a gift horse."

Led/Lead

Led (pronounced like *head*) is the past tense of *lead* (pronounced like *need*):

> General Washington *led* the army into battle.

Lead is a heavy metal:

> *Lead* pipes are no longer used in plumbing.

EXERCISE 16   Identifying Correct Word Choice

Underline the correct word in the parentheses.

1. In 1914, Carl Eric Wickman couldn't sell his Hupmobile—a seven-passenger automobile—which (lead/<u>led</u>) him to start a bus service with it.

2. The bus (lead/led) its passengers on a two-mile trip between two small towns in Minnesota.

3. After Wickman added more and larger buses, their long, sleek appearance and (lead/led)-gray color caused someone to say that they looked like "greyhounds streaking by."

4. The comment, of course, (lead/led) to the name "Greyhound Bus."

Lie/Lay

Lie means "to recline":

> I am going to *lie* down.
> The pen is *lying* on top of the book.

The forms of *lie* are as follows:

Present tense	Past tense	Past participle
lie, lies	lay	lain

Lay, which usually means "put," is something you do to an object:

> I am going to *lay* this book on the table.

Its forms are as follows:

Present tense	Past tense	Past participle
lay, lays	laid	laid

TIPS

For *Lay/Lie*
The chicken *laid* an egg, and then she *lay* down to sleep.

EXERCISE 17   Identifying Correct Word Choice

Underline the correct word in the parentheses.

1. The continents of the earth (<u>lie</u>/lay) on huge slabs of rock—or plates—that slide over the earth's core very slowly, at a rate of one to eight inches a year.

2. Sometimes this movement of the continents causes earthquakes, which result from the pressure of one plate (lying/laying) against another as they move.

3. Other times, this movement causes a gap between plates, and the hot melted rock that has (laid/lain) beneath the plates shoots out in the form of a volcano.

4. Geologists believe that the continents all (lay/laid) in one large land mass, called *Pangaea,* about 230 million years ago.

5. The continent of North America, like the other continents, is not (lying/laying) still. It drifts away from Europe at a rate of three inches a year.

Lose/Loose

Lose means "to misplace" or "not to win":

> Did you *lose* your book? Did you *lose* the game?

TIPS

For *Lose/Loose*
Loose as a *goose.*

Loose is an adjective that means "not tight":

> My pants are *loose*.

EXERCISE 18   Identifying Correct Word Choice

Underline the correct word in the parentheses.

1. If you were to bet that the Baby Ruth candy bar was named after the baseball player Babe Ruth, you would (<u>lose</u>/loose).

2. Don't (lose/loose) track of the actual facts: the candy was named after the oldest daughter of President Grover Cleveland.

3. Tell somebody the true story. What do you have to (lose/loose)?

Mine/Mind

Mine is a possessive word:

> This pen is *mine*.

Mind as a noun means your "brain" or "intellect." As a verb, it means "to object":

> Einstein had a brilliant *mind*.
> Do you *mind* if I close this window?

> **✓ TIPS**
> **For** *Mine/Mind*
> A good *mind* is not hard to *find*. It's *mine!*

EXERCISE 19   Identifying Correct Word Choice

Underline the correct word in the parentheses.

1. Nowadays it's common to think that you should look out for your best interests, and I'll look out for (<u>mine</u>/mind).

2. This brings to (mine/mind) the expression, "Charity begins at home."

3. Ironically, the phrase, first written in 1642 by Sir Thomas Browne, was not intended to praise selfishness. Browne was discouraged that so many people didn't seem to (mind/mine) their own poverty or ignorance and would not try to better themselves.

4. Therefore, he (reminded/remined) his readers, "How shall we expect charity toward others when we are so uncharitable to ourselves? 'Charity begins at home' is the voice of the world; yet is every man his greatest enemy, and, as it were, his own executioner?"

Passed/Past

Passed is the past tense and past participle of the verb *to pass*:

> We *passed* the house.

TIPS

For *Passed/Past*

The verb *pass*—without a *–t*—is *passed*.

Past is a preposition meaning "beyond." It can also be a noun or adjective meaning "before the present":

> We went *past* (beyond) that house.
> That is *past* (before the present) history.

EXERCISE 20   Identifying Correct Word Choice

Underline the correct word in the parentheses.

1. The sewing needle appeared very early in humankind's (<u>past</u>/passed).

2. Needles of ivory, bone, and walrus tusk have been found in caves from 40,000 years in the (past/passed).

3. But almost that many years had (past/passed) before people created a better way than sewing by hand.

4. In 1830, a tailor named Barthélemy Thimmonier, of Lyon, France, invented a simple sewing machine that far sur(past/passed) the speed with which an experienced tailor could make stitches.

5. Only a short time had (past/passed) before Thimmonier was turning out military uniforms for the government.

6. However, an angry mob of tailors, who were afraid of being put out of business, stormed (past/passed) the entrance to his factory, destroyed all eighty of his machines, and nearly killed the inventor.

7. Thimmonier fled to another town, where he died in poverty, but the idea of a sewing machine was (past/passed) on to many others, including two men from Boston: Elias Howe and Isaac Singer.

Quiet/Quite/Quit

Quiet means "not noisy." Notice the ending, *–iet*. The two vowels are pronounced as separate syllables:

> It was a *quiet* night.

Quite means "very" or "a great deal of." Notice the ending, *–ite*. The ending is a silent *–e:*

> He is *quite* tall. He has *quite* a problem going through doorways.

And *quit* means "to stop" or "resign." Notice the ending, *–it:*

> Maria *quit* smoking, and Ralph *quit* his job.

TIPS

For *Quiet/Quite/Quit*

It was *quite* a *bite*, but he *quit* after a *bit*—and then was *quiet*.

EXERCISE 21   Identifying Correct Word Choice

Underline the correct word in the parentheses.

1. The man who invented Birds Eye frozen foods was, (quiet/<u>quite</u>/quit) naturally, named Clarence Birdseye.

2. He was an explorer who, in 1916, was able to keep meat and vegetables (quiet/quite/quit) fresh by storing them in freezing water.

3. Back in the United States, he started a frozen-food company that became (quiet/quite/quit) successful.

4. In 1929, Birdseye decided to (quiet/quite/quit) the business and sold it to the Postum Company.

5. When Postum split the trademark into two words—Birds Eye—Clarence Birdseye kept (quiet/quite/quit) about the change, for his family had originally spelled its name that way.

Rise/Raise

Rise means "to get up without help":

> The sun *rises* in the east.

TIPS

For *Rise/Raise*
He always *pays* when he gets a *raise.*

Raise as a verb means "to lift or increase something." As a noun, it means "an increase in pay":

> *Raise* your hand if you know the answer.
> Susan just got a *raise,* so she can afford a larger apartment.

EXERCISE 22   Identifying Correct Word Choice

Underline the correct word in the parentheses.

1. The origin of the expression "Steal my thunder" might (rise/<u>raise</u>) a few eyebrows.

2. John Dennis, an English playwright 200 years ago, created a method of (raising/rising) a noise like a thunderclap and used it in his new play.

3. The thunder was a great success, but the play didn't (raise/rise) enough money to continue beyond a few performances.

4. A short time later, Dennis attended a performance of Shakespeare's *Macbeth,* only to discover that the director was using his method of making thunder. He (raised/rose) to his feet and proceeded to (raise/rise) a ruckus.

5. "That's my thunder, by God!" he said, with his voice (raising/rising) louder and louder. "The villains will not play my play, but they steal my thunder."

TIPS
For *Sit/Set*
Set the bet down.

Sit/Set

Sit means "to seat yourself":

> Please *sit* down.

Set means "to put something down":

> Please *set* the glass on the table.

EXERCISE 23   Identifying Correct Word Choice

Underline the correct word in the parentheses.

1. The first photograph was made in 1826, when a French inventor coated a metal sheet with a special solution, exposed it to light, and (sit/<u>set</u>) it on a windowsill to dry.

2. He photographed an object, of course, since no person could (sit/set) still for as long as it took to make an exposure.

3. Motion pictures began in America some time between 1867 and 1871, when one man bet another that a running horse couldn't lift all four legs off the ground at once. They (sit/set) up a series of cameras along a racetrack, which photographed the horse as it galloped past—with, at various points, all four legs off the ground.

4. Edwin Land invented the Polaroid camera in 1947. He wanted to take a picture of his daughter and develop it while she was still (sitting/setting).

Then/Than

Then is a time expression meaning "afterward" or "later":

> I studied for two hours and *then* took a break.

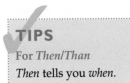

TIPS
For *Then/Than*
Then tells you *when*.

Than is used in a comparison:

> Juan gets higher grades *than* anyone else in class.

EXERCISE 24   Identifying Correct Word Choice

Underline the correct word in the parentheses.

1. In the music world, composers who write nine symphonies seem to be cursed. Six composers have done so and (<u>then</u>/than) died.

2. Ludwig van Beethoven (1770–1827) is more famous (then/than) the other five. The composer had just completed his ninth symphony and was planning a tenth, but (then/than) he caught a cold. He died a few months later.

3. Anton Bruckner (1824–1896), an Austrian, was almost unknown until the end of his life; (then/than) he was recognized as a great composer. He died while finishing his ninth symphony.

4. (Then/Than) came Antonin Dvorák (1841–1904). His ninth symphony, *From the New World,* was performed in New York in 1893, but he died a little more (then/than) eleven years later without completing another symphony.

5. The other three composers were, first, the Russian A. K. Glazunov (1865–1936); (then/than), the Bohemian Gustav Mahler (1860–1911); and finally, the British Ralph Vaughan Williams (1872–1958).

6. Mahler suffered from heart disease and was terrified of the curse of the ninth symphony. Therefore, he completed his ninth and (then/than) immediately began work on a tenth, but the effort was more (then/than) his heart could take. He soon died.

There is/It is

There is/are and *it is* aren't look-alikes or sound-alikes, but some people confuse the two expressions. Both usually function as sentence-starters; that is, they have no meaning in themselves but merely begin a sentence. Don't use them often, but when you do, use them properly.

You may begin a statement with *there is* or *there are* to show the location or to say that something or someone exists:

> *There is* a knife in the drawer under the sink.
> *There are* only two solutions (in existence) to the problem.

Use *it is* when you want to express an attitude or opinion:

> *It is* too bad that he is sick.
> *It is* a shame that he can't come to the graduation.

And use *it is* to discuss weather, temperature, conditions, distance, and time:

> *It is* cold today.   *It is* 78 degrees in this room.
> *It is* dark and wet outside.   *It is* three miles from here to the bank.
> *It is* 3:15.

Don't confuse *it is* expressions with *there is/are*:

> *Incorrect:*   It's a lot of chores that I have to do.
> *Correct:*   *There are* a lot of chores that I have to do.

✓ **TIPS**

For *There is/It is*
There is a *bear* in *here.*

EXERCISE 25   Identifying Correct Word Choice

Underline the correct word in the parentheses.

1. (It's/<u>There's</u>) hardly anything simpler than the brown paper bag.

2. (It's/There's) so popular that Americans use more than forty billion a year.

3. Charles Stilwell invented a machine to make paper bags in 1883, when he realized that (it was/there was) a need for the product.

4. (It was/There were) paper bags before Stilwell's invention, but (it was/there were) two problems with them: they couldn't stand up on their own, and they couldn't be easily folded or stacked.

5. (It was/There was) brilliant of Stilwell to make flat-bottomed bags that could stand up by themselves; (it was/there was) the most attractive feature to grocers and market baggers.

6. When supermarkets opened in the early 1930s, (it was/there was) a big increase in the number of items sold and packaged in stores, so (it was/there was) a big increase in the sales of paper bags.

Whether/Weather

Whether suggests a choice; it is used in the same way as *if* in indirect questions:

> I don't know *whether* he can afford a vacation.
> He wanted to know *whether* the test was hard.

Weather refers to the temperature and atmospheric conditions:

> The *weather* has been mild this year.

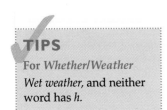

TIPS

For *Whether/Weather*
Wet weather, and neither
word has *h*.

EXERCISE 26   Identifying Correct Word Choice

Underline the correct word in the parentheses.

1. Most historians claim that General William T. Sherman said, "War is hell," but he was never sure (<u>whether</u>/weather) he really said it.

2. Before his death in 1891, the general looked through all his private papers to determine (whether/weather) the words were actually his.

3. There are several accounts of when the words were said. One version goes back to 1863 in the Civil War, when Sherman's troops were crossing a bridge in bad (whether/weather). The commander supposedly said to the passing soldiers, "War is hell, boys."

4. It's debatable (whether/weather) he made the statement then. Two other claims are that he used the expression at a military academy graduation in 1879 or in a speech to Union veterans in 1880.

5. In fact, no one can prove (whether/weather) Sherman ever said, "War is hell."

IN SUMMARY   To Distinguish Sound-alikes and Look-alikes from Each Other

1. Contractions with *to be*, such as *it's* and *they're*, should not be confused with similar words such as *its* or *their*.
2. *To, two,* and *too* are spelled differently and have different meanings.
3. The contraction for *have, 've*, sounds like *of* but should not be replaced with *of*.
4. Other words discussed in this chapter can be confused, but if you follow the tips and are careful in your word choice, you can avoid picking the wrong word.

EDITING FOR MASTERY

Mastery Exercise 1

Editing for Correct Word Choice

The following passage contains eighteen errors in sound-alike and look-alike words, aside from the first error, which has been corrected for you as an example. Correct each error above the line.

The Mysterious Disappearance of Amelia Earhart (1897–1937)

(1) Perhaps ^no ~~know~~ American woman of the 1930s was as famous as the flier Amelia Earhart, who's accomplishments were well known and admired buy women and men. (2) She was born in Kansas, graduated high school in Chicago in 1915, and then took up flying. (3) In 1928, her flight across the Atlantic with two men lead to her fame as an outspoken model of "rugged feminism." (4) She married the rich publisher George Putnam in 1931. (5) But she refused to except the role of a housewife and continued to fly. (6) She set the record for a flight across the Atlantic Ocean in 1932, and her later achievements where almost as impressive.

(7) By 1937 she was use to taking risks, so she attempted a more difficult feat then any she had done in the passed: an around-the-world flight with navigator Fred Noonan. (8) There departure from Miami in June attracted great attention. (9) The world applauded when Earhart reached New Guinea and then set off for an island in the Pacific on July 1. (10) Within a short time, however, she would loose radio contact with people on the ground. (11) No one new weather she had crashed or made and emergency landing, and the Navy could not fine any sign of the plane. (12) The newspapers were

COLLABORATIVE ACTIVITY 2

Checking Your Answers
Compare your answers to Mastery Exercise 1, and report your results to the class.

filled with theories about Earhart's fate for months. (13) While many people believed that she was a great pilot, others said she wasn't and had tried to difficult a task. (14) Perhaps she simply ran out of fuel and ended in a watery grave.

(15) To this day, it's a lot of difference theories about what happened to her. (16) Did the Japanese capture and murder her? (17) Did she land on some remote island and die a quite death? (18) The mystery of Earhart's disappearance may never be solved.

Scorecard: Number of errors found and corrected _____

Mastery Exercise 2

Editing for Correct Word Choice

The following passage contains eighteen errors in sound-alike and look-alike words, aside from the first error, which has been corrected for you as an example. Correct each error above the line.

The Beginning of the Elvis Era: 1956

(1) ^It's an excepted fact that Elvis Presley became the first superstar of rock in 1956. (2) Without his influence, popular music might of followed a much difference course. (3) Presley, more then anyone else, defined the age of rock 'n' roll with his first hit, "Heartbreak Hotel." (4) The knew record quickly raised to the top of the record charts in February. (5) Hardly any time had past before this twenty-one-year-old singer released another song, an then another, and another. (6) He let lose a barrage of nineteen songs in twelve months, and three songs rose to number one. (7) His sexy movements on stage also lead TV shows to change there photography of live performances.

(8) Elvis Aron Presley, who use to be a truck driver for the Crown Electric Company of Memphis, Tennessee, also appeared in his first movie, *Love Me Tender,* in 1956. (9) And nothing was quiet as eagerly anticipated as his appearance on Ed Sullivan's show in September. (10) As cameras shot Presley from the waist up, the teen-aged audience went out of their mines. (11) There screaming drowned out his singing. (12) *The New York Times* called his behavior "burlesque," and *Music Journal* later labeled his performances "filthy," with their "whining, moaning, and suggestive lyrics." (13) Only Jackie Gleason, who booked Presley for a television show in 1956, wasn't prejudice against him. (14) Gleason didn't think the young singer was to wild and called him "a guitar-playing Marlon Brando."

(15) Presley didn't understand the criticism. (16) He later said of himself: "I never thought of my performing style as wicked. Wicked? I don't even smoke or drink." (17) After two breatheless years on the pop scene, Elvis Presley sold and amazing 28 million records and appeared on bestseller charts fifty-five times. (18) He earned a fortune, became a legend, and took the title of "the King." (19) Popular music would never be the same again.

Scorecard: Number of errors found and corrected _____

CHAPTER 30

Keeping Verbs in Order

You probably already know a great deal about verbs and word order even if you can't explain every grammatical rule. For example, you wouldn't say or write the following combination of words:

> Friend my to the drove some store groceries for.

Rearranged, these words make a sentence. Try unscrambling them. _____

_____

Did you write "My friend drove to the store for some groceries"? If so, you applied many grammatical rules in order to create that sentence.

If you feel less than confident about verb forms and related matters, however, this chapter will help build your confidence by

- explaining verb tenses and phrases
- giving you practice in understanding and writing complex verb forms
- suggesting different ways to phrase questions
- clarifying sentence order when you use objects and adverbs
- explaining how to express negative statements

THE CONTINUOUS TENSES

The two most common continuous tenses, present and past, are formed in similar ways.

In the Present

There are two present tenses in English, but they communicate entirely different meanings.

The **simple present tense** discusses habitual actions—actions that happen all of the time, most of the time, or some of the time:

> I *go* to my English class three days a week.
> My instructor usually *assigns* a short composition on Fridays.

It can also discuss current feelings, observations, facts, or statements involving no action:

> I *like* cauliflower, but I *hate* spinach. (feelings)
> I *hear* a noise, but I *don't see* anything. (observations)
> The earth *revolves* around the sun, and the moon *orbits* the earth. (facts)
> We *don't have* a car. Cars *cost* too much. (statements involving no action)

Notice that present-tense verbs have only two endings. Verbs that agree with *I, we, you,* or *they* do not end in *–s.* Verbs that agree with *he, she,* or *it* must end in *–s.* In most questions or negative statements, they take the helping verb *do* or *does,* based on the same subject-verb agreement. (See Chapter 10.)

The **present continuous** (or **progressive**) **tense** discusses actions that are happening now or planned for the future.

> *I'm going* to my English class now.
> *We're handing* in our compositions on Monday.

Verbs in the present continuous tense always include two parts: a present-tense form of the verb *to be* (*am, is,* or *are*) + an *–ing* word.

EXERCISE I   Writing Present Tenses

Rewrite each of the following sentences, changing from the simple present to the present continuous tense, or vice versa.

Simple present tense	Present continuous tense
1. We often walk home after classes.	1. *We're walking home after classes today.*
2. My brother-in-law sleeps fourteen hours a day.	2. _____ right now.
3. _____ every week.	3. My father is washing the car now.
4. Jason often has a party on the weekend.	4. _____ this Saturday.
5. Mrs. Highnose doesn't watch television.	5. _____ now.
6. It gets cold in here once in a while.	6. _____ today.

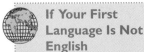

If Your First Language Is Not English

In many languages, the *forms* of words—their beginnings, endings, or internal changes—convey a great deal of grammatical information. But in English, the *order* of words often determines how they function grammatically. Take, for example, the word *wash.* If you shift it to different positions in a sentence, it can be a noun, a verb, or an adjective—even though its form doesn't change:

As a verb: I always *wash* clothes on Saturday.

As a noun: When do you do the *wash*?

As an adjective: Saturday is my *wash* day.

The rules that govern English word order are generally consistent, so you can master them.

In the Past

Like the two present tenses, the two most important past tenses express entirely different meanings.

The **simple past tense** discusses a completed action or situation in the past, often at a stated time:

> Stanislav *passed* the test yesterday and *felt* wonderful.
> We *didn't see* the movie.

Most verbs in the simple past tense end in *–ed,* but some are **irregular,** meaning they show past tense in some other way (see Chapter 11). In questions or negative statements, past-tense verbs take the helping verb *did.*

The **past continuous** (or **progressive**) **tense** discusses actions in progress at a specific time or period of time in the past:

> I *was studying* at midnight.
> They *were working* all day yesterday.

The past continuous tense often appears in combined sentences joined by *when, while,* or *as:*

> I *was taking* a shower *when* the telephone *rang.*
> Tom *tried* to study *while* his sister *was watching* TV.

Verbs in the past continuous tense always include two parts: a past-tense form of the verb *to be* (*was* or *were*) + an *–ing* word.

EXERCISE 2   Writing Past Tenses

Rewrite each of the following sentences, changing the simple past tense to the past continuous tense, or vice versa.

Simple past tense

1. I studied for the test this morning.

2. _____ yesterday.

3. _____ every day last week.

4. Bill got a haircut yesterday.

5. They didn't listen to the news during dinner.

Past continuous tense

1. I was studying for the test when you called.

2. Our telephone wasn't working for several hours.

3. They were doing the wash again this morning.

4. _____ when the barbershop caught on fire.

5. _____ last night.

6. _____   6. Who was watching the children

when _____   while you were shopping?

this morning?

E X E R C I S E   3   Combining Sentences About the Past

Combine each of the following pairs of sentences, using *when* or *while.*

1. Mario had dinner. His cat sat down in his spaghetti. *Mario was having dinner when his cat sat down in his spaghetti.*

2. I talked to my friend. Several hundred-dollar bills dropped from my pocket. _____

_____

3. Mr. Gotbucks smoked a cigar. His chauffeur drove the car. _____

_____

4. They fell in love. They danced cheek to cheek. _____

_____

5. His wife washed the dishes, swept the floor, and threw out the garbage. Mr. Hogg

read the paper. _____

_____

6. I took a bath. The house caught on fire. _____

_____

MORE VERB PHRASES

COLLABORATIVE ACTIVITY I

Writing in the Present and Past

Write eight affirmative statement sentences—two in the simple present tense, two in the present continuous tense, two in the simple past tense, and two in the past continuous tense. Exchange papers and

1. Correct any errors you find.
2. Change each sentence into a negative statement.
3. Change each sentence into a question.

Then exchange papers again for a third student to check.

A verb can contain as many as four words, which together make a **verb phrase.** The last word in a verb phrase is called the **main verb;** all the other words in the phrase are called **helping verbs.** Although verb phrases may seem complicated, the rules for writing them are entirely consistent. We'll examine those rules as follows.

Two-Word Verb Phrases

There are four categories of two-word verbs: *to be* as the helping verb, *to have* as the helping verb, *to do* as the helping verb, and fixed-form helping verbs.

To Be.   The helping verb is *to be,* followed by one of the two verb forms:

1. An **–*ing* word,** which creates a continuous tense:

he is I am they are	seeing (present continuous tense)
she was you were	seeing (past continuous tense)

2. A **past participle,** which forms the **passive voice** (see Chapter 11):

she is
I am   } seen (present tense, passive voice)
we are

I was
they were } seen (past tense, passive voice)

To Have.   The helping verb is *to have,* followed by one of two verb forms:

1. A **past participle,** which creates a **perfect tense** (see Chapter 11):

he has
they have } seen (present-perfect tense)

we had   seen (past-perfect tense)

2. An **infinitive,** which in the present tense expresses the same meaning as *must* (The infinitive is actually two words, since it begins with *to*):

she has
they have } to see (must see)

I had   to study (This past-tense idea cannot be expressed with *must.*)

EXERCISE 4   Writing in the Perfect Tenses

Complete each of the following sentences by including a verb phrase in the present-perfect or past-perfect tense.

1. I don't want to see that movie because ___*I've seen it before.*___

2. Bill apologized for being rude after he _____

_____

3. I can't take a coffee break now because _____

_____ already.

4. Carmen felt terrible after _____

_____

5. Wilbur couldn't drive a car after_____

_____

6. All the students were overjoyed because _____

_____

EXERCISE 5   Writing Statements with *Have to*

Complete each of the following sentences by including a verb phrase with have to, has to, *or* had to. *In these sentences, the verb means* must.

1. I couldn't watch television last night because ____*I had to study for an examination.*____

2. That is a very dangerous intersection, so drivers _____

_____

3. If they want to avoid an accident, _____

_____

4. I have a paper due tomorrow, so _____

_____

5. When you visit Europe, you _____

_____

6. Mr. Kim was very sick yesterday, so _____

_____

7. If you need to pay your tuition, _____

_____

COLLABORATIVE ACTIVITY 2

Writing Two-Word Verb Forms

Write sentences with two-word verbs—two with *to be*, two with *to have*, two with *to do*, and two with the fixed-form helping verbs. Exchange papers and do the following:

1. Correct any errors you find.
2. Change each sentence into a negative statement—or each negative into an affirmative.
3. Change each sentence into a question.

Then exchange papers again for a third student to check.

To Do.   The helping verb is *to do*—for questions, negative statements, or emphasis with any main verb except *to be*.

1. In questions:

> *Do* you *like* sports? *Does* he *like* sports? *Did* he *eat* dinner?

2. In negative statements:

> I *don't like* sports. He *doesn't like* sports. He *didn't eat* dinner.

3. For emphasis in affirmative statements:

> I *do like* sports. Oh yes, he *does like* sports. You're wrong; he *did eat* dinner.

Notice that in all three categories:

- The first verb (the helping verb) determines the tense and subject-verb agreement.
- The second verb (the main verb) never changes for tense or subject-verb agreement.

EXERCISE 6   Writing Negatives with *Do*

Write an appropriate negative statement after each of the following statements.

1. I worked yesterday. ____*I didn't get much rest.*____

2. Abraham Lincoln died in office. _____

_____

3. It often rains in Oregon during the winter. _____

_____

4. In Europe, most children start school when they are seven. _____

_____

5. Most college students these days hold part-time or full-time jobs. _____

_____

_____

6. I drove to work this morning. _____

_____

Fixed-Form Verbs.   The helping verb is a fixed-form verb, which never changes its form (although we express the past-tense meanings of *can* and *will* with the verbs *could* and *would*). The main verb is a partial infinitive (without *to*), so it cannot change for tense or agreement:

I, we, you he, she, they	{ can could will would shall should may might must }	go, have, be

Exception: Ought is *followed by a complete infinitive:* ought to go *or* ought to be

The main function of these verb phrases is to discuss ability, possibility, obligation, choice, or necessity in the present or future:

Ability:	I	can	study now (or later).
Possibility:	I	{ may might could }	study now (or later).
Obligation:	I	{ ought to would should shall }	study now (or later) if I had the chance. study now (or later).
Choice:	I	{ may will might }	study now or later.
Necessity:	I	must	study now (or later).

EXERCISE 7   Writing Helping Verbs

Each of the sentences below already has a helping verb. Complete each one, using an appropriate main verb.

1. I am ___*composing great sentences now.*___

2. At 8:00 P.M. yesterday, we were _____

3. I've_____ many times.

4. Has our teacher _____ yet?

5. I had _____ before coming to school today.

6. I could _____ many years ago.

7. You should _____

Three-Word Verb Phrases

There are two main groups of three-word verbs: those for the active voice and those for the passive voice. In the **active voice,** the subject performs the action of the verb, and in the **passive voice,** the subject is passive—it receives the action of the verb. We'll examine both main groups here.

Active-Voice Phrases.   You've already seen these combinations in two-word verbs:

1. a fixed-form helping verb + short infinitive
2. *have* + a past participle or full infinitive
3. *be* + an *–ing* word

Three-word verbs in the active voice simply extend these combinations:

Fixed-form verb	Have	Past participle or full infinitive
might, may, could, etc.	have	{ done to go

Fixed-form verb	Be	*–ing* word
might, may, could, etc.	be	doing

Here is how these verb phrases function.
    Three-word verb phrases with *have* interpret past actions or circumstances:

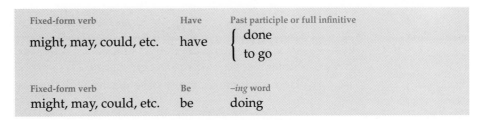

Bill didn't feel well yesterday, so he	{ must have been sick. could have had a cold. might have had the flu. may have had the flu. should have stayed home.

Or they describe a change in a past action or condition beginning with the conditional word *if:*

| If I had known that Bill was sick, I | would have called him. could have taken him to the doctor. might have gone to his house. |

Or, with *will have* and the past participle, they form the **future-perfect tense,** which describes an action or event already completed before a later time in the future.

| Ten years from now, Joe | will have graduated from college. will have gotten a good job. will have married and (will have) had children. |

Three-word verb phrases with *be* express possibilities, conclusions, or plans about the present or future:

| I don't know where Bill is now. He | could be working. might be working. ought to be working. may be gone. |

| Bill isn't home now, so he | must be working. |
| By this time next week, | Young will be flying to Korea. |

Passive-Voice Phrases.   Three-word verbs in the **passive voice**—in which the subject is being acted upon—discuss a continuing action. To do so, these verb phrases also extend patterns you've already seen:

1. *be* + an –*ing* word (this forms a continuous tense)
2. *be* + a past participle (this creates the passive voice)

The passive-voice continuous tenses combine the patterns with forms of *be* as the first word and the –*ing* word, followed by the past participle:

COLLABORATIVE ACTIVITY 3

Writing More Three-Word Verbs
Write six sentences with three-word verbs—three in the active voice, and three in the passive voice. Exchange papers and check each other's work.

Be	–*ing* word	Past participle
am, is, are was, were	being	done, served, taken, tested, etc.

Here are some examples of sentences with three-word verbs in the passive voice:

The food *is being prepared* now.
The instructions *were being explained* when I left.

EXERCISE 8   Writing Three-Word Verb Phrases

Complete each of the following sentences, using an appropriate three-word verb phrase. The first word of the phrase has been provided.

1. You can't drive on Wilson Avenue now. _It is being repaired._____

2. Fidel isn't at his desk. He could_____

3. Please don't go into the kitchen. The floor is _____

_____

4. When I last saw my old car, it was _____

5. If I had known that you couldn't use your car, I would _____

_____

6. By this time next year, I will _____

Four-Word Verb Phrases

Four-word verbs are extensions of three-word verbs. The first helping verb must be fixed-form, and the second word must be *have*. Then comes *been*, the past participle of *be*:

> might have been

Either an *–ing* word or past participle can complete the verb phrase:

> might have been going   might have been gone

These four-word verbs express meanings similar to those of three-word verbs. Four-word verb phrases that end with *–ing* words interpret the past but express continuous actions:

COLLABORATIVE ACTIVITY 4

Writing More Four-Word Verbs

Write six sentences with four-word verbs—three in the active voice, and three in the passive voice. Exchange papers and check each other's work.

Manuel wasn't home yesterday. He	could have been working. must have been working. might have been working. may have been working.
However, Manuel was sick yesterday. He	should have been resting.
If Manuel had been smart, he	would have been resting.

Four-word verbs ending in past participles are passive-voice expressions that interpret the past:

The radio didn't work. It	could have been dropped on the floor. might have been broken by my son. must have been broken by someone.
The radio wasn't fixed, but	it should have been fixed.

EXERCISE 9   Writing Four-Word Verb Phrases

Complete each of the following sentences, using an appropriate four-word verb phrase.

1. Norma was watching wrestling on TV last night when she _should have been studying._

2. I didn't receive my final grades last week. They _____

_____

3. Claudia came home with many grocery bags, so she _____ in the afternoon.

4. Main Street was still closed to traffic last week. It _____ three weeks ago.

5. This song wasn't written by Mozart, but it _____ _____ by Haydn.

6. Your telephone line was busy all last night. Your teenage son _____ _____

INDIRECT QUESTIONS

As you know, some sentences ask a question:

> How can I get to the train station?

But some sentences imply that a question is asked without really asking it:

> I want to know how I can get to the train station.

This is an **indirect question**. It is actually part of a statement, so its word order and end punctuation follow the pattern for statements, not direct questions. Compare these sentences:

> *Direct question:*   Where is the office?
> *Indirect question:*   I wonder where the office is.

Note these differences:

- A **direct question** ends in a question mark and begins with a verb before the subject.
- An **indirect question**—since it is a statement—ends in a period and begins with the subject before the verb:

An indirect question can also be included in a statement that makes a request, or even as a dependent clause in a direct question. Here are examples:

> *Request:*   Please tell me *where the registrar's office is.*
> *Question:*   Can you tell me *where the registrar's office is?*

Finally, *quoted* direct questions differ from indirect questions in word order, punctuation, and verb tense. Quotations reproduce the exact words of the speaker, in the same order and tense. But indirect questions adjust word order and tense to fit within the statement that introduces them. Carefully note the tense differences in the following examples:

Direct question	Indirect question
He asked me, "Are you all right?"	He asked me if I was all right.
He asked me, "Were you working?"	He asked me if I had been working.
He asked me, "Will you come?"	He asked me if I would come.

COLLABORATIVE ACTIVITY 5

Writing More Questions
Write nine sentences—three direct questions, three indirect questions, and three sentences with quoted direct questions. Exchange papers and rephrase the sentences. Make direct questions into indirect questions, indirect questions into direct questions, and quoted direct questions into indirect questions that aren't quoted. Exchange papers again so a third student checks your work.

He asked me, "Can you come?"	He asked me if I could come.
He asked me, "Did you come?"	He asked me if I had come.
He asked me, "Have you finished?"	He asked me if I had finished.

EXERCISE 10   Writing Indirect Questions

Rewrite each of the following direct questions as an indirect question, beginning with the words provided.

1. Do you need any help? I want to know ____ *if you need any help.* ____

2. How are your parents? I would be interested to hear _____

    _____

3. Where is room 814? Can you tell me _____

4. When does the class begin? He asked me _____

5. Did you study for the final examination? I wanted to know if _____

    _____

6. When can I call the doctor? He inquired about when _____

    _____

OBJECTS AFTER VERBS

Objects, which receive the action of verbs, can be placed between or after verbs, depending on the type of verbs. We'll look at both situations here.

Objects with Phrasal Verbs

When you write a sentence using an action verb (that tells what a subject *does, did,* or *will do*), the normal word order is subject-verb-object. The object can be a noun or pronoun.

Subject	Verb	Noun object	Pronoun object
We	picked	some grapes	(them).
Bill	dropped	the plate	(it)
I	took	the dishes	(them).

Suppose, however, that you change the meaning of a verb by adding another word that looks like a preposition:

| picked up | dropped off | took out |

These two-word expressions are called **phrasal verbs,** and with them the placement of the object is more complicated. With many phrasal verbs, a noun-object can precede or follow the second verb word:

I *picked up* some grapes at the store. I *picked* some grapes *up* at the store.
Bill *dropped off* the book at my house. Bill *dropped* the book *off* at my house.

Try writing the sentence "I _____ the dishes" in two ways, using *took away* as the verb.

_____

_____

Did you write, "I took away the dishes," and "I took the dishes away"? Then you understand the flexibility of noun-objects.

Unlike noun-objects, however, pronoun-objects *must* come between the two words of the phrasal verb:

> I *picked* them *up*.
> Bill *dropped* it *off*.
> I *took* them *out*.

But some phrasal verbs cannot be separated by objects in this way. In general, the following rules apply.

▶ A two-word verb that *moves or changes the condition* of an object can take a noun-object either before or after the second verb word.

> We *put* the dishes *away*. We *put away* the dishes. (The verb *put away* moved the dishes.)
> I *cheered* my friend *up*. I *cheered up* my friend. (The verb *cheered up* changed the mental condition of your friend.)

▶ A phrasal verb that *does not* move or change the condition of an object cannot be separated. In this case, the object must come after the complete verb.

> I *ran into* an old friend yesterday.
> I always *count on* you for help. (The objects don't move or change in these sentences.)

Common Phrasal Verbs

The following reference lists of common phrasal verbs may be helpful.

Separable verbs:

ask out	clean out, up	figure out
back up	cool off, up	fill in, out, up
blow up	cross off, out	find out
break down, off, up	cut off, up	fix up
bring about, out, up	do over	follow up
build up	dress up	get back, down, out
burn up	drink up	give away, up
buy out, up	drive back	hand in, out
call back	drop off	hang up
call off	dry off, up	have on
check out, over, up	dust off, up	help out
cheer up	eat up	hold up

keep down, on, up
knock out
leave on, out
let in, on, off,
   out, up
look over, up
make up
mix up
open up
pass out, up
pay off, out
pick out, up
plug in, up
point out

put aside, away, down,
   in, off, on, up
rub off
set up
shut down,
   off, out
slow down, up
speed up
stand up
straighten out, up
sweep out, up
take away, back,
   off, on, out,
   over, up

talk out, over, up
tear up
tell apart
think over
try on, out
turn around, down,
   in, up
use over, up
warm up
wash out, up
wear out
wipe off, up
work out
write down, off

Inseparable verbs:

agree on
allow for
amount to
ask for
back out of
become of
bump into
care about
come across
come along with
come back to, out of, over
   to, through with, up to
count on
deal in, with
do without
drop in, on, out of
   into, off, on, out, over

feel like
get ahead of
get into, off, on, out
   of, over, through
   with
go into, on with
grow out of
hear about
hold on to
keep on with, up with
look at, for, out for
meet with
occur to
part with
plan on
put up with
read up on

run into, across, off
   with, out of, over
see about
send for, away for
side with
speak about, for, of
stand by, up for
stick to
take up with
talk about, back to
think about, back on, of
try out for
turn into
wait for, on
walk out on
watch out for
work on

COLLABORATIVE ACTIVITY 6

Composing Sentences
Write at least ten sentences using different phrasal verbs from the lists just given. Then, exchange papers and check each other's work.

EXERCISE 11   Writing Phrasal Verbs

Write a sentence using each of the following phrasal verbs and its object.

1. (*verb*) make up (*object*) the examination _Alicia made up the examination she had missed._

2. (*verb*) put off (*object*) studying _____

   _____

3. (*verb*) look up (*object*) it_____

   _____

4. (*verb*) throw away (*object*) an old dress_____

_____

5. (*verb*) try on (*object*) them_____

_____

6. (*verb*) take out (*object*) the lettuce_____

_____

7. (*verb*) do over (*object*) it _____

_____

8. (*verb*) find out (*object*) the secret of long life_____

_____

9. (*verb*) get back (*object*) him_____

_____

10. (*verb*) give up (*object*) smoking _____

_____

Direct and Indirect Objects

Many verbs take a **direct object,** which receives the action of the verb:

Subject	Verb	Direct object
1. A repairman	fixed	the broken window.
2. The company	will open	a branch store.

But some verbs take two objects: a direct object, which receives the action of the verb, and an **indirect object,** which receives the direct object.

Subject	Verb	Indirect object	Direct object
3. The repairman	sent	us	the bill.
4. The branch store	should offer	its customers	many services.

Notice the order of the objects in sentences 3–4: *the indirect object comes before the direct object.*

There is a second way to write a direct object and an indirect object in a sentence. You may write the direct object *first* and then follow it with *to* (or sometimes *for*) plus the indirect object:

Subject	Verb	Direct object	Indirect object
5. The repairman	sent	the bill	to us.
6. The branch store	should offer	many services	to its customers.
7. Richie	mixed	drinks	for his guests.

These are the only two ways to place direct and indirect objects. They should *never* be placed in this order: *to* (or *for*)—object—direct object.

Incorrect:	I lent to Juan my pen.
Correct:	I lent Juan my pen. I lent my pen to Juan.
Incorrect:	Richie mixed for his guests a drink.
Correct:	Richie mixed a drink for his guests.
	Richie mixed his guests a drink.

EXERCISE 12   Writing Two Objects

Rewrite the following sentences, reversing the order of the objects.

1. In 1837, the famous showman P. T. Barnum sold the public his first hoax. _In 1837, the famous showman P. T. Barnum sold his first hoax to the public._

2. Over 10,000 New Yorkers bought tickets for themselves. _____
_____

3. Barnum showed them a 161-year-old ex-slave. _____
_____

4. After her death and autopsy, the newspapers told her real age—eighty—to the public.
_____
_____

5. Naturally, Barnum did not give refunds to anyone. _____
_____

EXERCISE 13   Writing More Objects

Using the verbs in parentheses, write sentences containing both direct and indirect objects. Be sure to vary the object word order.

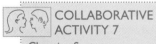

COLLABORATIVE ACTIVITY 7

Changing Sentences
Exchange the sentences you wrote in Exercise 13. Rewrite each, changing the order of the objects. Then have a third student check them.

1. (give) _Tomas gave me a piece of paper. or Tomas gave a piece of paper to me._

2. (tell) _____

3. (make) _____

4. (sell) _____

5. (send) _____

6. (bring) _____

ADVERBS

Remember that **adverbs** tell *when, where, why,* or *how* an action occurs. Phrases and even whole clauses can be adverbs:

(When) *After John Jacob Astor had made millions of dollars as a fur trader,* he opened the Astor Hotel (later the famous Waldorf-Astoria) in New York.

And single words (usually ending in *–ly*) or phrases can be adverbs:

Single words

(how much)	Eighteenth-century clock maker Levi Hutchins *intensely* disliked oversleeping.
(how)	He awoke *promptly* at 4:00 A.M. each day.
(when)	But *sometimes* he would sleep past his normal waking hour.

Phrases

(why and when)	*As a result,* Hutchins set out to invent the first alarm clock in 1787.
(how)	He combined a clock and a bell *in a unique way.*
(when)	He wrote, "It was simplicity itself to arrange the bell to sound *at the predetermined hour.*"

Single Adverbs

As the following examples show, you can place an adverb in many locations in a sentence for emphasis or variety:

Levi Hutchins *intensely* disliked . . . (between the subject and the verb)
He awoke *promptly* . . . (after the verb)
. . . *sometimes* he would sleep . . . (before the subject)
or
. . . he would *sometimes* sleep . . . (between the helping verb and the main verb)

However, an adverb rarely goes between a verb and its object or objects:

Incorrect: Levi Hutchins disliked intensely oversleeping.
Incorrect: He combined in a unique way a clock and a bell.

EXERCISE 14   Editing Misplaced Adverbs

Underline the adverb, the adverb phrase, or the adverb clause in each of the following sentences. Then draw an arrow to the spot where the misplaced adverb should be located in each sentence.

1. Three men and a giraffe shared <u>cheerfully</u> a box lunch.

2. Throw Momma from the train a kiss.

3. Smoking a hand-rolled cigarette, the man turned on quickly the radio.

4. The man walked down the block his dog.

5. I sent very promptly the answer he wanted to him.

6. Johnnie kissed on a moonlit night his girlfriend.

Placing Two or More Adverbs

When a sentence contains several adverbs, you may wish to spread them around for variety or emphasis, as in this example:

> when   where   why
> *In 1843,* a man *in Troy, Ohio,* was fined $10 *for kissing a married lady.*

Or you could put them all at the end of the sentence:

> A man was fined $10 *in Troy, Ohio, in 1843 for kissing a married lady.*

But when you stack up all the adverbs at the end of a sentence, the choices become more limited. In a sentence with no object after the verb, place the adverbs in this order: verb—how—where—when—(why). For example:

>   verb   where   when
> The first U.S. bank robbery occurred *in New York in 1831.*
>
>   verb   how   where   when
> President W. H. Harrison died *of pneumonia in Washington after only thirty days in office.*
>
>   verb   where   when   why
> Private bathtubs appeared *in a New York hotel in 1844, perhaps for sanitary reasons.*

In a sentence with an object after the verb, place the adverbs in this order: how—verb—object—where—when—(why). For example:

>   how   verb   object   where   when
> Robert M. Green *happily* invented the ice-cream soda in *Philadelphia in 1874.*
>
>   verb   object   where   when   why
> Whitcomb Judson put the first zipper *on boots in 1893 so people would not have to tie their shoes.*

EXERCISE 15   Writing Adverbs

Write five sentences. Each must include at least two adverbs from the following list.

happily   loudly

slyly   briskly

COLLABORATIVE ACTIVITY 8

Changing Sentences
Exchange the sentences you wrote in Exercise 15. Rewrite any in which the adverbs can be placed differently. Then discuss and compare the first and second versions to see which are most graceful.

uneasily	on several occasions
smartly	from one place to another
swiftly	to his high-rise apartment
drowsily	fourteen hours a day
in May of this year	from Nevada to California
on the sidewalk	after the term ends
since he called his parents	although he walks like a three-legged turtle
because he is always tired	at work
in more than one way	when Manuel saw the ten-dollar bill

PAST PARTICIPLES AND PRESENT PARTICIPLES

Past participles (such as *spoken, seen, tired*) and *–ing* words, or **present participles,** are formed from verbs. But they often function as adjectives. Here's how to distinguish between their meanings.

- Present participles express a feeling or action created by the noun they modify:

> We heard some *shocking* news. (The news created shock in the people who heard it.)
> The book was *interesting*. (The book created interest in me.)

COLLABORATIVE ACTIVITY 9

Correcting Sentences
Write five sentences, each of which uses one of the following words as an adjective: *exciting, baked, married, boring,* and *written*. Exchange papers and correct the sentences.

Often that feeling or action is continuing, was continuing, or will be continuing:

> Don't touch that pot of *boiling* eggs.
> I tried to stay out of the *falling* rain.

- Past participles express a feeling or action received by the noun they modify:

> The *shocked* man couldn't believe the news. (The man received the shock.)
> I am *interested* in the book. (I receive the interest from the book.)

Often that feeling or action is completed, was completed, or will be completed:

> These *boiled* eggs are cold.
> I will pick up some *fallen* rocks by the side of the road.

EXERCISE 16   Writing Present or Past Participles

Complete each of the following sentences with the appropriate past- or present-participle form of the verb in parentheses.

1. The man sounds (irritate) _irritated._

2. The movie was very (interest) _____ to me.

3. I always enjoy well-(perform) _____ plays.

4. The (explode) _____ bomb is not dangerous now, but it hurt several soldiers.

5. Three (injure) _____ soldiers had to be taken to the hospital.

6. The (break) _____ branch made a loud noise.

7. The (bore) _____ audience slept through the lecture.

DOUBLE NEGATIVES

In most languages, a statement can have two, three, or even four negatives. In English, though, a negative statement can have only one negative word. The word may be *not*, which makes the verb negative:

> I did *not* do anything last night. I did*n't* have any money.

Or the negative word (usually *no, nothing, nowhere,* or *no one*) may appear elsewhere in a sentence with an affirmative verb:

> I did *nothing* last night. I had *no* money.

You *cannot* use two negatives to express a negative idea. That is an error called a **double negative:**

> *Incorrect:* I did*n't do nothing* last night.
> *Correct:* I *didn't do anything* last night. Or I *did nothing* last night.

In fact, two negatives can actually express an affirmative idea:

> *Correct:* It's *not uncommon* to see ducks in the pond. (It's quite common to see the ducks.)
> *Correct:* I never do nothing. (I always do something.)

Here is a list of the most common negative words, along with their affirmative versions:

Negatives	Affirmatives
no one	anyone
nobody	anybody
nothing	anything
nowhere	anywhere
no	any

none	any
never	ever

Two other words are negative in meaning: *hardly* and *scarcely*. They mean *almost no, almost none,* or *almost never:*

I had *hardly any* homework this week. (almost no homework)
The Wilsons *scarcely ever* go out. (almost never)

Like other negative words, they need to stand alone. They cannot be used with another negative:

Incorrect:	We didn't have hardly any money.
Correct:	We had *hardly any* money.

EXERCISE 17 Eliminating Double Negatives

Cross out one of the two negatives in each of the following sentences and write any changes above the line.

1. Nobody ever says ^anything ~~nothing~~ unkind to Bruno.

2. Reno never has no luck at cards.

3. When Mr. Swift explains something, it doesn't make no sense.

4. I've scarcely spent no money this week.

5. I don't like to borrow nothing from other people.

6. We didn't go nowhere on our vacation.

7. You can't hardly find an honest person these days.

8. I didn't notice no difference between those two pizzas—I ate them both.

IN SUMMARY   To Keep Verbs in Order

1. Write continuous tenses with the present- or past-tense forms of *to be* + *–ing* to express continuing actions in the present or past.
2. Form two-word verbs with these patterns:
   a. *be* + *–ing* (for continuous tenses)
   b. *be* + past participle (for passive voice)
   c. *have* + past participle (for perfect tenses)
   d. *have* + infinitive (for obligation or necessity)
   e. *do* + simple form of the verb (for negatives in present or past tense)
   f. fixed-form verbs + simple form of the verb (for ability, possibility, obligation, choice, or necessity)

3. Form three-word verbs with these patterns:

   a. fixed-form helping verb + *be* + *–ing* (for active voice) or past participle (for passive voice)

   b. fixed-form helping verb + *have* + past participle (for active voice), or fixed-form helping verb + *be* + *being* + past participle (for passive voice)

4. Form four-word verbs with these patterns:

   a. fixed-form helping verbs + *have* + *been* + *–ing* (for continuous tenses)

   b. fixed-form helping verbs + *have* + *been* + past participle (for passive voice)

5. Write direct questions using this word order: verb-subject-verb? Write indirect questions with this word order: subject-verb.

6. When a phrasal verb moves or changes the condition of the object, place a noun object after or between the parts of the verb, and place a pronoun object only after the verb. When a phrasal verb *does not* move or change the condition of the object, place both noun and pronoun objects after the verb.

7. Place direct and indirect objects in either of these patterns:

   a. verb-indirect object-direct object

   b. verb-direct object-*to* (or *for*)-indirect object

8. Place a short adverb

   a. before the subject

   b. between the subject and verb

   c. after the verb (unless the verb takes an object);

9. When there is no object after the verb, use this order: verb-how-where-when-(why).

10. When there is an object after the verb, use this order: how-verb-object-where-when-(why).

11. Use past participles as adjectives to express a completed action or an action that the modified noun did not perform; use present participles as adjectives to express a continuing action that the modified noun is performing.

12. Make a negative with *not* on the verb or with *no* before a noun or pronoun—but *don't make the negative twice.*

EDITING FOR MASTERY

MASTERY EXERCISE 1   ***Editing Verb Forms and Word Order***

The following passage contains fourteen errors in verb forms, placement of adverbs, placement of direct and indirect objects, use of phrasal verbs, use of past and present participles as adjectives, and use of negatives—aside from the first error, which has been corrected as an example. Make your corrections above the lines.

The Real Discoverers of the "New World"

(1) On October 12, 1492, ⋀The natives ~~on October 12, 1942,~~ of a small island in the central Bahamas discovered Christopher Columbus. (2) They found him on their beach, along with several of his equally pale companions who had on very strange clothing. (3) If the natives could

had understood these visitors, they would have being surprised. (4) Although he did know where he was, Columbus was saying that this island now belonged to something called "Spain." (5) And he gave to the natives the name "Indians."

(6) Columbus didn't discover no "new world" on October 12, 1492. (7) In fact, Columbus didn't even discover the Central Bahamas. (8) The Tiano natives who were migrated from South America beat him to it by 800 years.

(9) Long before Columbus arrived, early settlers had begin raising for food plants throughout the Americas. (10) The settlers formed villages and cities that turned into great empires. (11) By 1492, more than 600 separate cultures had in the Americas developed. (12) Their inhabitants were merchants, farmers, hunters, artisans, religious leaders, and warriors.

(13) No doubt, the island natives who greeted Columbus and his crew were impressing by the crew's appearance, but that appearance didn't intimidate probably them. (14) The Tiano natives were much taller than their European visitors. (15) Due to a healthy diet of berries, fruit, and fish, the average male Tiano stood nearly six feet tall. (16) By contrast, the sailors who came along with Columbus averaged about five feet, three inches in height. (17) Some of the older Tiano were in their seventies. (18) But hardly any Europeans of that era did not live to be fifty, because of their poor diets and frequent plagues that swept through for centuries the filthy cities of Europe. (19) In fact, Columbus would be dead at fifty-six after suffering from severe arthritis.

(20) Who were these tan, gentle natives of the Americas? (21) We know that their ancestors had from Asia migrated by crossing the Bering Strait. (22) But we are still trying to solve the mystery of when did they come and how did their cultures evolve. (23) Anthropologists and archaeologists still debate this mystery.

COLLABORATIVE ACTIVITY 10

Checking Your Answers
Compare your answers to Mastery Exercise I and report your result to the class.

Scorecard: **Number of errors found and corrected** _____

MASTERY EXERCISE 2

Editing Verb Forms and Word Order

The following passage contains fifteen errors in verb forms, placement of adverbs, placement of direct and indirect objects, use of phrasal verbs, use of past and present participles as adjectives, and use of negatives—aside from the first error, which has been corrected as an example. Make your corrections above the lines.

National Horsefly Day

(1) No one seems to know how it happened, but^ the United States has been
                                                      for more than 200 years
celebrating ~~for more than 200 years~~ its independence from Great Britain on the wrong day: July 4, 1776. (2) U.S. independence was declared actually on July 2. (3) Hardly nothing important took place on July 4, 1776, except for approval of the wording of

the Declaration of Independence by the Continental Congress. (4) In fact, the most important event of that day might had grown out of an invasion of giant horseflies in Independence Hall in Philadelphia.

(5) When the Continental Congress met on June 7, 1776, Richard Henry Lee of Virginia stood up and talked about the need for independence from England. (6) Many of the representatives agreed with him, but his demand presented to them a problem. (7) To vote yes would have being an act of treason, punishable by death. (8) So the assembly did what politicians traditionally do when faced with a tough decision: They tabled (delayed) Lee's motion to study it further.

(9) By the time that the Congress met again on July 2, the representatives had changed their minds. (10) Recent actions by the British had been angered everyone. (11) Therefore, they all agreed on Lee's motion for a declaration of independence.

(12) On July 4, the Continental Congress met for only one item of business. (13) Thomas Jefferson had been asked if could he produce a formal declaration, so he had written one. (14) The delegates were there to talk over its contents and approve the final language. (15) They had read already Jefferson's Declaration before the meeting, and everyone was wanting to add some language or take out it.

(16) It was humid in Philadelphia that day, so the delegates opened windows, which let in hundreds of giant horseflies from a nearby stable. (17) As the hungry horseflies attacked the founding fathers, no one seemed interesting in the debate any more. (18) A very uncomfortable delegate said that Jefferson's declaration seemed suitable to him. (19) Most of the others agreed and approved quickly the document. (20) Just as quickly, the delegates went out of the building.

(21) The actual signing of the Declaration of Independence would took place on August 18, 1776, and some members added to it their names later. (22) In reality, then, there isn't no clear date that marks the independence of the states.

(23) Although we managed to get the date wrong, July 4, 1776, remains an important day in American history, and every citizen should be grateful to the horseflies for their contribution.

Scorecard: Number of errors found and corrected _____

CHAPTER 31

Mastering the Little Words: Articles and Prepositions

No one notices articles and prepositions when you use them correctly. But when you don't, your writing sounds odd and even unclear. This chapter will examine some solutions to typical "little word" problems. You'll learn

■ when to use *a/an*, *the*, or no article

■ when to use which prepositions for time, place, and other special meanings

ARTICLES

The **articles**—*a*, *an*, and *the*—help your reader understand whether you are using a noun in a general or a specific way. But some people confuse *a* with *an*, and many nonnative speakers of English have difficulty distinguishing when to use *a/an*, *the*, or no article at all.

The articles entered English long ago simply as different pronunciations of the words *one* ("an") and *that* ("the"). So in actual usage, *a/an* replaces *one*, and *the* replaces *that*. We'll be looking more specifically at the rules for using these articles. Although the rules, unfortunately, don't explain all the uses of the articles, they explain most of the uses.

A/An

▶ Use *a* before consonant sounds, *an* before vowel sounds.

Remember that the articles entered the language as sounds, and sound still determines their use. The beginning sound—not the spelling—of a word determines whether *a* or *an* precedes it. *An* goes before *vowel sounds:*

an elephant	*an* awful experience
an enormous task	*an* overcharge

And for ease of pronunciation, *a* goes before *consonant sounds:*

a lesson	*a* shoe
a chair	*a* doctor

> When a word beginning with a *u* sounds as if it begins with *y*, use the article *a*.

Long *u* is pronounced like the word *you*, so its sound begins with the sound *y*, a consonant sound. Therefore, *a* precedes words beginning with long *u*:

a unit	*a* unique experience	*a* useful product
but		
an uncle	*an* unusual experience	*an* ugly mess

> When an *h* at the beginning of a word is silent, use the article *an*.

The first sound of words beginning with silent *h* is a vowel. Therefore, *an* precedes these words:

an hour	*an* honor	*an* heir
but		
a happy moment	*a* humorous story	*a* historian

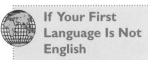

If Your First Language Is Not English

Be aware that many languages—Russian, Polish, and Persian, for example—do not use articles or use them in different ways from the way English does. And many languages do not use prepositions in the same way English does.

E X E R C I S E 1   Writing *A* or *An*

Place a *or* an *before each of the following words or phrases.*

1. _____ child

2. _____ hour

3. _____ elephant

4. _____ lion tamer

5. _____ unit of instruction

6. _____ historic event

7. _____ humid day

8. _____ unique environment

9. _____ urban setting

10. _____ ironing board

Singular Countable Nouns: *A/An* versus *The*

> With singular countable nouns, use *a* or *an* to mean "any one."

There are two kinds of nouns in English:

1. **countable nouns** (you can put a number before them): one day, three apples, five people
2. **uncountable nouns** (you cannot put a number before them): water, music, honesty, luggage

As you know, the article *a/an* means the same thing as the number *one*. Therefore, use *a/an* only before a singular countable noun.

Here are some examples of *a/an*, meaning "any one" or "one of many":

> Take *a* pencil. (any one pencil; there are many choices)
> I just ate *an* apple. (one of many possible apples)
> *A* robin built its nest in that tree. (not a specific robin; it could be any one robin)

If Your First Language Is Not English

In many languages, you can write "I am student," but in English, you must include the *a* because you mean "I am one of many students." Here are further examples:

He is *a* lawyer.

It is *an* adjective.

She is only *a* little girl.

The

Use *the* to point out a specific one.

Unlike *a*, which means "any one," *the* points to something specific—as does the word *that*. So *the* means a *specific one* or a *particular one*. Note that in the following examples the phrase or clause after the noun makes it specific:

> What is *the* assignment for Wednesday? (specifies and distinguishes it from other assignments, such as those for Monday and Friday)
>
> *The* new Chevrolet that Linda bought is beautiful. (specifies and distinguishes it from other cars or Chevrolets)
>
> Let's eat *the* pie your mother made. (specifies and distinguishes it from other pies, perhaps made by someone else)

EXERCISE 2   Writing *The*

Make each of the following general nouns specific by changing a/an *to* the *and adding a descriptive phrase or clause after the noun. Use several different structures throughout.*

General	Specific
1. a red book	**1.** the red book on the table
	or
	the red book that I bought yesterday
	or
	the red book sitting in my room
2. a new car	**2.** _____
3. an old woman	**3.** _____
4. a gardening tool	**4.** _____
5. a large table	**5.** _____
6. an oddly shaped pear	**6.** _____

Use *the* when you mean *the only one*.

Sometimes, there is only one of something in a room, a house, or the whole world. In such cases, the noun is specific—because there is no other choice. So the article *the* precedes the noun:

> *The roof* of this house leaks. (The house has only one roof.)
> What time does *the clock* say? (There is only one clock in the room.)
> *The* sky is cloudy today. (There is only one sky.)

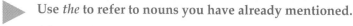

Use *the* to refer to nouns you have already mentioned.

After you've mentioned a noun, you've specified which one you mean. Therefore, use *the* if you discuss it further:

> Would you buy *a used car* from that man?
> Yes, but only if *the car* (now specified) had a five-year guarantee.

EXERCISE 3   Adding Articles

Write the omitted articles a/an or the above the lines.

1. In 1843, *a*ᐱ gentleman from Abbeville, South Carolina, refused *a*ᐱ challenge to *a*ᐱ duel. As *a*ᐱ result, his neighbors were so happy that they gave him *a*ᐱ barbecue.

2. In 1849, Elizabeth Blackwell was first woman doctor to practice in the United States.

3. In 1862, twenty-three-year-old man invested $4,000 of his life's savings in oil refinery. His name was John D. Rockefeller.

4. In 1864, motto "In God We Trust" appeared on coins for first time.

5. In 1870, Mississippi sent new senator to the U.S. Congress. He was Hiram R. Revels, first black man ever to serve in Senate.

6. In 1871, fire started in barn on West Side of Chicago. It swept through city, destroying $200 million in property.

Plural Countable Nouns and Uncountable Nouns: Using *The* or Nothing

▶ Use *the* before all specific nouns; use no article before general plural countable or uncountable nouns.

You cannot place *a/an* before a plural noun. So you must use *the* or no article at all. *The* indicates a specific plural noun; no article indicates a nonspecific (or general) plural noun. Compare these examples:

> *The three birds on the windowsill* (specific) are pigeons.
>   *but*
> *Birds* (in general) are interesting animals.
> *The people on my block* (specific) are friendly.
>   *but*
> *People* (in general) are attending college in larger numbers.

Don't place an article before an uncountable noun used in a general sense. Compare these examples:

> *The water* in Lake Erie (specific) is polluted.
>   *but*
> *Water* (in general) covers most of the Earth.

COLLABORATIVE ACTIVITY I

Adding Articles

Write five sentences, leaving out the articles. Include examples of all the rules just given. Exchange papers and add articles where they are needed. Then exchange papers again for a third student to check.

EXERCISE 4   Adding *The*

Write the above the lines where the is needed in the following sentences.

1. I loved ᐱ*the* movie I saw this weekend.

2. Beginning of movie was particularly exciting.

3. I attend church on Main Street.

4. You should read newest book on fat-free cooking.

5. You ought to try new high-protein diet mentioned in today's newspaper.

6. Dogs make good pets.

Additional Advice about *A/An* and *The*

 Some names require *the*.

Use *the* before the names of countries that end in –s or contain the word *Republic*:

> *the* Netherlands (but just Holland)
> *the* British Isles (but just Great Britain)
> *the* People's Republic of China (but just China)

Use *the* before the names of rivers, oceans, and seas (but not lakes):

> *the* Nile River   *the* Mediterranean Sea
> *the* Atlantic Ocean   Lake Superior
> *Exception: the* Great Salt Lake

Use *the* before college names that begin with the words *College or University*:

> *the* University of Illinois   *the* College of Liberal Arts and Sciences
> *but*
> Boston College   Indiana University

EXERCISE 5   Adding Missing Articles

Write the *on the lines where it is needed.*

1. _The_____ Caspian Sea

2. _____ University of Pittsburgh

3. _____ Lake Ontario

4. _____ Germany

5. _____ Northwestern University

6. _____ Canada

7. _____ Republic of Bolivia

8. _____ Atlantic Ocean

9. _____ College of DuPage

10. _____ United Arab Republic

 Some words replace articles before nouns.

When you place one of the following words before a noun, you cannot use an article. All of these words specify the noun in some way:

every	any	much
each	no	which
either	enough	what
neither	many	his, her, their, and so forth
some	more	Bill's, Mary's, and so forth

Some words go before articles.

Articles usually precede adjectives before a noun:

> *the* large, round bowl
> *a* dirty old T-shirt

But don't confuse the following five words with adjectives. They're actually adverbs that precede articles:

> both *(the)*   half *(the* or *a)*   all *(the)*   many *(a)* such *(a)*
> *Examples:*   *Both the* men are here.   *Half the* pie is gone.
>   I never saw *such a* fight before.   *Many a* problem can be
>   solved.

PREPOSITIONS

A **preposition** is a little word such as *in, on, off, under,* and *through.* It goes before (*pre–* means "before") a noun or pronoun to show the *position* of the noun or pronoun in space or time within a sentence. For example, phrases containing a preposition + a noun added to the sentence "I saw a fire" can locate the position of the fire and locate the time the action occurred:

> I saw a fire *in* the attic *on* Wednesday.

There are many prepositions and thousands of expressions that use them. Those uses can be confusing, but they're not impossible to learn. We'll look at some of the most common prepositions and their uses. For a list of common expressions using prepositions, see Appendix E.

To Indicate Time

1. *At* a specific or precise time:

> Class ends *at* 3:50 P.M.
> *At* midnight, the next day begins.

2. *By* a specific time (means no later than that time):

> Jill said she might be ready as early as 4:30 but certainly *by* 6:00.

3. *Until* a specific time (continuing up to that time):

> Last night Juanita studied *until* 11:00.

4. *In* a specific time period (usually measured in hours, minutes, days, months, or years):

> I will be leaving *in* five minutes.
> World War II ended *in* 1945.
> *in* the morning, *in* the afternoon, or *in* the evening (but *at* night)

5. *For* a duration of time:

> I have been a student *for* thirteen years.
> We have been best friends *for* a long time.

6. *Since* a starting date or time:

> They have been living next door to us *since* 1991.
> No one has eaten *since* 8:15.

7. *On* a specific day or date:

> Most people are paid *on* Friday.
> The doctor can see you *on* June 12.

8. *During* a continuing time period (or within the time period):

> I was ill *during* the night.
> We'll be away from the office *during* the next few hours.

9. Miscellaneous time expressions:

> *on* time (that is, promptly)
> *in* a while
> *at* the beginning or end (of a day, month, or year)
> *in the* middle (of a day, month, or year)
> *from* time to time (that is, occasionally)

EXERCISE 6   Writing Prepositions

Write an appropriate preposition to indicate time in each blank space.

1. _On_____ August 1, 1903, a car arrived in New York, completing the first
   cross-country automobile trip. It had been traveling _____ July 11, when
   it left San Francisco.

2. _____ June 1905, the Pennsylvania Railroad opened its route between
   New York and Chicago. The first train made its trip _____ eighteen hours.
   _____ the next week the New York Central Railroad started its own
   eighteen-hour train service. Both trains operated _____ only two weeks,
   after they had both crashed, killing nineteen people.

3. Most cars _____ the first years of the twentieth century were expensive,
   costing as much as $2,800. Then came Henry Ford's "universal car," the Model T.
   _____ several years his cars were priced at $850, but later, the Model T
   sold for $290.

To Indicate Place

1. *In* a country, area, state, city, or neighborhood:

in France   *in* Michigan   *in* Boston   *in* Lincoln Square

2. *On* (the surface of) a street or block:

We live *on* Wells Avenue.   They work *on* Main Street.

3. *At* a specific address:

We live *at* 1621 Wells Avenue.   We work *at* 945 Main Street.

4. *At* an intersection of two streets:

Let's meet *at* (the corner of) Main Street and Madison.

E X E R C I S E   7   Writing More Prepositions

Write an appropriate preposition in each space.

The Origin of a Song

(1) In 1939, the Montgomery Ward store, located __*on*____ State Street _____ Chicago, was looking for something unusual for its Santa Claus to give to parents and children. (2) Robert May, who worked _____ the store _____ the advertising department, suggested an illustrated poem, printed _____ a booklet, that families would want to keep _____ their homes and reread each holiday season. (3) May recommended a shiny-nosed reindeer, a Santa's helper; and an artist friend of May's spent hours _____ a local zoo creating sketches of reindeer. (4) May thought about names for his character everywhere he went: _____ work, _____ home, even while standing _____ the corner waiting for a bus. (5) Finally, one day his four-year-old daughter said that she preferred Rudolph.

(6) That Christmas, 2.4 million copies of the "Rudolph" booklet were handed out _____ Montgomery Ward stores everywhere _____ the country. (7) In 1949, a song about Rudolph became so popular that the red-nosed celebrity became a familiar image _____ Germany, Holland, Denmark, Sweden, Norway, England, Spain, Austria, and France.

For Vehicles and Chairs

1. *In(to)* and *out of* for small vehicles (like cars) and chairs with arms:

I got *in(to)* the cab as someone else was getting *out of* it.
My father likes to sit *in* his big, comfortable chair.

2. *On* and *off* (*of*) for large vehicles (such as planes, trains, buses, and boats) and armless chairs or any long seat (such a bench or a sofa):

> We rode *on* the subway and got *off* at our stop.
> He's sitting *on* that bench over there.
> The man *on* the wooden chair is his brother.

E X E R C I S E 8   Writing More Prepositions

Write the correct preposition in each space.

1. Years ago, people came to the United States *on*_____ ocean liners. Now almost

everyone comes here _____ a plane.

2. We took a ride _____ our new car. We got _____ it at the park and

walked around for a while.

3. Some of the people are sitting _____ the couch, and some of them are sitting

_____ armchairs.

4. Where do you usually get _____ the bus? Where do you get _____ it?

5. Would you please get _____ that table and sit _____ a chair.

Other Prepositions

1. *For* a reason or *for* someone who benefits:

> Bill went to the barber *for* a haircut.
> I bought a present *for* my sister.

2. *About* a subject (or *on* a subject):

> We were talking *about* our plans for next week.
> I recently read an article *about* (or *on*) space travel.

3. *Between* two; *among* three or more:

> We shared the sandwich *between* the two of us.
> The five members of the board discussed it *among* themselves.

4. *From* a starting point; *to* a destination:

> We drove *from* Kansas *to* Alaska.

5. *Toward* (in the direction of) a place:

> I walked *toward* the beach but turned south before I arrived at the beach.

6. *Into* (entering) a place or space:

> He just went *into* that room through the back door.

7. *In* (inside of) a place or space:

> He has been running *in* the gym; he hasn't gone outside.

COLLABORATIVE ACTIVITY 2

Adding Prepositions
Write ten sentences, leaving out the prepositions. Include examples of all the prepositions explained in this chapter. Exchange papers and add the missing prepositions. Then exchange papers again for a third student to check.

8. *On* a surface:

> The book is *on* the table.
> The portrait is hanging *on* the wall.

9. *Off* a surface:

> I took the book *off* the table.
> The painting fell *off* the wall.

E X E R C I S E   9   Writing Still More Prepositions

If Your First Language Is Not English

You may confuse the prepositions *on* and *in* with each other, especially if your first language is Spanish. Note these differences:

1. To show place relationships:
   a. *On* generally means "on the surface of" or "on top of": *on* the floor, *on* a street
   b. *In* generally means "inside of" or "within": *in* a room, *in* the water

2. To show time relationships:
   a. *On* refers to a day or a date: *on* Saturday, *on* July 5, 1990
   b. *In* generally means "within a period of time," including a month or a season: *in* January, *in* summer, *in* an hour

Write an appropriate preposition in each of the following spaces.

The United States Enters World War II

(1) Japan made an alliance to fight *with* Germany and Italy _____ 1940. (2) Throughout 1941, the United States moved closer and closer _____ war, but it didn't join the fighting. (3) _____ March 1941, the United States passed a law that allowed supplies to go from the United States _____ Britain.

(4) President Franklin D. Roosevelt began to make a number of speeches _____ the possibility of war. (5) _____ Sunday, December 7, 1941, General George C. Marshall received a message _____ a Japanese attack _____ the Pacific. (6) He sent messages of warning _____ the Philippines, the Panama Canal Zone, and San Francisco. (7) However, the warning didn't get _____ Pearl Harbor _____ Hawaii. (8) _____ 7:55 that same morning, Japanese planes flew _____ Pearl Harbor, filled with bombs _____ the American ships. (9) By 10:00 A.M., eighteen ships were sunk or badly damaged, and about 2,500 people were killed. (10) When President Roosevelt heard _____ the attack, he immediately went on radio _____ the purpose _____ informing the American people of the Japanese attack. (11) The next day, Congress declared war _____ Japan and its allies.

E X E R C I S E   1 0   Writing *In* or *On*

Write on *or in* in each space below.

1. You will find the book _on_____ the desk and find the papers in the drawer.

2. I will meet you _____ the corner of Fifth and Main.

3. The new table is _____ the corner of the room.

4. I think I left my book _____ my bed.

5. Bill isn't feeling well; he is staying _____ bed today.

6. We haven't gone to a movie _____ a month.

7. Sue is usually _____ time, so she should be here _____ a few minutes.

8. Who is _____ charge of this department?

To Repeat the Meanings of Prefixes

A **prefix** is something attached to the beginning of a word. For example, the prefix *re–* means "again," so the word *review* literally means "view again." Many prefixes in English came from Latin:

Prefix	Meaning	Examples
ad–, ac–, ap–, a–	to	admit, acceptable, apply, agree
con–, com–	with	converse, communicate
ex–, e–	from	excuse, emigrate, exit
in–, im–	in	involved, implicit

Many times—but not always—a word with one of these prefixes also repeats the meaning of the prefix in a preposition following the word:

ad mitted *to* a school; *ac* ceptable *to* me; *ap* ply *to* the school; *a* gree *to* a contract

con versed *with* me; *com* municated *with* a friend

ex cused *from* class; *e* migrate *from* a country

in volved *in* a crime; *im* plicit *in* his statement

A large list of common expressions using prepositions is in Appendix E on pages 446–447. You may wish to memorize these expressions, perhaps in groups of ten at a time. Or you may use the list for a reference as you write and edit your papers.

IN SUMMARY   ## Mastering the Little Words

To use articles with singular nouns

1. Place *a* before consonant sounds, including long *u*.
2. Place *an* before vowel sounds and silent *h*.

3. With singular countable nouns, use *a/an* when you mean "one of many."
4. Use *the*
   a. to point out a specific or particular one.
   b. when you mean the only one.
   c. to refer to nouns you have already mentioned.

To use articles with plural and uncountable nouns
1. Place *the* before specifics.
2. Use no article before unspecifics.

To use articles with names
1. Use *the* with country names ending in *–s* or containing the word *Republic*.
2. Use *the* with river, ocean, or sea names—but not names of lakes.
3. Use *the* with college names beginning with the words *College* or *University*.

To use prepositions
Consult the guidelines found in this chapter.

EDITING FOR MASTERY

Mastery Exercise 1

Supplying Articles and Prepositions

Insert the twenty-five missing articles and prepositions in the blank spaces.

The Ford Model T (1908–1928)

The Model T Ford was a fragile-looking automobile, but it became ___*the*___ most popular car in American history. Henry Ford sold almost 16 million Model T's (1) _____ years 1908 and 1928. (2) _____ Model T was introduced (3) _____ 1908 and cost $850. It was (4) _____ immediate best-seller, not only because of its low price, but because it was powerful, dependable, and simple enough to make it practical (5) _____ the average American to own and drive.

The Model T, whose nickname was (6) "Tin Lizzie," sold well (7) _____ the farms and (8) _____ small towns where half (9) _____ country lived. Furthermore, people could drive it (10) _____ the rough roads (11) _____ rural America (12) _____ the early 1900s. And people could depend (13) _____ the Model T. As (14) _____ popular joke expressed it, (15) _____ Model T owner wanted to be buried (16) _____ his Tin Lizzie. When friends asked why, he replied, "Oh, because (17) _____ thing pulled me out of every hole I ever got into, and it ought to pull me out of this one."

Henry Ford didn't invent the Model T; it was developed (18) _____ a team of engineers (19) _____ his Ford Motor Company plant. But he brought together

COLLABORATIVE ACTIVITY 3

Checking Your Answers
Compare your answers to Mastery Exercise 1 and report your results to the class.

brilliant people who found ways to mass-produce (20) _____ car on (21) _____ moving assembly line. He cut costs by building only one model and developing new methods (22) _____ production. He would then lower (23) _____ price of his cars, which increased sales. In 1924, Americans bought as many Tin Lizzies as all other cars combined, and next year the Model T sold for (24) _____ all-time low price of $290. Ford told Americans: "I am going to democratize the automobile, and when I'm through, everybody will be able to afford one and about everybody will have one." (25) _____ the time he died in 1947, he had fulfilled his promise.

Scorecard: Number of errors found and corrected _____

Mastery Exercise 2

Supplying Articles and Prepositions

Insert the twenty-five missing articles and prepositions in the blank spaces.

Cornelius Vanderbilt (1794–1877): A Rich American

Cornelius Vanderbilt, who later became known as _the_ "Commodore" because of his success in shipping, was born in New York, on May 27, 1794. As a young man, he was dedicated (1) _____ making money fast. He quit school (2) _____ the age of eleven and was working (3) _____ himself at sixteen. He bought (4) _____ small boat using money he borrowed (5) _____ his parents and took passengers (6) _____ Staten Island (7) _____ Manhattan daily. He quickly succeeded (8) _____ this business and bought three sailing boats. But he sold (9) _____ boats in 1817 to take advantage of the opportunity to learn the steamboat business.

For several years, Vanderbilt took care of (10) _____ steamboats of another man. But he started his own steamboat business (11) _____ 1829. By 1835, he was earning $60,000 a year, and by 1846 the Commodore was (12) _____ millionaire. (13) _____ main reason (14) _____ his success was that he destroyed his competitors. He cut his fares and offered better service to drive (15) _____ competition out of business. He soon owned more than a hundred boats.

When gold was discovered in California in 1849, Vanderbilt quickly increased his wealth. He established the Accessory Transit Company, which took gold hunters to California (16) _____ boat and on land. His company charged $300 for (17) _____ entire trip, by far the cheapest rate available. Soon Vanderbilt was making (18) _____ million dollars yearly, and he bragged in 1853 that he was worth $11 million.

In 1860, Vanderbilt lost interest (19) _____ boats and decided to enter the railroad business. Looking (20) _____ a bargain, he bought two railroads and then made them into one profitable company. He also purchased the New York Central Railroad (21) _____ spite of efforts to stop him, and he eventually began (22) _____ first route (23) _____ New York and Chicago.

When he died (24) _____ January 4, 1877, the eighty-two-year-old Vanderbilt was the richest man in the United States. He left a fortune to Central University in Nashville, Tennessee, which later changed its name (25) _____ Vanderbilt University. His son William Henry Vanderbilt inherited more than $90 million.

Scorecard: Number of errors found and corrected _____

Use these checklists as you edit your paragraphs and essays. Read over your drafts more than once, checking for a different group of items each time. As the term progresses, you should become more efficient in this practice. Highlight the items on the lists that especially apply to you, and narrow your focus to those items in the repeated readings.

PARAGRAPHS

- [ ] Are my paragraphs unified and coherent? (see pp. 33–35)

- [ ] Have I joined sentences correctly? (see pp. 70–78, 82–89)

- [ ] Are my sentences varied? (see pp. 201–207)

- [ ] Have I eliminated unnecessary repetition? (see pp. 207–209)

ARTICLES AND PREPOSITIONS

- [ ] Have I used the articles *a/an* and *the* correctly? (see pp. 388–393)

- [ ] Have I used prepositions correctly? (see pp. 393–398)

VERBS

- [ ] Are my verb tenses correct and consistent? (see pp. 364–374)

- [ ] Do my subjects and verbs agree? (see pp. 116–128)

- [ ] Are my verb endings and irregular verb forms correct? (see pp. 138–148, 382–383)

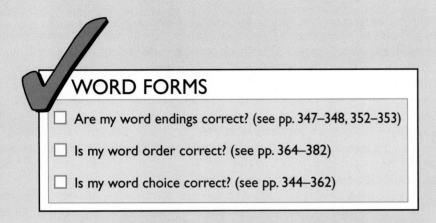

✓ WORD FORMS

- ☐ Are my word endings correct? (see pp. 347–348, 352–353)
- ☐ Is my word order correct? (see pp. 364–382)
- ☐ Is my word choice correct? (see pp. 344–362)

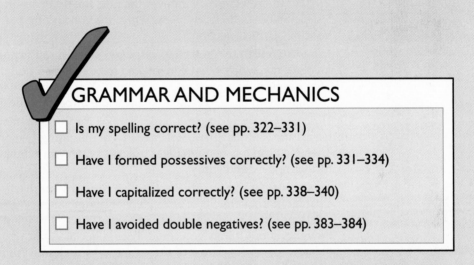

✓ GRAMMAR AND MECHANICS

- ☐ Is my spelling correct? (see pp. 322–331)
- ☐ Have I formed possessives correctly? (see pp. 331–334)
- ☐ Have I capitalized correctly? (see pp. 338–340)
- ☐ Have I avoided double negatives? (see pp. 383–384)

✓ PUNCTUATION

- ☐ Have I used commas correctly? (see pp. 300–307)
- ☐ Is my end punctuation (. ? !) correct? (see pp. 307–309)
- ☐ Have I handled direct quotations correctly? (see pp. 314–318)
- ☐ Have I punctuated contractions correctly? (see pp. 334–335)

Reading Selections

Every good writer is a good reader. Reading provides you with models of writing, along with inspiration to write, ideas to write about, and information to discuss in writing. And reading helps you learn what other people have learned and wish to share with you in their writing. The following selections should interest you. The authors are professional writers—many of them famous—and even students like you, who had great stories to tell and worked hard to tell them well. Each selection discusses issues that you face each day—or issues that perhaps you've never considered.

Read each selection at home and consider the questions that follow it. The questions—as well as the suggestions for writing—will give you additional practice in building the skills you've been working on throughout this book.

The key to reading well is to *read with a purpose.* You should know what to look for and how to understand a reading. Here's some advice to follow as you read these selections—and any other selections any time:

1. **Preread the selection.** Skim over the title, the first paragraph, the first and last sentences of the body paragraphs, the concluding paragraph, and any headings in the selection.

2. **Expect to return to a selection after you've read it.** Purposeful reading involves reviewing what you've read to be sure you understand its ideas. That's especially important as you study. You don't have to reread every word, but you have to be able to locate the important ideas.

3. **Highlight or underline main ideas.** Look for thesis statements and topic sentences and identify them, either with a highlighting pen or by underlining. Then, you can locate main ideas quickly, when you return to the selection for further review and study.

4. **Make notes in the margins of the text.** Record your reactions to a sentence or a paragraph: statements of agreement or disagreement ("great!" "yeah, right!"); reactions ("this reminds me of . . ."); objections ("but what about . . . ?"); thoughts about things you could discuss in class or in writing ("how about the issue of . . . ?"). Think of these notes as a dialogue you're having with the author of the text. The purpose of reading is to get you to think, not simply to swallow ideas, so record your thoughts.

5. **Reread while you're reading.** If you don't understand a sentence or idea, go back and reread the sentence or sentences that precede it. The puzzling passage may then make more sense. But if it doesn't, note the problem in the margin so you can return to it later, or perhaps discuss it with others.

6. **Circle or underline unfamiliar words, and try to determine their meaning in context**—from the sentence and the paragraph they're in. If you must look them up, do so after you finish reading. Then reread the selection. You'll go much faster—and understand much more.

7. **Make journal entries in response to readings.** If the selection raises questions or ideas, capture them in writing. Discuss the questions in class and collect ideas that you can use later if you write about the selection for homework or a quiz.

8. **Know how fast you read—and how fast you read different things.** One of the keys to success in school is budgeting your time effectively. So you ought to know how long it takes you to read twenty pages in social science or twenty pages in history. Time yourself with each textbook. How many pages have you finished in fifteen minutes or an hour? That way, you can set aside

enough time to read carefully and thoroughly so you can plan your week's activities.

9. **Take frequent breaks.** Don't try to read a long, difficult selection straight through. Reading with a purpose can be hard work. Pause and rest every fifteen minutes or half hour. But don't take long breaks, or you'll find excuses not to read.

My Prison Studies
Malcolm X with Alex Haley

* * * *

Malcolm X was an extraordinary leader of the black power movement in the 1960s. The son of a Baptist minister, he was born Malcolm Little in 1925 in Omaha, Nebraska. He dropped out of school in the eighth grade and moved to New York. There he became involved with drugs and was arrested and sentenced for burglary in 1946. While serving a ten-year sentence in prison, he became a member of Elijah Muhammad's Black Muslim sect, which preached that all whites are evil. Eventually he became disillusioned with Muhammad's teachings and made a pilgrimage to Mecca, Islam's holiest city. Prior to his murder in 1964, he advocated black self-help and education and began working to establish cooperative relationships between blacks and whites.

In this excerpt from his autobiography, Malcolm X describes how he taught himself to read in prison. As you read it, notice the stages involved in his processes of learning.

1   Many who today hear me somewhere in person, or on television, or those who read something I've said, will think I went to school far beyond the eighth grade. This impression is due entirely to my prison studies.

2   It had really begun back in the Charlestown Prison, when Bimbi [a prison inmate] first made me feel envy of his stock of knowledge. Bimbi had always taken charge of any conversation he was in, and I had tried to emulate him. But every book I picked up had a few sentences which didn't contain anywhere from one to nearly all of the words that might as well have been in Chinese. When I just skipped those words, of course, I really ended up with little idea of what the book said. So I had come to the Norfolk Prison Colony still going through only book-reading motions. Pretty soon, I would have quit even these motions, unless I had received the motivation that I did.

3   I saw that the best thing I could do was get hold of a dictionary—to study, to learn some words. I was lucky enough to reason also that I should try to improve my penmanship. It was sad. I couldn't even write in a straight line. It was both ideas together that moved me to request a dictionary along with some tablets and pencils from the Norfolk Prison Colony school.

4   I spent two days just riffling uncertainly through the dictionary's pages. I'd never realized so many words existed! I didn't know which words I needed to learn. Finally, to start some kind of action, I began copying.

5   In my slow, painstaking, ragged handwriting, I copied into my tablet everything printed on that first page, down to the punctuation marks.

6   I believe it took me a day. Then, aloud, I read back, to myself, everything I'd written on the tablet. Over and over, aloud, to myself, I read my own handwriting.

7   I woke up the next morning, thinking about those words—immensely proud to realize that not only had I written so much at one time, but I'd written words that I never knew were in the world. Moreover, with a little effort, I also could remember what many of these words meant. I reviewed the words whose meanings I didn't remember. Funny thing, from the dictionary first page right now, that "aardvark" springs to my mind. The dictionary had a picture of it, a long-tailed, long-eared, burrowing African mammal, which lives off termites caught by sticking out its tongue as an anteater does for ants.

8   I was so fascinated that I went on—I copied the dictionary's next page. And the same experience came when I studied that. With every succeeding page, I also learned of people and places and events from history. Actually the dictionary is like a miniature encyclopedia. Finally the dictionary's A section had filled a whole tablet—and I went on into the B's. That was the way I started copying what eventually became the entire dictionary. It went a lot faster after so much practice helped me to pick up handwriting speed. Between what I wrote in my tablet, and writing letters, during the rest of my time in prison I would guess I wrote a million words.

9   I suppose it was inevitable that as my word-base broadened, I could for the first time pick up a book and read and now begin to understand what the book was saying. Anyone who has read a great deal can imagine the new world that opened. Let me tell you something; from then until I left that prison, in every free moment I had, if I was not reading in the library, I was reading on my bunk. You couldn't have gotten me out of books with a wedge. Between Mr. Muhammad's teachings, my correspondence, my visitors—usually Ella and Reginald—and my reading of books, months passed without my even thinking about being imprisoned. In fact, up to then, I never had been so truly free in my life.

10 The Norfolk Prison Colony's library was in the school building. A variety of classes was taught by instructors who came from such places as Harvard and Boston universities. The weekly debates between inmate teams were also held in the school building. You would be astonished to know how worked up convict debaters and audiences would get over subjects like "Should babies be fed milk?"

11 Available on the prison library's shelves were books on just about every general subject. . . . Some of them looked ancient: covers faded, old-time parchment-looking binding. . . . Any college library would have been lucky to get that collection.

12 As you can imagine, especially in a prison where there was heavy emphasis on rehabilitation, an inmate was smiled upon if he demonstrated an unusually intense interest in books. There was a sizable number of well-read inmates, especially the popular debaters. Some were said by many to be practically walking encyclopedias. They were almost celebrities. No university would ask any student to devour literature as I did when this new world opened to me, of being able to read and *understand*.

13 I read more in my room than in the library itself. An inmate who was known to read a lot could check out more than the permitted maximum number of books. I preferred reading in the total isolation of my own room.

14 When I had progressed to really serious reading, every night at about ten P.M. I would be outraged with the "lights out." It always seemed to catch me right in the middle of something engrossing.

15 Fortunately, right outside my door was a corridor light that cast a glow into my room. The glow was enough to read by, once my eyes adjusted to it. So when "lights out" came, I would sit on the floor where I could continue reading in that glow.

16 At one-hour intervals the night guards paced past every room. Each time I heard the approaching footsteps, I jumped into bed and feigned sleep. And as soon as the guard passed, I got back out of bed onto the floor area of that light-glow, where I would read for another fifty-eight minutes—until the guard approached again. That went on until three or four every morning. Three or four hours of sleep a night was enough for me. Often in the years in the streets I had slept less than that. . . .

17 I have often reflected upon the new vistas that reading opened to me. I knew right there in prison that reading had changed forever the course of my life. As I see it today, the ability to read awoke inside me some long dormant craving to be mentally alive. I certainly wasn't seeking any degree, the way a college confers a status symbol upon its students. My homemade education gave me, with every additional book that I read, a little bit more sensitivity to the deafness, dumbness, and blindness that was afflicting the black race in America. Not long ago, an English writer telephoned me from London, asking questions. One was, "What's your alma mater?" I told him, "Books." You will never catch me with a free fifteen minutes in which I'm not studying something I feel might be able to help the black man.

Questions for Analysis

1. What is the thesis statement in the first paragraph? Underline it.

2. What, according to Malcolm X, made him decide that he had to learn to read?

3. What at first stopped Malcolm X from reading? What did he have to do before he could progress in reading?

4. How many steps or stages in the process of learning to read does Malcolm X discuss? Number them.

5. At one point he explains, "I never had been so truly free in my life." What makes him feel this way?

6. What point does Malcolm X make at the end of this excerpt?

Suggestions for Writing

1. Malcolm X claims that college is mostly a status symbol. Do you agree or disagree? Explain your position.

2. Has anyone ever inspired you to learn something new or to achieve something difficult? Describe how the person inspired you.

3. Describe the process you went through to learn a new skill—whether in school, at home, or in some sport.

How to Write with Style
Kurt Vonnegut
★ ★ ★ ★

Kurt Vonnegut (1922–2007), the author of many science fiction novels and short stories, is greatly admired for his imagination, insight, and humor—as well as for the clarity and simplicity of his style. He survived as a prisoner of war during the firebombing of Dresden, Germany, in World War II and based his novel, Slaughterhouse-Five, *in part on that experience. In the following essay, Vonnegut offers plainspoken and entirely sensible advice on what makes writing effective. Note the clarity of his advice, especially as it relates to choosing a subject and addressing the concerns of readers. Note, too, that just as he tells you to sound like yourself, he does the same—with candor, wit, and specific examples.*

Before reading the essay, use your dictionary to look up the following words:

1. reputable
2. piquant
3. locution
4. exasperate

1 Newspaper reporters and technical writers are trained to reveal almost nothing about themselves in their writings. This makes them freaks in the world of writers, since almost all of the other ink-stained wretches in that world reveal a lot about themselves to readers. We call these revelations, accidental and intentional, elements of style.

2 These revelations tell us as readers what sort of person it is with whom we are spending time. Does the writer sound ignorant or informed, stupid or bright, crooked or honest, humorless or playful? And on and on.

3 Why should you examine your writing style with the idea of improving it? Do so as a mark of respect for your readers, whatever you're writing. If you scribble your thoughts any which way, your readers will surely feel that you care nothing about them. They will mark you down as an egomaniac or a chowderhead—or worse, they will stop reading you.

4   The most damning revelation you can make about yourself is that you do not know what is interesting and what is not. Don't you yourself like or dislike writers mainly for what they choose to show you or make you think about? Did you ever admire an empty-headed writer for his or her mastery of the language? No.

5   So your own winning style must begin with ideas in your head.

Find a subject you care about.

6   Find a subject you care about and which you in your heart feel others should care about. It is this genuine caring, and not your games with language, which will be the most compelling and seductive element in your style.

7   I am not urging you to write a novel, by the way—although I would not be sorry if you wrote one, provided you genuinely cared about something. A petition to the mayor about a pothole in front of your house or a love letter to the girl next door will do.

Do not ramble, though.

8   I won't ramble on about that.

Keep it simple.

9   As for your use of language: Remember that two great masters of language, William Shakespeare and James Joyce, wrote sentences which were almost childlike when their subjects were most profound.

> *"Should I act upon the urgings that I feel, or remain passive and thus cease to exist?"*
> *"To be or not to be?"*

"To be or not to be?" asks Shakespeare's Hamlet. The longest word is three letters long.

10   Joyce, when he was frisky, could put together a sentence as intricate as a necklace for Cleopatra, but my favorite sentence in his short story "Eveline" is this one: "She was tired." At that point in the story, no other words could break the heart of a reader as those three words do.

11   Simplicity of language is not only reputable, but perhaps even sacred. The Bible opens with a sentence well within the writing skills of a lively fourteen-year-old: "In the beginning God created the heaven and the earth."

Have the guts to cut.

12.   It may be that you, too, are capable of making necklaces for Cleopatra, so to speak. But your eloquence should be the servant of the ideas in your head. Your rule might be this: If a sentence, no matter how excellent, does not illuminate your subject in some new and useful way, scratch it out.

Sound like yourself.

13   The writing style which is most natural to you is bound to echo the speech you heard when a child. English was the novelist Joseph Conrad's third language, and much that seems piquant in his use of English was no doubt colored by his first language, which was Polish. And lucky indeed is the writer who has grown up in Ireland, for the English spoken there is so amusing and musical. I myself grew up in Indianapolis, where common speech sounds like a band saw cutting galvanized tin, and employs a vocabulary as unornamental as a monkey wrench.

14   In some of the more remote hollows of Appalachia, children still grow up hearing songs and locutions of Elizabethan times. Yes, and many Americans grow up hearing a language other than English, or an English dialect a majority of Americans cannot understand.

15   All these varieties of speech are beautiful, just as the varieties of butterflies are beautiful. No matter what your first language, you should treasure it all your life. If it happens

not to be standard English, and if it shows itself when you write standard English, the result is usually delightful, like a very pretty girl with one eye that is green and one that is blue.

16   I myself find that I trust my own writing most, and others seem to trust it most, too, when I sound most like a person from Indianapolis, which is what I am. What alternatives do I have? The one most vehemently recommended by teachers has no doubt been pressed on you, as well: to write like cultivated Englishmen of a century or more ago.

Say what you mean to say.

17   I used to be exasperated by such teachers, but I am no more. I understand now that all those antique essays and stories with which I was to compare my own work were not magnificent for their datedness or foreignness, but for saying precisely what their authors meant them to say. My teachers wished me to write accurately, always selecting the most effective words, and relating the words to one another unambiguously, rigidly, like parts of a machine. The teachers did not want to turn me into an Englishman after all. They hoped that I would become understandable—and therefore understood.

18   And there went my dream of doing with words what Pablo Picasso did with paint or what any number of jazz idols did with music. If I broke all the rules of punctuation, had words mean whatever I wanted them to mean, and strung them together higgledy-piggledy, I would simply not be understood. So you, too, had better avoid Picasso-style or jazz-style writing, if you have something worth saying and wish to be understood.

19   Readers want our pages to look very much like pages they have seen before. Why? This is because they themselves have a tough job to do, and they need all the help they can get from us.

Pity the readers.

20   They have to identify thousands of little marks on paper, and make sense of them immediately. They have to read, an art so difficult that most people don't really master it even after having studied it all through grade school and high school—twelve long years.

21   So this discussion must finally acknowledge that our stylistic options as writers are neither numerous nor glamorous, since our readers are bound to be such imperfect artists. Our audience requires us to be sympathetic and patient teachers, ever willing to simplify and clarify—whereas we would rather soar high above the crowd, singing like nightingales.

22   That is the bad news. The good news is that we Americans are governed under a unique Constitution, which allows us to write whatever we please without fear of punishment. So the most meaningful aspect of our styles, which is what we choose to write about, is utterly unlimited.

For really detailed advice.

23   For a discussion of literary style in a narrower sense, I commend to your attention *The Elements of Style*, by William Strunk, Jr. and E. B. White. E. B. White is, of course, one of the most admirable literary stylists this country has so far produced.

24   You should realize, too, that no one would care how well or how badly Mr. White expressed himself, if he did not have perfectly enchanting things to say.

Questions for Analysis

1. Kurt Vonnegut defines elements of *style* as "revelations, accidental and intentional." What does he mean?

2. What, according to Vonnegut, is the role of style as it relates to readers?

3. Like most good writers, Vonnegut likes to explore opposing ideas. Find several examples. Why does he create these oppositions?

4. Vonnegut discusses the differing views he had and has toward teachers of writing. How has his viewpoint changed?

5. What do you consider to be the best or the most important advice Vonnegut offers?

Suggestions for Writing

1. Kurt Vonnegut gives advice on developing a personal style and uses himself as an example. Discuss how your writing style is emerging from your background and your experiences with writing.

2. Describe an early experience you had with writing. How did it affect you—either positively or negatively?

3. Give advice to someone on the best practices in planning, drafting, and writing. Explain the process that works best for you.

4. Give advice on some other subject, based on your own experience: how to juggle a job and college successfully, how to study for a test, how to take good notes on a reading, how to eat properly on a busy schedule, how to get enough of the right kind of exercise, and so on. Choose any of these topics or choose your own.

Doing Laundry Comes with a Load of Rules
Dawn Turner Trice

* * * *

The duel between mother and child over neatness is almost universal. Living in the here and now, the child is careless and thoughtless: dropping clothes on the floor, misplacing all sorts of articles—no matter what their value—and expecting mom to be the maid and personal servant. The mother struggles to "civilize" her children, to make them realize they are not the center of the universe, and that they have responsibilities to others with whom they live. In the following column, which appeared in the Chicago Tribune *on April 2, 2007, Dawn Turner Trice lays out a set of rules for children (and, it seems, husbands) on the care and treatment of laundry.*

Dawn Turner Trice (born 1965), who was a participant in the Iowa Writers' Workshop, is a columnist for the Chicago Tribune *and for National Public Radio's* Morning Edition. *She is the author of the novel* Only Twice I've Wished for Heaven.

Before reading the article, use your dictionary to look up the following words:

1. compilation	5. ferret (as a verb)
2. albeit	6. corollary
3. dysfunctional	7. divine (as a verb)
4. rummage	8. temperament

1   When I was young, I could get out of doing household chores by reading. That was one of my mother's many rules. If you read, you didn't have to wash the dishes, mop the floor, do the laundry. Consequently, my sister and I read voraciously.

2   The only exception to the "Read Rather Than Do Chores Rule" came during spring break, or Clean-Up Week as we knew it back then. During Clean-Up Week, you cleaned. It was the perfect time for my mother to exercise her cleaning rules. Perhaps no chore came with as detailed a list of rules as doing laundry.

3   Here's a new and improved list of laundry rules. It's a compilation that includes items from my mother, my own experience and a few friends.

4   No. 1: All money—and that includes coins, paper bills and checks—left in pockets belongs to the person doing the laundry. That person is henceforth known as the launderer.

All money will be considered payment (albeit insufficient) for the launderer performing a thankless task.

5   No. 2: All cell phones, iPods, cameras and other digital devices left in pockets and rendered dysfunctional after the spin cycle are not the fault of the launderer, who shouldn't be expected to rummage through pockets ferreting out said devices. The launderer, however, will reserve the right to complain about such gross negligence and say things like: "Your next cell phone should be the model up from the tin can and string."

6   No. 3: Unless you put your underwear and pants on at the same time, there's no reason to take them off that way and expect the launderer to separate said articles of clothing.

7   No. 4: Allowing clothes to sit for days in smelly piles in a bedroom or a bathroom instead of in the laundry room will be considered an act of aggression and will be met with equal force.

8   No. 5: If you wake up in the morning and suddenly realize you have no clean under-wear, after the launderer expressly stated (the night before) that you should lay out all appropriate clothing—translation: every article of clothing that qualifies you as being fully dressed—then you will be relegated to wearing swimming attire.

9   No. 6: Be advised that the launderer will only wash laundry if there is enough for a full load. Also be advised that sorting clothes results in more than just two piles (lights and darks); therefore, doing the laundry takes time. So plan accordingly.

10   No. 7: A corollary to No. 5 and No. 6: If you have no clean underwear, no clean swim-ming attire and don't have enough clothes to make a full load, you (O pathetic one) are allowed just one purchase of underwear per month. Anything more merely adds to your slovenliness and you should be ashamed.

11   No. 8: Nobody worries anymore about ring around the collar, which is so 1970s. Wash your neck and any other body part that may leave a ring.

12   No. 9: These days most clothes—and not just the ultracheap ones—are made of shoddy material and should be washed in cold water and not placed in a dryer.

13   No. 10: This means that those in the house (members of the male species) inclined to wash everything in harsh detergent, warm water and then heap the load into the dryer should not be permitted to do the laundry except under extraordinary circumstances.

14   No. 11: A corollary to No. 10. Even under extraordinary circumstances, the aforemen-tioned group should not be allowed to wash the launderer's "unmentionables."

15   No. 12: The launderer refuses to wash clothes and fold them too. If you can't help fold the laundry, you deserve to wear your clothes looking wrinkled and rough-dried.

16   No. 13: The launderer refuses to mate socks. If you can't mate socks, then it's not the launderer's concern when you're running late for work or school and can't divine mates.

17   No. 14: The launderer has no mending skills—has never, ever had mending skills—therefore, if something needs to be sewn, sew it yourself or toss it out.

18   No. 15: The launderer will not pre-treat a stain. Shout it out yourself.

19   Please note that the launderer reserves the right to change the rules without notice and at any moment totally dependent on her temperament.

20   Thank you.

Questions for Analysis

1. Dawn Turner Trice begins her article by describing the "rules" from her childhood, especially the rule about reading. Why do you think she empha-sizes that rule?

2. Trice obviously intends her article to be funny. But does she have another purpose?

3. The language of Trice's list of rules is very formal and stiff. Cite some examples. Why does she use this formal language?

4. But Trice then begins to mix the formal language with the informal use of "you" and even, at one point to "O pathetic one." Who is the "you" in her audience, and is there more than one "you"? What is the reason for this mixture?

Suggestions for Writing

1. Trice lists fifteen rules, but they could be grouped into categories. Establish and explain those categories in a summary of the article.

2. For a specific audience, write out a set of rules for an everyday activity. Aim to be humorous.

3. Based on the article, contrast the implied definitions of "launderer"—from several points of view, including the members of Trice's household and Trice herself.

4. Write a narrative about a conflict over responsibilities for doing chores in your household (or at work) and how you resolved the conflict.

The Struggle to Be an All-American Girl
Elizabeth Wong

* * * *

Many people in the United States are bilingual, speaking one language at home or in their community and another language at school or work. And many people face conflicts between the traditions and desires of their parents and their own desires to assimilate—fit in—within the "all-American" culture. Elizabeth Wong was one of those people. Her mother insisted that Elizabeth and her brother attend a Chinese language school, and the essay that follows explores the conflicts involved. As you read it, notice the physical description that reinforces Wong's feelings toward the school. Notice the contrasts between the lessons of the Chinese school and the American school, the life in Chinatown and outside of Chinatown, and the attitudes toward speaking Chinese and speaking English.

Elizabeth Wong, who grew up in Los Angeles's Chinatown, is an award-winning Chinese playwright whose works focus on Asian American subject matter. Among her plays are China Doll, Letters to a Student Revolutionary, *and* Kimchee & Chitlins. *She was the staff writer for the television sitcom* All-American Girl.

Before reading the essay, use your dictionary to look up the following words:

1. stoic
2. dissuade
3. repress
4. maniacal
5. ideograph
6. pedestrian (adjective)
7. pidgin
8. exasperation

1   It's still there, the Chinese school on Yale Street where my brother and I used to go. Despite the new coat of paint and the high wire fence, the school I knew 10 years ago remains remarkably, stoically the same.

2   Every day at 5 P.M., instead of playing with our fourth- and fifth-grade friends or sneaking out to the empty lot to hunt ghosts and animal bones, my brother and I had to go to Chinese school. No amount of kicking, screaming, or pleading could dissuade my mother, who was solidly determined to have us learn the language of our heritage.

3   Forcibly, she walked us the seven long, hilly blocks from our home to school, depositing our defiant tearful faces before the stern principal. My only memory of him is that he swayed on his heels like a palm tree, and he always clasped his impatient twitching hands behind his back. I recognized him as a repressed maniacal child killer, and knew that if we ever saw his hands we'd be in big trouble.

4   We all sat in little chairs in an empty auditorium. The room smelled like Chinese medicine, an imported faraway mustiness. Like ancient mothballs or dirty closets. I hated that smell. I favored crisp new scents. Like the soft French perfume that my American teacher wore in public school.

5   There was a stage far to the right, flanked by an American flag and the flag of the Nationalist Republic of China, which was also red, white and blue but not as pretty.

6   Although the emphasis at the school was mainly language—speaking, reading, writing—the lessons always began with an exercise in politeness. With the entrance of the teacher, the best student would tap a bell and everyone would get up, kowtow, and chant, "Sing san ho," the phonetic for "How are you, teacher?"

7   Being 10 years old, I had better things to learn than ideographs copied painstakingly in lines that ran right to left from the tip of a *moc but,* a real ink pen that had to be held in an awkward way if blotches were to be avoided. After all, I could do the multiplication tables, name the satellites of Mars, and write reports on *Little Women* and *Black Beauty.* Nancy Drew, my favorite book heroine, never spoke Chinese.

8   The language was a source of embarrassment. More times than not, I had tried to disassociate myself from the nagging loud voice that followed me wherever I wandered in the nearby American supermarket outside Chinatown. The voice belonged to my grandmother, a fragile woman in her seventies who could outshout the best of the street vendors. Her humor was raunchy, her Chinese rhythmless, patternless. It was quick, it was loud, it was unbeautiful. It was not like the quiet, lilting romance of French or the gentle refinement of the American South. Chinese sounded pedestrian. Public.

9   In Chinatown, the comings and goings of hundreds of Chinese on their daily tasks sounded chaotic and frenzied. I did not want to be thought of as mad, as talking gibberish. When I spoke English, people nodded at me, smiled sweetly, said encouraging words. Even the people in my culture would cluck and say that I'd do well in life. "My, doesn't she move her lips fast," they would say, meaning that I'd be able to keep up with the world outside Chinatown.

10 My brother was even more fanatical than I about speaking English. He was especially hard on my mother, criticizing her, often cruelly, for her pidgin speech—smatterings of Chinese scattered like chop suey in her conversation. "It's not 'What it is,' Mom," he'd say in exasperation. "It's 'What is it, what is it, what is it!'" Sometimes Mom might leave out an occasional "the" or "a," or perhaps a verb of being. He would stop her in mid-sentence: "Say it again, Mom. Say it right." When he tripped over his own tongue, he'd blame it on her: "See, Mom, it's all your fault. You set a bad example."

11 What infuriated my mother most was when my brother cornered her on her consonants, especially "r." My father had played a cruel joke on Mom by assigning her an American name that her tongue wouldn't allow her to say. No matter how hard she tried, "Ruth" always ended up "Luth" or "Roof."

12 After two years of writing with a moc but and reciting words with multiples of meanings, I finally was granted a cultural divorce. I was permitted to stop Chinese school.

13 I thought of myself as multicultural. I preferred tacos to egg rolls; I enjoyed Cinco de Mayo* more than Chinese New Year. At last, I was one of you; I wasn't one of them. Sadly, I still am.

*Fifth of May, which is a Mexican national holiday celebrating its independence from France in 1862.

Questions for Analysis

1. What is the thesis—the main point—of the essay? Wong develops her essay through a series of contrasts, often using very specific details. Underline each one. How do these contrasts support the thesis?

2. Wong's story combines description, narration, and comparison-contrast. What comparisons or contrasts does she make? Underline them.

3. What did Wong learn in Chinese school? Was it only the Chinese language?

4. Wong says in the eighth paragraph that Chinese "was a source of embarrassment." Why?

5. What do you think Wong means by comments in paragraph 13, especially the concluding sentence?

Suggestions for Writing

1. Explain why Elizabeth Wong was embarrassed by her grandmother's and mother's speech. Cite examples from Wong's essay to support your explanation.

2. Wong probably would never go back to the Chinese language school. Describe a place that you would never go back to again and make clear to the reader why.

3. Describe a behavior of an adult (a parent, perhaps) that used to embarrass you and explain why. Or describe some aspect of your background that used to embarrass you and explain why.

4. Visit a place from your childhood that you haven't been to in a long time. Describe it now and compare it to how you remembered it.

My Fifteen Minutes of Fame
Mark Schlitt

* * * *

Sometimes an (almost) innocent moment can turn into a long nightmare. That's what happened to Mark Schlitt, a former student at Truman College. He survived the experience and went on to a successful college career. As you read his story, notice how Mark gets ever deeper into trouble. And notice how the trouble unfolds in specific details: characters, places, and objects have names.

1   When I was eleven, my brother and I became famous in one day. It all started because we felt persecuted by our mother's mad obsession with wholesome food. Even my little sister stared blankly at her lima beans. We wanted ice cream and my father hadn't uttered the code word—ice—for what seemed like years. We sat in the summer heat and swallowed our vegetables with disgust. Something had to be done, so after dinner we began plotting.

2   The next day my brother kept mom busy while I slid into her bedroom. After finding her purse, I gently pulled a bill from her wallet, put the purse back, and retreated into the hallway. I took a deep breath, stuffed the bill in my pocket, and tried to walk casually past mom without looking at her face.

3   As I went out the front door I gave my brother the sign. He ran out to the curb where I was waiting and panted, "Whaddya get?"

4   Glancing at the kitchen window nervously I said, "She didn't have any change; all I got was a buck." I held out a crumpled bill.

5   "That ain't a buck; that's ten bucks!" my brother said in amazement. Then he looked at me and said, "You're gonna get in trouble for this." I looked at the kitchen window again for signs of my mother. My brother stood on the curb waiting until he asked, "Well, whad're we gonna do now?" I felt like strangling him. My hand fidgeted with the bill in my pocket as I imagined the business end of my mother's ruler on my butt. "Are ya gonna get ice?" my brother said, interrupting my reverie. Then the taste of ice cream mixed with Bosco came to mind. Every time my mother caught me in a lie she washed my mouth out with Lava soap. I imagined looking innocent and saying, "I found the money, Ma; I didn't take it." The Lava soured the Bosco in my brain.

6   But my mom's face never appeared in the window and the sun kept telling me how good and cold ice cream would be.

7   We took off for town, arguing all the way. We decided to change the bill at the Ben Franklin, but we had to buy something to look legitimate. A Duncan see-through yo-yo caught my brother's eye. We argued, agreed on co-ownership, sealed it with spit-on-the-palm, and left. Eight dollars and some change remained. We were rich.

8   The saleslady in the Ben Franklin stared at us like goldfish in her five-and-ten fish bowl as we stood on the sidewalk tearing the plastic wrapper off the yo-yo. I pointed to a

sign on Jansma's Bakery window across the street: "Chocolate Eclairs—Four for a Dollar." We weren't allowed these cream-filled dreams at home—my mother was too mean—so we had to make up for lost time. After buying four eclairs we stood on the boulevard imitating pus-filled sores at each other.

9   But ice cream was still on my mind, so like two millionaires we strolled down to Rexall's. My mother's words, "Thou shalt not . . ." were lost in the noise of the swarm of kids inside the drugstore. My brother and I debated over the cooler filled with ice cream. We couldn't agree on what kind to buy. A small crowd gathered. We decided on a whole carton of Fudgsicles. Suddenly everyone liked us.

10   Even Gustuli, the kid that used to beat me up every day, was my pal. The power of money made my head swell and I couldn't see myself sitting down to lima beans ever again. We were now philanthropists, revered and respected for our wealth. In the alley behind the drugstore we stood like Mafia bosses, Fudgsicles jutting from our mouths.

11   Someone had fireworks for sale, but the deal had to be made in a secret place. We decided to meet in Hank's barn. My brother and I got there before anyone else, so we sat in the sun-lit straw and waited. Hank never seemed to be around and it looked like he never used the barn. As big to me as a cathedral and filled with dark corners and a nice musty smell, Hank's barn was one of my favorite places.

12   We were forbidden to play in the barn because it was dangerous and Hank didn't like trespassers. I sucked on a Fudgsicle and thought about the time Hank had caught my brother and me in his pear tree. He looked old and angry while pointing his gun at us. I thought he would shoot, but he let us down and told us to "get."

13   Finally, the kid with the firecrackers showed up, accompanied by a bunch of other guys. I bought some Chasers and Black Cats while my brother and the other kids ran around the barn hollering. Someone with a deck of cards suggested a poker game. We played cards in the tiny loft room, filled with streaming sun and straw dust, while the little kids played their games on the barn floor. My brother kept taunting me to walk the beam. Bored with cards, I finally agreed, but dared my brother to walk it with me. We went out, one at a time, tippy-toeing over the narrow joist above the barn floor to stand in the middle, where we had to raise one leg and then get back to the wall without falling off.

14   Walking the beam was exciting, but the fireworks in my pocket promised new thrills. My brother and I talked about throwing some in a huge barrel, but someone suggested putting one in a rat-hole. Toward the back of the barn, in one of the stalls, we found a huge rat-hole. We rigged a string of firecrackers together, lit the wick, jammed them into the hole, and backed away as the fireworks fizzled. Smoke trailed from the rat's front door. I looked for water in the barn, but the only buckets around were filled with dust. We tried to smother the fire by stuffing the hole shut. Our friends vanished. A disoriented rat appeared from nowhere and ran for the door where Hank stood holding a shovel.

15   I can't recall much of what happened after that, except the look of sadness on my mom's face when the police officer opened the back door to let us out of the squad car.

Questions for Analysis

1. In the first sentence of the story, what does the word *famous* mean? What kinds of "fame" have the brothers experienced by the end of the story?

2. The opening paragraph establishes a story's setting, telling *where, when, what,* and *who.* Examine the first paragraph of the story. How does each introduce the four Ws of its setting?

3. Soon after the story begins, you probably guess that Mark Schlitt is going to get deeper and deeper into trouble. What, therefore, creates the suspense and tension in the story?

4. The ending of the story is puzzling—and intriguing. Does the barn burn down? Has Mark been arrested? Why do you think Mark decided not to reveal these details?

5. Mark uses a lot of slang when he quotes the dialogue of the speakers. What effect does the slang create?

6. Examine each quotation carefully for its use of capitalization, punctuation, quotation marks, and paragraphing. Make a list of the "rules" for handling quotations. You may wish to compare your list with those of your classmates.

Suggestions for Writing

1. Mark Schlitt doesn't plan on getting into deep trouble, but each event seems to cause another. Summarize these events.

2. Tell the story about a time when you accepted a dare that led to trouble. Don't try to write as long a story as Mark Schlitt's (which actually was eight handwritten pages long).

3. Use dialogue as the primary way to tell the story of a funny moment from your childhood.

Tough Pitches
Ehsan Ghoreishi

* * * *

We sometimes find talent in unexpected places. In the following essay, Ehsan Ghoreishi, a student at Truman College in Chicago, describes an unusual performer. As you read his description, notice the contrasts he draws throughout. Notice, too, how he describes the changing sound of the clarinet and how he analyzes the skill of the performer.

1   Street music performers are all self-employed but not necessarily very talented. Some of those you hear in the subway or on the sidewalk sound like a fifteen-minute-long tape going in loops. Most pedestrians who pass them by pay little attention, but I pay attention because I'm a musician myself. One uniquely talented performer in particular catches my ear.

2   Kaliq plays the clarinet, but not the way you'd hear it in orchestra halls or Jewish weddings. His music is not tied to a music score or a tradition. His clarinet is wild like an alley cat trying to survive on the streets. The notes unexpectedly follow each other. They flow step-by-step, half-note-by-half-note, to the edge of the range of the instrument. Then the sound falls all the way to the low G. After he takes another breath, notes start in motion again, but this time they curve and rise like a Middle Eastern tune until he reaches a high pitch. He holds that pitch while glimpsing at the bucket in front of him. It's lined with a piece of rug so the sound of quarters and dimes won't distract others from adding more to it. Then the high pitch stops without any transition. He puts the clarinet aside and reaches inside the bucket. Then the singles and change all disappear into his pocket.

3   The next song will be as unpredictable as the amount of money thrown in the bucket. The clarinet rises in pitch again. Kaliq gives it a lot of freedom. He improvises and plays along with the traffic, the sirens of ambulances, and the chops of conversations fading away as people walk by. He can't wear gloves in the cold; only his bare fingertips can work on those holes and keys. As a green paper falls in the bucket, he nods to the pedestrians while blowing through the mouthpiece.

4   There are more than five saxophone players in downtown Chicago. Kaliq is the only street performer on clarinet. It's a difficult instrument to master: the clarinet requires a good amount of pressure from the lips and stomach. In fact, one of the main differences between a professional and a non-professional is endurance. And Kaliq's downtown performances last longer than a Wagner opera. He's not a perfectionist, however, for perfectionism can't exist on the street. The streets are too noisy, dusty, and rough.

5   Musicians who play on stage in theaters and clubs are most likely appreciated by the audience who choose to listen to them, but we don't get to choose everything that we

appreciate, like a fine spring day, a beautiful picture on a wall, or a pleasant sound emerging from a clarinet.

Questions for Analysis

1. List the contrasts Ehsan Ghoreishi makes throughout the essay. Why does he make these contrasts?

2. Ehsan also makes some comparisons. Underline them. What function do these comparisons serve?

3. The title of this essay might have more than one meaning. What meanings does it suggest?

4. Do you think that Ehsan believes Kaliq is "professional" in his playing? Why or why not?

5. What challenges does Ehsan say a street musician faces in performing?

6. What point is Ehsan making at the end of his essay? Explain it in your own words.

Suggestions for Writing

1. Explain what makes Kaliq's talent so unique. What makes him different from other players?

2. Describe the talents of an amateur you know. The person could be a musician, athlete, chef, artist, dancer, or any other gifted individual. Give examples to support your description.

3. Have you observed the same homeless person several times? Write a description of the person and his or her activities. Or take ten minutes to walk around or sit in a busy area until you observe someone interesting. (Don't stare, though; you don't want to offend or provoke a fight.) When you get home, write a description of the person you observed. What makes the person interesting?

Two Views of the Mississippi
Mark Twain

* * * *

The context in which we view anything determines how we interpret what we see. How does what we see affect our lives at that moment? In the following essay, Mark Twain contrasts his youthful admiration for the Mississippi River with his adult concerns for navigating a boat across the river. As you read the essay, notice the order in which he first presents the details—and how he later establishes contrasts by presenting the details in precisely the same order. Notice how the word choice in the first description reinforces the beauty and poetry of the river, while the word choice in the later description reinforces the practical applications of what Twain sees.

Mark Twain (1835–1910) was the pen name of Samuel Langhorne Clemens, and, as you can guess from this essay, he worked on a riverboat when he was young. He is the author of many novels, including Tom Sawyer *and* Huckleberry Finn, *and of countless short stories and essays.*

Before reading the essay, use your dictionary to look up the following words:

1. shoal
2. compass (verb)
3. sow (verb)

1   Now when I had mastered the language of this water, and had come to know every trifling feature that bordered the great river as familiarly as I knew the letters of the alphabet, I had made a valuable acquisition. But I had lost something which could never be restored to me while I lived. All the grace, the beauty, the poetry, had gone out of the majestic river! I still keep in mind a certain wonderful sunset which I witnessed when steamboating was new to me. A broad expanse of the river was turned to blood; in the middle distance the red hue brightened into gold, through which a solitary log came floating black and conspicuous; in one place a long, slanting mark lay sparkling upon the water; in another the surface was broken by boiling, tumbling rings that were as many tinted as an opal; where the ruddy flush was faintest was a smooth spot that was covered with graceful circles and radiating lines, ever so delicately traced; the shore on our left was densely wooded, and the somber shadow that fell from this forest was broken in one place by a long, ruffled trail that shone like silver; and high above the forest wall a clean-stemmed dead tree waved a single leafy bough that glowed like a flame in the unobstructed splendor that was flowing from the sun. There were graceful curves, reflected images, woody heights, soft distances; and over the whole scene, far and near, the dissolving lights drifted steadily, enriching it every passing moment with new marvels of coloring.

2   I stood like one bewitched. I drank it in, in a speechless rapture. The world was new to me, and I had never seen anything like this at home. But as I have said, a day came when I began to cease from noting the glories and the charms which the moon and the sun and the twilight wrought upon the river's face; another day came when I ceased altogether to note them. Then, if that sunset scene had been repeated, I should have looked upon it without rapture, and should have commented upon it, inwardly, after this fashion: "This sun means that we are going to have wind tomorrow; that floating log means that the river is rising, small thanks to it; that slanting mark on the water refers to a bluff reef which is going to kill somebody's steamboat one of these nights, if it keeps on stretching out like that; those tumbling 'boils' show a dissolving bar and a changing channel there; the lines and circles in the slick water over yonder are a warning that that troublesome place is shoaling up dangerously; that silver streak in the shadow of the forest is the 'break' from a new snag, and he has located himself in the very best place he could have found to fish for steamboats; that tall dead tree, with a single living branch, is not going to last long, and then how is a body ever going to get through this blind place at night without the friendly old landmark?"

3   No, the romance and beauty were all gone from the river. All the value any feature of it had for me now was the amount of usefulness it could furnish toward compassing the safe piloting of a steamboat. Since those days, I have pitied doctors from my heart. What does the lovely flush in a beauty's cheek mean to a doctor but a "break" that ripples above some deadly disease? Are not all her visible charms sown thick with what are to him the signs and symbols of hidden decay? Does he ever see her beauty at all, or doesn't he simply view her professionally, and comment upon her unwholesome condition all to himself? And doesn't he sometimes wonder whether he has gained most or lost most by learning his trade?

Questions for Analysis

1. What is the thesis of the essay? Where in the first paragraph does Twain state the thesis? Where (in the third paragraph) does he state it more explicitly?

2. What sentence in the second paragraph establishes the transition from a poetic view of the Mississippi to a matter-of-fact, practical view?

3. Compare the language of the two views of the Mississippi. Make a grid on a sheet of paper by drawing a line down the middle. On one side, list the

details of the first description, and on the other side list the parallel details of the second. What do you notice about the language Twain uses for each?

4. At the end of his essay, Twain says he pities doctors. Why? How does the point relate to his two views of the Mississippi?

Suggestions for Writing

1. Discuss whether Twain lost or gained something important as he saw the Mississippi in a different light as an adult.

2. Describe a place that you view differently as an adult from the way you viewed it as a child. Contrast the two views and explain why they have changed.

3. Describe a place that you view differently from the way someone else views it. Explain why your views differ.

Divining the Strange Eating Habits of Kids
Ellen Goodman

* * * *

Everyone who has teenage children or has ever been a teenager should enjoy and understand this essay. As you read it, notice how Ellen Goodman first establishes a "problem" that she then tries to solve. Notice how she then explains her mistaken interpretation of the cause of the problem. Finally, notice her categories or classifications of real causes for the problem.

Ellen Goodman, who was born in 1941, is a Pulitzer Prize winning columnist and the author of many books, including Value Judgments *and (with co-author Patricia O'Brien)* I Know Just What You Mean: The Power of Friendship in Women's Lives. *She has received many awards for her work in furthering the causes of civil rights and the rights of women.*

Before reading the essay, use your dictionary to look up the following words:

1. refrain
2. dire
3. divine (verb)
4. anthropology
5. intrinsic
6. nomadic

1   As a parent who works with words for a living, I have prided myself over many years for a certain skill in breaking the codes of childspeak. I began by interpreting baby talk, moved to more sophisticated challenges like "chill out" and I graduated with "wicked good."

2   One phrase, however, always stumped me. I was unable to crack the meaning of the common cry echoing through most middle-class American households: "There's Nothing to Eat in This House!"

3   This exclamation becomes a constant refrain during the summer months when children who have been released from the schoolhouse door grow attached to the refrigerator door. It is during the summer when the average taxpayer realizes the true cost-effectiveness of school: It keeps kids out of the kitchen for roughly seven hours a day. A feat no parent is able to match.

4   At first, like so many others, I assumed that "NETH!" [as in "Nothing to Eat in This House"] was a straightforward description of reality; if there was NETH, it was because the children had eaten it all. After all, an empty larder is something you come to expect when you live through the locust phase of adolescence.

5   I have one friend with three teenage sons who swears that she doesn't even have to unload her groceries anymore. Her children feed directly from the bags, rather like ponies. I have other friends who buy ingredients for supper only on the way home so that supper doesn't turn into lunch.

6 Over the years, I have considered color-coding food with red, yellow and green stickers. Green for eat. Yellow for eat only if you are starving. Red for "touch this and you die."

7 However, I discovered that these same locusts can stand in front of a relatively full refrigerator while bleating the same pathetic choruses of "NETH! NETH!" By carefully observing my research subjects, I discovered that the demand of "NETH!" may indeed have little to do with the supply.

8 What then does the average underage eater mean when he or she bleats "NETH! NETH!" You will be glad to know that I have finally broken the code for the "nothing" in NETH and offer herewith, free of charge, my translation.

9 NETH includes:

10 1. Any food that must be cooked, especially in a pan or by convectional heat. This covers boiling, frying or baking. Toasting is acceptable under dire conditions.

11 2. Any food that is in a frozen state with the single exception of ice cream. A frozen pizza may be considered "something to eat" only if there is a microwave oven on hand.

12 3. Any food that must be assembled before eaten. This means tuna that is still in a can. It may also mean a banana that has to be peeled, but only in extreme cases. Peanut butter and jelly are exempt from this rule as long as they are on the same shelf beside the bread.

13 4. Leftovers. Particularly if they must be reheated. [See 1.]

14 5. Plain yogurt or anything else that might have been left as a nutrition trap.

15 6. Food that must be put on a plate, or cut with a knife and fork, as opposed to ripped with teeth while watching videos.

16 7. Anything that is not stored precisely at eye level. This includes:

17 8. Any item on a high cupboard shelf, unless it is a box of cookies and:

18 9. Any edible in the back of the refrigerator, especially on the middle shelf.

19 While divining the nine meanings of "NETH!" I should also tell you that I developed an anthropological theory about the eating patterns of young Americans. For the most part, I am convinced, Americans below the age of 20 have arrested their development at the food-gathering stage.

20 They are intrinsically nomadic. Traveling in packs, they engage in nothing more sophisticated than hand-to-mouth dining. They are, in effect, strip eaters who devour the ripest food from one home, and move on to another.

21 Someday, I am sure they will learn about the use of fire, not to mention forks. Someday, they will be cured of the shelf-blindness, the inability to imagine anything hidden behind a large milk carton. But for now, they can only graze. All the rest is NETHing.

Questions for Analysis

1. Who is Ellen Goodman's audience, and what is her purpose in writing to them? Where does she state her point, and what is it?

2. Goodman writes a classification with nine categories. She does not state her criterion for classification. What is it?

3. After listing the nine meanings of NETH, Goodman makes several other observations. Are they irrelevant to her point? Why or why not?

4. How would you describe Goodman's attitude toward teenagers? What evidence from the essay supports your viewpoint?

5. Goodman writes several sentence fragments. Underline them. Why do you think she chooses to do so?

Suggestions for Writing

1. Why do you think that, in Goodman's words, "Americans below the age of 20 have arrested their development at the food-gathering stage"? What from Goodman's categories supports your argument?

2. Write a paragraph or an essay in which you categorize the items that do not get put away or thrown out in a typical teenager's room.

3. Why do teenagers tend to "travel in packs"? Cite examples from your own experience or the experience of people you know to support your explanation.

Sorry for Not Being a Stereotype
Rita Pyrillis

* * * *

The image most Americans have of Indians—or Native Americans—has probably been shaped by movies, myths, and sports teams. Rita Pyrillis, a member of the Cheyenne River Sioux Tribe, has been fighting against stereotyping all her life. As you read her essay, which first appeared in the Chicago Sun-Times, *note her descriptions of how people characterize Indians and how she contrasts those characterizations with her experiences and some facts about Native Americans.*

1 How many of you would know an American Indian if you saw one? My guess is not many. Certainly not the bank teller who called security when an Indian woman—a visiting scholar—tried to cash a check with a tribal identification card. When asked what the problem was, the teller replied: "It must be a scam. Everyone knows real Indians are extinct."

2 And not the woman who cut in front of me at the grocery checkout a few months ago. When I confronted her, she gave me the once over and said: "Why don't you people just go back to your own country."

3 OK, lady, after you, I said, when I thought of it the next morning.

Even though I was born and raised in Chicago, strangers sometimes assume I'm a foreigner. For the record, I'm Native American or Indian—take your pick. I prefer Lakota.

4 Sometimes strangers think I'm from another time. They wonder if I live in a teepee or make my own buckskin clothes or have ever hunted buffalo. They are surprised when I tell them that most Indians live in cities, in houses, and some of us shop at the Gap. I've never hunted a buffalo, although I almost hit a cow once while driving through South Dakota.

5 Sometimes, people simply don't believe I'm Indian. "You don't look Indian," a woman told me once. She seemed disappointed. I asked her what an Indian is supposed to look like. "You know. Long black hair, braids, feathers, beads."

6 Apparently, as Indians go, I'm a flop, an embarrassment to my racial stereotype. My hair is shoulder-length, and I don't feather it, unless you count my unfortunate Farrah Fawcett period in junior high.

7 When you say you're Indian, you better look the part or be prepared to defend yourself. Those are fighting words. When my husband tells people he's German, do they expect him to wear lederhosen and a Tyrolean hat? Of course not. But such are the risks when you dare to be Indian. You don't tug on Superman's cape, and you don't mess around with a man's stereotype.

8 Native American scholar Vine Deloria wrote that of all the problems facing Indian people, the most pressing one is our transparency. Never mind the staggering suicide rate among Native youth, or the fact that Indians are the victims of violent crimes at more than twice the rate of all U.S. residents—our very existence seems to be in question.

9 "Because people can see right through us, it becomes impossible to tell truth from fiction or fact from mythology," he wrote. "The American public feels most comfortable with the mythical Indians of stereotype-land who were always THERE."

10 Sure. Stereotypes don't have feelings, or children who deserve to grow up with images that reflect who they are—not perfect images, but realistic ones. While Little Black Sambo and the Frito Bandito have gone the way of minstrel shows, Indians are still battling a red-faced, big-nosed Chief Wahoo and other stereotypes. No wonder people are confused

about who Indians really are. When we're not hawking sticks of butter, or beer or chewing tobacco, we're scalping settlers. When we're not passed out drunk, we're living large off casinos. When we're not gyrating in Pocahoochie outfits at the Grammy Awards, we're leaping through the air at football games, represented by a white man in red face. One era's minstrel show is another's halftime entertainment. It's enough to make Tonto speak in multiple syllables.

11   And it's enough to make hard-working, decent Indian folks faced with more urgent problems take to the streets in protest. Personally, I'd rather take in my son's Little League game, but as long as other people insist on telling me when to be honored or offended, or how I should look or talk or dance, I will keep telling them otherwise. To do nothing would be less than honorable.

Questions for Analysis

1. Why does Rita Pyrillis begin by addressing her audience as *you* and then tell two short stories about her experiences?

2. Pyrillis develops her thesis through a number of contrasts. Find several of these contrasts and place a star next to them.

3. What are some of the stereotypes about Native Americans that Pyrillis cites?

4. Halfway through the essay, Pyrillis makes this rather puzzling comment: "Native American scholar Vine Deloria wrote that of all the problems facing Indian people, the most pressing one is our transparency." What do you think this means? How does the rest of the quotation help you understand?

5. Pyrillis doesn't state her thesis directly but suggests it in the last two paragraphs. Write a statement of the thesis in a sentence or two.

Suggestions for Writing

1. Describe a time when you or someone you know suffered (or benefited) from stereotyping. What happened? How did the incident end?

2. Contrast one or two incorrect perceptions some people may have about you with how your perceive yourself.

3. Define *stereotype*. Develop your definition through examples.

4. Rita Pyrillis has encountered many instances of stereotyping but doesn't consider herself a "victim." Based on her essay, write a description of Pyrillis.

5. Pyrillis refers to some stock characters and stereotypes of the past. Look up Farrah Fawcett, Little Black Sambo, Frito Bandito, and Tonto on the Web. What kind of stereotype does each represent (one is a real person)? Classify each as a stereotype, and explain how stereotypes limit real people.

The Writing on the Wall
Adapted from *The People's Almanac*

* * * *

There are many things around us that we see every day but don't think about very much. One of the traits of a good writer is to consider and analyze these things and to discuss them in ways that make us think about them. The following essay on graffiti is an example. As you read it, notice that it begins with a definition and then continues with a three-part classification. Notice the examples of each part of the classification. And notice the purpose of the essay—to entertain.

Before you read the essay, use your dictionary to define the following words:

1. archaeologist
2. motive
3. vandalism

1   The term *graffiti*—a plural noun, by the way—comes from an Italian word that means scribbling or scratching, and archaeologists use it to refer to the writings and drawings on the walls of caves or ancient buildings. Most people, however, are familiar with modern graffiti, such as the writings and pictures found on the walls of washrooms, buildings, subway cars, and billboards. Those with a mind toward classifying these scribbles have divided them into three types, based on the motives of the graffiti-maker: identity graffiti, message or opinion graffiti, and art graffiti. A fourth type, dialogue graffiti, overlaps the other three.

2   Identity graffiti represent an attempt by someone (let's assume he is male) to immortalize his existence by writing his name and the date, announcing his current romance ("John loves Mary"), or simply stating, "I was here." This urge to leave a personal imprint seems to be old as the human race. Signatures of ancient Greek soldiers are still scratched on the sphinx and on the Great Pyramid at Giza in Egypt.

3   The writer of messages or opinions likes to tell the world exactly what is on his or her mind. Most message graffiti make political statements, although some also deal with philosophy, religion, the arts, and sex. Here are a few examples:
     "We are the people our parents warned us about."
     "Carry me back to old virginity."
     "May your life be like a roll of toilet paper—long and useful."

4   The drawers of art graffiti display their greatest achievements in big cities, where inner-city kids decorate walls with spray-painted creations. Instead of leaving a simple message, these unpaid exterior decorators write their own names (or the names of their gangs) in swirls, curlicues, and flourishes of all colors. Some graffiti artists cover a building wall with complex designs or murals. Although most of these graffiti are only vandalism, some spray-painters have been paid to do murals for office buildings. An art gallery in New York even held a graffiti exhibit.

5   Sometimes graffiti-makers start talking back to each other, and a graffiti dialogue is born. These dialogues can develop into long-winded conversations, with several scribblers getting into the act. A subway poster for a job retraining program showed a complicated electrical unit with a question written underneath: "When this circuit learns your job, what are you going to do?" Then came the graffiti responses: "Go on relief," "Pull the plug," and "Become a circuit breaker." Another poster asked, "Did you make New York dirty today?" and received the obvious comeback: "New York makes me dirty every day."

6   No matter what their purpose, graffiti are ways for ordinary people to communicate. Graffiti have several advantages: they are free, uncensored, and available to everyone. Graffiti have been both hated and enjoyed throughout history and will no doubt survive, in spite of occasional cleanup and paint jobs. A scribbler in a New York washroom summed it up: "Everything has its place, even the stupid writings in this cold john."

Questions for Analysis

1. What are the four categories of graffiti discussed in the essay? What criterion is used for classifying them? Why does the fourth type overlap the other categories?

2. What phrases at the beginning of paragraphs 2 through 5 introduce the category to be explained and illustrated? Are any of the categories defined? Which ones?

3. What examples for each category does the essay cite? Do any paragraphs include more than one example?

Suggestions for Writing

1. In your own words, write a summary of the reasons that people make graffiti. Do not copy from the essay.

2. Choose another way that people often communicate: by letters, memos, e-mails, text messaging, telephone, messages left on the refrigerator, or messages left on telephone answering machines. Divide the subject into categories (for example, the types of messages left on the refrigerator) and illustrate each category with one or more examples.

3. Do you or the people you know speak differently to different groups—to people your age of the same sex or opposite sex, to parents, to grandparents, to young bosses, to teachers? Choose several ways in which the speaking is different, and illustrate each one.

Running with Walker
Robert Hughes

* * * *

Walker Hughes was born with a rare genetic deficiency: autism. Now over twenty-one years of age, with an IQ of 129, he rarely talks, does not seem to respond to people in normal ways, and often seems to panic in unfamiliar situations. Despite enormous obstacles, his parents, Ellen and Robert Hughes, have struggled to provide Walker with a stable, loving environment—and to understand and interpret Walker's attempts to communicate with them and others. Unfortunately, doctors, psychiatrists, and ordinary people have been less informed about Walker's condition and less understanding. The following excerpt from Running with Walker *describes one of Hughes's encounters with people who see Walker as some kind of freak—and how Hughes responds to their response.*

Before reading the selection, use your dictionary to look up the following words:

1. extravaganza
2. mockery
3. belligerent
4. obsess

1   On a lovely spring day at the south end of Lincoln Park, Walker and I were going along in our fashion: I was jogging, Walker was skip-leaping with his fingers in his ears and grinning. Three young men between eighteen and twenty-two or so approached us from the opposite direction and one of them pointed at Walker and laughed. He started to mimic Walker; then one of his pals joined in. Soon all three were skip-leaping with their fingers in their ears. Instantly furious despite the fact that such open mockery is very rare, I made an effort to ignore them. I thought, *Don't stoop to their level, Bob.* As they passed I smiled at Walker, then looked ahead. When they were behind us I said: "Those guys are jerks, Walker. Don't let them bother you."

2   But deep in my brain I was busy stooping to their level as fast as I could. I started inventing put-downs that would leave them feeling guilty about their behavior and their puny worthless selves. *That's really big of you pathetic little twits, mocking a handicapped child.* [pregnant pause] *Have a nice day!*

3   Ever the English teacher, I wasn't satisfied with this. As we passed the statue of Abraham Lincoln I worked on my scathing speech some more. I decided my first draft wasn't sarcastic enough. *Very clever, gentlemen. It takes really big men to mock a disabled child.* [Longer, more threatening pause. They think, Will he hurt us?] *Have a nice day!*

4   I was satisfied with this for a moment or two, but somehow it lacked real bite. The "Have a nice day," I decided, was terrific, but there was something wrong. By now we were in front of the Cardinal's mansion and Walker was jubilant: smiling, looking at the Victorian

redbrick many-chimneyed extravaganza with great pleasure. He probably expected me to say something about it as I usually did, but I had my work cut out for me.

5   Too wordy, I concluded. Better just to stop in front of the punks, hold Walker's hand, and stare at them until they look at me in stunned fright. Then pause a few moments, smile a little half smile, and say, *Have a nice day.*

6   How perfect! I thought. That's the ticket! But still . . .

7   As we rounded the corner and passed the International College of Surgeons on the inner drive, I was again fussing with my draft. Walker was smiling at the huge statue of a noble surgeon gallantly lifting a sick man; only today the good doctor was sporting two pigeons on his head. But I was full of one thought: the joy of putting those creeps in their place with the brilliant sting of my sarcasm.

8   *I'll teach 'em to mess with an English professor!*

9   We made our way to Chicago and State, a very long distance for us, and down the stairs to the subway platform. After a few minutes Walker got tired of waiting, or maybe my obsessed mood had finally become too much for him. He started yelling and attacking me, trying to bite my hand and flailing around. This had happened before on subway platforms and it always drove me nuts: the danger of falling onto the tracks, the amplified sound of his shouting, the alarm on the faces of the waiting passengers, the need for me to pretend to be in control—it was all more than I could deal with.

10   While I wrestled with him I heard a deep voice shout: "WHAT'S THE MATTER WITH HIM?" It didn't sound like the voice of help. It was a new tone to me, something like belligerent curiosity. Somebody actually expected me to carry on a shouting conversation about Walker's condition! As I struggled with Walker, again I heard: "I'm TALKING to you! I SAID, What's the MATTER with him!"

11   Standing behind Walker now, pinning his arms behind him and pushing his head down, I muttered: "None of your business."

12   "WHA'D YOU SAY!" the voice bellowed, this time with straight belligerent belligerence.

13   Then I saw him. He was built like an NFL lineman, slightly taller than I and a good forty pounds heavier. He was dressed in a dirty army fatigue jacket and dirty black sweatshirt and he was walking rapidly toward us. "WHA'D YOU SAY? NOBODY TALKS TO ME LIKE THAT!" For some reason my exquisite put-down—"Have a nice day!"—did not spring to my lips. I seized Walker's hand and ran with him, yanking him up the stairs: "Let's go, man! Go . . . go . . . go!" while the angry voice echoed up from the tunnel below.

14   When we got through the turnstile, up another flight of steps and back out on the street, I saw to my relief that he hadn't followed us. (It's one thing to kill a guy, apparently, but another to pay train fare twice in order to do it.) Walker was in a completely different mood, laughing and relaxed. I started laughing too.

15   I made a resolution: *Bob, from this moment on, you will control your anger. You will not obsess about people who annoy you. You will be happy in your heart, for Walker's sake and for your own.*

16   And for the next day or so, that was precisely what I did.

Questions for Analysis

1. Underline the words or phrases that establish the four Ws—*who, what, where,* and *when.*

2. What conflict does Robert Hughes introduce in the first paragraph? What other conflicts occur throughout the story? How are these conflicts resolved?

3. Walker doesn't act "normal" at several points in the story. What in his behavior seems unusual?

4. People with autism supposedly don't notice and react to the feelings of others, but Walker certainly does. How does his father feel at various stages in the story, and how does Walker react to those feelings?

5. Hughes, the professor of English, plans what he will say to the young men as if he were drafting and revising an essay. Identify his "drafts" and "revisions."

Suggestions for Writing

1. In the story you've just read, the young men react in different ways to the behavior of Walker and his father. Analyze those reactions, explaining why you think they occurred.

2. Describe a time when you witnessed an act of cruelty. Explain what happened and why you think it happened.

3. Have you ever helped someone in a dangerous or threatening situation? Describe what happened.

Block That Ringtone!
Sam Lubell

* * * *

The cellphone has become a large part of our lives, but not always in helpful ways. The following article, which appeared in the New York Times *on April 8, 2004, discusses ways in which businesses and other institutions (and some people) are trying to limit the use of cellphones. As you read it, note how it explores the pros and cons of limiting cellphone use—and how it discusses the legal issues involved.*

Before reading the article, use your dictionary to look up the following words:

1. aria
2. disrupt
3. render
4. inoperable
5. proponent
6. rudimentary
7. desist
8. deride

1 It could happen on a train, in a restaurant or during an awe-inspiring aria at a performance of "Carmen": a neighbor's cellphone starts bleating the theme song from "Friends," disrupting the mood and setting nerves on edge. Wouldn't it be great, you think to yourself, if this couldn't happen?

2 Others are thinking likewise, including companies and researchers developing or already selling devices that render cellphones inoperable in certain locations. Methods include jammers that interfere with cellphone frequencies, routing systems that mute phones' ringers in specific places, sensors that detect active cellphones and building materials that block cellphone waves.

3 Proponents say that such measures are more effective than "no cellphone" signs, "quiet cars" on trains or even legal restrictions (like a law prohibiting cellphone use during performances, enacted by the New York City Council last year).

4 The concerns go beyond mere annoyance: casinos are seeking to stop phone-based cheating; prison authorities want to guard against phone use by inmates for drug deals or other forms of wrongdoing. With the rise of camera cellphones have come privacy concerns that have made locker rooms and other areas no-phone zones.

5 "At some point the American public will become so frustrated with the abuse of cellphones that it will rise up and yell that something must be done," said Dave Derosier, chief executive of Cell Block Technologies, based in Fairfax, Va., which is developing a transmitter the size of a smoke detector that relays signals of "no service" to cellphone frequencies, prompting them to send calls to voice mail.

6 Cell Block's products are slightly more sophisticated versions of what is probably the most widespread method of stopping cellphone use, called jamming, which renders phones inoperable by disrupting the connection between cellphone towers and cellphones. Jamming devices overpower phones' frequencies with especially strong signals and

often with loud noise. Such devices can be found on eBay and at Web sites like global-gadgetuk.com.

7   That site says it has sold thousands of devices to theaters, businesses, military users and individuals. The jammers range from $200 for a rudimentary hand-held model to nearly $10,000 for suitcase-sized gear sold to governments and the military, with the price usually based on the signal range and the likelihood of disrupting cellular activity.

8   Other means are also in development, from devices that merely detect cellphone use (and prompt users to desist) to construction methods that render cellphones inoperable.

9   But not everyone finds this trend encouraging. Cellphone industry experts and federal regulators deride jammers in particular as unlawful, unethical and even dangerous.

10   "You're not allowed to barricade the street in front of your house because you don't like hearing an ambulance," said Travis Larson, a spokesman for the Cellular Telephone Industry Association, who asserts that blocking systems inhibit customers' rights and can block emergency calls. "Just like roads, the airwaves are public property."

11   The Federal Communications Commission points specifically to the Federal Communications Act of 1934, which says that "no person shall willfully or maliciously interfere with or cause interference to any radio communications" licensed by the government.

12   "It is the FCC's authority and obligation to determine which transmissions are lawful," said Lauren Patrich, a spokeswoman for the commission's wireless bureau. "If the FCC doesn't have that authority, then what's its point?" Fines for violations can reach $11,000 for a single offense.

13   Mr. Derosier said that devices like Cell Block's are "questionably legal" in the United States, but he added that with proper disclosure and provisions made for emergencies, there is no reason that they should not be used. The devices are legal in Japan, France and Eastern Europe, and in most of South Asia, Africa and the Middle East, he said.

14   Mr. Derosier said that prospective buyers in those areas included prisons, mosques, banks and embassies. Globalgadgetuk's owner, Michael Menage, said he believes that "people should be able to do whatever they want in their own spaces." He said his largest group of customers comes from the United States, which he said is evidence that there is a need for such technology here.

Questions for Analysis

1. Sam Lubell begins the article by addressing the reader directly (with "you think to yourself"). Why?

2. What general problem does Sam Lubell establish at the beginning of the article, and what proposed solution does he identify?

3. What two organizations, specifically, does Lubell say would like to block cellphone use? Why?

4. Which organizations have bought cellphone jamming devices?

5. Lubell cites arguments for and against blocking cellphone use. Does he seem to favor one argument over the other? How do you know?

6. What countries already use jamming devices and where do they install them?

Suggestions for Writing

1. Summarize the main arguments for and against blocking cellphone signals in Sam Lubell's article.

2. Describe how the cellphone has changed the way we act in business or in social situations.

3. Explain how a cellphone has benefited you or someone else. Perhaps you could discuss a time when it helped in an emergency or in some other situation.

Homeless
Anna Quindlen

* * * *

Because homeless people in the United States do not register with any government bureau or have any "official" status, it is impossible to determine how many people live on the streets, in cars, or in shelters throughout the country. Indeed, estimates of the number of homeless people range from 150,000 to 3.5 million. The homeless are certainly visible to us as they sit or sleep on park benches and beg on the streets. But how often do we tend to ignore them, as if they were invisible—people without past lives, present concerns, and personal futures? Anna Quindlen refuses to do so. In the following essay, which appears in her book Thinking Out Loud, *she demands that we recognize their humanity. As you read the essay, note how she supports her claims through contrasts between her life and the lives of the homeless—and, more importantly, through specific examples.*

Anna Quindlen (born 1952) was a reporter for the New York Post *and the* New York Times, *and, for many years, a columnist for the* Times. *She is the author of four novels, four nonfiction books, and two children's books. She currently writes a biweekly column for* Newsweek *magazine.*

1   Her name was Ann, and we met in the Port Authority Bus Terminal several Januarys ago. I was doing a story on homeless people. She said I was wasting my time talking to her; she was just passing through, although she'd been passing through for more than two weeks. To prove to me that this was true, she rummaged through a tote bag and a manila envelope and finally unfolded a sheet of typing paper and brought out her photographs.

2   They were not pictures of family, or friends, or even a dog or cat, its eyes brown-red in the flashbulb's light. They were pictures of a house. It was like a thousand houses in a hundred towns, not suburb, not city, but somewhere in between, with aluminum siding and a chain-link fence, a narrow driveway running up to a one-car garage and a patch of backyard. The house was yellow. I looked on the back for a date or a name, but neither was there. There was no need for discussion. I knew what she was trying to tell me, for it was something I had often felt. She was not adrift, alone, anonymous, although her bags and her raincoat with the grime shadowing its creases had made me believe she was. She had a house, or at least once upon a time had had one. Inside were curtains, a couch, a stove, potholders. You are where you live. She was somebody.

3   I've never been very good at looking at the big picture, taking the global view, and I've always been a person with an overactive sense of place, the legacy of an Irish grandfather. So it is natural that the thing that seems most wrong with the world to me right now is that there are so many people with no homes. I'm not simply talking about shelter from the elements, or three square meals a day or a mailing address to which the welfare people can send the check—although I know that all these are important for survival. I'm talking about a home, about precisely those kinds of feelings that have wound up in cross-stitch and French knots on samplers over the years.

4   Home is where the heart is. There's no place like it. I love my home with a ferocity totally out of proportion to its appearance or location. I love dumb things about it: the hot-water heater, the plastic rack you drain dishes in, the roof over my head, which occasionally leaks. And yet it is precisely those dumb things that make it what it is—a place of certainty, stability, predictability, privacy, for me and for my family. It is where I live. What more can you say about a place than that? That is everything.

5   Yet it is something that we have been edging away from gradually during my lifetime and the lifetimes of my parents and grandparents. There was a time when where you lived often was where you worked and where you grew the food you ate and even where you were buried. When that era passed, where you lived at least was where your parents had lived and where you would live with your children when you became enfeebled. Then, suddenly, where you lived was where you lived for three years, until you could move on to something else and something else again.

6   And so we have come to something else again, to children who do not understand what it means to go to their rooms because they have never had a room, to men and women whose fantasy is a wall they can paint a color of their own choosing, to old people reduced to sitting on molded plastic chairs, their skin blue-white in the lights of a bus station, who pull pictures of houses out of their bags. Homes have stopped being homes. Now they are real estate.

7   People find it curious that those without homes would rather sleep sitting up on benches or huddled in doorways than go to shelters. Certainly some prefer to do so because they are emotionally ill, because they have been locked in before and they are damned if they will be locked in again. Others are afraid of the violence and trouble they may find there. But some seem to want something that is not available in shelters, and they will not compromise, not for a cot, or oatmeal, or a shower with special soap that kills the bugs. "One room," a woman with a baby who was sleeping on her sister's floor, once told me, "painted blue." That was the crux of it; not size or location, but pride of ownership. Painted blue.

8   This is a difficult problem, and some wise and compassionate people are working hard at it. But in the main I think we work around it, just as we walk around it when it is lying on the sidewalk or sitting in the bus terminal—the problem, that is. It has been customary to take people's pain and lessen our own participation in it by turning it into an issue, not a collection of human beings. We turn an adjective into a noun: the poor, not poor people; the homeless, not Ann or the man who lives in the box or the woman who sleeps on the subway grate.

9   Sometimes I think we would be better off if we forgot about the broad strokes and concentrated on the details. Here is a woman without a bureau. There is a man with no mirror, no wall to hang it on. They are not the homeless. They are people who have no homes. No drawer that holds the spoons. No window to look out upon the world. My God. That is everything.

Questions for Analysis

1. Why does Anna Quindlen begin her essay with the story of Ann? If she had started instead with paragraph 3 ("I've never been very good at looking at the big picture . . ."), how would that have affected our reactions?

2. In paragraph 2, Quindlen describes specific details about the house in the pictures. What effects do these have on us?

3. Throughout the essay, Quindlen cites specific examples to back up her claims. Locate these examples, and discuss their role in her argument.

4. In the last paragraphs of the essay, Quindlen contrasts "broad strokes" with "details"—and returns to the story of Ann. What point is she making?

5. In the next-to-last sentence, Quindlen says, "My God." What effect does that expression have?

Suggestions for Writing

1. What is a home? Write a paragraph or an essay comparing or contrasting Quindlen's viewpoint with your own.

2. Quindlen claims that turning homelessness into "an issue" avoids the problem. Explain what she means, and give examples from the essay or your own experience to support your explanation.

3. Discuss another important issue today (health care, street crime, unemployment, college tuition, racial discrimination, gay marriage—you choose the topic), and cite examples that support your claims. Consider using Quindlen's strategy of focusing on one individual or family.

The Power of One: The $10 Solution
Jeffrey D. Sachs

* * * *

The gap between the developed nations and the poor nations of Africa—especially in terms of disease and hunger—is widening so much that we as individuals may feel powerless to act. But Jeffrey D. Sachs knows otherwise. In the following article, which appeared in Time *magazine on January 15, 2007, he proposes a simple solution for eradicating a terrible disease affecting large segments of Africa: malaria. As you read his argument, notice how he establishes a cause-and-effect relationship between the disease, poverty, overpopulation, and violent political unrest.*

Jeffrey D. Sachs (born 1954) is the director of the Earth Institute at Columbia University and the president and cofounder of the Millennium Promise Alliance, which aims to eliminate extreme poverty around the world. He is the author of hundreds of articles and many books, including The End of Poverty. *In 2004 and 2005* Time *magazine named as one of the world's 100 most influential leaders.*

Before reading the article, use your dictionary to look up the following words:

1. ineffable
2. succumb
3. insidious
4. jihad
5. paradoxically
6. ecological

1   Listen for a moment to the beautiful and dignified voices of Africa's mothers. Despite their burdens of poverty and hunger, they will tell you not of their endless toil but of their hopes for their children. But softly, ever so softly, they will also recount the children they have lost, claimed by a sudden fever, children who died in their arms as they were carried in a desperate half-day's journey by foot from the village to the nearest clinic.

2   This is the ineffable sadness of malaria. Another African child has died of malaria since you started reading this article. Perhaps 2 million children in all will succumb this year.

3   The long-term consequences are insidious as well as tragic and even relate to the ability of the U.S. to prevail against the jihadists. Not only does malaria sap worker productivity and scare away business investment, but also, paradoxically, increases the rate of population growth. Instead of having two or three children, couples in a malarial region often choose to have six or seven—unsure how many will survive.

4   Malaria also helps create a poverty trap with special ferocity in Africa. By a quirk of ecological fate, Africa has the world's heaviest toll of this disease, the result of its tropical climate, its specific types of mosquitoes, and its limitless mosquito-breeding sites. Children are struck down in unmatched numbers. And Africa's disease toll from malaria may be even higher than previously recognized. Recent research has found that malaria infection increases the likelihood that an HIV-infected individual will transmit the AIDS virus to others. Many millions are also infected simultaneously with malaria and worm infections, multiplying the disease burden.

5   Osama bin Laden has called for jihad in Africa, trying to capitalize on its extreme poverty. Here's how we can respond. While malaria has shaped Africa's poverty trap, it is a trap that can finally be unlocked. Spectacular technological advances, some stunningly simple, offer practical and low-cost solutions. The most obvious one is insecticide-treated bed nets, now cleverly engineered to last up to five years. The cost to manufacture, ship, and distribute each net is $10. A new generation of medicines based on artemisinin, an extract from a traditional Chinese herbal remedy, is remarkably effective in treating cases of the disease, at a cost of about a dollar per treatment.

6   Yet these solutions still aren't reaching the vast proportion of Africans in need. Hard as it is for us to imagine, Africa's households simply can't afford even $10 for a net, or a dollar for medicines when a child falls sick. Nor can African governments carry these costs on meager budgets or take extra vital steps to train local health workers and ensure that every village has reliable access to effective medicines.

7   Here is where you and I come in. Considering the costs of the nets, medicines and other components of malaria control, a comprehensive program would cost about $4.50 per African at risk, or about $3 billion a year for the whole continent. This is an amount that is too large for Africa but truly tiny for the rich world.

8   Let me put the $3 billion in perspective: there are a billion of us in the high-income world—that amounts to $3 a person, or one Starbucks coffee a year. It's around 12.5% of the estimated $24 billion in Wall Street's Christmas bonuses.

9   We should bring forth armies of Red Cross volunteers to distribute bed nets and to offer village-based training for tens of thousands of villages across Africa. In a brilliant demonstration of people power and modern logistics, Red Cross volunteers distributed nets to more than half the households of Togo in 2004 and Niger in 2005 in a matter of a few days in each country. That successful delivery model should be replicated across Africa, by 2010 if not earlier, but this will depend on mobilizing the needed resources.

10   New citizens' movements, including Malaria No More *(malarianomore.org)* and Nothing but Nets *(nothingbutnets.net)*, have been established to achieve the needed breakthrough. We can each contribute $10 for a bed net. We can each learn more about the disease and become antimalaria leaders in our communities, schools, churches and businesses. We can urge our governments to work with the private sector and citizen's groups to win the fight against malaria during this decade. President Bush recently took a good step in scaling up the U.S. government's malaria-control efforts, but much more needs to be done to ensure that aid reaches the hundreds of millions of Africans at risk.

11   Together we can choose peace over jihad and life over violence. Through our common resolve, we can prove the power we each have to save a life.

Questions for Analysis

1. In the opening paragraph, Jeffrey D. Sachs describes the voices of Africa's mothers as "beautiful and dignified," and says they speak "softly, ever so softly." Why?

2. At several places, Sachs makes a point through comparisons. What comparisons do you find, and what points do they make?

3. Sachs develops his argument largely by describing the effects of malaria. What are those effects, and are they limited only to death from disease?

4. Sachs ends his article for a plea for us to choose "peace over jihad and life over violence." What is he referring to?

Suggestions for Writing

1. Write a one-paragraph summary of the main points of Sachs's article. Then respond to some aspect of his argument. Do you agree or disagree? Explain why, and support your claims with specific references to the article (facts, figures, even short quotations).

2. Describe a time when a small act of kindness (an action, a gift, a loan) helped someone. What happened, and what were the effects of that act?

3. Consider a problem in your community or at your college that could be solved or at least made better through some simple plan of action. Explain that plan and how it would work. But don't try to be a "great philosopher"; keep the plan simple.

This Man

Gary Soto

* * * *

How do we deal with aftermath of a tragedy, whether we caused it or were its victims? Do we feel guilt, shame, anger, or something else? And how do we express, or try to avoid expressing, those feelings? Gary Soto explores this complex question in the following essay from his memoir, The Effects of Knut Hamsun on a Fresno Boy, *published in 1983. As you read the essay, note the contrasting feelings and actions that Soto explores, and note, too, how he explores them through specific detail, both real and imagined.*

1   My father died in an accident, and it was no accident that the man who fell on him and broke my father's neck never again came to our house, though he was a friend of the family who lived only five houses away. He was that person who walked past our house every day on his way to Charlie's Grocery for meat, a head of lettuce, milk for his children. After our father's death he took a different route; he chose instead Sarah Street to get to the grocery.

2   I wonder how it was for him, what he felt. Nearly thirty years later I can see him in my mind. He's on the couch, tired from the work of candling eggs for Safeway, his boots off and shirt open; or it's summer, hot, and he's in the back yard staring transfixed at the water running from a hose into the garden. I see his wife shout from the kitchen that she needs butter. He gets up slowly and laces up his boots; he turns away from the river of water, already drying between the rows of squash and tomato plants, and coils the hose. He takes the quarter from his wife and starting off to the store, thinks of Manuel, our father, maybe sees his face whole, maybe sees his face twisted and on the ground, the blood already drying like the water in the garden. But how much? How much of our father was on his mind? Did the kids in the street distract him, the neighbors on porches, a barking dog? Did he sing inside his head, worry about bills, maybe think of work and the eggs that traveled endlessly on the conveyor? He bought his butter, went home to eat with his children, who after the accident never came over to play with us. We waved to them when we walked past their yard and, behind their fence, they waved back.

3   Shortly after the accident we moved away from our south Fresno neighborhood, and he and his family became those names we never said in our house. Something happened in our family without us being aware, a quiet between mother and children settled on us like dust. We went to school, ate, watched television that wasn't funny, and because Mother never said anything, Father, too, became that name we never said in our house. His grave was something we saw in photographs; his remembrance those clothes hanging in the back of the closet.

4   I remembered this man from the old street when I saw him years later buying cigarettes at a gas station. I was filling the tires on my bike. His car was large, and he himself was large, his girth like a tree: I like to think he was eating for two, himself and father, who was inside like a worm taking his share; that after all those years he still thought of Manuel and the afternoon when he climbed that ladder with a tray of nails on his shoulder, lost his balance, and fell. This is my hope, for my sake and this man's, because we should remember the dead, call them back in memory to feel their worth.

5   He must have felt guilt and shame, or otherwise he would have walked up our street to the grocery or said more than "Hi" to me at the gas station. But it's not guilt or shame that I want to feel for him but sadness, that a man like so many others is dead and the photographs we own do no good in assembling Father once again into flesh and bone. We lived poor years because he died. We suffered quietly and hurt even today. Shouldn't this mean something to him?

6   Sadness not guilt. I have felt both. As a kid I often thought about the sea, yearned for the sea, and imagined that where I lived was the wrong place; that being poor and Mexican was wrong. During those years I thought of the sea a lot, not of Father, and am ashamed of this. It's so strange to me now: I had maps of the sea, books, model ships I set proudly on doilies for visitors to notice. I had questions for teachers—How big was

Atlantis? Did the Vikings really discover America? Are Eskimos Chinese who live in the cold? This went on for years, my fascination with the sea, and for years I never dared mention my father to my mother or my sister and brother. He was gone, and we were here, and the man who did this to us was nowhere to be found.

7   It would take a doctor to explain our loss, or a wise man to sit me down and quiet my nervous knee that I can't stop. It's strange; my brother has the same tic. When we meet for Thanksgiving, his knee, like mine, jumps up and down. It won't stop. When I ask, "What's wrong," he says, with his arms folded behind his head, "Nothing. Nothing at all."

Questions for Analysis

1. Gary Soto claims that "it was no accident" that the man responsible for his father's death "never again came to our house." What do you think Soto means by this claim?

2. In paragraph 2, Soto cites a long imaginary example of the man doing simple, even trivial, household tasks. Why?

3. In paragraph 6, Soto claims he feels sadness and guilt. About whom does he feel sadness? And about whom does he feel guilt?

4. In the same paragraph, Soto also claims he feels ashamed. Is this feeling justified?

Suggestions for Writing

1. How does Soto feel about the man who accidentally killed his father? How do you know?

2. Central to Soto's essay is the refusal—or inability—to discuss the past. How might his feelings have changed if the family had been able to communicate with each other?

3. Describe a time when you or someone close to you was involved in an accident (it doesn't have to be tragic). What happened, and what did people do to help—or not help?

4. Describe a time when you felt guilty or ashamed for something that was not your fault. What happened, and why did you have these feelings?

The Boy Left Behind
Sonia Nazario

* * * *

Illegal immigration, especially from Latin America, is one of the most controversial issues of our times. Whatever opinions people may hold on the subject, however, they cannot ignore the horrible conditions, and incredible risks, many of the immigrants endure as they cross the border between Mexico and the United States. The following excerpt from Enrique's Journey *relates the true story of a seventeen-year-old Honduran boy who succeeds in his eighth attempt to locate his mother in North Carolina, despite terrible hardships—wading through chest-deep water (he couldn't swim), clinging to the sides or tops of boxcars, encountering bandits and corrupt police, and working at odd jobs to pay for his food and shelter.*

Sonia Nazario (born 1960), a reporter and feature writer for the Los Angeles Times, *won the Pulitzer Prize for Feature Writing in 2003 for a series of articles on Latin American children who immigrate to the United States in hopes of reuniting with their parents. The series won more than a dozen additional awards, including a second Pulitzer Prize for Feature Photography. In 2006, Nazario expanded her series into the full-length book from which this excerpt is taken.*

Before you begin reading, use your dictionary to look up the term Holy Grail.

1   The boy does not understand.

2   His mother is not talking to him. She will not even look at him. Enrique has no hint of what she is going to do.

3   Lourdes knows. She understands, as only a mother can, the terror she is about to inflict, the ache Enrique will feel, and finally the emptiness.

4   What will become of him? Already he will not let anyone else feed or bathe him. He loves her deeply, as only a son can. With Lourdes, he is openly affectionate, "*Dame pico, mami.* Give me a kiss, Mom," he pleads, over and over, pursing his lips. With Lourdes, he is a chatterbox. "*Mira, mami.* Look, Mom," he says softly, asking her questions about everything he sees. Without her, he is so shy it is crushing.

5   Slowly, she walks out onto the porch. Enrique clings to her pant leg. Beside her, he is tiny. Lourdes loves him so much she cannot bring herself to say a word. She cannot carry his picture. It would melt her resolve. She cannot hug him. He is five years old.

6   They live on the outskirts of Tegucigalpa, in Honduras. She can barely afford food for him and his sister, Belky, who is seven. She's never been able to buy them a toy or a birthday cake. Lourdes, twenty-four, scrubs other people's laundry in a muddy river. She goes door to door, selling tortillas, used clothes, and plantains.

7   She fills a wooden box with gum and crackers and cigarettes, and she finds a spot where she can squat on a dusty sidewalk next to the downtown Pizza Hut and sell the items to passersby. The sidewalk is Enrique's playground.

8   They have a bleak future. He and Belky are not likely to finish grade school. Lourdes cannot afford uniforms or pencils. Her husband is gone. A good job is out of the question.

9   Lourdes knows of only one place that offers hope. As a seven-year-old child, delivering tortillas her mother made to wealthy homes, she glimpsed this place on other people's television screens. The flickering images were a far cry from Lourdes's childhood home: a two-room shack made of wooden slats, its flimsy tin roof weighted down with rocks, the only bathroom a clump of bushes outside. On television, she saw New York City's spectacular skyline, Las Vegas's shimmering lights, Disneyland's magic castle.

10 Lourdes has decided: She will leave. She will go to the United States and make money and send it home. She will be gone for one year—less, with luck—or she will bring her children to be with her. It is for them she is leaving, she tells herself, but still she feels guilty.

11 She kneels and kisses Belky and hugs her tightly. Then she turns to her own sister. If she watches over Belky, she will get a set of gold fingernails from *el Norte.*

12 But Lourdes cannot face Enrique. He will remember only one thing that she says to him: "Don't forget to go to church this afternoon."

13 It is January 29, 1989. His mother steps off the porch.

14 She walks away.

15 *"¿Dónde está mi mami?"* Enrique cries, over and over. "Where is my mom?"

16 His mother never returns, and that decides Enrique's fate. As a teenager—indeed, still a child—he will set out for the United States on his own to search for her. Virtually unnoticed, he will become one of an estimated 48,000 children who enter the United States from Central America and Mexico each year, illegally and without either of their parents. Roughly two thirds of them will make it past the U.S. Immigration and Naturalization Service.

17 Many go north seeking work. Others flee abusive families. Most of the Central Americans go to reunite with a parent, say counselors at a detention center in Texas where the INS houses the largest number of the unaccompanied children it catches. Of those, she counselors say, 75 percent are looking for their mothers. Some children say they need to find out whether their mothers still love them. A priest at a Texas shelter says they often bring pictures of themselves in their mothers' arms.

18   The journey is hard for the Mexicans but harder still for Enrique and the others from Central America. They must make an illegal and dangerous trek up the length of Mexico. Counselors and immigration lawyers say only half of them get help from smugglers. The rest travel alone. They are cold, hungry, and helpless. They are hunted like animals by corrupt police, bandits, and gang members deported from the United States. A University of Houston study found that most are robbed, beaten, or raped, usually several times. Some are killed.

19   They set out with little or no money. Thousands, shelter workers say, make their way through Mexico clinging to the sides and tops of freight trains. Since the 1990s, Mexico and the United States have tried to thwart them. To evade Mexican police and immigration authorities, the children jump onto and off of the moving train cars. Sometimes they fall, and the wheels tear them apart.

20   They navigate by word of mouth or by the arc of the sun. Often, they don't know where or when they'll get their next meal. Some go days without eating. If a train stops even briefly, they crouch by the tracks, cup their hands, and steal sips of water from shiny puddles tainted with diesel fuel. At night, they huddle together on the train cars or next to the tracks. They sleep in trees, in tall grass, or in beds made of leaves.

21   Some are very young. Mexican rail workers have encountered seven-year-olds on their way to find their mothers. A policeman discovered a nine-year-old boy near the downtown Los Angeles tracks. "I'm looking for my mother," he said. The youngster had left Puerto Cortes in Honduras three months before. He had been guided only by his cunning and the single thing he knew about her: where she lived. He had asked everyone, "How do I get to San Francisco?"

22   Typically, the children are teenagers. Some were babies when their mothers left; they know them only by pictures sent home. Others, a bit older, struggle to hold on to memories: One has slept in her mother's bed; another has smelled her perfume, put on her deodorant, her clothes. One is old enough to remember his mother's face, another her laugh, her favorite shade of lipstick, how her dress felt as she stood at the stove patting tortillas.

23   Many, including Enrique, begin to idealize their mothers. They remember how their mothers fed and bathed them, how they walked them to kindergarten. In their absence, these mothers become larger than life. Although in the United States the women struggle to pay rent and eat, in the imaginations of their children back home they become deliverance itself, the answer to every problem. Finding them becomes the quest for the Holy Grail.

Questions for Analysis

1. The passage begins with a scene in which Enrique's mother, Lourdes, cannot talk or look at him. Why has she chosen to abandon him? Why does she ignore him as she prepares to leave?

2. The passage contrasts Lourdes's childhood home with the images of the United States she sees on television—that is, Las Vegas and Disneyland. What point about the perceptions of the United States is Sonia Nazario making?

3. Nazario chooses to tell the story in the present tense. How does this affect our reaction to the story?

4. Although Nazario tells Enrique's story, she later broadens the focus to discuss the "estimated 48,000 children who enter the United States . . . illegally and without either of their parents." Why does she do this?

5. Nazario is a reporter, so she cites experts and authorities at various points in the narrative. Where do these citations occur, and what is their function?

Suggestions for Writing

1. Write a single paragraph describing your emotional response to the story—and why you responded as you did. Then write a second paragraph analyzing what you believe Nazario wants you to do in light of that response.

2. The last two paragraphs of the passage from *Enrique's Journey* describe how children like Enrique come to idealize their mothers so that they become "larger than life." What do you think would be the consequences of those beliefs if and when they actually meet their mothers?

3. Enrique's mother intends to live and work in the United States for only a year, but stays for eleven. Defend or attack her decision to remain in the United States without her son.

Preparing Portfolios

In many composition classes, end-of-term portfolios play a large role in determining student success. A **portfolio** is a representative sample of a person's best work and has long been required of artists, actors, and people in the professions to demonstrate their accomplishments and potential. Likewise, portfolios can show what students can do and how well they have done it.

THE RATIONALE FOR THE PORTFOLIO

Often, unfortunately, the first—and often the only—thing that some students look at on a returned assignment is the grade. They may ignore or misinterpret the instructor's comments, suggestions for improvement, and even encouraging words that accompany the grade. For these students, the grade conveys a simple message: "I've failed," "I'm okay," or "I'm surprised." These students tend to view the grade as a judgment rather than an opportunity to improve through further revision.

Revision, however, is the key to writing. As *Writing with Confidence* emphasizes, writers don't simply draft a paper once and expect perfection. Instead, they consider what they're going to say. They plan how to say it (but know they'll change their plans). They compose a rough draft. They show it to other people for reactions and suggestions. And they revise the draft many times over a period of days, weeks, or even months. The revision, and learning, process shouldn't screech to a halt simply because a paper has been marked by an instructor.

Furthermore, because writing is a skill that develops over time, no single paper should be judged in isolation. The work you produce by the end of the term may be significantly better than your work at the beginning. If you've improved, you should be able to demonstrate that improvement. But how, exactly, do you demonstrate it? That's where the portfolio comes in.

The end-of-term portfolio gives you the opportunity to explain what you have learned, and to select and revise papers to back up your claims. You'll include papers that show your writing at its best. You'll revise those papers again, confident in your ability to identify and resolve problems in structure and grammar. The portfolio, therefore, consists of two sections: (1) an introductory essay in which you reflect on and assess what you have learned; and (2) final revisions of papers that demonstrate that learning.

Section 1: The Self-Assessment Essay

There is no single format for a self-assessment essay, but it should demonstrate that you have evaluated your work and can identify your improvements as a writer as well as the areas you must continue to work on.

Think of it this way: Writing is an activity, but readers see only the *result* of that activity, not how you have reached that result. They haven't watched you plan, draft, and revise. They haven't seen what suggestions you've received from friends or peer-group members, or how you've reacted to them. They haven't seen the changes you've incorporated from one draft to the next: the sharpening of focus, the improved support for claims, the addition of transitions, and editing and proofreading for grammar, mechanics, and clarity. Therefore, it's important that you *explain* all these things to readers. You can do so in the self-assessment essay.

The essay will call upon a number of the skills you have practiced during the term. You will be considering the audience for the essay—your instructor—and your purpose: to persuade him or her that you have mastered the skills of the course. You will be making and supporting claims, citing examples from the papers you have chosen to include in the portfolio. You will be classifying your strengths and weaknesses. You may be describing the process of how you have improved as a writer. You will be contrasting the earlier drafts with the final revisions, indicating how they differ.

Here are some possible ideas to consider in planning and writing the essay:

1. How has your writing process changed as a result of this class? In what ways has it changed?
2. What do you consider to be your strengths as a writer?
3. Which writing skills do you feel need more improvement?
4. What peer or instructor comments to your papers have been most important to you during the term? Have they revealed persistent problems (and strengths)?
5. Therefore, which of your papers during the term have you chosen to revise and include? Why? What does each of these papers demonstrate?

Section 2: The Revised Papers

Your instructor will determine how many revised papers the portfolio should contain, and may require that certain papers be included. In either case, you must revise each paper fully and submit a proofread, clean copy. Each submission must also include all the earlier drafts, arranged from the most recent to the beginning ones.

Use a photocopy of the Final Essay Progress Log (p. 439) as a cover sheet for each essay. Answer its questions honestly. Not only will the answers help you determine the success of each revised paper, but they will also help your instructor determine how insightful you are in evaluating your own writing.

Final Essay Progress Log

Date of completion prior to submission in the portfolio: _____

1. Reason I've chosen to include this paper in the portfolio: _____

   _____

2. My intended audience for the paper: _____

3. Goal(s) I hoped to accomplish for this audience: _____

   _____

4. Strategies I used for prewriting: _____

5. Number of drafts I worked through before including this paper in the portfolio: _____

   _____

6. People who have responded to my draft(s):

   a. instructor _____

   b. tutor _____

   c. peer-group members _____

   d. friend or relative _____

7. Main revisions I have made to this final submission:_____

   _____

   _____

8. Strengths of the final submission: _____

   _____

   _____

   _____

9. Weakness of the final submission—or changes I would like to make if I continue to work on it again: _____

   _____

   _____

The Portfolio as a Semester-Long Project

The portfolio isn't a last-minute project; it must evolve over the course of the term. Buy a soft-cover folder with side pockets, and, if you wish, a center three-ring binder. Store all your drafts of all your papers in the pockets—date each draft, and keep them organized.

When you prepare the final portfolio, use dividers or tabs to label each of the components: the Self-Assessment Essay, the first revised paper, the second revised paper, and so on. The table of contents will look like this:

1. Self-Assessment Essay
2. First Revised Paper: Title
   a. Final Submission
   b. Last Graded Revision
   c. Early Drafts and Notes
3. Second Revised Paper: Title
   a. Final Submission
   b. Last Graded Revision
   c. Early Drafts and Notes

(And further revised papers)

Be organized and neat; this is, after all, your best and final chance to show what you can do.

Pronouns

Personal Pronouns. These stand in for persons as subjects or objects.

	SUBJECT PRONOUNS		OBJECT PRONOUNS	
	Singular	Plural	Singular	Plural
First Person	I	we	me	us
Second Person	you	you	you	you
Third Person	he, she, it	they	him, her, it	them

EXAMPLES:

Mark gave *the books* to *Sylvia.*   *Sylvia* got *the books* from *Mark.*

He gave *them* to *her.*   *She* got *them* from *him.*

Possessive Pronouns. These show ownership or possession. They can function as adjectives before nouns or stand alone to replace nouns:

POSSESSIVE PRONOUNS BEFORE NOUNS

	Singular	Plural	Noun
First Person	my	our	
Second Person	your	your	house
Third Person	his, her, its	their	

EXAMPLE: The house belongs to us. It is *our* house.

POSSESSIVE PRONOUNS REPLACING THE NOUN

	Singular	Plural
First Person	mine	ours
Second Person	yours	yours
Third Person	his, hers, its	theirs

EXAMPLES: Your car is new. My car is old. *Yours* is new, but *mine* is old.

Demonstrative Pronouns. These pronouns identify or refer to a noun:

Singular	Plural
this	these
that	those

EXAMPLE: I want *this* book, but I don't need *those.*

Interrogative Pronouns. These pronouns begin a question:

> who, whom, whose, which, what
> ———————————————————
> EXAMPLES: *Who* is the oldest person in the class? *Which* book did you read?

Relative Pronouns. These pronouns relate information back to a noun or pronoun:

> who, whom, whose, which, that
> ———————————————————
> EXAMPLE: Annamarie, *who* is from Romania, came here three years ago.

Indefinite Pronouns. These pronouns refer to a category of people or things. They do not refer to a specific person or thing:

> Singular
> anyone, anybody, no one, nobody, anything, nothing, everyone, everybody, someone, somebody, something, nothing, either, neither, none, another
>
> Plural
> all, both, some, a few, many
> ———————————————————
> EXAMPLES: Did *anyone* lose a pen? *Somebody* found one in the classroom.

Reflexive Pronouns. These pronouns repeat the subject as an object (or repeat a noun or pronoun for emphasis):

	Singular	Plural
First Person	myself	ourselves
Second Person	yourself	yourselves
Third Person	himself, herself, itself	themselves

EXAMPLES: *I* looked at *myself* in the mirror.

You both can help *yourselves* to some food.

My friend likes big cars, but I, *myself*, prefer smaller ones.

Common Irregular Verbs

Present tense	Past tense	Past participle
be (am, are, is)	was, were	been
beat	beat	beaten
become	became	become
begin	began	begun
bend	bent	bent
bet	bet	bet
bind	bound	bound
bite	bit	bitten
bleed	bled	bled
blow	blew	blown
break	broke	broken
breed	bred	bred
bring	brought	brought
build	built	built
burst	burst	burst
buy	bought	bought
cast	cast	cast
catch	caught	caught
choose	chose	chosen
come	came	come
cost	cost	cost
creep	crept	crept
cut	cut	cut
deal	dealt	dealt
dig	dug	dug
do	did	done
draw	drew	drawn
dream	dreamt (dreamed)	dreamt (dreamed)
drink	drank	drunk
drive	drove	driven
eat	ate	eaten
fall	fell	fallen
feed	fed	fed
feel	felt	felt
fight	fought	fought
find	found	found

Present tense	Past tense	Past participle
fit	fit	fit
flee	fled	fled
fly	flew	flown
forget	forgot	forgotten
forgive	forgave	forgiven
freeze	froze	frozen
get	got	gotten
give	gave	given
go	went	gone
grind	ground	ground
grow	grew	grown
hang	hung, hanged	hung, hanged
have	had	had
hear	heard	heard
hide	hid	hidden
hit	hit	hit
hold	held	held
hurt	hurt	hurt
keep	kept	kept
know	knew	known
lay	laid	laid
lead	led	led
leave	left	left
lend	lent	lent
let	let	let
lie	lay	lain
light	lit (or lighted)	lit (or lighted)
lose	lost	lost
make	made	made
mean	meant	meant
meet	met	met
pay	paid	paid
put	put	put
quit	quit	quit
read	read	read
ride	rode	ridden
ring	rang	rung

Present tense	Past tense	Past participle
rise	rose	risen
run	ran	run
say	said	said
see	saw	seen
sell	sold	sold
send	sent	sent
set	set	set
shake	shook	shaken
shed	shed	shed
shine	shone, shined	shone, shined
shoot	shot	shot
show	showed	shown
shrink	shrank	shrunk
shut	shut	shut
sing	sang	sung
sink	sank	sunk
sit	sat	sat
slay	slew	slain
sleep	slept	slept
slide	slid	slid
slit	slit	slit
speak	spoke	spoken
spend	spent	spent
spin	spun	spun
split	split	split
spread	spread	spread

Present tense	Past tense	Past participle
stand	stood	stood
steal	stole	stolen
stick	stuck	stuck
sting	stung	stung
stink	stank	stunk
strike	struck	struck
strive	strove	striven
swear	swore	sworn
sweep	swept	swept
swim	swam	swum
swing	swung	swung
take	took	taken
teach	taught	taught
tear	tore	torn
tell	told	told
think	thought	thought
throw	threw	thrown
thrust	thrust	thrust
understand	understood	understood
wake	woke	woken
wear	wore	worn
weave	wove	woven
win	won	won
wind	wound	wound
withdraw	withdrew	withdrawn
write	wrote	written

Commonly Misspelled Words

Add your own words to the list as you look up their correct spelling.

absenCe
aCCept
aCCoMModate
aCComplish
aCCurate
achIEvement
acquaintANCE
aCRoss
adverTISEment
adVICE/adVISE
A LOT
AnSWer
aPPropriate
arGUment
artiCLE
aTHLete
attenDANCE
availABLE
bEAUtiful
begiNNing
behaVIOR
breaTH/breathE
BUSIness
calENDAR
cEIling
certAINly
chIEf
choiCe
chOOse/chOse
coMMerCIAL
coMMiTTee
compETItion
conCentrate
congRATulate
conSCIENCE
conSCIOUS
conSENSus
consEquently

convenIEnce
counSelor
criticiSM/critiCIZE
deFINITEly
dESCribe
desPErate
develOP
diffERent/diffERence
diSAPPoint
DISease
doESN'T
duRing
eiGHTH
embaRRass
enTRANCE
enveLOPE
enviRONment
especIALLY
exaGGerate
EXcept
existENCE
exPERIENCE
exPERIment
exPLANAtion
exTREMEly
familIAR
faSCinate
FeBRUary
forEIGN
genIUS
goVERNment
gramMAR
guarANtee
hEIGHT
iMMediate
imporTANT
indepenDENCE
inTEGration

inTELLectual
inTERest/inTEResting
inTERfere
inteRRupt
iRRELevant
jEWELry
jUDGment
knowLEDGE
laBORATory
leiSURE
liCenSe
lONELiness
lOOse/lOse
mainTENance
maTHEmatics
miLLeNNium
misCHIEF
miSSpell
nIEce
ninETY
ninTH
oCCasion
oCCuRRENCE
opINion
oPPortunity
opTImist
oRIGinal
partiCULAR
PAStime
PERform
PERhaps
phoNY
phySICAL
poSSess
preFER
prejUDicED
PREscription
preVALENT

priviLEGE
proBABly
proNUNciation
PSYchology
PURsue
quIET/quITE
realIZE
reCEIve
recoMMend
RHyTHM
ridicULOUS
scenERy
SCHEDule
SECRETary
SePArate
sIEge
simILAR
sinCE
sinCEREly
spEEch
straiGHT
strenGTH
SURpriSE
temPERature
thoROUGH
THROUGH
ThurSday
toMoRRow
unNECESsary
UNusually
WedNESday
Your own words:

_____

_____

_____

_____

_____

_____

Appendix E

Common Expressions Using Prepositions

accuse someone *of* something
acquaintance *with* someone or something
affection *for* someone
afraid *of* something
agree *with* someone about something
alarmed *at* something
a lot *of* something
amazed *at* something
amused *at* or *by* someone or something
angry *at* someone
angry *with* something
approve *of* someone or something
argue *about* something
argue *with* someone *for* (or *about*) something
arrive *at* a place *in* a city or country
ashamed *of* something
ask someone *for* something
ask something *of* someone
associate *with* someone *in* some activity
assure someone *of* something
at the top *of*
aware *of* someone or something
bargain *with* someone *for* something
because *of* something or someone
believe *in* something
blame someone *for* something
by means *of*
call *on* someone socially
call *to* someone *from* a distance
call *up* someone *on* the telephone
capable *of* something
certain *of* something
challenge someone *to* something
characteristic *of* something
cheat someone *out of* something
close *to* something or someone
comment *on* someone or something
communicate something *to* someone
comparable *to* something
complain *to* someone *about* something
composed *of* something

conceive *of* something
concerned *about* someone or something
confess *to* someone
confidence *in* someone or something
confident *of* something
congratulate someone *on* something
conscious *of* something
consideration *for* someone
contempt *for* someone or something
contribute *to* something
control *over* someone or something
convict someone *of* something
copy *from* someone
correspond *with* someone
count *on* someone *for* something
cure *for* something
cure someone *of* something
deal *with* someone or something
decide *on* something
dedicate something *to* someone
defend someone *from* something or *against* something
delighted *with* someone or something
delight *in* someone or something
demand something *of* someone
depend *on* someone *for* something
deprive someone *of* something
designed *for* something
desire *for* something
die *of* or *from* a disease
different *from* someone or something
disagree *with* someone *about* something
disappointed *in* something
disappointed *with* someone
disgusted *with* someone or something
displeased *with* someone or something
distrust *of* someone or something
do something *about* something
doubt *about* someone or something
dream *of* or *about* something
due *to* someone or something
duty *to* someone

engaged *to* someone
escape *from* something
excel *in* something
exception *to* something
excuse *for* something
excuse someone *from* something
explain something *to* someone
failure *of* someone *in* something
faithful *to* someone or something
fall *in* love *with* someone
fascinated *with* someone or something
fearful *of* something
fond *of* someone
for the purpose *of*
for the sake *of*
full *of* something
grateful *to* someone *for* something
guard *against* something
guess *at* something
hear *about* something
hear *of* something
hint *at* something
horrified *at* something
in case *of*
in common *with*
independent *of* someone or something
in favor *of*
influence *over* someone
inform someone *of* something
in place *of*
inquire *into* something
in search *of*
in spite *of*
in the course *of*
intent *on* something
interfere *with* someone or something
introduce someone *to* someone
invite someone *to* something
irrelevant *to* something
knock *at* or *on* a door
laugh *at* something or someone
lecture *on* or *about* something
listen *to* someone or something
look *at* someone or something
look *for* something or someone
look up something *in* a reference book
made *of* something
make something *for* someone
mistaken *for* someone
need *for* something
obligation *to* someone
on account *of*
opportunity *for* someone or something
opposition *to* someone or something

pay someone *for* something
pay something *to* someone
pity *for* someone
point *at* someone or something
popularity *with* someone
prefer something *to* something
prejudiced *against* someone or something
protect someone *from* something
provide something *for* someone
punish someone *for* something
qualification *for* a job
quarrel *with* someone *over* something
quote something *from* someone
reason *for* something
reason *with* someone *about* something
recover *from* an illness
related *to* someone
rely *on* someone or something
remind someone *of* something
reply *to* someone *about* something
require something *of* someone
research *in* something
responsible *to* someone *for* something
result *from* a cause
result *in* a consequence
result *of* a cause
rob someone *of* something
satisfactory *to* someone
search *for* something
send *for* something
shocked *at* something
shocking *to* someone
similar *to* someone or something
smile *at* someone
stare *at* someone
start *with* something
supply someone *with* something
sure *of* something
sympathy *with* or *for* someone or something
take advantage *of* someone or something
take care *of* someone or something
talk *over* something *with* someone
talk *to* someone *about* something
tell someone *of* or *about* something
thankful *for* something
think *of* or *about* or *over* something
threaten someone *with* something
tired *of* something
trust *in* something or someone
trust someone *with* something
wait *for* someone or something
weary *of* something
work *for* or *on behalf of* someone or something
worry *about* something

Answers to Chapter Exercises

(Odd Numbered Items Only) and to Mastery Exercise 1 in All Chapters

Chapter 2

Exercise 2

3. to inform

5. to inform or to entertain

Exercise 5

1. to entertain—and persuade students to do well in school

3. that students fail because they don't try and they can succeed if they do try

Chapter 3

Exercise 1

Possible answers

3. a trend in music; a trend in dress; surfing the Internet.

5. how the writer became interested in a hobby; typical experiences with the hobby.

Exercise 2

Paragraph C Sentence 1

Paragraph E Sentence 1

Paragraph G Sentence 1

Paragraph H Sentence 7

Exercise 3

Sample answers

3. People who bury their pets in cemeteries have too much time and money on their hands.

5. Sports are boring.

Exercise 4

Sample topic sentences

Paragraph C Cats probably emerged as pets much later than dogs.

Paragraph E Cats later suffered much worse fates outside of Egypt.

Exercise 8

Paragraph 3 The origins of nursery rhymes
Delete sentence c.

Paragraph 5 came about for a number of reasons
Delete sentence d.

Exercise 9

1. Sentence 17—the final sentence

3. (1) the chocolate chip cookie (2) chocolate (3) chocolate chip cookie, *xocoati* (4) *xocoatl, chocolati* (6) chocolate powder (7) solid chocolate (8) hard chocolate, chocolate chip (9) the cookie (10) first chocolate chip cookie, Toll House Inn (11) the inn's owner (12) chocolate pieces . . . butter cookies . . . the Toll House Inn cookie (13) For chocolate bits, the Nestlé Company's, Chocolate Bar (14) Nestlé . . . bar (15) chocolate (16) The cookie . . . chocolate chips (17) . . . chocolate

5. The Aztecs, the Spanish, a candy maker in Holland, a British company, (possibly) Ruth Wakefield, the Nestlé Company

Chapter 4

Exercise 1

1. three points: extraordinary attractiveness, incredible physical talent, and exemplary character. The opening sentences are introductory and serve to attract the reader's interest.

3. (2) handsome, magnificent body on his 6½-foot frame, shaves his hair, broad shoulders and rippling muscles (3) dodges defense and makes spectacular shots, scores a lot of points . . . top scorer, "Air Jordan" moves . . . agility and leaping ability, jumps in air and can stay there for a long time, smart . . . and tries to keep his teammates disciplined (4) team captain shows cool and controlled leadership and gentility, never fights, and calms down teammates, puts on his suit and politely answers questions, donates money to charity, sponsors community services.

Exercise 2

1. **Paragraph 2** A description of the role of the executive branch and how it provides checks and balances against the remaining two branches.

   Paragraph 3 A description of the role of the judicial branch and how it provides

checks and balances against the remaining two branches.

3. **Paragraph 1**   A discussion of the way we get our
news.

Paragraph 2   A discussion of the way we
communicate.

Paragraph 3   A discussion of the way we view
entertainment.

Paragraph 4   A discussion of the way we listen to
entertainment.

Exercise 3

3. *Revision*: *My pet dog* (or *cat*) was my best friend for
ten years.

Chapter 5

Exercise 2

3. The Republican party

5. Two of his generals

7. He

9. The future president

Exercise 4

3. would be [to die]

5. would die [being]

7. held [dying]

9. would have been [to outlive, coming, according]

Exercise 5

Possible answers

3. put

5. was

7. wanted

9. hoped

11. won

Exercise 6

3. Lee resigned, accepted

5. He had graduated, sworn

7. did he believe, states had

9. I have been, he wrote

Exercise 7

3. Mary (fragment)

5. attended (fragment)

7. <u>husband</u> appeared

9. <u>Mumler</u> produced

Exercise 8

Possible answers

3. *He* lifted . . .   5. no error   7. no error

Exercise 9

3. battlefront, he went . . .

5. downstairs when the sobbing grew louder,
although . . .

Exercise 10

3. soldiers who were acting as guards told him . . .
president who had . . .

5. . . . story, which the president . . .

Exercise 11

3. sentence   5. fragment (add a clause)

Mastery Exercise 1

Possible changes

South (3) *now* that . . .

4. he *was* telling . . . (5) *by* preparing . . .

7. post, (8) either

9. rang out, (10) *Lincoln* fell forward . . .

11. stage, (12) *in* the process . . .

14. horse, (15) *which* was . . .

16. theater (17) *where* he died . . . next morning,

18. throwing . . .

19. or another, (20) *Abraham* Lincoln . . .

21. discovered: (22) *John* Wilkes Booth . . .

24. to be hanged, (25) *including* Mary Surratt . . .

Chapter 6

Exercise 1

3. for   5. but   7. nor   9. and

Exercise 2

3. . . . the cash box, *but* he did not harm . . .

5. . . . an angry poem, *but* it also contained . . .

7. . . . not amused, *so (and)* it offered . . .

9. . . . handkerchief, *or* he might . . .

11. . . . passenger, *nor* have I ever treated . . .

Exercise 6

3. . . . possible; *therefore,* he . . .

5. . . . brave; *otherwise,* they would never . . .

7. . . . water; *nevertheless,* they were . . .

Exercise 8

Sample combinations

3. . . . freedom, *so* she returned [freedom; *therefore,*
she returned] . . .

5. . . . how it happened, *for* [or *but*]the slaves
returned . . .

7. . . . made a slave in the South, *yet* she returned
[made a slave in the South; *nevertheless,* she
returned] . . .

9. . . . would endanger the others, *so* whenever they
turned back [would endanger the others; *therefore,*
whenever they turned back] . . .

Mastery Exercise 1

Possible answers

2. . . . on this door, *and* Tubman . . .

3. . . . was a secret message; it was her "ticket" . . .

4. no change

5. . . . no tracks or trains; *nevertheless,* it took . . .

6. . . . Underground railroad, *for* (or *and*) by the 1830s . . .

7. . . . from captivity, *and* they guided . . .

8. no change

9. . . . had timetables; they showed . . .

10. . . . the long winter nights, *and* the slaves followed . . .

11. no change

12. . . . a brilliant planner, *for* (or *so*) she carried fake passes . . .

13. . . . her former masters lived; *therefore,* she dressed . . .

14. . . . walking toward her, *so* she quickly released . . .

Chapter 7

Exercise 1

3. I. C. . . . Owens felt tense . . . D. C. *because* a German . . .

5. D. C. *Although* Hitler claimed . . . , I. C. the meaning . . .

7. D. C. *When* the track . . . , I. C. Jesse Owens . . .

Exercise 2

Possible answers

3. . . . to participate *because* he had sprained . . .

5. *When (Because, After)* he got off to a perfect start, . . .

7. *When* Owens won the 200-yard dash . . .

9. *As (When)* Owens completed four events in forty-five minutes . . .

Exercise 4

Possible answers

3. *Although planning* to become a tailor at Carlisle, Thorpe attracted . . .

5. *While continuing* to compete . . .

Exercise 5

Possible answers

3. *When (After)* the world later learned . . . the world was astonished.

5. *Although* Thorpe played for only a few dollars, he was technically . . .

Mastery Exercise 1

Possible answers

3. . . . was thrilled when . . . (omit comma)

4. The Bulgarians drew loud cheers (5) *when* they marched . . . (join)

6. were jeered *because* they didn't (omit semicolon)

8. *Although* his fellow African-American teammate . . . (omit *but*—or retain *but* and omit *Although*) . . .

9. . . . for the broad jump, (10) Owens fouled . . . (add comma and join)

11. . . . tired (12) *because* he had just run . . . (join)

13. *When* Owens felt a hand on his shoulder, (14) *he* turned . . . (join)

17. . . . his second jump (18) *although* Luz Long tied it . . . (join and omit comma)

20. *After* landing on his final jump, (21) *Owens* was congratulated . . . (join)

22. *While* collecting four gold medals in all, (23) Owens didn't receive . . . (join)

Chapter 8

Exercise 1

3. . . . January 1, *which* was . . .

5. . . . to parties, *that* didn't exist . . .

7. . . . the custom, *which* went on . . .

Exercise 2

3. who seemed to sneeze just before dying from illness.

5. , who had basically similar ideas,

7. that killed many people in Italy

Exercise 5

3. Pardon me, are you the student whose books are lost?

5. Relative clauses whose meaning is unclear can be confusing.

Exercise 8

Possible answers

3. A few months later, de Mistral thought of a better way to fasten fabrics when he was on a hunting trip with his dog.

5. De Mistral noticed tiny hooks on their ends while examining the burrs under a microscope.

Mastery Exercise 1

Possible answers

2. . . . many things *that* they were thankful for . . .

3. . . . Indian named Squanto, *who* would stay . . .

4. . . . to America, (5) *who* sold him into slavery (add comma and join) . . .

7. During the year *that* the Pilgrims were . . .

8. . . . a new governor, *whose* name was William . . .

9. . . . in their small town, (10) *which* had [add comma and join]

13. However, the "turkeys" *in* which [or *that*] they found . . .

14. . . . any form of the bird, *which* included ducks . . .

16. The four Pilgrim women and two teenage girls, whom the previous winter had not killed, prepared . . . [add commas after *girls* and *killed*]

Chapter 9

Exercise 1

Possible answers

3. The governor was *furious; he* put Pep on trial and sentenced the dog to life imprisonment.

5. The story has a happy *ending; Pep's* fellow inmates loved him, and he could switch cellmates at will.

Exercise 2

Possible answers

CS 3. Every evening *when* he returned on a train, Hachi was always there to greet him.

CS 5. Hachi, *who* lived for ten more years, went to the train station every evening and patiently waited for his master.

CS 7. *Because* Hachi always met the evening trains, he became a familiar sight to Japanese travelers.

9. correct

Exercise 3

Possible answers

3. They kept repeating in *Swahili, a language* he did not know well, that Dian was dead until he finally understood them.

5. *Four days later,* the fifty-four-year-old woman was buried in the station's animal cemetery in a spot next to the graves of some mountain gorillas that she loved so dearly.

7. McGuire was accused of a crime and fled the *country; however,* there were other, more obvious suspects.

Mastery Exercise 1

Possible answers

2. . . . gorillas; *consequently,* they . . .

3. . . . world *although* there were only 250 . . .

5. . . . distance, *but* later on she . . .

6. . . . body language, *and* she also nibbled . . .

7. . . . understandable; *she* had been . . .

8. . . . goldfish, *and* when it died . . .

9. *After* she saw gorillas . . .

10. She left Africa *but then* returned . . .

11. . . . the poachers who were killing the animals.

13. . . . authorities *who* wanted (remove comma) . . .

14. . . . attractions, *and* she threatened . . .

Chapter 10

Exercise 1

3. areas   5. females   7. lions; zebras

Exercise 2

1. hunt   3. lives, joins   5. kills

Exercise 3

1. women   3. lice   5. teeth

Exercise 4

3. own   5. rains   7. write

Exercise 5

3. make   5. seems

Exercise 6

3. is ('s)   5. are ('re)   7. are ('re)

Exercise 7

3. *There are also* small . . .

5. *They're* kept . . .

7. . . . leopards *are*

Exercise 8

3. don't   5. don't   7. doesn't

Exercise 9

3. has

5. don't have (haven't)

7. doesn't have (haven't)

9. have

Exercise 10

1. Are   3. Do   5. Does

Exercise 11

3. are   5. are

Exercise 14

3. ~~of this social club~~ don't

5. ~~of pizzas, french fries, garlic bread, onion rings, and nachos~~ usually *disappears*

Mastery Exercise 1

1. . . . cats *have* always . . .

2. . . . some *cats* . . . others *work* . . .

3. . . . job . . . these days *is* . . .

4. . . . but it *doesn't* . . .

5. . . . some tests of intelligence *show* . . .

7. . . . everyone *knows* . . .

8. There *are* . . . all the breeds *have* . . .

9. *They're* the only animals . . . that *walk* . . .

11. . . . it *has* . . .

13. *It's* the only animal . . .

14. . . . *are* the female cat and the male cat?

17. . . . he *doesn't* stick . . .

Chapter 11

Exercise 1

3. Pr   5. P

Exercise 2

3. showered, rushed

5. started

7. developed, crumbled

9. spread

11. called, changed

13. baked, received

15. piled

17. visited, watched, considered

19. criticized, adopted

Exercise 4

3. were   5. was   7. was   9. were, was

Exercise 5

3. Bill wants to know if he can borrow your car.

5. Jeannette thinks that she will graduate in two years.

Exercise 6

3. They *have remained* . . .   5. . . . *has served* . . .

Exercise 7

3. protected

5. have searched, have discovered

7. have guarded

Exercise 8

3. haven't been   5. hasn't been

Exercise 9

1. was   3. (had) worked, sent

Exercise 10

3. laid   5. paid   7. heard

Exercise 11

3. bought   5. felt   7. lost, taught, meant

Exercise 12

3. became, led

5. fought, found

7. wound, was, had

9. came

11. wound, had

Exercise 13

3. rang   5. sank, handed

Exercise 14

3. put   5. quit   7. cut, spread, shut

Exercise 15

3. drew, fell

5. broke, swore, overate

7. had done, wrote, had grown

Mastery Exercise 1

2. . . . Ponce de Leon *discovered* Florida . . .

5. The king of Spain *had* removed . . .

6. . . . he *could* find.

7. . . . didn't *mention* . . .

9. . . . had *sought* . . .

10. . . . had *gone* looking for the fountain.

14. That attraction *drew* . . .

15. . . . Louella McConnell *told* . . .

16. She *saw* . . .

17. . . . from a box *buried* near the tree.

21. . . . a millionaire *named* Henry Flagler . . .

22. . . . where McConnell *charged* admission . . .

24. . . . he *gave* up his plans . . .

25. . . . who *made* . . .

26. . . . was *discovered* . . .

Chapter 12

Exercise 1

3. . . . and *he* . . .

5. *He and I* . . .

7. . . . *they* are . . .

Exercise 2

Possible sentences

3. Sam works harder than we (do).

5. The counselor talks to you more often than (she does) to me.

Exercise 3

Possible changes

3. . . . until *the company* could fix the problem

5. . . . which outsold *them* all.

7. no change

Exercise 4

Possible changes

3. . . . *people* don't repair calculators; . . .

5. . . . *the industry* think of next?

Exercise 5

Possible changes

3. ~~He~~ *The attendant* then strolled . . .

5. ~~he~~ *the person* must not assume . . .

Exercise 6

Possible changes

3. . . . gazed at *his or her* image . . .

5. *If people* dropped . . . *they* would soon die, or that the gods were sparing *them* . . .

7. . . . that *people's* health changed . . . that *they* could determine *their* condition from it.

Exercise 8

3. yourselves   5. himself (or herself)   7. I

Exercise 10

Possible answers

3. However, we do know the identity of the man *who first called a bagel a "bagel."*

5. In 1683, the first coffeehouse in Vienna was opened by a Polish man *who introduced a new bread called the* beugel.

Mastery Exercise 1

Possible revisions

2. . . . where *Edison and his coworkers* invented . . .

4. . . . because *Edison* was . . .

6. . . . *the person* made *Edison's* hearing worse.

7. . . . educating *himself* . . .

8. . . . *these* experiments . . . *the company* fired him.

12. . . . his assistants and *he* perfected.

13. . . . *was* earning him national fame.

14. . . . for *himself or herself.*

15. . . . *these* sudden changes . . .

17. . . . for *him* (or *himself*) . . .

Chapter 13

Exercise 1

3. peacefully   5. badly

Exercise 2

3. This man <u>in simple clothes</u>

5. Settlers <u>on the frontier,</u> began calling him Johnny Appleseed <u>in a spirit of humor or ridicule</u>

7. buried <u>in Johnny Appleseed Park, <near Fort Wayne, Indiana</u>

Exercise 3

3. Jefferson <u>wearing plain working clothes</u> . . .

5. formed . . . <u>offering their services</u> . . .

Exercise 4

3. myth, <u>invented by writer George Lippard</u> . . .

5. was coined <u>to refer</u> . . .

Exercise 5

3. Dr. Richard Schuckburgh <u>who wrote the first version of "Yankee Doodle"</u>

5. song <u>that made fun of the colonials' appearance</u>

Exercise 6

Possible answers

3. Sam Wilson served as the drummer boy *at the age of eight* . . .

5. . . . been settled with the *Treaty of Paris* in 1783 . . .

7. Another war, *which was also fought against Britain,* . . .

9. One day, *when asked by government inspectors what the "U.S." stood for,* a meat packer . . .

Exercise 7

Possible revisions

3. *At the age of thirty-five,* Adams . . .

5. Ironically, John Adams died *at 6:00 in the evening* . . .

Exercise 8

Possible revisions

3. Unhappy with both teaching and the clergy, *Adams turned to his true love, the law.*

5. His reputation and political future could have been damaged *when he defended* the British soldiers who shot some Massachusetts citizens in the Boston Massacre.

Exercise 9

Possible combinations

3. Because this brilliant and very patriotic young man was sure that a national language would unify the country, he began his research in 1803.

5. Webster then began to work on a much longer dictionary, which he finished two decades later.

7. When Webster died in 1843, George and Charles Merriam bought the rights to Webster's dictionary.

Mastery Exercise 1

Possible revisions

2. . . . a man without a beard *in a solid black hat and topcoat.*

3. no change

4. The first pictures of him *in a red hat* . . .

5. The flowing beard, *which appeared during Abraham Lincoln's presidency,* was inspired . . .

6. Uncle Sam was such a popular figure *in the late nineteenth century* . . .

7. no change

8. Pictures of a tall, thin man, *who resembled the original Uncle Sam,* Sam Wilson, . . .

9. However, the most famous portrayal of Uncle Sam, *the one most frequently reprinted and most widely recognized,* . . .

10. no change

11. The poster *showing Uncle Sam dressed in his full flag costume* sold four million copies . . .

12. *Contrary to the popular belief,* Flagg's Uncle Sam . . .

Chapter 14

Exercise 1

3. larger   5. more popular

Exercise 3

3. the gentlest   5. the longest

Exercise 4

Possible answers

3. the least talented   5. less than her siblings.

Exercise 6

3. more commonly   5. more likely

Exercise 7

3. well, better   5. bad, the worst   7. badly, the worst

Mastery Exercise 1

2. . . . disappeared so *quickly.*

3. . . . *harder* to believe.

9. . . . *more complete* . . .

11. . . . lived *happily* . . .

12. . . . hurt their crops *badly* . . .

13. . . . the *most* important part of the colonists' diet.

14. . . . the same *as* chicken but was a little *tougher.*

18. . . . device that worked *well* . . .

19. . . . called very *loudly* . .

Chapter 15

Exercise 1

3. we   5. her

Exercise 2

Possible answers

3. It serves great burgers and fries.

5. A person who wants to enjoy himself or herself should go to the new Sixteen Flags Over the Grand Canyon. It has the best and scariest rides.

Exercise 4

3. was   5. thought, was   7. knew, could

Exercise 6

3. . . . but she *would* eventually become . . .

7. . . . so she *could* explore Tibet without him for fourteen years.

11. . . . until he *died* . . .

15. after she *had* emerged from the cave in 1916.

Exercise 7

1. avoid the accident

3. a good student

5. exhausted

7. ran back

Exercise 10

Possible answers.

3. . . . and also *their customs.*

5. . . . and *called* on Alexandra . . .

7. . . . remained in their disguises and *were* undetected.

9. . . . made her return to Tibet and *live* there . . .

Mastery Exercise 1

2. . . . *people* could hear . . .

3. . . . *was* awakening from . . .

4. . . . and *blotted* out the sun.

5. . . . and then *fell* back into the volcano.

6. . . . and *rained* stones all over the mountainside.

7. . . . and *escaped* in their boats.

8. *They* lived to tell . . .

9. . . . or *in the public baths.*

11. . . . and *set* others on fire.

12. . . . and *suffocated* the rest.

14. . . . *would* be preserved in the ash . . .

15. . . . *people* could visit the city . . .

Chapter 16

Exercise 1

Possible answers

3. larger   5. more popular

Exercise 2

Possible answers

3. constructed, erected, assembled, threw together

5. lifted, swiped, stole, looted, boosted

Exercise 3

3. My friend can balance spoons on his nose.

5. My car belongs in the museum of ancient, worthless machines.

Exercise 5

3. Martin Luther King was an inspiring leader.

5. The afternoon talk shows on television are ridiculous.

Exercise 6

3. Fourteen girls, fifteen guys, and a large turtle were packed into my minivan.

5. A new musical will be opening on Broadway this month.

Exercise 8

3. Bus fare is pretty expensive in this city.

5. Stretch Everest, the center on our basketball team, attracts attention when he plays.

Exercise 9

Possible revisions

3. I like art because it allows me to be creative.

5. Anita seems to have a lot of self-confidence.

Exercise 10

Possible combinations

3. When his host showed him an easy target, a baby bear (or cub), Roosevelt refused to shoot it.

5. Morris Michtom, the owner of a toy store in Brooklyn, New York, was so inspired by the cartoon that he and his wife made a soft brown bear.

7. The bear and many more sold quickly, developing a fad that became very popular.

9. The president sent a handwritten note to Michtom granting him permission.

Exercise 11

3. Getting rid of every cliché is difficult.

5. Honest politicians are rare.

Mastery Exercise 1

Possible revisions, which reflect goals that students probably will only approximate.

2. Germans surrounded the Americans and attacked them.

3. Furthermore, the American division also was getting "friendly fire" from their own army.

4. The division commander Major Charles W. Whittlesey knew that many of his men had been killed or hurt, and they had almost run out of rations and medical supplies.

5. To stop more "friendly fire" from coming at the division, Whittlesey decided to write a note to his superiors at division headquarters in Rampont.

6. He asked them to stop bombing the division.

7. The only way to get the message to headquarters twenty-five miles away was to send it by carrier pigeon.

8. Whittlesey sent up five pigeons with the message, but German marksmen killed each one of them immediately.

9. He put the message inside a capsule attached to the leg of the only pigeon left, Cher Ami, which means "dear friend" in French.

10. After a short flight, Cher Ami landed on the branch of a nearby tree and decided to groom his feathers.

11. Major Whittlesey knew that this situation was so bad, he had to make the bird fly.

Chapter 27

Exercise 1

3. Catherine of Aragon, Anne Boleyn, Jane Seymour, Anne of Cleves, Catherine Howard, *and* Catherine Parr.

Exercise 2

5. . . . (later Tuskegee), *and* his mother . . .

11. . . . and sympathized with him, *for* they were convinced . . .

Exercise 3

Possible changes

3. *When his friends and neighbors talked*, he no longer heard . . .

5. . . . an alphabet as a syllabary, *eighty-six characters representing all the sounds of spoken Cherokee.*

7. The task took Sequoyah twelve years *in all*.

Exercise 4

Odd numbered items only

5. Within a few months, *a group* of almost entirely . . .

7. *In 1828,* Sequoyah and other Cherokees arrived . . .

9. Charles Bird King, *a famous painter,* asked him to sit . . .

11. Although most Cherokees refused to leave Tennessee and Alabama, *Sequoyah's* . . .

Exercise 5

3. no commas

5. an awkward, tall basketball player

Exercise 6

3. After December 5, 2011, Kathy will be an attorney.

5. July 4, 1776, in Philadelphia, Pennsylvania.

Exercise 7

Odd numbered items only

3. *Consequently,* a large battalion . . .

7. . . . over the *land,* over the members of the local government, *and* over many other matters.

9. At the meeting of the entire *tribe,* all the groups agreed to live in peace.

11. *However,* Sequoyah still could not rest.

13. Where were these lost Cherokees, *who did not know of his alphabet or the new Nation?*

Exercise 8

3. NBC

5. The Environmental Protection Agency is called the EPA.

Exercise 9

3. other.   5. forest?

Exercise 10

3. population.   5. today.

Exercise 11

3. . . . into the ground; however, their council house . . .

5. . . . religious ceremonies; each contained . . .

Exercise 12

1. Nathaniel Hawthorne, *The Scarlet Letter;* Mark Twain, *Huckleberry Finn;* Herman Melville, *Moby-Dick;* William Faulkner, *The Sound and the Fury;* F. Scott Fitzgerald, *The Great Gatsby;* and Ernest Hemingway, *For Whom the Bell Tolls.*

3. Bear Wallow, Kentucky; Pewee, Kentucky; Bulls' Gap, Tennessee; Difficult, Tennessee; Hot House,

North Carolina; Improve, Mississippi; Scratch Ankle, Alabama; and Dime Box, Texas.

Exercise 13

3. fashions: a neon T-shirt, jeans torn at the knees, orange and green spiked hair, and seventeen pierces in her left ear.

5. take one from column A, two from column B, and your choice of two from column C or D.

Exercise 14

3. (the first planet beyond normal eyesight to be observed)

5. —in fact there is no wind, no sound, no life.

Exercise 15

3. The Da Vinci Code

5. High School Musical is a very popular Broadway production.

Exercise 17

3. Martha told me, "I have been working late."

5. Mr. Joseph asked where the registrar's office was (is).

Exercise 18

3. "Well, . . . night," murmured . . . author. "When will this end?"

5. servants, "Why . . . immortal?"

7. "Please," mumbled Theodore Roosevelt, "put . . . lights."

Mastery Exercise 1

Possible Answers:

3. When he decided to make the world, he went . . . [add comma]

7. Since that time, the rocks have not changes; they have become harder. [add comma and semicolon]

8. The Great Chief Above made trees, berries . . . [add comma]

9. . . . a ball of mud. [add period] Then he told the man to take a fish from the waters [omit comma] and deer and other game.

10. When the man said, "I am lonely," the Great Chief Above . . . [reverse comma and end quotation marks]

12. He showed her how to cook the salmon and the animals . . . [omit semicolon]

13. When the woman prayed to the Great Chief, [add comma and join] (14) she said, "Please answer my prayer. [omit quotation marks] (15) I need help in having children."

19. The rocks that fell . . . [delete comma]

20. Buried under the rocks and the mountains . . . [omit comma]

22. . . . tops of the mountains, watching their children . . . [change semicolon to comma]

24. . . . hear spirits reply; therefore, they know . . . [change comma to semicolon and add comma]

27. No one knows when . . . [omit comma]

Chapter 28

Exercise 2

3. conceit   5. chief   7. deceive

Exercise 3

3. selves   5. shelves

Exercise 4

3. beauties   5. taxes   7. roses   9. breathes

Exercise 5

3. application

5. payment

7. flier (or flyer)

9. happily

Exercise 6

3. dancing   5. famous   7. dining

Exercise 7

3. usually   5. angrily   7. really

Exercise 8

3. writing   5. running   7. heating

Exercise 9

3. paralleling   5. preference

Exercise 10

3. stubborn   5. writing   7. occurred   9. bitten

Exercise 11

3. innumerable

5. dissatisfied

7. immaterial

9. mistake

Exercise 12

3. a lot

5. athlete

7. beginning

9. brilliant

11. carefully

13. chosen

15. competition

17. dealt

19. dining

21. describe

23. eighth

25. environment

27. explanation
29. finally
31. government
33. height
35. hoping
37. intellectual
39. jewelry
41. locally
43. misspell
45. occasion
47. prefer
49. potato
51. privilege
53. received
55. sacrifice
57. separate
59. sincerely
61. succeed
63. temperature
65. tomato
67. tries
69. written

Exercise 13
3. *Willie's* work
5. *Maria's* apartment
7. Mr. *Johnson's* statement

Exercise 14
3. Ms. *Jones's* house
5. *Mother's* Day
7. *Texas's* law

Exercise 15
3. A few *hours'* work   5. The *car's* front fenders

Exercise 16
3. runs   5. city's   7. leaves

Exercise 17
3. it's   5. we're   7. you're   9. doesn't

Exercise 18
3. *We'll* . . .   5. *don't . . . you're* . . .   7. *Who's* . . .

Exercise 19
3. forty-six   5. three-fourths

Exercise 20
3. a self-made millionaire   5. a pro-Russian speech

Exercise 21
Possible compound words.
3. fleabitten
5. newspaper

7. chairman
9. halftime

Exercise 22
3. stepped
5. wa-tered
7. ex-president
9. guard-house

Exercise 23
3. *Prairie Road* and *Central Street*
5. no capitalization
7. *I* . . .
9. *Spanish*

Exercise 24
3. *August*   5. no capitalization   7. *The*

Mastery Exercise 1
Only corrected words appear
1. parties . . . receive . . . it's
3. entering . . . classroom . . .
4. different
5. African-American
6. fifty-seven
7. written . . . lyrics
9. appeared . . . their . . . Coleman's
11. several
13. musical
14. royalties
16. . . . paid
18. delivered . . . stopped
20. its
21. seventy-eight

Chapter 29

Exercise 1
3. where   5. their   7. you're

Exercise 2
3. two   5. to, too

Exercise 3
3. have   5. have   7. have

Exercise 4
3. use, prejudice   5. accustomed

Exercise 5
3. acceptable

Exercise 6
3. advice

Exercise 7
3. affected   5. affect

Exercise 8

3. an   5. and, and, an

Exercise 9

3. breathe

Exercise 10

3. by, buy   5. by

Exercise 11

3. clothes

Exercise 12

3. unconsciously

Exercise 13

3. excellent   5. elegant

Exercise 14

3. fine

Exercise 15

3. knew   5. no

Exercise 16

3. lead

Exercise 17

3. lain   5. lying

Exercise 18

3. lose

Exercise 19

3. mind

Exercise 20

3. passed   5. passed   7. passed

Exercise 21

3. quite   5. quiet

Exercise 22

3. raise   5. rising

Exercise 23

3. set

Exercise 24

3. then   5. then

Exercise 25

3. there was   5. It was, it was

Exercise 26

3. weather   5. whether

Mastery Exercise 1

1. whose, by

3. led

5. accept

6. were

7. used, than, past

8. Their

10. lose

11. knew, whether, an, find

13. too

15. there's, different

17. quiet

Chapter 30

Exercise 1

3. My father washes the car every week.

5. Mrs. Highnose isn't watching television now.

Exercise 2

3. They did the wash every day last week.

5. They weren't listening to the news last night.

Exercise 3

Possible answers

3. While Mr. Gotbucks was smoking his cigar, his chauffeur was driving the car.

5. While his wife was washing the dishes, sweeping the floor, and throwing out the garbage, Mr. Hogg read the paper.

    (His wife was washing the dishes, sweeping the floor, and throwing out the garbage when Mr. Hogg read the paper.)

Exercise 5

Possible answers

3. they have to be careful.

5. have to go to Paris.

7. you have to save money.

Exercise 6

Possible answers

3. The sun doesn't shine very much.

5. They don't have much time to relax.

Exercise 7

Possible answers

3. eaten at that restaurant

5. eaten breakfast

7. take a vacation

Exercise 8

Possible answers

3. is being mopped

5. have lent you mine

Exercise 9

Possible answers

3. must have been shopping

5. could have been written

Exercise 10

3. where room 814 is.

5. you had studied for the final examination.

Exercise 12

3. a 161-year-old ex-slave to them.

5. did not give anyone refunds.

Exercise 14

3. the man [quickly] turned on the radio [quickly].

5. I [very promptly] sent the answer to him [very promptly].

Exercise 16

3. performed   5. injured   7. bored

Exercise 17

Possible answers

3. it doesn't make *any* sense.

5. I don't like to borrow *anything* . . .

7. You *can* hardly find . . .

Mastery Exercise 1

3. If the natives could *have* understood . . . they would have *been* surprised.

4. . . . Columbus *said* that this island . . .

5. And he gave *the name "Indians" to the natives.*

6. Columbus didn't discover *any* "new world" . . .

8. The Tiano natives who *migrated* . . .

9. . . . had *begun* raising *plants for food* . . .

11. . . . 600 separate cultures *had developed* in the Americas.

13. . . . crew were *impressed* by the crew's appearance, that appearance *probably didn't intimidate* them.

18. But hardly any Europeans of that era *lived* to be fifty; swept through *the filthy cities for centuries* . . .

21. . . . their ancestors *had migrated* from Asia . . .

22. . . . the mystery of *when they came* and *how their cultures evolved* . . .

Chapter 31

Exercise 1

1. a   3. an   5. a   7. a   9. an

Exercise 3

3. *a* twenty-three-year-old, *an* oil refinery

5. *a* new senator, *the* first, *the* Senate

Exercise 4

3. *the (a)* church on Main Street.

5. *the* new high-protein diet mentioned in today's newspaper.

Exercise 5

3. _____

5. _____

7. the

9. the

Exercise 6

1. *since* July 11   3. *in* the first. *For* several

Exercise 7

1. in   3. at   7. in

Exercise 8

1. on   3. on, in (on)   5. off (off of), in (on)

Exercise 9

1. in

3. In, to

5. On, about, in

7. to, in

11. against (on)

Exercise 10

3. in   5. in   7. on, in

Mastery Exercise 1

1. in the

2. The (3) in

4. an (5) for

7. on

8. in

9. the

10. on

11. in

12. in

13. on

14. a

15. a

16. in

17. the

18. by

19. at

20. the

21. a

22. of

23. the

24. the (an)

25. by

Glossary

A

Acronym: A word in which each letter represents a word, such as *FBI*, for *Federal Bureau of Investigation*.

Action verb: a verb that states what a subject does, did, or will do.

Active voice: a sentence structure in which the subject performs the action of the verb.

Adjective: a word or group of words that describe a noun or pronoun.

Adverb: a word or group of words that describe a verb (or a word formed from a verb, such as *–ing word* or an *infinitive*), telling *when, where, why, how,* or *how often* the action happens or happened. Adverbs (especially adverbs such as *very, really, too,* and *somewhat*) can also describe adjectives or other adverbs.

Adverb clause: a clause beginning with a subordinating conjunction such as *if, because, when,* or *before* that functions as an adverb.

Antecedent: the word or words that come before a pronoun and which the pronoun refers to.

Apostrophe: a punctuation mark ['] that shows possession before or after *–s* on nouns, replaces omitted letters in contractions, or forms the plurals of letters before adding *–s*.

Appositive: a noun that adds identifying information about a noun that precedes it.

Articles: the words *a, an,* and *the,* which determine whether a noun is specific or not specific.

B

Body: the central part of a paragraph or essay that develops and explains the topic sentence of the paragraph or the thesis statement of the essay.

Brainstorming: a part of prewriting in which you list thoughts as they come to you.

C

Case: the grammatical role of a pronoun as subject, object, possessive, and so on.

Causal analysis: an organization that examines the causes of an event or the results of an event, or both. It is also called *cause–effect organization*.

Cause–effect organization: see *causal analysis*.

Chronological order: an organization of events according to how they occur in a time sequence. This organization is most often found in narratives, process analysis, and cause–effect papers.

Claim: a statement (such as a topic sentence or thesis statement) that needs support in the body of a paragraph or throughout an essay.

Classification: an organization that divides the subject matter into categories determined by one criterion, or standard.

Clause: a group of words containing both a subject and a verb. Every sentence must contain at least one clause, although many sentences contain more than one.

Cliché: a tired and overused expression.

Climax order: an organizational arrangement going from the least important to the most important information and often ending dramatically.

Clustering: a part of prewriting in which you explore and organize your thoughts in a chart. Begin by writing and circling the topic in the middle of the page, and then draw lines (or branches) to circles in which you write related ideas. You can also draw branches and attach circles to each of the related ideas until you fill up the whole page.

Coherence: a quality in which the relationship between ideas is clear throughout a paragraph or essay.

Collective noun: a noun such as *class, orchestra,* or *team* that represents a group of people or things. Most—but not all—collective nouns are grammatically singular.

Colon: a punctuation mark [:] that functions like an equal sign. It is most often used to show that the last words of a grammatically complete statement are equal to what follows—usually a list or long quotation.

Comma: a punctuation mark [,] used for separating ideas or, with two commas, enclosing ideas.

Comma-spliced sentence: a sentence containing two independent clauses incorrectly joined by a comma. This is a serious, but common, grammatical error.

Common noun: a noun that represents but does not name something and is therefore not capitalized.

Comparative form: the form of an adjective or adverb ending in *–er* or preceded by *more,* showing that the two things being compared are not equal.

Comparison–contrast: an organization that shows similarities and differences between two or more subjects. The organization can be whole-to-whole or part-to-part.

Complex sentence: a sentence containing an independent clause and a dependent clause that begins with a word such as *after, because, if, who, that,* or *which*.

Compound predicate: a predicate containing two or more verbs.

Compound sentence: a sentence containing two independent clauses, each of which could be a sentence by itself.

Compound subject: a subject consisting of two or more nouns and/or pronouns joined by *and*.

Compound word: a word formed by joining two complete words—sometimes with a hyphen and sometimes without.

Conclusion: the last sentence of a paragraph or last paragraph of an essay, which ties together the preceding ideas and gracefully ends the work.

Conjunction: a joining word or phrase (see *coordinating conjunctions* and *subordinating conjunctions*).

Conjunctive adverb: a word that often follows a semicolon to explain how or in what way the two clauses joined by the semicolon are logically related. A conjunctive adverb is also called a *transitional word*.

Consonant: a sound represented by any of the letters of the alphabet that do not represent the vowel sounds.

Contraction: a joining of two words that requires the omission of a letter or several letters from the second word. An apostrophe occupies the spot of the missing letter(s).

Coordinating conjunction: a word that joins grammatically equal structures. There are only seven coordinating conjunctions: *for, and, nor, but, or, yet, so.*

Coordination: the joining of two or more grammatically equal structures, usually with a coordinating conjunction or a semicolon.

Countable nouns: nouns that can be either singular or plural.

Criterion: the method used in classifying things—such as by size, frequency, or age.

D

Dangling modifier: a modifier that does not modify any word or phrase in a sentence.

Dash: a punctuation mark [—] used to separate and enclose items that dramatically interrupt a sentence. Internal items require two dashes, while end items require one.

Definition: an explanation of a term's meaning, either through a synonym or a formal statement of definition.

Demonstrative adjectives: the pronouns *this, that, these,* and *those,* which go before nouns—as in "this man" or "these cars."

Demonstrative pronouns: the pronouns *this, that, these,* and *those* that are used without nouns (see *demonstrative adjectives*).

Dependent clause: a clause that cannot stand alone as a sentence but must be joined to an independent clause to complete its meaning. Most dependent clauses begin with words such as *because, although, if, that, which,* or *who.*

Description: writing that creates a mental picture, often of a scene.

Detail: a smaller part of something larger. Details usually support generalizations.

Direct object: the word or words (usually nouns or pronouns) following and receiving the action of an action verb, following a word formed from a verb

(such as an infinitive, a past participle, or an *-ing* word), or following a preposition.

Direct question: a question that forms a complete sentence ending in a question mark and in which the verb (or first helping verb) precedes the subject.

Direct quotation: the exact words of a speaker or writer, placed in quotation marks.

Double negative: a type of grammatical error in which two negative words express one negative idea. Only one negative word should be used.

E

Editing: one of the last steps in the writing process, in which you check over your second or third draft for misspelled words, words left out or repeated, grammatical errors, missing word endings, incomplete sentences, and incorrect punctuation.

Effect: the result of some action or event (see *causal analysis*).

Ellipsis marks: three dots [. . .] indicating that words have been omitted, especially in quotations.

Essay: an organized discussion of a topic in a series of paragraphs—usually at least five paragraphs and often many more. Ideally, the introductory paragraph attracts the readers' attention, states the thesis of the essay, and outlines its structure. The body paragraphs present each main supporting point of the thesis. The concluding paragraph summarizes the ideas and brings the paper to a graceful end.

Example: a specific illustration of a concept.

Exclamation point: an end punctuation mark [!] that shows strong emotion.

Exclamatory sentence: a statement or strong emotion ending in an exclamation point [!].

Exemplification: the use of examples to illustrate or clarify a general idea or claim.

Expository writing (exposition): informative writing, the primary purpose of which is to explain something.

F

Fact: a statement that can be proven to be true.

Figure: a number or percentage.

Formal statement of definition: defining a term by placing it in a category or class and then specifying characteristics that distinguish the term from other items in the category or class.

Four Ws: *who, what, where, when*—usually included in a description of a scene or a narrative.

Fragment: an incomplete sentence because (1) it is missing either a subject, a verb, or both; (2) the verb is incomplete; or (3) it is only a dependent clause and must be attached to an independent clause.

Freewriting: exploring your ideas in paragraph form without concern for grammar, spelling, or organization.

Future-perfect tense: a tense referring to an action or event completed before a later time in the future. This tense always contains three words: *will* + *have* + past participle.

H

Helping verb: the parts of the verb before the main verb, conveying the most important information about verb tense or mood.

Hyphen: a punctuation mark [-] used for joining words and word parts separated between syllables at the end of a line.

I

Indefinite pronoun: a pronoun such as *everyone, nowhere,* or *something* that does not refer to a specific person, place, or thing.

Independent clause: a clause that can stand alone as a sentence.

Indirect object: a noun or pronoun following a verb that receives a direct object.

Indirect question: a question contained within a larger statement that uses the word order of a statement. An indirect question does not end with a question mark.

Infinitive: a word formed from a verb but that does not have a tense and that functions as an adjective, adverb, or noun.

–ing **word:** a word formed from a verb that functions either as a noun, an adjective, or an adverb. An *–ing* word can also be part of a verb if some form of *to be* precedes it, such as *is going, was going,* or *will be going* (see *present participle*).

Introduction: the beginning of a paragraph or essay, which attracts the readers' interest and usually makes the central claim of the paragraph in a topic sentence or, for an essay, in a thesis statement.

Irregular nouns: nouns that do not form plurals by adding *–s.*

Irregular verbs: (1) verbs that do not simply add *–s* for present-tense subject–verb agreement but make larger changes, or (2) verbs that do not form the past tense or past participle by adding *–ed.* These verbs change internally or do not change form at all.

L

Linking verb: a verb that does not express action but merely links the subject to the word or words that describe the subject. The most common linking verbs are *to be* (*is, am, was, were,* etc.) and the verbs representing the five senses: *look, feel, smell, sound,* and *taste.*

M

Main verb: the last word in a verb phrase, conveying the most important information about the action the verb expresses.

Metaphor: a way to make writing livelier by discussing your actual topic (such as *thinking*) in terms of another (*brewing up* or *cooking up ideas*).

Modifier: a word or group of words that function as an adjective or an adverb.

N

Narration: a story, usually told in chronological order, or a sequence of consecutive events building to a climax, which ends the story. A narration often includes dialogue.

Nonrestrictive relative clause: a clause that provides information not essential to the meaning of the noun it relates to, so the clause is enclosed by two commas.

Noun: a word that functions as a subject or an object and can be replaced by a pronoun. A noun usually represents a person, place, idea, or thing.

Noun clause: a clause that functions as a noun, usually beginning with *what, that, where, why,* or *when.*

Number: the singular or plural forms of nouns or pronouns.

O

Object: a word or words (usually nouns or pronouns) following action verbs; words formed with verbs (*–ing* words, past participles, and infinitives); prepositions; or other objects (see *direct object* and *indirect object*).

Objective: reporting or summarizing without including any opinions or interpretations.

Object pronoun: a pronoun form (*me, us, you, him, her, it,* or *them*) that follows verbs, prepositions, or words formed from verbs.

P

Paragraph: a group of sentences that discuss a topic. A paragraph can contain many sentences—or as few as one sentence—especially when used for dialogue in a story. In most circumstances, paragraphs are smaller divisions of an essay.

Parallel construction (parallelism): the repetition of the same grammatical structure for coherence or emphasis.

Paraphrase: restating ideas in your own words and sentence structure—as opposed to quoting the ideas.

Parentheses: punctuation marks [( )] that enclose incidental information in a sentence. They always come in pairs.

Part-to-part organization: a way of making comparisons and contrasts between subjects by examining one part of each subject, then examining the second part of each, and so on.

Passive voice: a clause in which the subject does not act, but is acted upon. The passive voice is formed from *be* and the past participle of the verb in any tense, such as *has been done, is done, was done,* or *will be done.*

Past continuous (or progressive) tense: a tense showing an action in progress in the past, formed from the helping verbs *was* or *where* and an *–ing* word.

Past participle: a verb form that ends in *–ed* for regular verbs, although there are more than 100 irregular forms. The past participle functions as a main verb in perfect tenses (such as the present-perfect *has known,* or the past-perfect *had known*), and in the passive voice (such as *is known* or *was known*). The past participle is also used as an adjective (a *well-known* man).

Past-perfect tense: a tense used to describe past action or an event occurring prior to a later time in the past. The past-perfect tense is formed from *had* and the verb's past participle.

Past tense: a tense used to discuss completed actions in the past. All regular past-tense verbs end in *–ed.* There are more than 100 irregular verbs (see *simple past tense*).

Period: a punctuation mark [.] that ends a complete statement or is included in an abbreviation.

Person: a way of classifying personal pronouns: first person, *I* and *we;* second person, *you;* third person: *he, she, it,* and *they.*

Personal pronoun: a pronoun such as *I, we, you, he, she, it, they* or *me, us, him, her, them* that refers to people.

Phrasal verb: a two-word (and sometimes three-word) expression such as *get up,* which combines a verb with a second word to change the meaning of the verb.

Phrase: a group of two or more words. Unlike a clause, it does not contain a complete subject and verb.

Plural: more than one. Most plural nouns end in *–s,* but two or more nouns or pronouns can be joined to make a plural by *and.* Present-tense plural verbs do not end in *–s.*

Portfolio: a representative sample of a person's best work, which usually includes a self-assessment essay and several fully revised papers.

Possessive: a word that shows ownership or possession.

Possessive adjective: a possessive word—actually a pronoun, such as *my, our, your, his, her, its,* and/or *their,* that shows possession before a noun (see *possessive pronoun*).

Possessive noun: a possessive word formed by adding *–'s* to singular nouns or *–'* to plural nouns ending in *–s.*

Possessive pronoun: a possessive word, such as *mine, ours, yours, his, hers, its,* and *theirs,* which replaces a possessive noun or possessive adjective and the noun.

Predicate: the words that make a statement or ask a question about the subject. A predicate begins with a verb.

Prefix: an addition to the beginning of a root word.

Preposition: a small word such as *in, of, on, at,* or *around* that precedes a noun or pronoun object (for example: *on the roof, by the road, under the rug, in a year*). The preposition and its object, called a *prepositional phrase,* modify a noun or a verb.

Present continuous (or progressive) tense: a tense that discusses actions that are happening now or are planned for the future. All verbs in this tense include the helping verb *is, am,* or *are* and an *–ing* word.

Present participle: an *–ing* word that functions as an adjective or adverb.

Present-perfect tense: a tense used to describe an action or condition in the past that continues up to the present. The tense is formed with *has/have* and the past participle.

Present tense: see *simple present tense.*

Prewriting: the step in the writing process in which you think about your topic, purpose, and audience, and then explore your ideas through brainstorming, clustering, or freewriting.

Process analysis: an organizational structure that explains how to do something or how something works.

Proofreading: the last step in the writing process in which you examine the final copy for small errors and omissions.

Pronoun: a word that replaces a noun as a subject, object, or possessive word. Some pronouns have additional functions (see *relative pronouns, demonstrative pronouns,* and *reflexive pronouns*).

Proper noun: a noun that names someone or something and is therefore capitalized.

Purpose: what your paragraph or essay should achieve, usually to inform, persuade, or entertain.

Q

Question mark: a punctuation mark [?] that ends direct questions.

Quotation: the use of the exact words, capitalization, spelling, and punctuation found in the writing or speech of someone. The words are enclosed in quotation marks [""].

Quotation marks: punctuation marks [""] that enclose direct quotations, titles of short works, definitions, and words used in special ways.

R

Reflexive pronoun: a pronoun that both performs and receives the action of the verb (such as "I wouldn't do that to myself"). The pronoun's singular forms end in *–self,* and its plural forms end in *–selves.*

Regular verb: a verb that ends in *–ed* in the past participle, or that forms its third-person-singular form by adding *–s* or *–es.*

Relative clause: a clause that functions like an adjective, relating its information back to the noun that, in most cases, immediately precedes it.

Relative pronoun: the word that begins a relative clause, which relates its information back to a noun preceding the clause. The most common relative pronouns are *who, which, that,* and *whom.*

Report: a summary of decisions taken at a meeting, the details of some incident, the results of an experiment, or a set of observations.

Reported speech: a retelling in your own words of what the speaker or writer says or said. Reported speech never uses quotation marks.

Restrictive relative clause: a clause that provides essential information about the noun it relates to, so the clause is not enclosed in commas.

Root word: a word to which a suffix or prefix is added.

Run-on sentence: a sentence containing two independent clauses but joined together by nothing. This is a very serious grammatical error.

S

Semicolon: a punctuation mark [;] that most commonly joins two independent clauses or, less commonly, separates items in a series that contains internal commas.

Sentence: a complete statement or question containing a subject (usually a noun or subject pronoun) and a verb, which begins the statement or question about the subject.

Sequential order: an organization in which ideas are presented in consecutive steps or a sequence.

Simile: a comparison using *like* or *as,* such as "He ran *like a deer.*"

Simple past tense: a tense that shows a completed action or idea in the past. Regular verbs in the simple past tense end in *–ed,* but more than 100 past-tense verbs are irregular.

Simple present tense: a tense used to discuss habitual actions, or state facts or conditions that are true of the present. All third-person-singular present-tense verbs end in *–es.*

Singular: only one. Singular nouns usually do not end in *–s,* but the present-tense verbs that agree with them do end in *–s.*

Spatial order: an organization that presents details in space according to some arrangement, such as top to bottom, left to right, or front to back. This organization occurs most often in description.

Speaker tag: The phrase that identifies the speaker of a question, such as *he said,* or *she asked.*

Subject: the topic (*who* or *what*) a clause makes a statement or asks a question about. Most often the subject is a noun or subject pronoun. In statements, the subject usually precedes the verb; in questions, the verb precedes the subject.

Subjective: personal interpretation, evaluation, or opinion in the discussion of facts or ideas.

Subject pronoun: a word that replaces a noun as the subject of a verb. The list of subject pronouns includes *I, we, you, he, she, it,* and *they.*

Subject–verb agreement: matching of singular subjects with singular verbs or plural subjects with plural verbs. With the exception of *to be (was/were)* in the past tense, only present-tense verbs change form to agree with their subjects.

Subordination: joining two clauses by making one clause dependent on the other clause.

Subordinating conjunction: a word that joins two clauses by making one clause lower in importance and dependent on the second clause. The second clause is independent and completes the meaning of the dependent clause.

Suffix: an ending added to a root word.

Summary: a shorter version of a longer piece of information; it objectively presents the main idea and the most important supporting information.

Superlative forms: the adjective or adverb form ending in *–est* or preceded by *most,* used to show that one of three or more things in a comparison is greater than the others.

Syllable: a grouping of one or more letters that contain a single vowel sound.

Synonym: a word with the same or nearly the same meaning as another word.

T

Tense: the form of the verb that shows when an action or idea occurs or occurred—in the *present, past, future,* and so on. In two- or three-word verbs, the first word indicates the tense (*doesn't want*—simple present; *didn't want*—simple past; *is going*—present continuous; *was going*—past continuous; and so on).

Thesis statement: this sentence, included in the introductory paragraph of an essay, makes the central claim of the essay and often outlines the organization of the essay.

Topic sentence: a sentence that makes a claim or states the main idea, or point, of a paragraph, which the body of the paragraph develops. Most topic sentences come at the beginning of a paragraph.

Transitional word: a word that explains how or in what way two ideas are logically related (see *conjunctive adverb*).

U

Uncountable nouns: nouns that represent an idea or subject that cannot be counted such as *air, water,* or *furniture.*

Unity: a trait of an effective paragraph, in which each sentence develops the main idea, or topic, which is often expressed in the topic sentence.

V

Verb: a word or phrase that usually follows the subject and expresses the action the subject performs. A few verbs also link descriptive words back to the subject. Verbs generally have a tense (present, past, future, etc.) and can contain as many as four words.

Verb Phrase: a verb made up of two, three, or four words.

Vowel: a sound represented by the letters *a, e, i, o, u* (or a combination of these letters) that involves the passage of air through the vocal cords.

W

Whole-to-whole organization: a way of making comparisons and contrasts between subjects by examining everything about one subject and then everything about the other.

Credits

Index